FOLK & FAIRY TALES

FOURTH EDITION

EDITED BY

MARTIN HALLETT & BARBARA KARASEK

broadview press

Library and Archives Canada Cataloguing in Publication
Folk & fairy tales / edited by Martin Hallett & Barbara Karasek.— 4th ed.
Includes bibliographical references.
ISBN 978-1-55111-898-7

1. Fairy tales. 2. Tales. 3. Folk literature—History and criticism. I. Hallett, Martin, 1944-   II. Karasek, Barbara, 1954-   III. Title: Folk and fairy tales.

PZ8.F65 2008   398.2   C2008-905672-8

Broadview Press acknowledges the financial support of the Government of Canada through the Book Publishing Industry Development Program (BPIDP) for our publishing activities.

Broadview Press is an independent, international publishing house, incorporated in 1985. Broadview believes in shared ownership, both with its employees and with the general public; since the year 2000 Broadview shares have traded publicly on the Toronto Venture Exchange under the symbol BDP.

We welcome comments and suggestions regarding any aspect of our publications—please feel free to contact us at the addresses below or at broadview@broadviewpress.com.

North America:
PO Box 1243, Peterborough, Ontario, Canada K9J 7H5
2215 Kenmore Ave.,Buffalo, NY, USA 14207
Tel: (705) 743-8990; Fax: (705) 743-8353; E-mail: customerservice@broadviewpress.com

UK, Ireland, and continental Europe:
NBN International, Estover Road, Plymouth, UK PL6 7PY
Tel: 44 (0) 1752 202300; Fax: 44 (0) 1752 202330; E-mail: enquiries@nbninternational.com

Australia and New Zealand:
UNIREPS, University of New South Wales, Sydney, NSW, Australia 2052
Tel: 61 2 9664 0999; Fax: 61 2 9664 5420; E-mail: info.press@unsw.edu.au

www.broadviewpress.com

Copy edited by Betsy Struthers
This book is printed on paper containing 100% post-consumer fibre.

Book design and composition by George Kirkpatrick
PRINTED IN CANADA

CONTENTS

CONTENTS

[9]

PREFACE

Things change; things remain the same.

WE HOPE THAT THIS TRUISM has some application to this new edition of *Folk and Fairy Tales* —that the changes and additions we have made result in an anthology that is a yet more effective and enjoyable introduction to the study of fairy tales.

In preparing a new edition, we have been careful to remind ourselves that this book is, first and foremost, an *introduction*. From the very beginning, we have seen the typical reader of *Folk and Fairy Tales* as a student returning—somewhat sceptically—to the fairy tale for the first time since elementary school or kindergarten—or perhaps even professing to remember nothing about fairy tales that wasn't derived from a Disney movie. Thus, to revise our selection of tales or criticism purely for the sake of modernity would have been inappropriate; in striving for that elusive happy balance, we have tried to avoid making changes for change's sake. For instance, we have retained the original spelling and punctuation of the tales as a reminder both of the different cultures and times from which they come and of the mediating voice of the transcriber or translator.

At the same time, the valuable and much appreciated feedback that we have received from those who have used *Folk and Fairy Tales* in the classroom has helped us greatly in adjusting both our selection of tales and the manner in which we present them, both to introduce some lesser known versions of famous tales and to encourage comparison between versions of one tale or categories of several.

The distinguished American critic Leslie Fiedler once observed that children's books introduce all the plots used in adult works and that adult responses are frequently based on forgotten or dimly remembered works from childhood. This is particularly true of fairy tales, which, in providing much of our earliest literary and imaginative experience, have surely exerted an enormous influence over us. The goal of this anthology, therefore, is to draw attention not only to the fascination inherent in the tales themselves but also to the insights of some critics who have demonstrated, from a variety of perspectives—folkloric, psychological, feminist, historical, and cultural—that fairy tales have a complexity belied by their humble origins.

Furthermore, fairy tales can have great pedagogical value for teachers and students of literature. The increasing multiculturalism of our society has brought with it many riches; at the same time, however, it presents a problem for the teacher who must endeavor to find some common ground for students from diverse cultural, social, and educational backgrounds. In this context, the fairy tale offers a unique opportunity to introduce students to a literary form that is familiar and simple, yet multi-dimensional. No student can claim to be wholly ignorant of fairy tales, but it is highly unlikely that he or she has ever gone beyond their surface simplicity to discover the surprisingly subtle complexities that lie beneath.

Because the pedagogical technique of challenging expectations has been a major principle influencing our choice and juxtaposition of tales, most of those selected will quickly be recognized as "classics." It must be pointed out, however, that despite their popularity, these well-known tales are not representative of the international body of fairy tales. We did not set out to make our selection comprehensive, since it was our feeling that the greatest advantage could be achieved by guiding students through familiar territory while introducing some new perspectives. It will be the students' task, then, to apply these and other critical approaches more widely, not only to other fairy tales, but also to the whole world of literature.

Those familiar with earlier editions of this book will note some changes in our presentation of the tales. The comparative sections remain but have been considerably expanded, not only with new tales but also with some that were previously to be found in the nineteenth- and twentieth-century sections. We felt that grouping all the versions of a particular tale or type was preferable to separating them chronologically. We have also re-organized the thematic sections that follow. Each group of tales is preceded by a short critical introduction that begins the process of placing the tale in context. We point out some of the issues that may well have inspired these stories in the first place and outline some of the reactions which they have in turn provoked. One of our objectives has been to show how the creative imagination has worked on and developed the fairy tale, as evidenced in the sampling of contemporary stories.

New to this edition is a third kind of grouping, entitled "Juxtapositions," which contains four pairs of tales that in some way invite direct comparison; our hope is that the variety of approaches implicit in these sections will illuminate at least a few of the many ways in which one can explore the ever-surprising world of the fairy tale.

As with the tales, so with the critical selections. Our goal remains to provide the student with a representative sampling of different critical analyses of the fairy tale. As before, our choice has been governed by the fact that this is an introductory anthology; thus, we have included several older essays or excerpts that in our view offer the clearest statement of a particular line of inquiry into the fairy tale.

We hope that the accompanying web site will provide access to some of the material that could not be included in this new edition. <www.broadviewpress.com/tales/index.htm>

ACKNOWLEDGEMENTS

WE WISH TO THANK THE staff of the Vaughan Memorial Library, Acadia University, the Vanier College Library (Montreal), the Westmount Public Library, and the Wolfville branch of the Annapolis Valley Regional Library for their diligent efforts to locate and acquire texts for us. Thanks are also due to our editor, Betsy Struthers, for reining in our stylistic excesses.

We want to put on record our appreciation of the support, patience, and technical assistance of our respective spouses, Barbara and Eugene. Without them, the fruits of our collaboration would undoubtedly have been lost in cyberspace.

Finally, we would like to express our gratitude to Karen Rowe, who gave most generously of her time and expertise in response to our request for some "minor" updates to her article "Feminism and Fairy Tales." Our anthology is the richer as a result.

INTRODUCTION

Fairy tale is a term that is often used rather loosely. A dictionary will probably tell us that it is a story about fairies (which is often not the case) or else that it is an unbelievable or untrue story (which reflects the rationalistic criticism to which the fairy tale has been subjected). This vagueness of definition has made the term something of a catch-all: Lewis Carroll, for instance, described *Through the Looking-Glass* as a fairy tale, and Andrew Lang saw fit to include an abridged version of Book 1 of Swift's *Gulliver's Travels* in his *Blue Fairy Book*. So let us clarify the subject a little by introducing two more specific terms: "folk tale" and "literary tale." Once we have established the essential difference between these two terms, we will be in a better position to recognize the many permutations that have evolved over the years.

"Folk tale" means exactly what it says: it's a tale of the folk. If we resort again to our dictionary, we will learn that "folk" signifies the common people of a nation— and the important point to realize here is that the "common people" were, in the past, generally illiterate. Consequently, their tales were orally transmitted; in other words, they were passed down from generation to generation by word of mouth, until they were eventually recorded and published by such famous individuals as Charles Perrault and Jacob and Wilhelm Grimm. Because we hear so often of "Perrault's Fairy Tales" or of "Grimms' Fairy Tales," it's natural to assume that these men actually made them up, but that isn't the case; while all three were highly accomplished literary men, none of them were fairy-tale writers. They wrote them *down*, thereby creating what we may term a literary folk tale.

Consider for a moment what happens when a tale is transposed from oral performance. Even if the collectors of earlier times had had modern recording devices at their disposal, they still could not have published the tales exactly as they had heard them, for the simple reason that the spoken language is very different from the written. The judicious collector therefore had (and has) the task of making the tale "read" properly, which naturally involves the exercise of personal judgement and taste, thus imposing the "imprint" of this new intermediary. Moreover, the number of separate recorded versions of a single folk-tale type is sometimes quite amazing, reaching well into the hundreds. They come from all over the world, which presents us with some clues—and also some conundrums about the universal use of story to help people come to terms with the fears, the challenges, and the mysteries that are all part of life.

In most cases, we have no idea how old folk tales are. Once a tale has been told, it is gone; no trace of it remains except in the memories of the teller and the audience. And for the great majority of people today, memory is a fickle instrument—we only have to think back to that examination, or to the last time we lost the shopping-list, to realize how quickly (and how thoroughly) we forget. We are thus confronted with the realization that the only authentic version of the folk tale is an oral version—and since one telling will necessarily differ from the next, we must confer authenticity equally on all tellings, or—even more problematic—on the first telling alone, wherever and whenever that may have taken place.

The children's party game "Broken Telephone" provides us with an idea of just how a folk tale may have evolved as it was passed on from generation to generation. The first player begins by whispering a phrase or sentence to his or her neighbor, who must then pass it on to the next, and so on, until it reaches the last individual in the chain. Needless to say, in the progress from first to last, the words undergo some startling and often amusing changes, as they are variously misheard, misunderstood, or improved upon. On the simplest level, the game entertains by allowing us to play around with language and intention; on a more sophisticated level, we might see those changes as reflecting the preoccupations (conscious or otherwise) of the players. To put it another way, our moods, desires, and emotions will inevitably affect what is heard; we hear what we want (or expect) to hear. So it is with the folk tale; what we find there is—in part—a fragment of psychic history. An archaeologist unearths a piece of pottery and uses his professional experience and knowledge to determine its significance and function in the wider context. In the same way, we can use our growing familiarity with folk tales to identify some of the psychological elements (the "preoccupations") that give each tale much of its energy and color.

The archaeologist's discoveries generally end up in a museum—and that, in a sense, is what happens to the folk tale as well. Why use a word like "museum"? Because a museum is a place where you store and exhibit interesting dead things—and that is exactly what a folk tale is, once it's between the covers of a book. Even though a tale's oral existence may of course continue (there are even instances of literary tales becoming part of the oral tradition), the gradual spread of literacy has turned the oral tale into an endangered species; once the tale has been "frozen" in print, it can no longer evolve with telling and re-telling, since one reading will be exactly the same as any other.

It would be an exaggeration, however, to claim that the oral tale is entirely a thing of the past. Although the urban legend is much more localized and anecdotal than the folk tale and is characterized by sensationalism and black humor, it too has its origins in aspects of life that provoke anxiety or insecurity, such as our ambivalence toward technology or our suspicion that beneath the veneer of normalcy lurk chaos and madness. Like the folk tale, its "orality" is short-lived, but the intriguing question arises as to whether the Internet—often the favored means of transmission for urban legends—is itself part of the story, a kind of post-literate flux where the word is neither oral nor literate but shares qualities of both.

Today, the status and role of the storyteller are rather different; he or she is more often to be found in the rarefied atmosphere of library or classroom than in the lively informality of market-place or communal festivity. However, there is a difference between what we might term "formal" and "informal" entertainment. "Formal" entertainment is that which we consciously seek out for ourselves, generally at some expense, such as a visit to the cinema or theater. There is a clear and traditional separation between performer and audience, in which the latter plays a passive role as consumer, purchasing the professional services of the entertainer. If we look at "informal" entertainment, however, we find ourselves in surroundings much more congenial to storytelling, because the grouping (as opposed to audience) is likely to be spontaneous and transitory, such as at a cafeteria table or a party. This is not to suggest that there will be an exchange of folk tales in these more intimate settings, but there may well be some storytelling, albeit of a very local and personal nature. Nevertheless, the point can be made that that's probably the way in which many tales originated; the great majority died as quickly as they were born, a few managed a brief existence, and a tiny number contained that mysterious seed of delight, universality, or wisdom that allowed them to beat the odds and survive.

What is emerging, then, is the fact that the fairy tale must be seen as a continuum. At one extreme we find the oral folk tale, which by its very nature cannot be represented in this book. As we have already observed, the oral tale's transformation into literary form requires careful analysis not only of the tale itself, but also of the motives and values of those responsible for its metamorphosis. At the other extreme there is the literary tale, written by a specific person at a specific time, which allows us readily to place the tale in its original context, as we might do in examining any other literary work. In between these two poles, however, we have an almost unlimited number of variations, as tradition blends with invention in the writer's mind. Given this wide range of possibilities, the more general term "fairy tale" is useful in its comprehensiveness.

The first two literary collections of fairy tales in the Western tradition are by Italians whose names are relatively unknown outside scholarly circles: Giovanni Francesco Straparola (c.1480-c.1557), who published *The Facetious Nights* (1550), and Giambattista Basile (1575-1632), the collector/writer of *The Pentamerone* (1634). Unfamiliar though these collections may be, they contain early versions of many tales that would later be made famous by Charles Perrault and the Grimm brothers. Both these men clearly recognized the vitality and appeal of folk tales and brought them to the attention of a literate *adult* audience, adapting and embellishing them as contemporary literary style and social taste demanded. Another similarity shared by these fairy-tale collections is that they are both built around a frame story—a third and celebrated example of which would arrive in the shape of Antoine Galland's translation into French of the *Arabian Nights* (1704).

Even before Perrault published his now-famous collection, the popularity of the fairy tale was growing among the French upper classes, who often gathered in fashionable "salons" to discuss matters of cultural and artistic interest. One outcome of these discussions was an enthusiasm—especially among aristocratic women such as Madame la Comtesse D'Aulnoy and Madame la Comtesse de Murat—for writing highly stylized literary tales based upon folk-tale models. Like Perrault, these aristocratic ladies saw the folk tale as in need of "improvement," and consequently their tales tell us a good deal about eighteenth-century aristocratic manners as well as present a "feminist" perspective that gives the tales a distinctly contemporary edge.

However, the most famous name among the French writer/collectors of fairy tales at the beginning of the eighteenth century was Charles Perrault (1628-1703). An influential government bureaucrat in Louis XIV's France, he was involved in a vigorous literary debate of the time known as the Quarrel of the Ancients and the Moderns, in which the "Ancients" were those who asserted the superiority of Classical literature and art, while the "Moderns" were of the view that contemporary works were pre-eminent, since they could draw on all the achievements of cultural and social progress. In publishing his collection of fairy tales, *Stories or Tales from Past Times, with Morals* (1697), Perrault made his Modernist credentials clear, since the tales were both French and very unclassical! Yet while this debate is now of interest only to literary historians, his introduction of these tales of the peasants into courtly society showed a little touch of genius. As the Opies observe, "The literary skill employed in the telling of the tales is universally acknowledged; yet it also appears that the tales were set down very largely as the writer heard them told."[1] At the same time, we should also assume that Perrault was familiar with the versions of these folk tales written by his predecessors Straparola and Basile—so that Perrault's particular achievement is one of synthesizing literary sophistication with oral simplicity. The daily lives of rural peasant and urban bourgeois (not to mention aristocrat) were literally worlds apart—and Perrault responded to that fact.

One hundred years later, the joint stimuli of nationalism and Romanticism were the driving forces behind the Grimm brothers' fascination with folk tales. At a time of great political and social upheaval, caused first by French occupation and then by the process of unification as the modern Germany was being forged out of a patchwork of tiny states and principalities, there was a growing need to answer a new question: what does it mean to be German? At the same time, they were responding to the contemporary Romantic creed that the true spirit of a people was to be found not in the palaces or even the cities, but in the countryside, far away from urban sophistication. Jacob and Wilhelm Grimm (1785-1863; 1786-1859) might be described as archaeologists of a sort—although contrary to what was once believed, they were rarely if ever involved with any "digs" that first discovered these tales among the unlettered country folk. Such is the pre-eminence of the Grimms' collection *Kinder- und Hausmärchen* (first published 1812-15; published later in English as *Tales for Young and Old*) that we tend to regard it as being almost as organic and timeless a phenomenon as the tales themselves. It is nevertheless a fact that in more recent times, controversy has swirled around the Grimms' methodology and motivation in assembling their collection. The image of the brothers roaming the German countryside, gathering the tales in remote villages and hamlets, is attractive but false; generally, they were contributed by literate, middle-class friends and relatives, who thus represent yet another intermediary stage between the genuine folk tale, on the one hand, and the literary tale on the other. Indeed, the claim made by the Grimms in the Preface to the Second Edition of their tales (1819)—"... we have not embellished any detail or feature of the story told itself, but rather rendered its content just as we received it"[2]—appears confusing, given ample evidence to the contrary. We should not forget, however, that the scholarly brothers were pioneers in revising these tales for an audience radically different from the illiterate country folk among whom they originated. Ralph Manheim, the translator of the Grimm tales in this anthology, asserts that the brothers' genius was in "mak[ing] us hear the voices of the individual storytellers ... In the German text the human voice takes on a wide variety of tones ... But everywhere—or almost—it is a natural human voice,

1   Iona and Peter Opie, *The Classic Fairy Tales* (London: Oxford University Press, 1974) 21.

2   Joyce Crick, *Jacob and Wilhelm Grimm Selected Tales* (London: Oxford University Press, 2005) 8. See also Zohar Shavit, *Poetics of Children's Literature* (Athens, GA and London: University of Georgia Press, 1986) 20-27.

speaking as someone might speak..."[1] And once their popularity among children became apparent, Wilhelm in particular assumed the responsibility of ensuring that the tales were made suitable for the eyes of the child, according to contemporary notions about children's reading.

Even when we come to the tales of Hans Christian Andersen (1805-75), the link with folk tale remains strong. We perceive Andersen as a writer of original fairy tales rather than as a collector, and we assume, therefore, that his tales were exclusively of his own invention. What we need to consider is that Andersen came from a poor, working-class background in which the oral folk tale was common currency; consequently, his imagination was well primed before the world of literacy opened up new vistas of fancy to him. So it is hardly surprising to discover that several of Andersen's better-known tales (such as "The Tinderbox" and "The Princess and the Pea") either allude to, or are re-tellings of, traditional stories—some that he heard, and some that he later read. We should bear in mind that Andersen was barely a generation younger than the Grimm brothers and was well-acquainted with them; ironically, it appears that on at least one occasion, the folk tale owed a debt to Andersen: the Opies remind us that in 1843 the Grimms published a tale that closely resembled "The Princess and the Pea." However, Andersen's literary contribution to the fairy tale differs from that of the Grimms in the sense that while the latter were primarily concerned with presenting their tales in the most acceptable form to the German people, Andersen had a much more personal involvement with his tales. In his hands, a tale, whatever its source, became yet another opportunity for self-revelation. (It is no coincidence that he entitled one of his autobiographies *The Fairytale of My Life*.) As we have already seen, a knowledge of the historical context of the tales adds an extra dimension to our appreciation of them; in the case of Andersen and the other fairy-tale writers, that aspect becomes more specific, in the sense that we can now place the tales in a personal context as well as a social one.

The fact is that some rather unlikely minds have been drawn to express themselves through fairy tale, suggesting that the form retains a freedom and energy that has survived the transformation of audience from rural simplicity to urban sophistication. What attraction could the fairy tale possibly have had for such an apparently worldly individual as Oscar Wilde (1854-1900), for instance? Yet his tales show a great deal of craft and attention to detail, which suggests that they meant more to him than mere occasional pieces. Wilde, like other well-known nineteenth-century writers such as George MacDonald, John Ruskin, and even Charles Dickens, regarded the fairy tale as one of many literary forms to choose from, with its own particular advantages and limitations.

---

1   Ralph Manheim, "Preface," *Grimms' Tales for Young and Old* (Garden City, NY: Anchor Press, 1977) 1.

There is no question, however, that these writers (with the possible exception of Wilde) saw their primary audience as children—in several cases, their tales were composed with specific children in mind. Even Charles Perrault, at the end of the seventeenth century, had some awareness of the appeal of fairy tales for children, as is indicated by the frontispiece of the 1697 edition of his tales, with its inscription "Contes de ma Mère L'Oye" ("Tales of Mother Goose") and its depiction of an old woman spinning while she spins her yarn (!) to a group of children. The assumption is extended by his addition of explicit morals to the tales, thus making them overtly cautionary in nature. It is the narrator's ironic tone and occasional comment that betray his interest in appealing to an older, more sophisticated audience.

In England, the presence of the fairy tale in children's literature of the eighteenth century likewise depended on its ability to provide moral instruction. With its fantastic and sometimes violent and amoral content, the fairy tale was disapproved of by both the upholders of Puritan attitudes and the growing advocates of the more rational outlook exemplified in the philosophy and influential educational theories of John Locke. In their efforts to provide children with stories of virtue and piety, both the Rational Moralists and Sunday School Moralists of the late eighteenth and nineteenth centuries also looked upon this popular literature with a consternation verging on horror. In the periodical *The Guardian of Education*, its editor, the influential Sarah Trimmer, warned parents and governesses of the dangers of fairy tales: "A moment's consideration will surely be sufficient to convince people of the least reflection, of the danger, as well as the impropriety, of putting such books as these into the hands of little children, whose minds are susceptible to every impression; and who from the liveliness of their imaginations are apt to convert into realities whatever forcibly strikes their fancy."[1]

Despite this persistent disapproval, however, the tales were made available to eighteenth-century children through a somewhat less "respectable" source of reading material—chapbooks. The purveyors of this popular literature would not have had the scruples of the more reputable publishers, such as John Newbery, who sought to uphold the current educational theories of Locke. Chapbook publishers recognized the attraction of tales of fantasy and imagination and sought to provide them cheaply—generally by means of travelling pedlars—to the folk, child and adult alike. Thus the folk tale had, in a sense, come full circle. In being written down, it had been taken from the illiterate folk; now, as literacy was spreading slowly through the population, the tale could be returned—at a price—from whence it came.

During the early years of the nineteenth century, the Romantics would counter

---

1   Sarah Trimmer, "Nursery Tales," *The Guardian of Education* 4 (1805) 74-75, as quoted in *Children and Literature: Views and Reviews*, ed. Virginia Haviland (Glenview, IL: Scott and Foresman, 1973) 7.

the prevailing criticism of fairy tales and, in their turn denounce the moralizing and utilitarian books that were being produced for children. In his affirmation of the value of fantasy in his early reading, the poet Samuel Taylor Coleridge reacted against the common disapproval of such literature: "Should children be permitted to read Romances, and Relations of Giants and Magicians and Genii?—I know all that has been said against it; but I have formed my faith in the affirmative—I know no other way of giving the mind a love of 'the great' and 'the Whole.'"[1]

Although resistance to the fairy tale continued throughout the nineteenth century, when Grimms' fairy tales appeared in England in 1823, they were immediately popular. In the preface to his translation of the tales, Edgar Taylor criticized, in Romantic fashion, the prevailing educational goals and defended the value of fairy stories: "philosophy is made the companion of the nursery; we have lisping chemists and leading-string mathematicians ... Our imagination is surely as susceptible of improvement by exercise as our judgement and our memory."[2] His one stricture on imaginative stories was that they not interfere with moral education. Despite the acceptance of the Grimm brothers' work, it would be another twenty years before the fairy tale was fully accepted as literature for children. During the 1840s, the translation into English of Andersen's literary tales gave rise to the publication of a number of fairy-tale collections, which reached its apogee almost fifty years later in Andrew Lang's "color" series, beginning with the *Blue Fairy Book* (1889). After the success of the Grimms' tales, the arrival of Andersen's work represented an important next step in the restitution of the fairy tale, although disapproving voices could still be heard. As Jack Zipes observes, "[Andersen's] unusual tales, which combined fantasy with a moral impulse in line with traditional Christian standards, guaranteed the legitimacy of the literary fairy tale for middle-class audiences."[3] Thus, after centuries of criticism and banishment to the trade of the chapman, fairy tales and fantasy finally achieved the status they have never since lost—that of "approved" literature for children.

The second half of the nineteenth century witnessed the period that is often referred to as the Golden Age of children's literature. It may also have been the time when the lines became blurred as to just what constituted a fairy tale, since many of the works published for children were fantasies, beginning with Lewis Carroll's *Alice's Adventures in Wonderland* (1865)—and as we have already noted, Carroll himself referred to its sequel *Through the Looking-Glass* (1871) as a fairy tale. Be that as it may,

---

1 Earl Leslie Griggs, ed., *Collected Letters of Samuel Taylor Coleridge, 1785-1800.* Vol. 1 (Oxford: Clarendon Press, 1956) 354.
2 Edgar Taylor, ed., *German Popular Stories* (London: John Camden Hotten, 1869) 90.
3 Jack Zipes, "Introduction," *Victorian Fairy Tales: The Revolt of the Fairies and Elves* (New York: Methuen, 1987) xviii.

the fairy tale evolved in several ways: it grew longer (as in the work of writers such as George MacDonald and Andrew Lang), more didactic (Charles Kingsley's *The Water Babies* [1863] and the stories of Mary Louisa Molesworth are examples), and more focused upon social issues (see the section "A Less Than Perfect World"). Indeed, this last point raises an interesting paradox in the literary tale's evolution from the folk tale. Despite the *collective* nature of the folk tale's composition, its concerns are generally those of the individual, such as growing up, establishing a relationship, and so on. When we turn to the literary tale, it is attributable to a *single* writer but now tends to deal with social (i.e., collective) subjects.

However, in the process of becoming so closely associated with children, fairy tales have all too often been dismissed as literature not worthy of serious attention on the part of adult readers. In his pioneering essay "On Fairy Stories," J.R.R. Tolkien, author of the fantasy works *The Hobbit* and *Lord of the Rings*, was among the first to point out that this association of fairy stories with children is a historical accident and that children "neither like fairy-stories more, nor understand them better than adults do; and no more than they like other things."[1] Tolkien saw fairy stories as a natural branch of literature sharing the same qualities as may be found in many other genres.

It certainly can be argued that the fairy tale has regained an adult audience in recent times, as the modern tales and poems in this anthology demonstrate. The surprise is in the fact that these tales have been out of favor for so long among older readers, since, as Max Lüthi observes, fairy tales present us with both adult and child triumphing over their (and our) deepest fears and desires. Perhaps we have been the victims of our own rationalistic preconceptions of what a fairy tale actually is and what it has to say to us. Bruno Bettelheim's observation that at each stage of our lives, fairy tales take on new significance and speak "simultaneously to all levels of the human personality, communicating in a manner which reaches the uneducated mind of the child as well as that of the sophisticated adult" (see p. 326) was hardly a revelation in itself, but the impact that his book *The Uses of Enchantment: The Meaning and Importance of Fairy Tales* made when it was published in 1976 suggested that the time was ripe for a reappraisal—a project that has produced a substantial body of scholarship.

This recognition of the ability of the fairy tale to appeal to both child and adult has resulted in a recent resurgence of publications that address both audiences. A quick survey of any bookstore will reveal a number of shelves in the children's section devoted to fairy tales. They will doubtless include classic tales by Perrault, the Grimms, and Andersen, most likely in the form of lavishly illustrated individual works. Also available will be versions that reflect a particular motivation in

---

1   J.R.R. Tolkien, "On Fairy Stories," *Tree and Leaf* 2nd ed (London: George Allen and Unwin, 1975) 38.

their tellers—feminist, psychological, or environmental, for instance—whose approach ranges from parody to realism. Nearby the browser will come across shelves devoted to novel-length retellings intended for the young-adult reader (female in particular) by authors such as Jane Yolen, Robin McKinley, and Donna Jo Napoli, whose work—not surprisingly—tends to focus upon those tales that deal with the challenges of growing up. The fairy tale has made inroads into adult fiction as well; several well-known novelists (Margaret Atwood, A.S. Byatt, and Gregory Maguire among them) have acknowledged the deep and abiding influence that fairy tales have had on their own writing. And for those who remain unconvinced about how deeply embedded the fairy tale is in our collective unconscious, we note that on more specialized shelves in our hypothetical bookstore may be found such titles as *From Cinderella to CEO: How to Master the 10 Lessons of Fairy Tales to Transform Your Work Life* (2005), *Teaching Thinking Skills with Fairy Tales and Fantasy* (2005)—or even *Erotic Fairy Tales: A Romp Through the Classics* (2001). What emerges is that the fairy tale remains as relevant, democratic, and adaptable as it has ever been in its long history.

Without a doubt, however, the most significant development for the fairy tale (and for culture in general) in the twentieth century came from the film medium. The screening of *Snow White and the Seven Dwarves* in 1937 initiated the phenomenal influence that the Walt Disney studios have exerted upon our experience of the fairy tale. Seventy years and numerous films later, the animated Disney fairy tale is the first, and often only, version with which North Americans are familiar. For better or for worse—like all storytellers, collectors, and re-writers—Walt Disney has put his own imprint upon the tales. However, unlike his predecessors, he chose to combine the power of the film medium with the Disney entertainment empire (Disney World, Disney Land, and Euro-Disney, where we can meet and dine with Cinderella and Sleeping Beauty), to both disseminate and consolidate his vision to an unprecedented degree. Although Disney's influence has provoked fierce criticism (see Betsy Hearne's article), it is only recently —through the medium of film of course—that Disney's twentieth-century hegemony over the fairy tale has been challenged. Replacing Disney's royal romances are the sophisticated fractured fairy tales such as the *Shrek* series (2001, 2004, 2007) and *Hoodwinked* (2005) (see James Poniewozik's article). Disney's apparently unassailable pairing of fairy tale and animation has now been broadened to include "realistic" fairy-tale films such as *Ever After* (1998) or *Enchanted* (2007) and fantasy television shows such as *The Tenth Kingdom* (2000). Not surprisingly, the wide range of approaches to be found in contemporary books is paralleled in the medium of film. Yet, as the example of Disney's influence so clearly demonstrates, film and television have emerged as the current media of popular culture. In so doing (criticism of Disney notwithstanding), they have made the fairy tale very much a part of mass culture, just as it once was a part of folk culture; in this respect, the folk tale has come full circle.

One essential feature that has hopefully been established in this introduction, and that will be confirmed in the sections that follow, is that fairy tales can come in a bewildering number of versions. It begins with the infinite variability of the oral folk tale, continues with the differing assumptions or agendas of collectors, translators, and editors as the tale takes on literary form, and then undergoes constant transformation as generations of writers and illustrators are drawn to this mother-lode of story. Exploring the world of fairy tale, therefore, becomes rather a different kind of challenge than reading a nineteenth-century novel, for instance. While we may choose to read other works by the same author or historical texts to understand the context of the novel, the fact remains that we are dealing with just one novel. That is rarely the case with the fairy tale—and so to base a theory on the evidence of one version alone may well be to build a house of cards, for who is to say that this version is more authentic than any other? In some cases it may be possible to demonstrate that a particular version is the oldest of known variants—but is age the only criterion? Is it even possible to think of one specific version of a folk tale as definitive? Thus, any theory that we may devise applies in the first instance only to one version of a particular tale; the challenge then is to see if it retains its validity on being applied to other versions and even other tales.[1]

---

1   See Alan Dundes's fuller discussion of this issue in his article "Fairy Tales from a Folkloristic Perspective," in the Criticism section, p. 335.

LITTLE RED RIDING HOOD

FOR WHAT IS UNQUESTIONABLY ONE of the classic fairy tales, "Little Red Riding Hood" is more surprising for what it lacks than for what it contains. There is no royalty, no enchantment, no romance—just a talking wolf with a big appetite. How then has the heroine of this tale become as famous a figure as her more glamorous cousins, Sleeping Beauty, Cinderella, and Snow White? What is so remarkable about this stark little tale that describes the dramatic confrontation between an innocent little girl and a wicked wolf? How has it come about that the line "Grandmother, what big teeth you have!" is one of the most anticipated and familiar moments in all of Western literature, let alone fairy tale?

First of all, this is not a real wolf—and arguably neither child nor adult reader ever takes him as such. The first story in this section actually identifies him as a "bzou" or werewolf ("wer" is Old English for "man"), and, as Jack Zipes points out in his discussion of this version in *The Trials and Tribulations of Little Red Riding Hood*,

> The direct forebears of Perrault's literary tale were not influenced by sun worship or Christian theology, but by the very material conditions of their existence and traditional pagan superstition. Little children were attacked and killed by animals and grown-ups in the woods and fields. Hunger often drove people to commit atrocious acts. In the 15th and 16th centuries, violence was difficult to explain on rational grounds. There was a strong superstitious belief in werewolves and witches, uncontrollable magical forces of nature, which threatened the lives of the peasant population…. Consequently, the warning tale became part of a stock oral repertoire of storytellers.[1]

---

1 Jack D. Zipes, ed., *The Trials and Tribulations of Little Red Riding Hood,* 2nd ed. (New York: Routledge, 1993) 18-20.

Although it was only recorded in 1885, scholars are in general agreement that "The Story of Grandmother" is likely very similar to the version that Perrault heard two hundred years earlier. There are several intriguing aspects to this early version of the tale. The representation of the two paths through the forest as being of needles and pins is no doubt a play on the pine needles that carpet the forest floor; it may also be a sly reference to one of the domestic tasks that awaits feminine maturity. This tale also has a crudeness that underlines its folk origins—a conclusion borne out by the fact that variants from other parts of the world contain similar scatological episodes. Paul Delarue, the editor of the collection from which this tale was taken, observes in his notes that "... the common elements that are lacking in [Perrault's] story are precisely those which would have shocked the society of his period by their cruelness [sic] ... and their impropriety."[1]

Thus, what we see in Perrault's version is the adaptation of a gross folk tale to the more sophisticated tastes of high society. He removes all overt human aspects of his antagonist, relying simply on the powerful archetypal image of the wolf as predator and interloper. By way of compensation for his excision of the tale's vulgarities, Perrault appears to be responsible for the artistic touch of the red riding hood; he would doubtless be both shocked and amused to learn how controversial an addition that turned out to be! He tells us that it's a "hood like the ones that fine ladies wear when they go riding," which suggests that he's again trying to link the tale with the world of his audience—but why is it *red*? We are confronted with a color symbolic of sexuality that provides a further hint about Perrault's own assumptions regarding this tale.

The ending of "The Story of Grandmother" catches our eye because its happy outcome is attributable to the girl's practical quick-wittedness—a quality that Perrault denies his heroine, in keeping with his bourgeois assumptions about female naïvety and vulnerability, which make Little Red Riding Hood into the wolf's unwitting accomplice. Perrault's tragic and presumably truncated ending, which catches the modern reader so much by surprise, goes against folk-tale custom, but it is clear that such an ending suited Perrault's purposes admirably, given the Moral that he appended to the tale: "Children, especially pretty, nicely brought-up young ladies, ought never to talk to strangers..." Just what induced Perrault to add his Morals to the tales is unclear, but it was surely a critical moment in the evolution of the fairy tale as children's literature; to this day, the belief has persisted that the purpose of a tale is to inculcate morals in young minds. We must remember that Perrault was a pioneer in recognizing the potential appeal of these tales and transforming them from an oral into a literary form. As Jack Zipes points out,

---

1   Paul Delarue, comp., *Borzoi Book of French Folk Tales,* trans. Austin E. Fife (New York: Knopf, 1956).

Perrault's tale of "Little Red Riding Hood" had an unusually successful reception in the 18th century. In fact, it was one of the few literary tales in history which, due to its universality, ambivalence, and clever sexual innuendos, was reabsorbed by the oral folk tradition. That is, as a result of its massive circulation in print in the 18th and 19th centuries and of the corroboration of peasant experience, it took root in oral folklore and eventually led to the creation of the even more popular Grimms' tale, which had the same effect.[1]

When we turn to the Grimms' version, published over a hundred years later, we find a synthesis of the other two, with some intriguing additions. (Despite the Grimms' insistence that they were capturing the essence of the German spirit in their tales, it is surely not coincidental that the family that contributed this tale was of French extraction.) The red garment remains, as does the wolf; like Perrault, the Grimms choose to gloss over the cannibalistic snack that the girl unwittingly makes of her grandmother, and the "happy" ending has been restored—but only through the intervention of the paternalistic hunter, in a scene derived, according to Paul Delarue, from another French tale, "The Goat and Her Kids."

Nevertheless, it can be argued that the Grimm version is the most balanced, at least to the contemporary reader. The hunter presents an image of male goodness that counters the male wickedness of the wolf; the mother appears concerned about her daughter's correct behavior, if not her welfare—and the less familiar appended story, describing the defeat of a second wolf through the strategy of a wiser girl and grandmother, sends a very different message from Perrault's harsh ending, reminding us that, having realized the popularity of their tales among children, the Grimms endeavored to select and edit them with desirable educational principles in mind.

The story of Little Red Riding Hood has for so long been an inescapable part of growing up in the English language that it is hard enough to contemplate its greater authenticity in French or German. It comes as an even greater shock, therefore, to realize how old and widespread the tale is in Asia; Delarue points out that versions of the tale are widely distributed in China, Japan, and Korea.[2]

"The Chinese Red Riding Hoods" also reveals significant structural differences, but, on closer examination, we may be surprised to discover just how many of the elements from the previous versions are to be found here: as in "The Story of Grandmother," the children escape from the wolf's clutches by means of a clever ruse, and his final demise is brought about by much the same strategy as in the conclusion to

---

1   Zipes, *The Trials and Tribulations* 31.
2   In Alan Dundes, ed., *Little Red Riding Hood: A Casebook* (Madison, WI: University of Wisconsin Press, 1989) 13.

"Little Red Cap"—that is, by exploiting the greed and self-indulgence that are central to the fairy-tale wolf's character.

In some respects, this Chinese version has a distinctly contemporary feel. The mother is described as a young widow who teaches her children carefully about the nature of the world; yet the time must come when her children will have to fend for themselves—and at that moment of crisis, the girls prove susceptible to the wolf's trickery. Despite their mistake, however, the sisters (led by the formidable Felice) are able to keep their wits about them and finally outsmart the deceitful wolf. The experience may have deprived them of at least some of their trust in those around them; by the same token, they will be less likely to be fooled a second time.

What is intriguing about "Flossie and the Fox," by Patricia McKissack, is that it presents us with yet another central character who, like her Chinese counterparts, follows in the female trickster tradition that emerged in "The Story of Grandmother." Not surprisingly, this tale too is close to the oral tradition, as McKissack explains in her Author's Note. Indeed, the setting of the rural American South may remind us of a considerably more notorious mischief-maker in the shape of Brer Rabbit—not least because Flossie's would-be antagonist is a rather supercilious fox instead of a wolf. The fact that Flossie has the situation fully under control signifies a complete reversal of the message of female helplessness in Perrault's tale, a conceptual shift that Angela Carter will bring to triumphant conclusion in "The Company of Wolves," as we shall see.

The concern with the suitability of the fairy tale for a younger audience, which began with Perrault and became increasingly a concern for the Grimms with each subsequent edition of their tales, is even more apparent in contemporary reworkings. A good example is to be found in the popular work of American writer-illustrator David McPhail. His adherence to the traditional non-specific setting ensures that his version (1995) is easily accessible, Little Red Riding Hood is clever and resourceful, the Wolf is outsmarted in comic fashion with no one getting hurt, and the moral messages are communicated without a hint of the violence and underlying sexuality that are so much a part of earlier versions of the tale. The goal, as the book jacket claims, is to provide "tales that are perfect for today's very young child."

By contrast, it is quickly apparent that Angela Carter (1940-92), in "The Company of Wolves" (1979), is not writing for the child reader: her diction is too sophisticated, her interpretation of the tale too complex and disturbing for the younger mind. It is as if Carter is returning the tale to something resembling its original condition, while recognizing that modern literate adults represent a very different audience from their ancestors who first *heard* them in a very different world. It is clearly the *real* world behind the folk tale that particularly fascinated Carter—that potent cocktail of superstition, fear, and primitive religion that together lead the human imagination to strange and disturbing places. Thus, the first part of her tale is devoted to creating a realistic context that is a far cry from the romantic dream-world which has become the customary backdrop to modern retellings of fairy tales. (Very different though the tales are, we may nevertheless detect a similarity with "Flossie and the Fox" in this regard.) Consequently, this story has a flesh-and-blood materiality that is just one among several reminders of "The Story of Grandmother." Carter's most significant revision of the tale comes at the end, however, when she startles us with what amounts to a radical reversal of sexual stereotypes. If we inject some ferocity into the female and some tenderness into the male, who knows what the outcome might be…

To this point, all the versions of Little Red Riding Hood have been set in rural surroundings, as befits their origins. The modern world, however, is essentially an urban one, and that fact is reflected in Francesca Lia Block's "Wolf" (2000), which takes place, at least in part, in the concrete jungle of Los Angeles. While Carter brings new life to the tale by creating a quasi-historical context, Block finds her perspective in the harsh light of social realism (Sarah Moon uses the medium of photography to much the same effect; see p. 300). For the first time, the story is told from the girl's point of view (and, like Carter, Block has chosen to add some years to her central character whose age, the "Little" in her name notwithstanding, has been ambiguous from the beginning). With this story of abuse, loneliness, and misery, we have come a long way from the fairy-tale world of Little Red Riding Hood, and yet the dark shadows are visible from the beginning; the fact that writers have chosen to peer more and more closely into that darkness says something both about us and about the remarkable potency of this encounter between a girl and a wolf.

We conclude this section on a lighter note. In "What Bugs Bunny Said to Red Riding Hood" (1999), Tim Seibles confronts one cultural icon with another; more particularly, he brings Bugs Bunny's worldly irreverence to bear on Red Riding Hood's risky undertaking. Despite its frivolous tone, the poem reveals quite effectively the elements of fantasy and reality that in combination can produce such an explosive effect and reminds us that it's not always sheep's clothing that conceals the wolf.

THE STORY OF GRANDMOTHER[1]

Paul Delarue

THERE WAS ONCE A WOMAN who had some bread, and she said to her daughter: "You are going to carry a hot loaf and a bottle of milk to your grandmother."

The little girl departed. At the crossroads she met the *bzou*, who said to her: "Where are you going?"

"I'm taking a hot loaf and a bottle of milk to my grandmother."

"What road are you taking," said the *bzou*, "the Needles Road or the Pins Road?" "The Needles Road," said the little girl.

"Well, I shall take the Pins Road."

The little girl enjoyed herself picking up needles. Meanwhile the *bzou* arrived at her grandmother's, killed her, put some of her flesh in the pantry and a bottle of her blood on the shelf. The little girl arrived and knocked at the door.

"Push the door," said the *bzou*, "it's closed with a wet straw."

"Hello, Grandmother; I'm bringing you a hot loaf and a bottle of milk."

"Put them in the pantry. You eat the meat that's in it and drink a bottle of wine that is on the shelf."

As she ate there was a little cat that said: "A slut is she who eats the flesh and drinks the blood of her grandmother!"

"Undress, my child," said the *bzou*, "and come and sleep beside me."

"Where should I put my apron?"

"Throw it in the fire, my child; you don't need it any more."

"Where should I put my bodice?"

"Throw it in the fire, my child; you don't need it any more."

"Where should I put my dress?"

"Throw it in the fire, my child; you don't need it any more."

"Where should I put my skirt?"

"Throw it in the fire, my child; you don't need it any more."

"Where should I put my hose?"

"Throw it in the fire, my child; you don't need it any more."

"Oh, Grandmother, how hairy you are!"

"It's to keep me warmer, my child."

"Oh, Grandmother, those long nails you have!"

"It's to scratch me better, my child!"

---

1 First collected in 1885; this text from Delarue, *The Borzoi Book of French Folktales*, trans. Austin E. Fife (New York: Knopf, 1956).

"Oh, Grandmother, those big shoulders that you have!"

"All the better to carry kindling from the woods, my child."

"Oh, Grandmother, those big ears that you have!"

"All the better to hear with, my child."

"Oh, Grandmother, that big mouth you have!"

"All the better to eat you with, my child!"

"Oh, Grandmother, I need to go outside to relieve myself."

"Do it in the bed, my child."

"Oh, Grandmother, I want to go outside."

"All right, but don't stay long."

The *bzou* tied a woolen thread to her foot and let her go out, and when the little girl was outside she tied the end of the string to a big plum tree in the yard. The *bzou* got impatient and said:

"Are you making cables?"

When he became aware that no one answered him, he jumped out of bed and saw that the little girl had escaped. He followed her, but he arrived at her house just at the moment she was safely inside.

LITTLE RED RIDING HOOD[1]

Charles Perrault

ONCE UPON A TIME, DEEP in the heart of the country, there lived a pretty little girl whose mother adored her, and her grandmother adored her even more. This good woman made her a red hood like the ones that fine ladies wear when they go riding. The hood suited the child so much that soon everybody was calling her Little Red Riding Hood.

One day, her mother baked some cakes on the griddle and said to Little Red Riding Hood:

"Your granny is sick; you must go and visit her. Take her one of these cakes and a little pot of butter."

Little Red Riding Hood went off to the next village to visit her grandmother. As she walked through the wood, she met a wolf, who wanted to eat her but did not dare to because there were woodcutters working nearby. He asked her where

---

1 First published in 1697. This text from *Sleeping Beauty and Other Favourite Fairy Tales,* trans. Angela Carter (London: Gollancz, 1982).

she was going. The poor child did not know how dangerous it is to chatter away to wolves and replied innocently:

"I'm going to visit my grandmother to take her this cake and this little pot of butter from my mother."

"Does your grandmother live far away?" asked the wolf.

"Oh yes," said Little Red Riding Hood. "She lives beyond the mill you can see over there, in the first house you come to in the village."

"Well, I shall go and visit her, too," said the wolf. "I will take *this* road and you shall take *that* road and let's see who can get there first."

The wolf ran off by the shortest path and Red Riding Hood went off the longest way and she made it still longer because she dawdled along, gathering nuts and chasing butterflies and picking bunches of wayside flowers.

The wolf soon arrived at Grandmother's house. He knocked on the door, rat tat tat.

"Who's there?"

"Your granddaughter, Little Red Riding Hood," said the wolf, disguising his voice. "I've brought you a cake baked on the griddle and a little pot of butter from my mother."

Grandmother was lying in bed because she was poorly. She called out: "Lift up the latch and walk in!"

The wolf lifted the latch and opened the door. He had not eaten for three days. He threw himself on the good woman and gobbled her up. Then he closed the door behind him and lay down in Grandmother's bed to wait for Little Red Riding Hood. At last she came knocking on the door, rat tat tat.

"Who's there?"

Little Red Riding Hood heard the hoarse voice of the wolf and thought that her grandmother must have caught a cold. She answered:

"It's your granddaughter, Little Red Riding Hood. I've brought you a cake baked on the griddle and a little pot of butter from my mother."

The wolf disguised his voice and said:

"Lift up the latch and walk in."

Little Red Riding Hood lifted the latch and opened the door.

When the wolf saw her come in, he hid himself under the bedclothes and said to her:

"Put the cake and the butter down on the bread-bin and come and lie down with me."

Little Red Riding Hood took off her clothes and went to lie down in the bed. She was surprised to see how odd her grandmother looked. She said to her:

"Grandmother, what big arms you have!"

"All the better to hold you with, my dear."

"Grandmother, what big legs you have!"

"All the better to run with, my dear."

"Grandmother, what big ears you have!"

"All the better to hear with, my dear."

"Grandmother, what big eyes you have!"

"All the better to see with, my dear!"

"Grandmother, what big teeth you have!"

"All the better to eat you up!"

At that, the wicked wolf threw himself upon Little Red Riding Hood and gobbled her up, too.

Moral

Children, especially pretty, nicely brought-up young ladies, ought never to talk to strangers; if they are foolish enough to do so, they should not be surprised if some greedy wolf consumes them, elegant red riding hoods and all.

Now, there are real wolves, with hairy pelts and enormous teeth; but also wolves who seem perfectly charming, sweet-natured and obliging, who pursue young girls in the street and pay them the most flattering attentions.

Unfortunately, these smooth-tongued, smooth-pelted wolves are the most dangerous beasts of all.

LITTLE RED CAP[1]

Jacob and Wilhelm Grimm

ONCE THERE WAS A DEAR little girl whom everyone loved. Her grandmother loved her most of all and didn't know what to give the child next. Once she gave her a little red velvet cap, which was so becoming to her that she never wanted to wear anything else, and that was why everyone called her Little Red Cap. One day her mother said: "Look, Little Red Cap, here's a piece of cake and a bottle of wine. Take them to grandmother. She is sick and weak, and they will make her feel better. You'd better start now before it gets too hot; walk properly like a good little girl, and don't leave the path or you'll fall down and break the bottle and there won't be anything

---

1 First published in 1812/15, in the first edition of *Kinder- und Hausmärchen*. This text from the second edition (1819), from *Grimms' Tales for Young and Old*, trans. Ralph Manheim (Garden City, NY: Anchor Press, 1977).

for grandmother. And when you get to her house, don't forget to say good morning, and don't go looking in all the corners."

"I'll do everything right," Little Red Cap promised her mother. Her grandmother lived in the wood, half an hour's walk from the village. No sooner had Little Red Cap set foot in the wood than she met the wolf. But Little Red Cap didn't know what a wicked beast he was, so she wasn't afraid of him. "Good morning, Little Red Cap," he said. "Thank you kindly, wolf." "Where are you going so early, Little Red Cap?" "To my grandmother's." "And what's that you've got under your apron?" "Cake and wine. We baked yesterday, and we want my grandmother, who's sick and weak, to have something nice that will make her feel better." "Where does your grandmother live, Little Red Cap?" "In the wood, fifteen or twenty minutes' walk from here, under the three big oak trees. That's where the house is. It has hazel hedges around it. You must know the place." "How young and tender she is!" thought the wolf. "Why, she'll be even tastier than the old woman. Maybe if I'm crafty enough I can get them both." So, after walking along for a short while beside Little Red Cap, he said: "Little Red Cap, open your eyes. What lovely flowers! Why don't you look around you? I don't believe you even hear how sweetly the birds are singing. It's so gay out here in the wood, yet you trudge along as solemnly as if you were going to school."

Little Red Cap looked up, and when she saw the sunbeams dancing this way and that between the trees and the beautiful flowers all around her, she thought: "Grandmother will be pleased if I bring her a bunch of nice fresh flowers. It's so early now that I'm sure to be there in plenty of time." So she left the path and went into the wood to pick flowers. And when she had picked one, she thought there must be a more beautiful one farther on, so she went deeper and deeper into the wood. As for the wolf, he went straight to the grandmother's house and knocked at the door. "Who's there?" "Little Red Cap, bringing cake and wine. Open the door." "Just raise the latch," cried the grandmother, "I'm too weak to get out of bed." The wolf raised the latch and the door swung open. Without saying a single word he went straight to the grandmother's bed and gobbled her up. Then he put on her clothes and her nightcap, lay down in the bed, and drew the curtains.

Meanwhile Little Red Cap had been running about picking flowers, and when she had as many as she could carry she remembered her grandmother and started off again. She was surprised to find the door open, and when she stepped into the house she had such a strange feeling that she said to herself: "My goodness, I'm usually so glad to see grandmother. Why am I frightened today?" "Good morning," she cried out, but there was no answer. Then she went to the bed and opened the curtains. The grandmother had her cap pulled way down over her face, and looked very strange.

"Oh, grandmother, what big ears you have!"

"The better to hear you with."

"Oh, grandmother, what big eyes you have!"

"The better to see you with."

"Oh, grandmother, what big hands you have!"

"The better to grab you with."

"But, grandmother, what a dreadful big mouth you have!"

"The better to eat you with."

And no sooner had the wolf spoken than he bounded out of bed and gobbled up poor Little Red Cap.

When the wolf had stilled his hunger, he got back into bed, fell asleep, and began to snore very very loud. A hunter was just passing, and he thought: "How the old woman is snoring! I'd better go and see what's wrong." So he stepped into the house and went over to the bed and saw the wolf was in it. "You old sinner!" he said, "I've found you at last. It's been a long time." He levelled his musket and was just about to fire when it occurred to him that the wolf might have swallowed the grandmother and that there might still be a chance of saving her. So instead of firing, he took a pair of scissors and started cutting the sleeping wolf's belly open. After two snips, he saw the little red cap, and after another few snips the little girl jumped out, crying: "Oh, I've been so afraid! It was so dark inside the wolf!" And then the old grandmother came out, and she too was still alive, though she could hardly breathe. Little Red Cap ran outside and brought big stones, and they filled the wolf's belly with them. When he woke up, he wanted to run away, but the stones were so heavy that his legs wouldn't carry him and he fell dead.

All three were happy; the hunter skinned the wolf and went home with the skin; the grandmother ate the cake and drank the wine Little Red Cap had brought her and soon got well; and as for Little Red Cap, she said to herself: "Never again will I leave the path and run off into the wood when my mother tells me not to."

Another story they tell is that when Little Red Cap was taking another cake to her old grandmother another wolf spoke to her and tried to make her leave the path. But Little Red Cap was on her guard. She kept on going, and when she got to her grandmother's she told her how she had met a wolf who had bidden her good day but given her such a wicked look that "if it hadn't been on the open road he'd have gobbled me right up." "Well then," said the grandmother, "we'll just lock the door and he won't be able to get in." In a little while the wolf knocked and called out: "Open the door, grandmother, it's Little Red Cap. I've brought you some cake." But they didn't say a word and they didn't open the door. So Grayhead circled the house once or twice and finally jumped on the roof. His plan was to wait until evening when Little Red Cap would go home, and then he'd creep after her and gobble her up in the darkness. But the grandmother guessed what he had in mind. There was a big stone trough in front of the house, and she said to the child: "Here's a bucket,

Little Red Cap. I cooked some sausages yesterday. Take the water I cooked them in and empty it into the trough." Little Red Cap carried water until the trough was full. The smell of the sausages rose up to the wolf's nostrils. He sniffed and looked down, and in the end he stuck his neck out so far that he couldn't keep his footing and began to slide. And he slid off the roof and slid straight into the big trough and was drowned. And Little Red Cap went happily home, and no one harmed her.

THE CHINESE RED RIDING HOODS[1]

Isabelle C. Chang

"Beware of the wolf in sheep's clothing."

MANY YEARS AGO IN CHINA there lived a young widow with her three children. On their grandmother's birthday, the mother went to visit her.

"Felice," she cautioned her oldest daughter before she left, "you must watch over your sisters Mayling and Jeanne while I am gone. Lock the door and don't let anyone inside. I shall be back tomorrow."

A wolf who was hiding near the house at the edge of the woods overheard the news.

When it was dark he disguised himself as an elderly woman and knocked at the door of the three girls' house.

"Who is it?" called Felice.

"Felice, Mayling, and Jeanne, my treasures, it is your Grammie," answered the wolf as sweetly as possible.

"Grammie," said Felice through the door, "Mummy just went to see you!"

"It is too bad I missed her. We must have taken different roads," replied the crafty wolf.

"Grammie," asked Mayling, "why is your voice so different tonight?"

"Your old Grammie caught cold and is hoarse. Please let me in quickly, for it is drafty out here and the night air is very bad for me."

The tenderhearted girls could not bear to keep their grandmother out in the cold, so they unlatched the door and shouted, "Grammie, Grammie!"

As soon as the wolf crossed the threshold, he blew out the candle, saying the light

---

1   From *Chinese Fairy Tales* (Barre, MA: Barre Publishers, 1965).

hurt his tired eyes. Felice pulled a chair forward for her grandmother. The wolf sat down hard on his tail hidden under the skirt.

"Ouch!" he exclaimed.

"Is something wrong, Grammie?" asked Felice.

"Nothing at all, my dear," said the wolf, bearing the pain silently.

Then Mayling and Jeanne wanted to sit on their Grammie's lap.

"What nice, plump children," said the wolf, holding Mayling on one knee and Jeanne on the other.

Soon the wolf said, "Grammie is tired and so are you children. Let's go to bed."

The children begged as usual to be allowed to sleep in the huge double bed with their Grammie.

Soon Jeanne felt the wolf's tail against her toes. "Grammie, what's that furry thing?" she asked.

"Oh, that's just the brush I always have by me to keep away mosquitoes and flies," answered the wolf.

Then Mayling felt the sharp claws of the wolf. "Grammie, what are these sharp things?"

"Go to sleep, dear, they are just Grammie's nails."

Then Felice lit the candle and caught a glimpse of the wolf's hairy face before he could blow out the light. Felice was frightened. She quickly grabbed hold of Jeanne and said, "Grammie, Jeanne is thirsty. She needs to get up to get a glass of water."

"Oh, for goodness sake," said the wolf, losing patience, "tell her to wait until later."

Felice pinched Jeanne so that she started to cry.

"All right, all right," said the wolf, "Jeanne may get up."

Felice thought quickly and said, "Mayling, hurry and help Jeanne get a glass of water!"

When the two younger ones had left the bedroom, Felice said, "Grammie, have you ever tasted our luscious gingko nuts?"

"What is a gingko nut?" asked the wolf.

"The meat of the gingko nut is softer and more tender than a firm baby and tastes like a delicious fairy food," replied Felice.

"Where can you get some?" asked the wolf, drooling.

"Those nuts grow on trees outside our house."

"Well, your Grammie is too old to climb trees now," sighed the wolf.

"Grammie, dear, I can pick some for you," said Felice sweetly.

"Will you, angel?" pleaded the wolf.

"Of course, I'll do it right now!" said Felice, leaping out of bed.

"Come back quickly," called the wolf after her.

Felice found Mayling and Jeanne in the other room. She told them about the wolf, and the three girls quickly decided to climb up the tallest gingko tree around their cottage.

The wolf waited and waited, but no one came back. Then he got up and went outside and shouted, "Felice, Mayling, Jeanne, where are you?"

"We're up in the tree, eating gingko nuts," called Felice.

"Throw some down for me," yelled the wolf.

"Ah, Grammie, we just remembered Mummy telling us that gingkos are fairy nuts. They change when they leave the tree. You'll just have to climb up and eat these mouthwatering nuts here."

The wolf was raging as he paced back and forth under the tree.

Then Felice said, "Grammie, I just had an idea. There is a clothesbasket by the door with a long clothesline inside. Tie one end to the handle and throw the end of the rope up to me. We shall pull you up here."

The wolf happily went to get the clothesbasket.

Felice pulled hard on the rope. When the basket was halfway up, she let go, and the wolf fell to the ground badly bruised.

"Boo hoo, hoo!" cried Felice, pretending to be very sorry. "I did not have enough strength to pull poor Grammie up!"

"Don't cry, Sister," said Mayling, "I'll help you pull Grammie up!"

The greedy wolf got into the basket again.

Felice and Mayling pulled with all their might. The wolf was two-thirds up the tree before they let go of the rope. Down he fell with a crash. He began to scold.

"Grammie, Grammie, please don't get so upset," begged Jeanne. "I'll help my sisters to pull you all the way this time."

"All right, but mind you be very careful or I'll bite your heads off!" screeched the wolf.

The three children pulled with all their strength.

"Heave ho, heave ho!" they sang in rhythm as they hauled the wolf up slowly till he was thirty feet high. He was just beyond reach of a branch when Felice coughed and everyone let go of the rope. As the basket spun down, the wolf let out his last howl.

When the children were unable to get any answer to their calls of "Grammie," they slid down the tree and ran into the house, latched the door and soon went to sleep.

FLOSSIE AND THE FOX[1]

Patricia C. McKissack

Author's Note

Long before I became a writer, I was a listener. On hot summer evenings our family sat on the porch and listened to my grandmother dramatize a Dunbar poem. But it was always a special treat when my grandfather took the stage. He was a master storyteller who charmed his audience with humorous stories told in the rich and colorful dialect of the rural South. I never wanted to forget them. So, it is through me that my family's storytelling legacy lives on.

Here is a story from my youth, retold in the same rich and colorful language that was my grandfather's. He began all his yarns with a question. "Did I ever tell you 'bout the time lil' Flossie Finley come out the Piney Woods heeling a fox?" I'd snuggle up beside him in the big porch swing, then he'd begin his tale...

"Flo-o-o-ossie!"

The sound of Big Mama's voice floated past the cabins in Sophie's Quarters, round the smokehouse, beyond the chicken coop, all the way down to Flossie Finley. Flossie tucked away her straw doll in a hollow log, then hurried to answer her grandmother's call.

"Here I am, Big Mama," Flossie said after catching her breath. It was hot, hotter than a usual Tennessee August day.

Big Mama stopped sortin' peaches and wiped her hands and face with her apron. "Take these to Miz Viola over at the McCutchin Place," she say reaching behind her and handing Flossie a basket of fresh eggs. "Seem like they been troubled by a fox. Miz Viola's chickens be so scared, they can't even now lay a stone." Big Mama clicked her teeth and shook her head.

"Why come Mr. J.W. can't catch the fox with his dogs?" Flossie asked, putting a peach in her apron pocket to eat later.

"Ever-time they corner that ol' slickster, he gets away. I tell you, that fox is one sly critter."

"How do a fox look?" Flossie asked. "I disremember ever seeing one."

Big Mama had to think a bit. "Chile, a fox be just a fox. But one thing for sure, that rascal loves eggs. He'll do most anything to get at some eggs."

---

1 Published in 1986 (New York: Dial).

Flossie tucked the basket under her arm and started on her way. "Don't tarry now," Big Mama called. "And be particular 'bout them eggs."

"Yes'um," Flossie answered.

The way through the woods was shorter and cooler than the road route under the open sun. *What if I come upon a fox?* thought Flossie. *Oh well, a fox be just a fox. That aine so scary.*

Flossie commenced to skip along, when she come upon a critter she couldn't recollect ever seeing. He was sittin' 'side the road like he was expectin' somebody. Flossie skipped right up to him and nodded a greeting the way she'd been taught to do.

"Top of the morning to you, Little Missy," the critter replied. "And what is your name?"

"I be Flossie Finley," she answered with a proper curtsy. "I reckon I don't know who you be either."

Slowly the animal circled round Flossie. "I am a fox," he announced, all the time eyeing the basket of eggs. He stopped in front of Flossie, smiled as best a fox can, and bowed. "At your service."

Flossie rocked back on her heels then up on her toes, back and forward, back and forward ... carefully studying the creature who was claiming to be a fox.

"Nope," she said at last. "I just purely don't believe it."

"You don't believe what?" Fox asked, looking way from the basket of eggs for the first time.

"I don't believe you a fox, that's what."

Fox's eyes flashed anger. Then he chuckled softly. "My dear child," he said, sounding right disgusted, "of course I'm a fox. A little girl like you should be simply terrified of me. Whatever do they teach children these days?"

Flossie tossed her head in the air. "Well, whatever you are, you sho' think a heap of yo'self," she said and skipped away.

Fox looked shocked. "Wait," he called. "You mean ... you're not frightened? Not just a bit?"

Flossie stopped. Then she turned and say, "I aine never seen a fox before. So, why should I be scared of you and I don't even-now know you a real fox for a fact?"

Fox pulled himself tall. He cleared his throat. "Are you saying I must offer proof that I am a fox before you will be frightened of me?"

"That's just what I'm saying."

Lil' Flossie skipped on through the piney woods while that Fox fella rushed away lookin' for whatever he needed to prove he was really who he said he was.

Meanwhile Flossie stopped to rest 'side a tree. Suddenly Fox was beside her. "I have the proof," he said. "See, I have thick, luxurious fur. Feel for yourself."

Fox leaned over for Flossie to rub his back.

"Ummm. Feels like rabbit fur to me," she say to Fox. "Shucks! You aine no fox. You a rabbit, all the time trying to fool me."

"Me! A rabbit!" he shouted. "I have you know my reputation precedes me. I am the third generation of foxes who have out-smarted and out-run Mr. J.W. Mc-Cutchin's fine hunting dogs. I have raided some of the best henhouses from Franklin to Madison. Rabbit, indeed! I am a fox, and you will act accordingly!"

Flossie hopped to her feet. She put her free hand on her hip and patted her foot. "Unless you can show you a fox, I'll not accord you nothing!" And without further ceremony she skipped away.

Down the road apiece, Flossie stopped by a bubbling spring. She knelt to get a drink of water. Fox came up to her and said, "I have a long pointed nose. Now that should be proof enough."

"Don't prove a thing to me." Flossie picked some wild flowers. "Come to think of it," she said matter-of-fact-like, "rats got long pointed noses." She snapped her fingers. "That's it! You a rat trying to pass yo'self off as a fox."

That near 'bout took Fox's breath away. "I beg your pardon," he gasped.

"You can beg all you wanna," Flossie say skipping on down the road. "That still don't make you no fox."

"I'll teach you a thing or two, young lady," Fox called after her. "You just wait and see."

Before long Flossie came to a clearing. A large orange tabby was sunning on a tree stump. "Hi, pretty kitty," the girl say and rubbed the cat behind her ears. Meanwhile Fox slipped from behind a clump of bushes.

"Since you won't believe me when I tell you I am a fox," he said stiffly, "perhaps you will believe that fine feline creature toward whom you seem to have some measure of respect."

Flossie looked at the cat and winked her eye. "He sho' use a heap of words," she whispered.

Fox beckoned for Cat to speak up. Cat jumped to a nearby log and yawned and stretched—then she answered. "This is a fox because he has sharp claws and yellow eyes," she purred.

Fox seemed satisfied. But Flossie looked at the cat. She looked at Fox, then once more at both just to be sure. She say, "All due respect, Miz Cat, but both y'all got sharp claws and yellow eyes. So ... that don't prove nothing, cep'n both y'all be cats."

Fox went to howling and running round in circles. He was plum beside himself. "I am a fox and I know it," he shouted. "This is absurd!"

"No call for you to use that kind of language," Flossie said and she skipped away.

"Wait, wait," Fox followed pleading. "I just remembered something. It may be the solution to this—this horrible situation."

"Good. It's about time."

"I—I—I have a bushy tail." Fox seemed to perk up. "That's right," he said. "All foxes are known for their fluffy, bushy tails. That has got to be adequate proof."

"Aine got to be. You got a bushy tail. So do squirrels." Flossie pointed to one overhead leaping from branch to branch in the tree tops. "Here, have a bite of peach," she said, offering Fox first bite of her treat.

But Fox was crying like a natural born baby. "No, no, no," he sobbed. "If I promise you I'm a fox, won't that do?"

Flossie shook her head no.

"Oh, woe is me," Fox hollered. "I may never recover my confidence."

Flossie didn't stop walking. "That's just what I been saying. You just an ol' confidencer. Come tellin' me you was a fox, then can't prove it. Shame on you!"

Long about that time, Flossie and the fox came out of the woods. Flossie cupped her hands over her eyes and caught sight of McCutchin Quarters and Miz Viola's cabin. Fox didn't notice a thing; he just followed behind Flossie begging to be believed.

"Give me one last chance," he pleaded.

Flossie turned on her heels. "Okay. But just this once more."

Fox tried not to whimper, but his voice was real unsteady-like. "I—I have sharp teeth and I can run exceedingly fast." He waited for Flossie to say something.

Slowly the girl rocked from heel to toe ... back and forward. "You know," she finally said, smiling, "it don't make much difference what I think anymore."

"What?" Fox asked. "Why?"

"'Cause there's one of Mr. J.W. McCutchin's hounds behind you. He's got sharp teeth and can run fast too. And, by the way that hound's lookin', it's all over for you!"

With a quick glance back Fox dashed toward the woods. "The hound knows who I am!" he shouted. "But I'm not worried. I sure can out-smart and out-run one of Mr. J.W. McCutchin's miserable mutts any old time of the day, because like I told you, I am a fox!"

"I know," said Flossie. "I know." And she turned toward Miz Viola's with the basket of eggs safely tucked under her arm.

LITTLE RED RIDING HOOD[1]

David McPhail

ONCE THERE WAS A GIRL called Little Red Riding Hood because, whenever she went out, she wore a pretty red cape.

One day her mother baked some cookies and asked Little Red Riding Hood to take them to Grandmother, who was ill and could not leave her bed.

"Stay on the path and don't dawdle," instructed Little Red Riding Hood's mother.

And the girl started off.

Little Red Riding Hood was about halfway to Grandmother's house when she met a wolf, but as she didn't know what a bad sort of animal he was, she did not feel afraid.

"Where are you off to so early this fine day?" inquired the wolf.

"I'm taking some cookies to my grandmother," answered Little Red Riding Hood.

"And where does your grandmother live?" the wolf persisted.

"Her house stands beneath the three oak trees," said Little Red Riding Hood.

As she was innocently explaining all this, the wolf was thinking, *If I can get there before her, I'll eat the grandmother for my main course and this tender young morsel for my dessert.*

"Your grandmother would surely love a bouquet of flowers," the wolf said to Little Red Riding Hood.

And that set Little Red Riding Hood to thinking about it.

So Little Red Riding Hood ventured farther and farther off the path to pick flowers, while the wolf went hastily to Grandmother's house and knocked on the door.

"Who's there?" called the grandmother in a very weak voice.

"It's your dear granddaughter," lied the wolf. "Please open the door."

"Come in," said the grandmother. "The door is not locked."

As soon as the door opened, the grandmother realized her mistake.

For instead of the darling Little Red Riding Hood, a wicked wolf stepped into the room. And though the grandmother's body was weak, she ran into the wardrobe and locked the door.

The wolf would have torn the door right off its hinges, but through the window, he saw Little Red Riding Hood walking down the path.

---

1   Published in 1995 (New York: Scholastic).

So the wolf put on the grandmother's cap and glasses, which had fallen to the floor, climbed into the bed, and pulled the covers up to his chin.

When she got to her grandmother's house, Little Red Riding Hood was surprised to see an open door. Nevertheless, she stepped inside.

"Good morning, Grandmother," she called. But there was no answer. Little Red Riding Hood stepped closer to the bed.

As the curtain had been drawn around the bed, Little Red Riding Hood could not see clearly in the dim light. "Oh, Grandmother," she exclaimed, "what big *ears* you have!"

"All the better to *hear* you with," said the wolf.

"Oh, Grandmother," said Little Red Riding Hood, "what big *eyes* you have!"

"All the better to *see* you with," said the wolf.

"Oh, Grandmother," said Little Red Riding Hood, "what big *teeth* you have!"

"All the better to *eat* you with!" said the wolf and he threw back the covers.

But Little Red Riding Hood was too quick for the wolf, and before he could catch her, she crawled under the bed.

The angry wolf went after her, but as he was much bigger than Little Red Riding Hood, he got stuck.

Little Red Riding Hood came out from under the bed and jumped on top of it. She jumped up and down, and shouted at the top of her voice, "Help! Help! There's a big bad wolf in here, and I fear he has eaten my grandmother!"

Little Red Riding Hood's grandmother, on hearing this, came out of the wardrobe.

Meanwhile, everyone who happened to be in the forest that day, including a woodcutter with a mighty sharp ax, heard Little Red Riding Hood's cries and ran to help.

They had nearly reached the cottage when the wolf finally managed to squeeze out from under the bed and stagger through the door.

The last time Little Red Riding Hood saw the wolf, he was running down the path, followed closely by a hostile crowd.

And Little Red Riding Hood never saw or heard from him again.

THE COMPANY OF WOLVES[1]

Angela Carter

O NE BEAST AND ONLY ONE howls in the woods by night.

The wolf is carnivore incarnate and he's as cunning as he is ferocious; once he's had a taste of flesh, then nothing else will do.

At night, the eyes of wolves shine like candle flames, yellowish, reddish, but that is because the pupils of their eyes fatten on darkness and catch the light from your lantern to flash it back to you—red for danger; if a wolf's eyes reflect only moonlight, then they gleam a cold and unnatural green, a mineral, a piercing color. If the benighted traveler spies those luminous, terrible sequins stitched suddenly on the black thickets, then he knows he must run, if fear has not struck him stock-still.

But those eyes are all you will be able to glimpse of the forest assassins as they cluster invisibly round your smell of meat as you go through the wood unwisely late. They will be like shadows, they will be like wraiths, gray members of a congregation of nightmare. Hark! his long, wavering howl ... an aria of fear made audible.

The wolfsong is the sound of the rendering you will suffer, in itself a murdering.

It is winter and cold weather. In this region of mountain and forest, there is now nothing for the wolves to eat. Goats and sheep are locked up in the byre, the deer departed for the remaining pasturage on the southern slopes—wolves grow lean and famished. There is so little flesh on them that you could count the starveling ribs through their pelts, if they gave you time before they pounced. Those slavering jaws; the lolling tongue; the rime of saliva on the grizzled chops—of all the teeming perils of the night and the forest, ghosts, hobgoblins, ogres that grill babies upon gridirons, witches that fatten their captives in cages for cannibal tables, the wolf is worst, for he cannot listen to reason.

You are always in danger in the forest, where no people are. Step between the portals of the great pines where the shaggy branches tangle about you, trapping the unwary traveler in nets as if the vegetation itself were in a plot with the wolves who live there, as though the wicked trees go fishing on behalf of their friends—step between the gateposts of the forest with the greatest trepidation and infinite precautions, for if you stray from the path for one instant, the wolves will eat you. They are gray as famine, they are as unkind as plague.

The grave-eyed children of the sparse villages always carry knives with them when they go out to tend the little flocks of goats that provide the homesteads with

---

1   From *The Bloody Chamber and Other Stories*, 1979 (London: Gollancz).

acrid milk and rank, maggoty cheeses. Their knives are half as big as they are; the blades are sharpened daily.

But the wolves have ways of arriving at your own hearthside. We try and try but sometimes we cannot keep them out. There is no winter's night the cottager does not fear to see a lean, gray, famished snout questing under the door, and there was a woman once bitten in her own kitchen as she was straining the macaroni.

Fear and flee the wolf; for worst of all, the wolf may be more than he seems.

There was a hunter once, near here, that trapped a wolf in a pit. This wolf had massacred the sheep and goats; eaten up a mad old man who used to live by himself in a hut halfway up the mountain and sing to Jesus all day; pounced on a girl looking after the sheep, but she made such a commotion that men came with rifles and scared him away and tried to track him into the forest but he was cunning and easily gave them the slip. So this hunter dug a pit and put a duck in it, for bait, all alive-oh; and he covered the pit with straw smeared with wolf dung. Quack, quack! went the duck, and a wolf came slinking out of the forest, a big one, a heavy one, he weighed as much as a grown man and the straw gave way beneath him—into the pit he tumbled. The hunter jumped down after him, slit his throat, cut off all his paws for a trophy.

And then no wolf at all lay in front of the hunter, but the bloody trunk of a man, headless, footless, dying, dead.

A witch from up the valley once turned an entire wedding party into wolves because the groom had settled on another girl. She used to order them to visit her, at night, from spite, and they would sit and howl around her cottage for her, serenading her with their misery.

Not so very long ago, a young woman in our village married a man who vanished clean away on her wedding night. The bed was made with new sheets and the bride lay down in it; the groom said he was going out to relieve himself, insisted on it, for the sake of decency, and she drew the coverlet up to her chin and lay there. And she waited and she waited and then she waited again—surely he's been gone a long time? Until she jumps up in bed and shrieks to hear a howling, coming on the wind from the forest.

That long-drawn, wavering howl has, for all its fearful resonance, some inherent sadness in it, as if the beasts would love to be less beastly if only they knew how and never cease to mourn their own condition. There is a vast melancholy in the canticles of the wolves, melancholy infinite as the forest, endless as these long nights of winter, and yet that ghastly sadness, that mourning for their own, irremediable appetites, can never move the heart, for not one phrase in it hints at the possibility of redemption; grace could not come to the wolf from its own despair, only through some external mediator, so that, sometimes, the beast will look as if he half welcomes the knife that dispatches him.

That young woman's brothers searched the outhouses and the haystacks but never found any remains, so the sensible girl dried her eyes and found herself another husband, not too shy to piss in a pot, who spent the nights indoors. She gave him a pair of bonny babies and all went right as a trivet until, one freezing night, the night of the solstice, the hinge of the year when things do not fit together as well as they should, the longest night, her first good man came home again.

A great thump on the door announced him as she was stirring the soup for the father of her children and she knew him the moment she lifted the latch to him although it was years since she's worn black for him and now he was in rags and his hair hung down his back and never saw a comb, alive with lice.

"Here I am again, missis," he said. "Get me my bowl of cabbage and be quick about it."

Then her second husband came in with wood for the fire and when the first one saw she'd slept with another man and, worse, clapped his red eyes on her little children, who'd crept into the kitchen to see what all the din was about, he shouted: "I wish I were a wolf again, to teach this whore a lesson!" So a wolf he instantly became and tore off the eldest boy's left foot before he was chopped up with a hatchet they used for chopping logs. But when the wolf lay bleeding and gasping its last, the pelt peeled off again and he was just as he had been, years ago, when he ran away from his marriage bed, so that she wept and her second husband beat her.

They say there's an ointment the Devil gives you that turns you into a wolf the minute you rub it on. Or that he was born feet first and had a wolf for his father and his torso is a man's but his legs and genitals are a wolf's. And he has a wolf's heart.

Seven years is a werewolf's natural span, but if you burn his human clothing you condemn him to wolfishness for the rest of his life, so old wives hereabouts think it some protection to throw a hat or an apron at the werewolf, as if clothes made the man. Yet by the eyes, those phosphorescent eyes, you know him in all his shapes; the eyes alone unchanged by metamorphosis.

Before he can become a wolf, the lycanthrope[1] strips stark naked. If you spy a naked man among the pines, you must run as if the Devil were after you.

It is midwinter and the robin, friend of man, sits on the handle of the gardener's spade and sings. It is the worst time in all the year for wolves, but this strong-minded child insists she will go off through the wood. She is quite sure the wild beasts cannot

---

1   *lycanthrope*: Werewolf.

harm her although, well-warned, she lays a carving knife in the basket her mother has packed with cheeses. There is a bottle of harsh liquor distilled from brambles; a batch of flat oat cakes baked on the hearthstone; a pot or two of jam. The flaxen-haired girl will take these delicious gifts to a reclusive grandmother so old the burden of her years is crushing her to death. Granny lives two hours' trudge through the winter woods; the child wraps herself up in her thick shawl, draws it over her head. She steps into her stout wooden shoes; she is dressed and ready and it is Christmas Eve. The malign door of the solstice still swings upon its hinges, but she has been too much loved ever to feel scared.

Children do not stay young for long in this savage country. There are no toys for them to play with, so they work hard and grow wise, but this one, so pretty and the youngest of her family, a little latecomer, had been indulged by her mother and the grandmother who'd knitted the red shawl that, today, has the ominous if brilliant look of blood on snow. Her breasts have just begun to swell; her hair is like lint, so fair it hardly makes a shadow on her pale forehead; her cheeks are an emblematic scarlet and white and she has just started her woman's bleeding, the clock inside her that will strike, henceforward, once a month.

She stands and moves within the invisible pentacle of her own virginity. She is an unbroken egg; she is a sealed vessel; she has inside her a magic space the entrance to which is shut tight with a plug of membrane; she is a closed system; she does not know how to shiver. She has her knife and she is afraid of nothing.

Her father might forbid her, if he were home, but he is away in the forest, gathering wood, and her mother cannot deny her.

The forest closed upon her like a pair of jaws.

There is always something to look at in the forest, even in the middle of winter—the huddled mounds of birds, succumbed to the lethargy of the season, heaped on the creaking boughs and too forlorn to sing; the bright frills of the winter fungi on the blotched trunks of the trees; the cuneiform slots of rabbits and deer, the herring-bone tracks of the birds, a hare as lean as a rasher of bacon streaking across the path where the thin sunlight dapples the russet brakes of last year's bracken.

When she heard the freezing howl of a distant wolf, her practiced hand sprang to the handle of her knife, but she saw no sign of a wolf at all, nor of a naked man, neither, but then she heard a clattering among the brushwood and there sprang onto the path a fully clothed one, a very handsome young one, in the green coat and wide-awake hat of a hunter, laden with carcasses of game birds. She had her hand on her knife at the first rustle of twigs, but he laughed with a flash of white teeth when he saw her and made her a comic yet flattering little bow; she'd never seen such a fine fellow before, not among the rustic clowns of her native village. So on they went together, through the thickening light of the afternoon.

Soon they were laughing and joking like old friends. When he offered to carry her basket, she gave it to him although her knife was in it because he told her his rifle would protect them. As the day darkened, it began to snow again; she felt the first flakes settle on her eyelashes, but now there was only half a mile to go and there would be a fire, and hot tea, and a welcome, a warm one, surely, for the dashing huntsman as well as for herself.

This young man had a remarkable object in his pocket. It was a compass. She looked at the little round glass face in the palm of his hand and watched the wavering needle with a vague wonder. He assured her this compass had taken him safely through the wood on his hunting trip because the needle always told him with perfect accuracy where the north was. She did not believe it; she knew she should never leave the path on the way through the wood or else she would be lost instantly. He laughed at her again; gleaming trails of spittle clung to his teeth. He said if he plunged off the path into the forest that surrounded them, he could guarantee to arrive at her grandmother's house a good quarter of an hour before she did, plotting his way through the undergrowth with his compass, while she trudged the long way, along the winding path.

I don't believe you. Besides, aren't you afraid of the wolves?

He only tapped the gleaming butt of his rifle and grinned.

Is it a bet? he asked her. Shall we make a game of it? What will you give me if I get to your grandmother's house before you?

What would you like? she asked disingenuously.

A kiss.

Commonplaces of a rustic seduction; she lowered her eyes and blushed.

He went through the undergrowth and took her basket with him, but she forgot to be afraid of the beasts, although now the moon was rising, for she wanted to dawdle on her way to make sure the handsome gentleman would win his wager.

Grandmother's house stood by itself a little way out of the village. The freshly falling snow blew in eddies about the kitchen garden and the young man stepped delicately up the snowy path to the door as if he were reluctant to get his feet wet, swinging his bundle of game and the girl's basket and humming a little tune to himself.

There is a faint trace of blood on his chin; he has been snacking on his catch.

Aged and frail, granny is three-quarters succumbed to the mortality the ache in her bones promises her and almost ready to give in entirely. A boy came out from the village to build up her hearth for the night an hour ago and the kitchen crackles with busy firelight. She has her Bible for company; she is a pious old woman. She is propped up on several pillows in the bed set into the wall peasant fashion, wrapped up in the patchwork quilt she made before she was married, more years ago than she cares to remember. Two china spaniels with liver-colored blotches on their coats and black noses sit on either side of the fireplace. There is a bright rug of woven rags on the pantiles. The grandfather clock ticks away her eroding time.

We keep the wolves out by living well.

He rapped upon the panels with his hairy knuckles.

It is your granddaughter, he mimicked in a high soprano.

Lift up the latch and walk in, my darling.

You can tell them by their eyes, eyes of a beast of prey, nocturnal, devastating eyes as red as a wound; you can hurl your Bible at him and your apron after, granny; you thought that was a sure prophylactic[1] against these infernal vermin ... Now call on Christ and his mother and all the angels in heaven to protect you, but it won't do you any good.

His feral muzzle is sharp as a knife; he drops his golden burden of gnawed pheasant on the table and puts down your dear girl's basket, too. Oh, my God, what have you done with her?

Off with his disguise, that coat of forest-colored cloth, the hat with the feather tucked into the ribbon; his matted hair streams down his white shirt and she can see the lice moving in it. The sticks in the hearth shift and hiss; night and the forest has come into the kitchen with darkness tangled in its hair.

He strips off his shirt. His skin is the color and texture of vellum. A crisp stripe of hair runs down his belly, his nipples are ripe and dark as poison fruit, but he's so thin you could count the ribs under his skin if only he gave you the time. He strips off his trousers and she can see how hairy his legs are. His genitals, huge. Ah! huge.

The last thing the old lady saw in all this world was a young man, eyes like cinders, naked as a stone, approaching her bed.

The wolf is carnivore incarnate.

When he had finished with her, he licked his chops and quickly dressed himself again, until he was just as he had been when he came through her door. He burned the inedible hair in the fireplace and wrapped the bones up in a napkin that he hid away under the bed in the wooden chest in which he found a clean pair of sheets. These he carefully put on the bed instead of the telltale stained ones he stowed away in the laundry basket. He plumped up the pillows and shook out the patchwork quilt, he picked up the Bible from the floor, closed it and laid it on the table. All was as it had been before except that grandmother was gone. The sticks twitched in the grate, the clock ticked and the young man sat patiently, deceitfully beside the bed in granny's nightcap.

Rat-a-tap-tap.

Who's there, he quavers in granny's antique falsetto.

---

1 *prophylactic*: Protective course of action.

[52]

Only your granddaughter.

So she came in, bringing with her a flurry of snow that melted in tears on the tiles, and perhaps she was a little disappointed to see only her grandmother sitting beside the fire. But then he flung off the blanket and sprang to the door, pressing his back against it so that she could not get out again.

The girl looked round the room and saw there was not even the indentation of a head on the smooth cheek of the pillow and how, for the first time she's seen it so, the Bible lay closed on the table. The tick of the clock cracked like a whip. She wanted her knife from her basket but she did not dare reach for it because his eyes were fixed upon her—huge eyes that now seemed to shine with a unique, interior light, eyes the size of saucers, saucers full of Greek fire, diabolic phosphorescence.

What big eyes you have.

All the better to see you with.

No trace at all of the old woman except for a tuft of white hair that had caught in the bark of an unburned log. When the girl saw that, she knew she was in danger of death.

Where is my grandmother?

There's nobody here but we two, my darling.

Now a great howling rose up all around them, near, very near, as close as the kitchen garden, the howling of a multitude of wolves; she knew the worst wolves are hairy on the inside and she shivered, in spite of the scarlet shawl she pulled more closely round herself as if it could protect her, although it was as red as the blood she must spill.

Who has come to sing us carols? she said.

Those are the voices of my brothers, darling; I love the company of wolves. Look out of the window and you'll see them.

Snow half-caked the lattice and she opened it to look into the garden. It was a white night of moon and snow; the blizzard whirled round the gaunt, gray beasts who squatted on their haunches among the rows of winter cabbage, pointing their sharp snouts to the moon and howling as if their hearts would break. Ten wolves; twenty wolves—so many wolves she could not count them, howling in concert as if demented or deranged. Their eyes reflected the light from the kitchen and shone like a hundred candles.

It is very cold, poor things, she said; no wonder they howl so.

She closed the window on the wolves' threnody[1] and took off her scarlet shawl, the color of poppies, the color of sacrifices, the color of her menses, and since her fear did her no good, she ceased to be afraid.

---

1   *threnody*: Song of lamentation for the dead.

What shall I do with my shawl?

Throw it on the fire, dear one. You won't need it again.

She bundled up her shawl and threw it on the blaze, which instantly consumed it. Then she drew her blouse over her head; her small breasts gleamed as if the snow had invaded the room.

What shall I do with my blouse?

Into the fire with it, too, my pet.

The thin muslin went flaring up the chimney like a magic bird and now off came her skirt, her woolen stockings, her shoes, and onto the fire they went, too, and were gone for good. The firelight shone through the edges of her skin; now she was clothed only in her untouched integument[1] of flesh. Thus dazzling, naked, she combed out her hair with her fingers; her hair looked white as the snow outside. Then went directly to the man with red eyes in whose unkempt mane the lice moved; she stood up on tiptoe and unbuttoned the collar of his shirt.

What big arms you have.

All the better to hug you with.

Every wolf in the world now howled a prothalamion[2] outside the window as she freely gave the kiss she owed him.

What big teeth you have!

She saw how his jaw began to slaver and the room was full of the clamour of the forest's *Liebestod*,[3] but the wise child never flinched, even when he answered:

All the better to eat you with.

The girl burst out laughing; she knew she was nobody's meat. She laughed at him full in the face, she ripped off his shirt for him and flung it into the fire, in the fiery wake of her own discarded clothing. The flames danced like dead souls on Walpurgisnacht[4] and the old bones under the bed set up a terrible clattering, but she did not pay them any heed.

Carnivore incarnate, only immaculate flesh appeases him.

She will lay his fearful head on her lap and she will pick out the lice from his pelt and perhaps she will put the lice into her own mouth and eat them, as he will bid her, as she would do in a savage marriage ceremony.

The blizzard will die down.

The blizzard died down, leaving the mountains as randomly covered with snow as if a blind woman had thrown a sheet over them, the upper branches of the forest pines limed, creaking, swollen with the fall.

---

1 *integument*: Natural outer covering, such as skin.

2 *prothalamion*: A song to celebrate a forthcoming wedding.

3 *Liebestod*: Love of death.

4 Walpurgisnacht: The eve of May 1, when witches are supposed to meet.

Snowlight, moonlight, a confusion of pawprints.

All silent, all still.

Midnight; and the clock strikes. It is Christmas Day, the werewolves' birthday; the door of the solstice stands wide open; let them all sink through.

See! Sweet and sound she sleeps in granny's bed, between the paws of the tender wolf.

WOLF[1]

Francesca Lia Block

THEY DON'T BELIEVE ME. THEY think I'm crazy. But let me tell you something it be a wicked wicked world out there if you didn't already know.

My mom and he were fighting and that was nothing new. And he was drinking, same old thing. But then I heard her mention me, how she knew what he was doing. And no fucking way was she going to sit around and let that happen. She was taking me away and he better not try to stop her. He said, no way, she couldn't leave.

That's when I started getting scared for both of us, my mom and me. How the hell did she know about that? He would think for sure I told her. And then he'd do what he had promised he'd do every night he held me under the crush of his putrid skanky body.

I knew I had to get out of there. I put all my stuff together as quick and quiet as possible—just some clothes, and this one stuffed lamb my mom gave me when I was little and my piggy-bank money that I'd been saving—and I climbed out the window of the condo. It was a hot night and I could smell my own sweat but it was different. I smelled the same old fear I'm used to but it was mixed with the night and the air and the moon and the trees and it was like freedom, that's what I smelled on my skin.

Same old boring boring story America can't stop telling itself. What is this sicko fascination? Every book and movie practically has to have a little, right? But why do you think all those runaways are on the streets tearing up their veins with junk and selling themselves so they can sleep in the gutter? What do you think the alternative was at home?

I booked because I am not a victim by nature. I had been planning on leaving, but I didn't want to lose my mom and I knew the only way I could get her to leave him was if I told her what he did. That was out of the question, not only because of what

---

1   From *The Rose and the Beast*, 2000 (New York: Harper Collins).

he might do to me but what it would do to her.

I knew I had to go back and help her, but I have to admit to you that at that moment I was scared shitless and it didn't seem like the time to try any heroics. That's when I knew I had to get to the desert because there was only one person I had in the world besides my mom.

I really love my mom. You know we were like best friends and I didn't even really need any other friend. She was so much fun to hang with. We cut each other's hair and shared clothes. Her taste was kind of youngish and cute, but it worked because she looked pretty young. People thought we were sisters. She knew all the song lyrics and we sang along in the car. We both can't carry a tune. Couldn't? What else about her? It's so hard to think of things sometimes, when you're trying to describe somebody so someone else will know. But that's the thing about it—no one can ever know. Basically you're totally alone and the only person in the world who made me feel not completely that way was her because after all we were made of the same stuff. She used to say to me, Baby, I'll always be with you. No matter what happens to me I'm still here. I believed her until he started coming into my room. Maybe she was still with me but I couldn't be with her those times. It was like if I did then she'd hurt so bad I'd lose her forever.

I figured the only place I could go would be to the desert, so I got together all my money and went to the bus station and bought a ticket. On the ride I started getting the shakes real bad thinking that maybe I shouldn't have left my mom alone like that and maybe I should go back but I was chickenshit, I guess. I leaned my head on the glass and it felt cool and when we got out of the city I started feeling a little better like I could breathe. L.A. isn't really so bad as people think. I guess. I mean there are gangs at my school but they aren't really active or violent except for the isolated incident. I have experienced one big earthquake in my life and it really didn't bother me so much because I'd rather feel out of control at the mercy of nature than other ways, if you know what I mean. I just closed my eyes and let it ride itself out. I kind of wished he'd been on top of me then because it might have scared him and made him feel retribution was at hand, but I seriously doubt that. I don't blame the earth for shaking because she is probably so sick of people fucking with her all the time— building things and poisoning her and that. L.A. is also known for the smog, but my mom said that when she was growing up it was way worse and that they had to have smog alerts all the time where they couldn't do P.E.[1] Now that part I would have liked because P.E. sucks. I'm not very athletic, maybe cause I smoke, and I hate getting undressed in front of some of those stupid bitches who like to see what kind of underwear you have on so they can dis you in yet another ingenious way. Anyway,

---

1   P.E.: Physical education class.

my smoking is way worse for my lungs than the smog, so I don't care about it too much. My mom hated that I smoke and she tried everything—tears and the patch and Nicorette and homeopathic remedies and trips to an acupuncturist, but finally she gave up.

I was wanting a cigarette bad on that bus and thinking about how it would taste, better than the normal taste in my mouth, which I consider tainted by him, and how I can always weirdly breathe a lot better when I have one. My mom read somewhere that smoker's smoke as a way to breathe more, so yoga is supposed to help, but that is one thing she couldn't get me to try. My grandmother, I knew she wouldn't mind the smoking—what could she say? My mom called her Barb the chimney. There is something so dry and brittle, so sort of flammable about her, you'd think it'd be dangerous for her to light up like that.

I liked the desert from when I visited there. I liked that it was hot and clean-feeling, and the sand and rocks and cactus didn't make you think too much about love and if you had it or not. They kind of made your mind still, whereas L.A.—even the best parts, maybe especially the best parts, like flowering trees and neon signs and different kinds of ethnic food and music—made you feel agitated and like you were never really getting what you needed. Maybe L.A. had some untapped resources and hidden treasures that would make me feel full and happy and that I didn't know about yet but I wasn't dying to find them just then. If I had a choice I'd probably like to go to Bali or someplace like that where people are more natural and believe in art and dreams and color and love. Does any place like that exist? The main reason L.A. was okay was because that is where my mom was and anywhere she was I had decided to make my home.

On the bus there was this boy with straight brown hair hanging in his pale freckled face. He looked really sad. I wanted to talk to him so much but of course I didn't. I am freaked that if I get close to a boy he will somehow find out what happened to me—like it's a scar he'll see or a smell or something, a red flag—and he'll hate me and go away. This boy kind of looked like maybe something had happened to him, too, but you can't know for sure. Sometimes I'd think I'd see signs of it in people but then I wondered if I was just trying not to feel so alone. That sounds sick, I guess, trying to almost wish what I went through on someone else for company. But I don't mean it that way. I don't wish it on anyone, believe me, but if they've been there I would like to talk to them about it.

The boy was writing furiously in a notebook, like maybe a journal, which I thought was cool. This journal now is the best thing I've ever done in my whole life. It's the only good thing really that they've given me here.

One of our assignments was to write about your perfect dream day. I wonder what this boy's perfect dream day would be. Probably to get to fuck Pamela Lee or something. Unless he was really as cool as I hoped, in which case it would be to wake up in a bed full of cute kitties and puppies and eat a bowl full of chocolate chip cookies in milk and get on a plane and get to go to a warm, clean, safe place (the cats and dogs would arrive there later, not at all stressed from their journey) where you could swim in blue-crystal water all day naked without being afraid and you could lie in the sun and tell your best friend (who was also there) your funniest stories so that you both laughed so hard you thought you'd pop and at night you got to go to a restaurant full of balloons and candles and stuffed bears, like my birthdays when I was little, and eat mounds of ice cream after removing the circuses of tiny plastic animals from on top.

In my case, the best friend would be my mom, of course, and maybe this boy if he turned out to be real cool and not stupid. I fell asleep for a little while and I had this really bad dream. I can't remember what it was but I woke up feeling like someone had been slugging me. And then I thought about my mom, I waited to feel her there with me, like I did whenever I was scared, but it was like those times when he came into my room—she wasn't anywhere. She was gone then and I think that was when I knew but I wouldn't let myself.

I think when you are born an angel should say to you, hopefully kindly and not in the fake voice of an airline attendant: Here you go on this long, long dream. Don't even try to wake up. Just let it go on until it is over. You will learn many things. Just relax and observe because there just is pain and that's it mostly and you aren't going to be able to escape no matter what. Eventually it will all be over anyway. Good luck.

I had to get off the bus before the boy with the notebook and as I passed him he looked up. I saw in his journal that he hadn't been writing but sketching, and he ripped out a page and handed it to me. I saw it was a picture of a girl's face but that is all that registered because I was thinking about how my stomach had dropped, how I had to keep walking, step by step, and get off the bus and I'd never be able to see him again and somehow it really really mattered.

When I got off the bus and lit up I saw that the picture was me—except way prettier than I think I look, but just as sad as I feel. And then it was too late to do anything because the bus was gone and so was he.

I stopped at the liquor store and bought a bag of pretzels and a Mountain Dew because I hadn't eaten all day and my stomach was talking pretty loud. Everything tasted of bitter smoke. Then after I'd eaten I started walking along the road to my grandma's. She lives off the highway on this dirt road surrounded by cactus and other desert plants. It was pretty dark so you could see the stars really big and bright, and I thought how cold the sky was and not welcoming or magical at all. It just made me feel really lonely. A bat flew past like a sharp shadow and I could hear owls and coyotes. The coyote howls were the sound I would have made if I could have. Deep and sad but scary enough that no one would mess with me, either.

My grandma has a used stuff store so her house is like this crazy warehouse full of junk like those little plaster statuettes from the seventies of these ugly little kids with stupid sayings that are supposed to be funny, and lots of old clothes like army jackets and jeans and ladies' nylon shirts, and cocktail glasses, broken china, old books, trinkets, gadgets, just a lot of stuff that you think no one would want but they do, I guess, because she's been in business a long time. Mostly people come just to talk to her because she is sort of this wise woman of the desert who's been through a lot in her life and then they end up buying something, I think, as a way to pay her back for the free counseling. She's cool, with a desert-lined face and a bandanna over her hair and long skinny legs in jeans. She was always after my mom to drop that guy and move out here with her but my mom wouldn't. My mom still was holding on to her secret dream of being an actress but nothing had panned out yet. She was so pretty, I thought it would, though. Even though she had started to look a little older. But she could have gotten those commercials where they use the women her age to sell household products and aspirin and stuff. She would have been good at that because of her face and her voice, which are kind and honest and you just trust her.

I hadn't told Grandma anything about him, but I think she knew that he was fucked up. She didn't know how much, though, or she wouldn't have let us stay there. Sometimes I wanted to go and tell her, but I was afraid then Mom would have to know and maybe hate me so much that she'd kick me out.

My mom and I used to get dressed up and put makeup on each other and. pretend to do commercials. We had this mother-daughter one that was pretty cool. She said I was a natural, but I wouldn't want to be an actor because I didn't like people looking at me that much. Except that boy on the bus, because his drawing wasn't about the outside of my body, but how I felt inside and you could tell by the way he did it, and the way he smiled, that he understood those feelings so I didn't mind that he saw them. My mom felt that I'd be good anyway, because she said that a lot of actors don't like people looking at them and that is how they create these personas to hide behind so people will see that and the really good ones are created to hide a lot of things. I guess for that reason I might be okay but I still hated the idea of going on auditions and having people tell me I wasn't pretty enough or something. My mom said it was interesting and challenging but I saw it start to wear on her.

Grandma wasn't there when I knocked so I went around the back, where she sat sometimes at night to smoke, and it was quiet there, too. That's when I started feeling sick like at night in my bed trying not to breathe or vomit. Because I saw his Buick sitting there in the sand.

Maybe I have read too many fairy tales. Maybe no one will believe me.

I poked around the house and looked through the windows and after a while I heard their voices and I saw them in this cluttered little storage room piled up with the stuff she sells at the store. Everything looked this glazed brown fluorescent color. When I saw his face I knew something really bad had happened. I remembered the dream I had had and thought about my mom. All of a sudden I was inside that room, I don't really remember how I got there, but I was standing next to my grandma and I saw she had her shotgun in her hand.

He was saying, Barb, calm down, now, okay. Just calm down. When he saw me his eyes narrowed like dark slashes and I heard a coyote out in the night.

My grandmother looked at me and at him and her mouth was this little line stitched up with wrinkles. She kept looking at him but she said to me, Babe, are you okay?

I said I had heard him yelling at mom and I left. She asked him what happened with Nance and he said they had a little argument, that was all, put down the gun, please, Barb.

Then I just lost it, I saw my grandma maybe start to back down a little and I went ballistic. I started screaming how he had raped me for years and I wanted to kill him and if we didn't he'd kill us. Maybe my mom was already dead.

I don't know what else I said, but I do know that he started laughing at me, this hideous tooth laugh, and I remembered him above me in that bed with his clammy hand on my mouth and his ugly ugly weight and me trying to keep hanging on because I wouldn't let him take my mom away, that was the one thing he could never do and now he had. Then I had the gun and I pulled the trigger. My grandma had taught me how once, without my mom knowing, in case I ever needed to defend myself, she said.

My grandma says that she did it. She says that he came at us and she said to him, I've killed a lot prettier, sweeter innocents than you with this shotgun, meaning the animals when she used to go out hunting, which is a pretty good line and everything, but she didn't do it. It was me.

I have no regrets about him. I don't care about much anymore, really. Only one thing.

Maybe one night I'll be asleep and I'll feel a hand like a dove on my cheekbone and feel her breath cool like peppermints and when I open my eyes my mom will be there like an angel, saying in the softest voice, When you are born it is like a long, long dream. Don't try to wake up. Just go along until it is over. Don't be afraid. You may not know it all the time but I am with you. I am with you.

WHAT BUGS BUNNY SAID TO RED RIDING HOOD[1]

Tim Seibles

SAY, GOOD LOOKIN, WHAT BRINGS you out thisaway
amongst the fanged and the fluffy?
Grandma, huh?
Some ol bag too lazy to pick up a pot, too feeble
to flip a flapjack—
and you all dolled up like a fire engine
to cruise these woods?

This was your **mother's** idea?
She been livin in a *CrackerJack* box or somethin?
This is a tough neighborhood, mutton chops—
you gotchur badgers, your wild boar, your
hardcore grizzlies   and lately,
this one wolf's been actin pretty big and bad.

I mean, what's up, doc?
Didn anybody ever tell you it ain't smart
to stick out in wild places?
Friendly? You want friendly you better
try Detroit. I mean
you're safe wit me, sweetcakes,
but I ain't a meat-eater.

You heard about Goldie Locks, didn'cha? Well,
didn'cha? Yeah, well, little Miss Sunshine—
little Miss *I'm-so-much-cuter-than-thee*—
got caught on one of her sneaky porridge runs
and the Three Bears weren't in the mood:
so last week the game warden nabs baby bear
passin out her fingers to his pals.

---

1   First published in 1999. Text taken from *The Poets' Grimm: Twentieth-Century Poems from Grimm Fairy Tales*, edited by Jeanne Marie Beaumont and Claudia Carlson (Ashland, OR: Story Line Press, 2003).

That's right. Maybe your motha should
turn off her soaps, take a peek at a newspaper,
turn on some cartoons, for Pete's sake:
this woyld is about teeth, bubble buns—who's bitin
and who's gettin bit. The noyve a'that broad
sendin you out here lookin like a ripe tomata.
Why don't she just hang a sign aroun your neck:
Get over here and bite my legs off!
Cover me wit mustid— call me a hotdawg!

Alright, alright, I'll stop.
Listen, Red, I'd hate for somethin unpleasant
to find you out here all alone. Grandma-shmandma— let'er call *Domino's*.
They're paid to deliver. Besides, toots,
it's already later than you think—
get a load a'that chubby moon up there.

Ya can't count on Casper tanight either.
They ran that potata-head outta town two months ago—
tryin to make friends all the time—
he makes you sick after awhile.

Look, Cinderella, I got some candles and some
cold uncola back at my place— whaddaya say?

Got any artichokies in that basket?

SLEEPING BEAUTY

Few fairy tales have achieved greater popularity—or provoked more controversy—than "Sleeping Beauty." The hundred-year enchanted sleep endured by the central character is at the same time a memorable narrative ploy and a vivid symbol of feminine passivity; it is no wonder, therefore, that feminist critics have seen a darker aspect to the tale's continued success.

As in the previous section, there can be little doubt that the earlier version (or versions) had a definite influence upon its successors, but in this case the result of that influence is clearly different. In the versions of "Little Red Riding Hood," we can see the process of literary refinement in the tale's elaboration; now that same process takes the opposite tack, as the tale undergoes significant shrinkage (particularly between Perrault and the Grimms) in the effort to make the tale suitable for its ever-younger audience.

Despite the obvious differences between these versions, the central image of the enchanted sleep remains constant and is arguably the key to the popularity of the tale. So the question arises: how could an image of extended inactivity be so crucial to the tale's success? One answer, as P.L. Travers points out in an insightful essay,[1]

---

1 P.L. Travers, *About the Sleeping Beauty* (New York: McGraw-Hill, 1975) 59-61. Travers takes pains to remind us of the multi-faceted nature of the symbol, which she illustrates most effectively in a list of famous sleepers whose concerns often have little to do with growing up: "The idea of the sleeper, of somebody hidden from mortal eye, waiting until the time shall ripen has always been dear to the folkly mind—Snow White asleep in her glass coffin, Brynhild behind her wall of fire, Charlemagne in the heart of France, King Arthur in the Isle of Avalon, Frederick Barbarossa under his mountain in Thuringia. Muchukunda, the Hindu King, slept through eons till he was awakened by the Lord Krishna; Oisin of Ireland dreamed in Tir n'an Og for over three hundred years. Psyche in her magic sleep is a type of Sleeping Beauty, Sumerian Ishtar in the underworld may be said to be another. Holga the Dane is sleeping and waiting, and so, they say, is Sir Francis Drake. Quetzalcoatl of Mexico and Virochocha of Peru are both sleepers. Morgan le Fay of France and England and Dame Holle of Germany are sleeping in raths and cairns" (51).

is that the central image of a sleeping princess awaiting the prince who will bring her (and her whole world) back to life has powerful mythic overtones of death and resurrection. On a more human level, the image is a metaphor of growing up: in each case the heroine falls asleep as a naïve girl and awakens as a mature young woman on the threshold of marriage and adult responsibility. For cultural reasons, the metaphor is generally seen as gender-specific, in that sleep denotes the decorous passivity expected of the virtuous young female—a characteristic that undoubtedly attracted nineteenth-century approval of this tale. By contrast, the young male must demonstrate his maturity through deeds of daring, manifested most effectively in Perrault's version of the tale.

Giambattista Basile (1575-1632) was a minor Neapolitan courtier and soldier who was among the first in the Western world to commit the folk tale to paper. It becomes quickly apparent, however, that Basile's tales in *The Pentamerone* (first published in 1634-36 as *Lo cunto li cunti*) are a good deal more sophisticated than we expect a fairy tale to be; their content, tone, and overall structure hearken back to Boccaccio and Chaucer rather than anticipate the fairy-tale collections that would follow. This quality is well illustrated by Basile's version of "Sleeping Beauty," which is a story of rape, adultery, sexual rivalry, and attempted cannibalism—a far cry from what we have come to expect in this famous tale!

Comparing Basile's tale with Perrault's "Sleeping Beauty in the Wood" provides a fascinating glimpse into the evolution of a tale in its literary form, as the Frenchman sets about revising it to match *his* assumptions about what a fairy tale is and who will read (or hear) it. In a nutshell, it might be said that Perrault's approach is rather more subtle than that of his Neapolitan predecessor. Clearly, Perrault wants no part of Basile's evident delight in the salacious aspects of his story. While as a royal courtier he was doubtless no stranger to confrontations between jealous wives and beautiful mistresses, his tale suggests that discretion and a sophisticated cynicism are now the rule in dealing with such matters; social diplomat that he is, Perrault favors the oblique comment, the aside that demonstrates the wit of the writer and makes an accomplice of the reader. Thus, Perrault's prince refrains—at least at the moment of discovery—from all physical contact with the sleeping princess (he is simply present when the enchantment reaches full term, whereas the spell-breaking kiss bestowed by the Grimms' prince implies an arousal that is sexual in nature). We may detect more than a trace of archness, however, when Perrault tells us that the young couple "...did not sleep much, that night; the princess did not feel in the least drowsy." Likewise, through his use of symbolism, Perrault finds a way to sublimate the sexual rivalry that gives Basile's more realistic tale much of its impact. In Perrault's version, the king's tigerish wife becomes the prince's ogress mother, which allows the retention of several significant elements (such as the cannibalism motif), while further deflecting the violence of the tale with a characteristic touch of sly humor: her intention to eat one of Sleeping Beauty's children is horrific, of course, but there is a certain Gallic *savoir faire* in the instruction to her steward to "… serve her up with sauce Robert."

To modern eyes, Perrault's alteration of the tale clearly invites a Freudian interpretation, as the prince's mother wages her ruthless campaign to destroy all rivals for her son's affections. As suggested above, the lesser-known sequel contains an intriguing insight into *male* maturation, counterpointing Sleeping Beauty's transformation by sleep. The crisis of this episode is brought on by the prince's assumption that becoming king is the external confirmation of his personal maturity; he therefore chooses this moment to reveal the existence of his wife and children to his mother. "Some time afterwards," we are told, in an apparent *non sequitur* that speaks volumes, "the king decided to declare war on his neighbor, the Emperor Cantalabutte"! Given the prince's awareness of his mother's appetites, how are we to explain such a decision? Is his departure an indication of his naïvety, in that he has no inkling of the rivalry that he leaves behind him—or is he in fact so aware of it that he reckons there's more peace to be found in the middle of a battlefield?

After all the excitement of the two earlier versions, it comes as something of a surprise to realize that the much shorter, blander version by the Brothers Grimm is by far the best known—perhaps for the very reason that the Grimms chose not to darken the blue sky of romance with the storm-clouds of jealousy and sexual rivalry that may loom up in human relationships (although, as we noted above, theirs is the version in which Sleeping Beauty's awakening has the clearest sexual connotation). Yet only a moment's thought is necessary to appreciate why they may have made the editorial decision to end the story there; once again, the central importance of the intended audience asserts itself. Perrault's claims notwithstanding, it was only with the Grimms that the fairy tale unequivocally entered the child's domain—and the Grimms took their responsibility seriously. Consequently, no trace of Basile's hand remains, and little enough of Perrault's either: a comparison of the gifts presented to Sleeping Beauty by the fairies in the Perrault and Grimm versions offers an intriguing insight into the different worlds from which these tales come. At the same time, it might be said that in Grimm we see the tale stripped down to its narrative core, revealing most clearly its *oral* origins.

"The Neapolitan Soldier," a tale from Italo Calvino's collection *Italian Folktales* (1956), brings a sturdily proletarian flavor to this otherwise aristocratic tale. The competitive antics of the three soldiers remind us of the more common three-brother motif, in which the smallest (and youngest?) is invariably the hero. Calvino (1923-85), like the Grimms before him, has "improved" the tale a little; he states in his Note that "The original shows the first two soldiers deriding the third because he is from Naples. I made these two Roman and Florentine respectively, to accentuate the spirit of the barracks."[1] And although royalty is indeed present in this version, their strategy for discovering the phantom lover—initiated by the princess herself— suggests a particularly egalitarian kind of rule.

Yet the story of Sleeping Beauty is by no means limited to the Western tradition. From the large and somewhat amorphous collection known as the *Arabian Nights* comes "The Ninth Captain's Tale,"[2] which contains a number of surprises in terms of what it reveals about the evolution of this tale. (Individual tales within the *Arabian Nights* differ considerably in age, but most were recorded long before the publication, in 1550, of the earliest Western fairy-tale collection, *The Facetious Nights*, by Straparola.) For instance, this version offers us a much fuller depiction of the prince and a much closer look at the nature of his relationship with the girl. Exotic and mysterious though it may seem at first glance, this tale—like so many others, from East or West—is about growing up. In this regard, it bears some resemblance to Perrault's "Sleeping Beauty in the Wood" in its insistence that a relationship cannot work unless both partners have achieved a level of maturity and understanding. In effect, both must go through a ritual death and rebirth (as occurs in initiation rites in traditional societies) to be ready for the responsibilities of an adult relationship.

When we turn to contemporary interpretations of the tale, we find a fascination—in this highly socialized age of ours—with the sheer separateness of Sleeping Beauty. For instance, Gabriel Garcia Marquez, in his short story "Sleeping Beauty and the Airplane" (1982), chooses to locate this encounter between fantasy and reality in that most surrealistic of settings, an aircraft cabin. Like Angela Carter, Marquez is a skilled proponent of that form of writing known as "magic realism," a term vividly exemplified by this short story. What better opportunity for the imagination to escape its bonds than in the tedium and discomfort of air travel, where personal identity is all but lost in transit? Marquez captures the fevered excitement of this unlikely prince as he contemplates the sleeping beauty beside him, but all flights of fancy must come to an end, and we return to earth—sometimes with a jolt!

Wilfred Owen (1893-1918) is remembered almost exclusively for the poetry he wrote as a soldier in World War I, in which he described the horrific reality of combat for a public still caught up in a fantasy of patriotism and comic-book bravado. Written in 1914, "The Sleeping Beauty" is undeniably old-fashioned in its tender lyricism and archaic diction; yet here, too, a moment of real experience is illuminated and perhaps comprehended through the fantasy of a fairy tale.

---

1   Italo Calvino, comp., *Italian Folktales*, trans. George Martin (New York: Pantheon, 1980) 736.
2   Since this tale appears in no other *Arabian Nights* collection, its origins continue to be debated.

It is intriguing that in both Marquez's story and Owen's poem, we see things from the "prince's" point of view—and in each instance, he perceives the female as sealed within a cocoon of perfection that he cannot bring himself to penetrate. Is this an indication of a change in male sensibility—and perhaps a hint of the loneliness that can come with perfect beauty?

SUN, MOON, AND TALIA (SOLE, LUNA, E TALIA)[1]
Giambattista Basile

THERE WAS ONCE A GREAT king who, on the birth of his daughter—to whom he gave the name of Talia—commanded all the wise men and seers in the kingdom to come and tell him what her future would be. These wise men, after many consultations, came to the conclusion that she would be exposed to great danger from a small splinter in some flax. Thereupon the King, to prevent any unfortunate accident, commanded that no flax or hemp or any other similar material should ever come into his house.

One day when Talia was grown up she was standing by the window, and saw an old woman pass who was spinning. Talia had never seen a distaff and spindle, and was therefore delighted with the dancing of the spindle. Prompted by curiosity, she had the old woman brought up to her, and taking the distaff in her hand, began to draw out the thread; but unfortunately a splinter in the hemp got under her fingernail, and she immediately fell dead upon the ground. At this terrible catastrophe the old woman fled from the room, rushing precipitously down the stairs. The stricken father, after having paid for this bucketful of sour wine with a barrelful of tears, left the dead Talia seated on a velvet chair under an embroidered canopy in the palace, which was in the middle of a wood. Then he locked the door and left forever the house which had brought him such evil fortune, so that he might entirely obliterate the memory of his sorrow and suffering.

It happened some time after that a falcon of a king who was out hunting in these parts flew in at the window of this house. As the bird did not return when called back, the King sent someone to knock at the door, thinking the house was inhabited. When they had knocked a long time in vain, the King sent for a vine-dresser's ladder,

---

1   First published in 1634-36. This text from *The Pentamerone*, trans. Benedetto Croce, ed. N.M. Penzer (London: John Lane, the Bodley Head, 1932).

so that he might climb up himself and see what was inside. He climbed up and went in, and was astonished at not finding a living being anywhere. Finally he came to the room in which sat Talia as if under a spell.

The King called to her, thinking she was asleep; but since nothing he did or said brought her back to her senses, and being on fire with love, he carried her to a couch and, having gathered the fruits of love, left her lying there. Then he returned to his own kingdom and for a long time entirely forgot the affair.

Nine months later, Talia gave birth to two children, a boy and a girl, two splendid pearls. They were looked after by two fairies, who had appeared in the palace, and who put the babies to their mother's breast. Once, when one of the babies wanted to suck, it could not find the breast, but got into its mouth instead the finger that had been pricked. This the baby sucked so hard that it drew out the splinter, and Talia was roused as if from a deep sleep. When she saw the two jewels at her side, she clasped them to her breast and held them as dear as life; but she could not understand what had happened, and how she came to be alone in the palace with two children, having everything she required to eat brought to her without seeing anyone.

One day the King bethought himself of the adventure of the fair sleeper and took the opportunity of another hunting expedition to go and see her. Finding her awake and with two prodigies of beauty, he was overpowered with joy. He told Talia what had happened and they made a great compact of friendship, and he remained several days in her company. Then he left her, promising to come again and take her back with him to his kingdom. When he reached his home he was forever talking of Talia and her children. At meals the names of Talia, Sun, and Moon (these were the children's names) were always on his lips; when he went to bed he was always calling one or the other.

The Queen had already had some glimmering of suspicion on account of her husband's long absence when hunting; and hearing his continued calling on Talia, Sun, and Moon, burned with a heat very different from the sun's heat, and calling the King's secretary, said to him: "Listen, my son, you are between Scylla and Charybdis,[1] between the doorpost and the door, between the poker and the grate. If you tell me with whom it is that my husband is in love, I will make you rich; if you hide the truth from me, you shall never be found again, dead or alive." The man, on the one hand moved by fear, and on the other egged on by interest, which is a bandage over the eyes of honour, a blinding of justice and a cast horseshoe to faith, told the Queen all, calling bread bread and wine wine.

---

1   Scylla and Charybdis: Two monsters of Greek mythology who lived on opposite sides of a narrow channel of water. The phrase "between Scylla and Charybdis" means having to choose between two undesirable situations.

Then she sent the same secretary in the King's name to tell Talia that he wished to see his children. Talia was delighted and sent the children. But the Queen, as soon as she had possession of them, with the heart of a Medea,[1] ordered the cook to cut their throats and to make them into hashes and sauces and give them to their unfortunate father to eat.

The cook, who was tender-hearted, was filled with pity on seeing these two golden apples of beauty, and gave them to his wife to hide and prepared two kids,[2] making a hundred different dishes of them. When the hour for dinner arrived, the Queen had the dishes brought in, and whilst the King was eating and enjoying them, exclaiming: "How good this is, by the life of Lanfusa! How tasty this is, by the soul of my grandmother!" she kept encouraging him, saying: "Eat away, you are eating what is your own." The first two or three times the King paid no attention to these words, but as she kept up the same strain of music, he answered: "I know very well I am eating what is my own; you never brought anything into the house." And getting up in a rage, he went off to a villa not far away to cool his anger down.

The Queen, not satisfied with what she thought she had already done, called the secretary again, and sent him to fetch Talia herself, pretending that the King was expecting her. Talia came at once, longing to see the light of her eyes and little guessing that it was fire that awaited her. She was brought before the Queen, who, with the face of a Nero[3] all inflamed with rage, said to her: "Welcome, Madame Troccola![4] So you are the fine piece of goods, the fine flower my husband is enjoying! You are the cursed bitch that makes my head go round! Now you have got into purgatory, and I will make you pay for all the harm you have done me!"

Talia began to excuse herself, saying it was not her fault and that the King had taken possession of her territory whilst she was sleeping. But the Queen would not listen to her, and commanded that a great fire should be lit in the courtyard of the palace and that Talia should be thrown into it.

The unfortunate Talia, seeing herself lost, threw herself on her knees before the Queen, and begged that at least she should be given time to take off the clothes she was wearing. The Queen, not out of pity for her, but because she wanted to save the clothes, which were embroidered with gold and pearls, said: "Undress—that I agree to."

Talia began to undress, and for each garment that she took off she uttered a shriek. She had taken off her dress, her skirt, and bodice and was about to take off her petticoat, and to utter her last cry, and they were just going to drag her away to reduce her

---

1 Medea: One of the great sorceresses in Greek mythology; when her husband left her, she ate their children.
2 Kid: Young goat.
3 Nero: A Roman emperor infamous for his cruelty.
4 Troccola: Busybody.

to lye ashes, which they would throw into boiling water to wash Charon's[5] breeches with, when the King saw the spectacle and rushed up to learn what was happening. He asked for his children, and heard from his wife, who reproached him for his betrayal of her, how she had made him eat them himself.

The King abandoned himself to despair. "What!" he cried, "am I the wolf of my own sheep? Alas, why did my veins not recognise the fountain of their own blood? You renegade Turk, this barbarous deed is the work of your hands? Go, you shall get what you deserve; there will be no need to send such a tyrant-faced one to the Colosseum to do penance!"

So saying, he ordered that the Queen should be thrown into the fire lighted for Talia, and that the secretary should be thrown in, too, for he had been her handle in this cruel game and the weaver of this wicked web. He would have had the same done to the cook who, as he thought, had cut up his children; but the cook threw himself at the King's feet, saying: "Indeed, my lord, for such a service there should be no other reward than a burning furnace; no pension but a spike-thrust from behind; no entertainment but that of being twisted and shrivelled in the fire; neither could there be any greater honour than for me, a cook, to have my ashes mingle with those of a queen. But this is not the thanks I expect for having saved your children from that spiteful dog who wished to kill them and return to your body what came from it."

The King was beside himself when he heard these words; it seemed to him as if he must be dreaming and that he could not believe his ears. Turning to the cook, he said: "If it is true that you have saved my children, you may be sure I will not leave you turning spits in the kitchen. You shall be in the kitchen of my heart, turning my will just as you please, and you shall have such rewards that you will account yourself the luckiest man in the world."

Whilst the King was speaking, the cook's wife, seeing her husband's difficulties, brought Sun and Moon up to their father, who, playing at the game of three with his wife and children, made a ring of kisses, kissing first one and then the other. He gave a handsome reward to the cook and made him Gentleman of the Bed-chamber. Talia became his wife, and enjoyed a long life with her husband and children, finding it to be true that:

Lucky people, so 'tis said,
Are blessed by Fortune whilst in bed.

---

1   Charon: The ferryman who rowed the souls of the dead across the river Styx to Hades.

THE SLEEPING BEAUTY IN THE WOOD[1]

Charles Perrault

ONCE UPON A TIME, THERE lived a king and a queen who were bitterly unhappy because they did not have any children. They visited all the clinics, all the specialists, made holy vows, went on pilgrimages and said their prayers regularly but with so little success that when, at long last, the queen finally did conceive and, in due course, gave birth to a daughter, they were both wild with joy. Obviously, this baby's christening must be the grandest of all possible christenings; for her godmothers, she would have as many fairies as they could find in the entire kingdom. According to the custom of those times, each fairy would make the child a magic present, so that the princess could acquire every possible perfection. After a long search, they managed to trace seven suitable fairies.

After the ceremony at the church, the guests went back to the royal palace for a party in honour of the fairy godmothers. Each of these important guests found her place was specially laid with a great dish of gold and a golden knife, fork and spoon studded with diamonds and rubies. But as the fairies took their seats, an uninvited guest came storming into the palace, deeply affronted because she had been forgotten—though it was no wonder she'd been overlooked; this old fairy had hidden herself away in her tower for fifteen years and, since nobody had set eyes on her all that time, they thought she was dead, or had been bewitched. The king ordered a place to be laid for her at once but he could not give her a great gold dish and gold cutlery like the other fairies had because only seven sets had been made. The old fairy was very annoyed at that and muttered threats between her teeth. The fairy who sat beside her overheard her and suspected she planned to revenge herself by giving the little princess a very unpleasant present when the time for present giving came. She slipped away behind the tapestry so that she could have the last word, if necessary, and put right any harm the old witch might do the baby.

Now the fairies presented their gifts. The youngest fairy said the princess would grow up to be the loveliest woman in the world. The next said she would have the disposition of an angel, the third that she would be graceful as a gazelle, the fourth gave her the gift of dancing, the fifth of singing like a nightingale, and the sixth said she would be able to play any kind of musical instrument that she wanted to.

But when it came to the old fairy's turn, she shook with spite and announced

---

1 First published in 1697. This text from *Sleeping Beauty and Other Favourite Fairy Tales,* trans. Angela Carter (London: Gollancz, 1982).

that, in spite of her beauty and accomplishments, the princess was going to prick her finger with a spindle and die of it.

All the guests trembled and wept. But the youngest fairy stepped out from behind the tapestry and cried out:

"Don't despair, King and Queen; your daughter will not die—although, alas, I cannot undo entirely the magic of a senior-ranking fairy. The princess *will* prick her finger with a spindle but, instead of dying, she will fall into a deep sleep that will last for a hundred years. And at the end of a hundred years, the son of a king will come to wake her."

In spite of this comfort, the king did all he could to escape the curse; he forbade the use of a spindle, or even the possession of one, on pain of death, in all the lands he governed.

Fifteen or sixteen years went by. The king and queen were spending the summer at a castle in the country and one day the princess decided to explore, prowling through room after room until at last she climbed up a spiral staircase in a tower and came to an attic in which an old lady was sitting, along with her distaff, spinning, for this old lady had not heard how the king had banned the use of a spindle.

"Whatever are you doing, my good woman?" asked the princess.

"I'm spinning, my dear," answered the old lady.

"Oh, how clever!" said the princess. "How do you do it? Give it to me so that I can see if I can do it, too!"

She was very lively and just a little careless; but besides, and most importantly, the fairies had ordained it. No sooner had she picked up the spindle than she pierced her hand with it and fell down in a faint.

The old lady cried for help and the servants came running from all directions. They threw water over her, unlaced her corsets, slapped her hands, rubbed her temples with *eau-de-cologne*—but nothing would wake her.

The king climbed to the attic to see the cause of the clamour and, sad at heart, knew the fairy's curse had come true. He knew the princess' time had come, just as the fairies said it would, and ordered her to be carried to the finest room in the palace and laid there on a bed covered with gold and silver embroidery. She was as beautiful as an angel. Her trance had not yet taken the colour from her face; her cheeks were rosy and her lips like coral. Her eyes were closed but you could hear her breathing very, very softly and, if you saw the slow movement of her breast, you knew she was not dead.

The king ordered she should be left in peace until the time came when she would wake up. At the moment the princess had pricked her finger, the good fairy who saved her life was in the realm of Mataquin, twelve thousand leagues away, but she heard the news immediately from a dwarf who sped to her in a pair of seven-league boots. The fairy left Mataquin at once in a fiery chariot drawn by dragons and arrived at the grieving court an hour later. The king went out to help her down; she approved of all his arrangements but she was very sensitive, and she thought how sad the princess would be when she woke up all alone in that great castle.

So she touched everything in the house, except for the king and queen, with her magic ring—the housekeepers, the maids of honour, the chambermaids, the gentlemen-in-waiting, the court officials, the cooks, the scullions, the errand-boys, the night-watchmen, the Swiss guards, the page-boys, the footmen; she touched all the horses in the stable, and the stable-boys, too, and even Puff, the princess' little lap-dog, who was curled up on her bed beside her. As soon as she touched them with her magic ring, they all fell fast asleep and would not wake up until their mistress woke, ready to look after her when she needed them. Even the spits on the fire, loaded with partridges and pheasants, drowsed off to sleep, and the flames died down and slept, too. All this took only a moment; fairies are fast workers.

The king and queen kissed their darling child but she did not stir. Then they left the palace forever and issued proclamations forbidding anyone to approach it. Within a quarter of an hour, a great number of trees, some large, some small, interlaced with brambles and thorns, sprang up around the park and formed a hedge so thick that neither man nor beast could penetrate it. This hedge grew so tall that you could see only the topmost turrets of the castle, for the fairy had made a safe, magic place where the princess could sleep her sleep out free from prying eyes.

At the end of a hundred years, the son of the king who now ruled over the country went out hunting in that region. He asked the local people what those turrets he could see above the great wood might mean. They replied, each one, as he had heard tell—how it was an old ruin, full of ghosts; or, that all the witches of the country went there to hold their sabbaths. But the most popular story was, that it was the home of an ogre who carried all the children he caught there, to eat them at his leisure, knowing nobody else could follow him through the wood. The prince did not know what to believe. Then an old man said to him:

"My lord, fifty years ago I heard my father say that the most beautiful princess in all the world was sleeping in that castle, and her sleep was going to last for a hundred years, until the prince who is meant to have her comes to wake her up."

When he heard that, the young prince was tremendously excited; he had never heard of such a marvelous adventure and, fired with thoughts of love and glory, he made up his mind there and then to go through the wood. No sooner had he stepped among the trees than the great trunks and branches, the thorns and brambles parted, to let him pass. He saw the castle at the end of a great avenue and walked towards it, though he was surprised to see that none of his attendants could follow him because the trees sprang together again as soon as he had gone between them. But he did not abandon his quest. A young prince in love is always brave. Then he arrived at a courtyard that seemed like a place where only fear lived.

An awful silence filled it and the look of death was on everything. Man and beast stretched on the ground, like corpses; but the pimples on the red noses of the Swiss guards soon showed him they were not dead at all, but sleeping, and the glasses beside them, with the dregs of wine still at the bottoms, showed how they had dozed off after a spree.

He went through a marble courtyard; he climbed a staircase; he went into a guardroom, where the guards were lined up in two ranks, each with a gun on his shoulder, and snoring with all their might. He found several rooms full of gentlemen-in-waiting and fine ladies; some stood, some sat, all slept. At last he arrived in a room that was entirely covered in gilding and, there on a bed with the curtains drawn back so that he could see her clearly, lay a princess about fifteen or sixteen years old and she was so lovely that she seemed, almost, to shine. The prince approached her trembling, and fell on his knees before her.

The enchantment was over; the princess woke. She gazed at him so tenderly you would not have thought it was the first time she had ever seen him.

"Is it you, my prince?" she said. "You have kept me waiting for a long time."

The prince was beside himself with joy when he heard that and the tenderness in her voice overwhelmed him so that he hardly knew how to reply. He told her he loved her better than he loved himself and though he stumbled over the words, that made her very happy, because he showed so much feeling. He was more tongue-tied than she, because she had had plenty of time to dream of what she would say to him; her good fairy had made sure she had sweet dreams during her long sleep. They talked for hours and still had not said half the things they wanted to say to one another.

But the entire palace had woken up with the princess and everyone was going about his business again. Since none of them were in love, they were all dying of hunger. The chief lady-in-waiting, just as ravenous as the rest, lost patience after a while and told the princess loud and clear that dinner was ready. The prince helped the princess up from the bed and she dressed herself with the greatest magnificence; but when she put on her ruff, the prince remembered how his grandmother had worn one just like it. All the princess' clothes were a hundred years out of fashion, but she was no less beautiful because of that.

Supper was served in the hall of mirrors, while the court orchestra played old tunes on violins and oboes they had not touched for a hundred years. After supper, the chaplain married them in the castle chapel and the chief lady-in-waiting drew the curtains round their bed for them. They did not sleep much, that night; the princess did not feel in the least drowsy. The prince left her in the morning, to return to his father's palace.

The king was anxious because his son had been away so long. The prince told him that he had lost himself in the forest while he was out hunting and had spent the night in a charcoal burner's hut, where his host had given him black bread and cheese to eat. The king believed the story but the queen, the prince's mother, was not so easily hoodwinked when she saw that now the young man spent most of his time out hunting in the forest. Though he always arrived back with an excellent excuse when he had spent two or three nights away from home, his mother soon guessed he was in love.

He lived with the princess for more than two years and he gave her two children. They named the eldest, a daughter, Dawn, because she was so beautiful, but they called their son Day because he came after Dawn and was even more beautiful still.

The queen tried to persuade her son to tell her his secret but he dared not confide in her. Although he loved her, he feared her, because she came from a family of ogres and his father had married her only because she was very, very rich. The court whispered that the queen still had ogrish tastes and could hardly keep her hands off little children, so the prince thought it best to say nothing about his own babies.

But when the king died and the prince himself became king, he felt confident enough to publicly announce his marriage and install the new queen, his wife, in his royal palace with a great deal of ceremony. And soon after that, the new king decided to declare war on his neighbour, the Emperor Cantalabutte.

He left the governing of his kingdom in his mother's hands and he trusted her to look after his wife and children for him, too, because he would be away at war for the whole summer.

As soon as he was gone, the queen mother sent her daughter-in-law and her grandchildren away to the country, to a house deep in the woods, so that she could satisfy her hideous appetites with the greatest of ease. She herself arrived at the house a few days later and said to the butler:

"I want to eat little Dawn for my dinner tomorrow."

"Oh my lady!" exclaimed the butler.

"She's just the very thing I fancy," said the queen mother in the voice of an ogress famished for fresh meat. "And I want you to serve her up with sauce Robert."

The poor man saw he could not argue with a hungry ogress, picked up a carving knife and went to little Dawn's room. She was just four years old. When she saw her dear friend, the butler, she ran up to him, laughing, threw her arms around his neck and asked him where her sweeties were. He burst into tears and the knife fell from his hands. He went down to the farmyard and slaughtered a little lamb instead. He served the lamb up in such a delicious sauce the queen mother said she had never eaten so well in her life and he spirited little Dawn away from harm; he handed her over to his wife, who hid her in a cellar, in the servants' quarters.

Eight days passed. Then the ogress said to the butler:

"I want to eat little Day for my supper."

The butler was determined to outwit her again. He found little Day playing at fencing with his pet monkey; the child was only three. He took him to his wife, who hid him away with his sister, and served up a tender young kid in his place. The queen mother smacked her lips over the dish, so all went well until the night the wicked ogress said to the butler:

"I want to eat the queen with the same sauce you made for her children."

This time, the poor butler did not know what to do. The queen was twenty, now, if you did not count the hundred years she had been asleep; her skin was white and lovely but it was a little tough, and where in all the farmyard was he to find a beast with skin just like it? There was nothing for it; he must kill the queen to save himself and he went to her room, determined he would not have to enter it a second time. He rushed in with a dagger in his hand and told her her mother-in-law had ordered her to die.

"Be quick about it," she said calmly. "Do as she told you. When I am dead, I shall be with my poor children again, my children whom I love so much."

Because they had been taken away from her without a word of explanation, she thought they were dead.

The butler's heart melted.

"No, no, my lady, you don't need to die so that you can be with your children. I've hidden them away from the queen mother's hunger and I will trick her again, I will give her a young deer for supper instead of you."

He took her to the cellar, where he left her kissing her children and weeping over them, and went to kill a young doe that the queen mother ate for supper with as much relish as if it had been her daughter-in-law. She was very pleased with her own cruelty and practiced telling her son how the wolves had eaten his wife and children while he had been away at the wars.

One night as she prowled about as usual, sniffing for the spoor of fresh meat, she heard a voice coming from the servants' quarters. It was little Day's voice; he was crying because he had been naughty and his mother wanted to whip him. Then the queen mother heard Dawn begging her mother to forgive the little boy. The ogress recognised the voices of her grandchildren and she was furious. She ordered a huge vat to be brought into the middle of the courtyard. She had the vat filled with toads, vipers, snakes and serpents and then the queen, her children, the butler, his wife and his maid were brought in front of her with their hands tied behind their backs. She was going to have them thrown into the vat.

The executioners were just on the point of carrying out their dreadful instructions when the king galloped into the courtyard. Nobody had expected him back so soon. He was astonished at what he saw and asked who had commanded the vat and the bonds. The ogress was so angry to see her plans go awry that she jumped head-first into the vat and the vile beasts inside devoured her in an instant. The king could not help grieving a little; after all, she was his mother. But his beautiful wife and children soon made him happy again.

Moral

A brave, rich, handsome husband is a prize well worth waiting for; but no modern woman would think it was worth waiting for a hundred years. The tale of the Sleeping Beauty shows how long engagements make for happy marriages, but young girls these days want so much to be married I do not have the heart to press the moral.

BRIER ROSE[1]

Jacob and Wilhelm Grimm

LONG, LONG AGO THERE LIVED a king and a queen, who said day after day: "Ah, if only we had a child!" but none ever came. Then one day when the queen was sitting in her bath a frog crawled out of the water and said to her: "You will get your wish; before a year goes by, you will bring a daughter into the world." The frog's prediction came true. The queen gave birth to a baby girl who was so beautiful that the king couldn't get over his joy and decided to give a great feast. He invited not only his relatives, friends, and acquaintances, but also the Wise Women, for he wanted them to feel friendly toward his child. There were thirteen Wise Women in his kingdom, but he only had twelve golden plates for them to eat from, so one of them had to stay home. The feast was celebrated in great splendour and when it was over the Wise Women gave the child their magic gifts; one gave virtue, the second beauty, the third wealth, and so on, until they had given everything a person could wish for in this world. When the eleventh had spoken, the thirteenth suddenly stepped in. She had come to avenge herself for not having been invited, and without a word of greeting, without so much as looking at anyone, she cried out in a loud voice: "When she is fifteen, the princess will prick her finger on a spinning wheel and fall down dead." Then without another word she turned around and left the hall. Everyone was horror-stricken. But the twelfth Wise Woman, who still had her wish to make, stepped forward, and since she couldn't undo the evil spell but only soften it, she said: "The

---

1   First published in 1812/15, in the first edition of *Kinder- und Hausmärchen*. This text from the second edition (1819), from *Grimms' Tales for Young and Old*, trans. Ralph Manheim (Garden City, NY: Anchor Press, 1977).

princess will not die, but only fall into a deep hundred-year sleep."

The king, who wanted to guard his beloved child against such a calamity, sent out an order that every spindle in the whole kingdom should be destroyed. All the Wise Women's wishes for the child came true: she grew to be so beautiful, so modest, so sweet-tempered and wise that no one who saw her could help loving her. The day she turned fifteen the king and the queen happened to be away from home and she was left alone. She went all over the castle, examining room after room, and finally she came to an old tower. She climbed a narrow winding staircase, which led to a little door with a rusty key in the lock. She turned the key, the door sprang open, and there in a small room sat an old woman with a spindle, busily spinning her flax. "Good day, old woman," said the princess. "What are you doing?" "I'm spinning," said the old woman, nodding her head. "And what's the thing that twirls around so gaily?" the princess asked. With that she took hold of the spindle and tried to spin, but no sooner had she touched it than the magic spell took effect and she pricked her finger.

The moment she felt the prick she fell down on the bed that was in the room and a deep sleep came over her. And her sleep spread to the entire palace. The king and queen had just come home, and when they entered the great hall they fell asleep and the whole court with them. The horses fell asleep in the stables, the dogs in the courtyard, the pigeons on the roof, and the flies on the wall. Even the fire on the hearth stopped flaming and fell asleep, and the roast stopped crackling, and the cook, who was about to pull the kitchen boy's hair because he had done something wrong, let go and fell asleep. And the wind died down, and not a leaf stirred on the trees outside the castle.

All around the castle a brier hedge began to grow. Each year it grew higher until in the end it surrounded and covered the whole castle and there was no trace of a castle to be seen, not even the flag on the roof. The story of Brier Rose, as people called the beautiful sleeping princess, came to be told far and wide, and from time to time a prince tried to pass through the hedge into the castle. But none succeeded, for the brier bushes clung together as though they had hands, so the young men were caught and couldn't break loose and died a pitiful death. After many years another prince came to the country and heard an old man telling about the brier hedge that was said to conceal a castle, where a beautiful princess named Brier Rose had been sleeping for a hundred years, along with the king and the queen and their whole court. The old man had also heard from his grandfather that a number of princes had tried to pass through the brier hedge and had got caught in it and died a pitiful death. Then the young man said: "I'm not afraid. I will go and see the beautiful Brier Rose." The good man did his best to dissuade him, but the prince wouldn't listen.

It so happened that the hundred years had passed and the day had come for Brier Rose to wake up. As the king's son approached the brier hedge, the briers turned into big beautiful flowers, which opened of their own accord and let him through, then closed behind him to form a hedge again. In the courtyard he saw the horses and mottled hounds lying asleep, and on the roof pigeons were roosting with their heads under their wings. When he went into the castle, the flies were asleep on the wall, the cook in the kitchen was still holding out his hand as though to grab the kitchen boy, and the maid was sitting at the table with a black hen in front of her that needed plucking. Going farther, he saw the whole court asleep in the great hall, and on the dais beside the throne lay the king and the queen. On he went, and everything was so still that he could hear himself breathe. At last he came to the tower and opened the door to the little room where Brier Rose was sleeping. There she lay, so beautiful that he couldn't stop looking at her, and he bent down and kissed her. No sooner had his lips touched hers than Brier Rose opened her eyes, woke up, and smiled sweetly. They went downstairs together, and then the king and the queen and the whole court woke up, and they all looked at each other in amazement. The horses in the courtyard stood up and shook themselves; the hounds jumped to their feet and wagged their tails; the pigeons on the roof took their heads from under their wings, looked around and flew off into the fields; the flies on the wall started crawling, the fire in the kitchen flamed up and cooked the meal; the roast began to crackle again, the cook boxed the kitchen boy's ear so hard that he howled, and the maid plucked the chicken. The prince and Brier Rose were married in splendour, and they lived happily to the end of their lives.

THE NEAPOLITAN SOLDIER[1]

Italo Calvino

THREE SOLDIERS HAD DESERTED THEIR regiment and taken to the open road. One was a Roman, one a Florentine, while the smallest was a Neapolitan. After traveling far and wide, they were overtaken by darkness in a forest. The Roman, who was the oldest of the three, said, "Boys, this is no time for us all three to go to sleep. We must take turns keeping watch an hour at a time."

He volunteered for the first watch, and the other two threw down their knapsacks,

---

1   From *Italian Folktales*, retold by Italo Calvino, trans. George Martin (New York: Pantheon, 1980).

unrolled their blankets, and went fast asleep. The watch was almost up, when out of the forest rushed a giant.

"What are you doing here?" he asked the soldier.

"None of your business," replied the soldier, without even bothering to turn around.

The giant lunged at him, but the soldier proved the swifter of the two by drawing his sword and cutting off the giant's head. Then he picked up the head with one hand and the body with the other and threw them into a nearby well. He carefully cleaned his sword, resheathed it, and called his companion who was supposed to keep the next watch. Before awakening him, though, he thought, I'd better say nothing about the giant, or this Florentine will take fright and flee. So when the Florentine was awake and asking, "Did you see anything?" the Roman replied, "Nothing at all, everything was as calm as could be." Then he went to sleep.

The Florentine began his watch, and when it was just about up, here came another giant exactly like the first, who asked, "What are you doing here?"

"That's no business of yours or anybody else's," answered the Florentine.

The giant sprang at him, but in a flash the soldier drew his sword and lopped off his head, which he picked up along with the body and threw into the well. His watch was up, and he thought, I'd better say nothing of this to the lily-livered Neapolitan. If he knew that things like this went on around here, he'd take to his heels and we'd never see him again.

So, when the Neapolitan asked, "Did you see any action?" the Florentine replied, "None at all, you've nothing to worry about." Then he went to sleep.

The Neapolitan watched for almost an hour, and the forest was perfectly still. Suddenly the leaves rustled and out ran a giant. "What are you doing here?"

"What business is it of yours?" replied the Neapolitan.

The giant held up a hand that would have squashed the Neapolitan flatter than a pancake, had he not dodged it, brandished his sword, and swept off the giant's head, after which he threw the remains into the well.

It was the Roman's turn once more to keep watch, but the Neapolitan thought, I first want to see where the giant came from. He therefore plunged into the forest, spied a light, hastened toward it, and came to a cottage. Peeping through the keyhole, he saw three old women in conversation before the fireplace.

"It's already past midnight, and our husbands are not yet back," said one.

"Do you suppose something has happened to them?" asked another. "It might not be a bad idea," said the third, "to go after them. What do you say?"

"Let's go right now," said the first. "I'll carry the lantern that enables you to see a hundred miles ahead."

"And I'll bring the sword," said the second, "which in every sweep wipes out an army."

"And I'll bring the shotgun that can kill the she-wolf at the king's palace," said the third.

"Let's be on our way." At that, they threw open the door.

Hiding behind the doorpost with sword in hand, the Neapolitan was all ready for them. Out came the first woman holding the lantern, and swish! her head flew off before she could say a single "Amen." Out came the second, and swish! her soul sped to kingdom come. Out came the third and went the way of her sisters.

The soldier now had the witches' lantern, sword, and shotgun and decided to try them out immediately. "We'll just see if those three dotards were telling the truth." He raised the lantern and saw an army a hundred miles away besieging a castle, and chained on the balcony was a she-wolf with flaming eyes. "Let's just see how the sword works." He picked it up and swung it around, then raised the lantern once more and peered into space: every last warrior lay lifeless on the ground beside his splintered lance and dead horse. Then the Neapolitan picked up the gun and shot the she-wolf.

"Now I'll go and see everything from close up," he said.

He walked and walked and finally reached the castle. His knocks and calls all went unanswered. He went inside and walked through all the rooms, but saw no one until he came to the most beautiful chamber of all, where a lovely maiden sat sleeping in a plush armchair.

The soldier went up to her, but she continued to sleep. One of her slippers had dropped off her foot, and the soldier picked it up and put it in his pocket. Then he kissed her and tiptoed away.

He was no sooner gone than the sleeping maiden awakened. She called her maids of honor, who were also sleeping in the next room. They woke up and ran to the princess, exclaiming, "The spell is broken! The spell is broken! We have awakened! The princess has awakened! Who could the knight be who freed us?"

"Quick," said the princess, "look out the windows and see if you see anyone."

The maids looked out and saw the massacred army and the slain she-wolf. Then the princess said, "Hurry to His Majesty, my father, and tell him a brave knight came and defeated the army that held me prisoner, killed the she-wolf that stood guard over me, and broke the evil spell by kissing me." She glanced at her bare foot and added, "And then he went off with my left slipper."

Overjoyed, the king had notices posted all over town: WHOEVER COMES FORWARD AS MY DAUGHTER'S DELIVERER SHALL HAVE HER IN MARRIAGE, BE HE PRINCE OR PAUPER.

In the meantime the Neapolitan had gone back to his companions in broad day-light. When he awakened them, they asked immediately, "Why didn't you call us earlier? How many hours did you watch?"

But he wasn't about to tell them all that had happened and simply said, "I was so wide-awake I watched the rest of the night."

Time went by without bringing a soul to town to claim the princess as his rightful bride. "What can we do?" wondered the king.

The princess had an idea. "Papa, let's open a country inn and put up a sign that reads: HERE YOU CAN EAT, DRINK, AND SLEEP AT NO CHARGE for three days. That will draw many people, and we'll surely hear something important."

They opened the inn, with the king's daughter acting as innkeeper. Who should then come by but our three soldiers as hungry as bears, and singing as usual, in spite of hard times. They read the sign, and the Neapolitan said, "Boys, here you can eat and sleep for nothing."

"Don't believe a word of it," replied his companions. "They just say that, the better to cheat people."

But the princess-innkeeper came out and invited them in, assuring them of the truth of every word of the sign. They entered the inn, and the princess served them a supper fit for a king. Then she took a seat at their table and said, "Well, what news do you bring from the world outside? Way off in the country like this, I never know what's going on elsewhere."

"We have very little of interest to report, madam," answered the Roman who then smugly told of the time he was keeping watch when suddenly confronted by a giant whose head he cut off.

"Zounds!" exclaimed the Florentine. "I too had something similar happen to me," and he told about his giant.

"And you, sir?" said the princess to the Neapolitan. "Has nothing ever happened to you?"

His companions burst out laughing. "You don't think he would have anything to tell, do you? Our friend here is such a coward he'd run and hide for a whole week if he heard a leaf rustle in the dark."

"Don't belittle the poor boy like that," said the maiden, who insisted that he too tell something.

So the Neapolitan said, "If you really want the truth, I too was confronted by a giant while you two were sleeping and I killed him."

"Ha, ha, ha!" laughed his companions. "You'd die of fright if you so much as saw a giant! That's enough! We don't want to hear any more, we're going to bed." And they went off and left him with the princess.

She served him wine and coaxed him to go on with his story. Thus, little by little, he came out with everything—the three old women, the lantern, the shotgun, the sword, and the lovely maiden he had kissed as she slept, and her slipper he had carried off.

"Do you still have the slipper?"

"Here it is," replied the soldier drawing it from his pocket.

Overjoyed the princess kept filling his glass until he fell asleep, then said to her valet, "Take him to the bedchamber I prepared especially for him, remove his clothes, and put out kingly garb for him on the chair."

When the Neapolitan awakened next morning he was in a room decorated entirely in gold and brocade. He went to put on his clothes and found in their place robes for a king. He pinched himself to make sure he wasn't dreaming and, unable to make heads or tails of a thing, he rang the bell.

Four liveried servants entered and bowed down to him. "At Your Highness's service. Did Your Highness sleep well?"

The Neapolitan blinked. "Have you lost your mind? What highness are you talking about? Give me my things so I can get dressed, and be done with this comedy."

"Calm down, Highness. We are here to shave you and dress your hair."

"Where are my companions? Where did you put my things?"

"They are coming right away, you will have everything immediately, but allow us first to dress you, Highness."

Once he realized there was no getting around them, the soldier let the servants proceed: they shaved him, dressed his hair, and clothed him in a kingly outfit. Then they brought in his chocolate, cake, and sweets. After breakfast he said, "Am I going to see my companions or not?"

"Right away, Highness."

In came the Roman and the Florentine, whose mouths flew open when they saw him dressed in such finery. "What are you doing in that costume?"

"You tell me. Your guess is as good as mine."

"Goodness knows what you've cooked up!" replied his companions. "You must have told the lady some pretty tall tales last night!"

"For your information, I told no tall tales to anyone."

"So how do you account for what's happening now?"

"I'll explain," said the king, coming in just then with the princess in her finest robe. "My daughter was under a spell, and this young man set her free."

By questions and answers, they got the entire story.

"I am therefore making him my daughter's husband," said the king, "and my heir. As for yourselves, have no fears. You will become dukes, since had you not slain the other two giants, my daughter would not be free today."

The wedding was celebrated to the great joy of all, and followed by a grand feast.

On the menu was chicken à la king:
Long live the queen!
Long live the king!

THE NINTH CAPTAIN'S TALE[1]

Arabian Nights

THERE WAS ONCE A WOMAN who could not conceive, for all her husband's assaulting. So one day she prayed to Allah, saying, "Give me a daughter, even if she be not proof against the smell of flax!"

In speaking thus of the smell of flax she meant that she would have a daughter, even if the girl were so delicate and sensitive that the anodyne smell of flax would take hold of her throat and kill her.

Soon the woman conceived and easily bore a daughter, as fair as the rising moon, as pale and delicate as moonlight.

When little Sittukhan, for such they called her, grew to be ten years old, the sultan's son passed beneath her window and saw her and loved her, and went back ailing to the palace.

Doctor succeeded doctor fruitlessly beside his bed; but, at last, an old woman, who had been sent by the porter's wife, visited him and said, after close scrutiny, "You are in love, or else you have a friend who loves you."

"I am in love," he answered.

"Tell me her name," she begged, "for I may be a bond between you."

"She is the fair Sittukhan," he replied; and she comforted him, saying, "Refresh your eyes and tranquilize your heart, for I will bring you into her presence."

Then she departed and sought out the girl, who was taking the air before her mother's door. After compliment and greeting, she said, "Allah protect so much beauty, my daughter! Girls like you, and with such lovely fingers, should learn to spin flax; for there is no more delightful sight than a spindle in spindle fingers." Then she went away.

At once the girl went to her mother, saying, "Mother, take me to the mistress."

"What mistress?" asked her mother.

"The flax mistress," answered the girl.

---

1   From *The Book of the Thousand Nights and One Night,* trans. E. Powys Mather, 2nd ed. (London: Routledge and Kegan Paul, 1964).

"Do not say such a thing!" cried the woman. "Flax is a danger to you. Its smell is fatal to your breast, a touch of it will kill you."

But her daughter reassured her, saying, "I shall not die," and so wept and insisted, that her mother sent her to the flax mistress.

The white girl stayed there for a day, learning to spin; and her fellow pupils marveled at her beauty and the beauty of her fingers. But, when a morsel of flax entered behind one of her nails, she fell swooning to the floor.

They thought her dead and sent to her father and mother, saying, "Allah prolong your days! Come and take up your daughter, for she is dead."

The man and his wife tore their garments for the loss of their only joy, and went, beaten by the wind of calamity, to bury her. But the old woman met them, and said, "You are rich folk, and it would be shame on you to lay so fair a girl in dust."

"What shall we do then?" they asked, and she replied, "Build her a pavilion in the midst of the waves of the river and couch her there upon a bed, that you may come to visit her."

So they built a pavilion of marble, on columns rising out of the river, and planted a garden about it with green lawns, and set the girl upon an ivory bed, and came there many times to weep.

What happened next?

The old woman went to the king's son, who still lay sick of love, and said to him, "Come with me to see the maiden. She waits you, couched in a pavilion above the waves of the river."

The prince rose up and bade his father's wazir[1] come for a walk with him. The two went forth together and followed the old woman to the pavilion. Then the prince said, "Wait for me outside the door, for I shall not be long."

He entered the pavilion and began to weep by the ivory bed, recalling verses in the praise of so much beauty. He took the girl's hand to kiss it and, as he passed her slim white fingers through his own, noticed the morsel of flax lodged behind one of her nails. He wondered at this and delicately drew it forth.

At once the girl came out of her swoon and sat up upon the ivory bed. She smiled at the prince, and whispered, "Where am I?"

"You are with me," he answered, as he pressed her all against him. He kissed her and lay with her, and they stayed together for forty days and forty nights. Then the prince took leave of his love, saying, "My wazir is waiting outside the door. I will take him back to the palace and then return."

He found the wazir and walked with him across the garden towards the gate, until

---

1   wazir: Prime minister.

he was met by white roses growing with jasmine. The sight of these moved him, and he said to his companion, "The roses and the jasmine are white with the pallor of Sittukhan's cheeks! Wait here for three days longer, while I go to look upon the cheeks of Sittukhan."

He entered the pavilion again and stayed three days with Sittukhan, admiring the white roses and the jasmine of her cheeks.

Then he rejoined the wazir and walked with him across the garden towards the gate, until the carob, with its long black fruit, rose up to meet him. He was moved by the sight of it, and said, "The carobs are long and black like the brows of Sittukhan. O wazir, wait here for three more days, while I go to view Sittukhan's brows."

He entered the pavilion again and stayed three days with the girl, admiring her perfect brows, long and black like carobs hanging two by two.

Then he rejoined the wazir and walked with him towards the gate, until a springing fountain with its solitary jet rose up to meet him. He was moved by this sight and said to the wazir, "The jet of the fountain is as Sittukhan's waist. Wait here for three days longer, while I go to gaze again upon the waist of Sittukhan."

He went up into the pavilion and stayed three days with the girl, admiring her waist, for it was as the slim jet of the fountain.

Then he rejoined the wazir and walked with him across the garden towards the gate. But Sittukhan, when she saw her lover come again a third time, had said to herself, "What brings him back?" So now she followed him down the stairs of the pavilion, and hid behind the door which gave on the garden to see what she might see.

The prince happened to turn and catch sight of her face. He returned toward her, pale and distracted, and said sadly, "Sittukhan, Sittukhan, I shall never see you more, never, never again." Then he departed with the wazir, and his mind was made up that he would not return.

Sittukhan wandered in the garden, weeping, lonely and regretting that she was not dead in very truth. As she walked by the water, she saw something sparkle in the grass and, on raising it, found it to be a talismanic ring. She rubbed the engraved carnelian of it, and the ring spoke, saying, "Behold here am I! What do you wish?"

"O ring of Sulaiman," answered Sittukhan, "I require a palace next to the palace of the prince who used to love me, and a beauty greater than my own."

"Shut your eye and open it!" said the ring; and, when the girl had done so, she found herself in a magnificent palace, next to the palace of the prince. She looked in a mirror which was there and marveled at her beauty.

Then she leaned at the window until her false love should pass by on his horse. When the prince saw her, he did not know her; but he loved her and hastened to his mother, saying, "Have you not some very beautiful thing which you can take as a present to the lady who dwells in the new palace? And can you not beg her, at the same time, to marry me?"

"I have two pieces of royal brocade," answered his mother, "I will take them to her and urge your suit with them." Without losing an hour, the queen visited Sittukhan, and said to her, "My daughter, I pray you to accept this present, and to marry my son."

The girl called her negress and gave her the pieces of brocade, bidding her cut them up for floor cloths; so the queen became angry and returned to her own dwelling.

When the son learned that the woman of his love had destined the cloth of gold for menial service, he begged his mother to take some richer present, and the queen paid a second visit, carrying a necklace of unflawed emeralds.

"Accept this gift, my daughter, and marry my son," she said; and Sittukhan answered, "O lady, your present is accepted." Then she called her slave, saying, "Have the pigeons eaten yet?"

"Not yet, mistress," answered the slave.

"Take them these green trifles!" said Sittukhan.

When she heard this outrageous speech, the queen cried, "You have humbled us, my daughter. Now, at least, tell me plainly whether you wish to marry my son or no."

"If you desire me to marry him," answered Sittukhan, "bid him feign death, wrap him in seven winding-sheets, carry him in sad procession through the city, and let your people bury him in the garden of my palace."

"I will tell him your conditions," said the queen.

"What do you think!" cried the mother to her son, when she had returned to him. "If you wish to marry the girl, you must pretend to be dead, you must be wrapped in seven winding-sheets, you must be led in sad procession through the city, and you must be buried in her garden!"

"Is that all, dear mother?" asked the prince in great delight. "Then tear your clothes and weep, and cry, 'My son is dead!'"

The queen rent her garments and cried in a voice shrill with pain, "Calamity and woe! My son is dead!"

All the folk of the palace ran to that place and, seeing the prince stretched upon the floor with the queen weeping above him, washed the body and wrapped it in seven winding-sheets. Then the old men and the readers of the Koran came together and formed a procession, which went throughout the city, carrying the youth covered with precious shawls. Finally they set down their burden in Sittukhan's garden and went their way.

As soon as the last had departed, the girl, who had once died of a morsel of flax, whose cheeks were jasmine and white roses, whose brows were carobs two by two, whose waist was the slim jet of the fountain, went down to the prince and unwrapped the seven winding-sheets from about him, one by one.

Then "Is it you?" she said. "You are ready to go very far for women; you must be fond of them!" The prince bit his finger in confusion, but Sittukhan reassured him, saying, "It does not matter this time!"

And they dwelt together in love delight.

SLEEPING BEAUTY AND THE AIRPLANE[1]

Gabriel Garcia Marquez

SHE WAS BEAUTIFUL AND LITHE, with soft skin the color of bread and eyes like green almonds, and she had straight black hair that reached to her shoulders, and an aura of antiquity that could just as well have been Indonesian as Andean. She was dressed with subtle taste: a lynx jacket, a raw silk blouse with very delicate flowers, natural linen trousers, and shoes with a narrow stripe the color of bougainvillea. "This is the most beautiful woman I've ever seen," I thought when I saw her pass by with the stealthy stride of a lioness while I waited in the check-in line at Charles de Gaulle Airport in Paris for the plane to New York. She was a supernatural apparition who existed only for a moment and disappeared into the crowd in the terminal.

It was nine in the morning. It had been snowing all night, and traffic was heavier than usual in the city streets, and even slower on the highway, where trailer trucks were lined up on the shoulder and automobiles steamed in the snow. Inside the airport terminal, however, it was still spring.

I stood behind an old Dutch woman who spent almost an hour arguing about the weight of her eleven suitcases. I was beginning to feel bored when I saw the momentary apparition who left me breathless, and so I never knew how the dispute ended. Then the ticket clerk brought me down from the clouds with a reproach for my distraction. By way of an excuse, I asked her if she believed in love at first sight. "Of course," she said. "The other kinds are impossible." She kept her eyes fixed on the computer screen and asked whether I preferred a seat in smoking or nonsmoking.

"It doesn't matter," I said with intentional malice, "as long as I'm not beside the eleven suitcases."

---

1 From *Strange Pilgrims: Twelve Stories*, trans. Edith Grossman (London: Cape, 1993).

She expressed her appreciation with a commercial smile but did not look away from the glowing screen.

"Choose a number," she told me: "Three, four, or seven."

"Four."

Her smile flashed in triumph.

"In the fifteen years I've worked here," she said, "you're the first person who hasn't chosen seven."

She wrote the seat number on my boarding pass and returned it with the rest of my papers, looking at me for the first time with grape-colored eyes that were a consolation until I could see Beauty again. Only then did she inform me that the airport had just been closed and all flights delayed.

"For how long?"

"That's up to God," she said with her smile. "The radio said this morning it would be the biggest snowstorm of the year."

She was wrong: it was the biggest of the century. But in the first-class waiting room, spring was so real that there were live roses in the vases and even the canned music seemed as sublime and tranquilizing as its creators had intended. All at once it occurred to me that this was a suitable shelter for Beauty, and I looked for her in the other waiting areas, staggered by my own boldness. But most of the people were men from real life who read newspapers in English while their wives thought about someone else as they looked through the panoramic windows at the planes dead in the snow, the glacial factories, the vast fields of Roissy devastated by fierce lions. By noon there was no place to sit, and the heat had become so unbearable that I escaped for a breath of air.

Outside I saw an overwhelming sight. All kinds of people had crowded into the waiting rooms and were camped in the stifling corridors and even on the stairways, stretched out on the floor with their animals, their children, and their travel gear. Communication with the city had also been interrupted, and the palace of transparent plastic resembled an immense space capsule stranded in the storm. I could not help thinking that Beauty too must be somewhere in the middle of those tamed hordes, and the fantasy inspired me with new courage to wait.

By lunchtime we had realized that we were ship-wrecked. The lines were interminable outside the seven restaurants, the cafeterias, the packed bars, and in less than three hours they all had to be closed because there was nothing left to eat or drink. The children, who for a moment seemed to be all the children in the world, started to cry at the same time, and a herd smell began to rise from the crowd. It was a time for instinct. In all that scrambling, the only thing I could find to eat were the last two cups of vanilla ice cream in a children's shop. The waiters were putting chairs on tables as the patrons left, while I ate very slowly at the counter, seeing myself in the mirror with the last little cardboard cup and the last little cardboard spoon, and thinking about Beauty.

The flight to New York, scheduled for eleven in the morning, left at eight that night. By the time I managed to board, the other first-class passengers were already in their seats, and a flight attendant led me to mine. My heart stopped. In the seat next to mine, beside the window, Beauty was taking possession of her space with the mastery of an expert traveler. "If I ever wrote this, nobody would believe me," I thought. And I just managed to stammer an indecisive greeting that she did not hear.

She settled in as if she were going to live there for many years, putting each thing in its proper place and order, until her seat was arranged like the ideal house, where everything was within reach. In the meantime, a steward brought us our welcoming champagne. I took a glass to offer to her, but thought better of it just in time. For she wanted only a glass of water, and she asked the steward, first in incomprehensible French and then in an English only somewhat more fluent, not to wake her for any reason during the flight. Her warm, serious voice was tinged with Oriental sadness.

When he brought the water, she placed a cosmetics case with copper corners, like a grandmother's trunk, on her lap, and took two golden pills from a box that contained others of various colors. She did everything in a methodical, solemn way, as if nothing unforeseen had happened to her since her birth. At last she pulled down the shade on the window, lowered the back of her seat as far as it would go, covered herself to the waist with a blanket without taking off her shoes, put on a sleeping mask, turned her back to me, and then slept without a single pause, without a sigh, without the slightest change in position, for the eight eternal hours and twelve extra minutes of the flight to New York.

It was an ardent journey. I have always believed that there is nothing more beautiful in nature than a beautiful woman, and it was impossible for me to escape even for a moment from the spell of that storybook creature who slept at my side. The steward disappeared as soon as we took off and was replaced by a Cartesian attendant who tried to awaken Beauty to hand her a toiletry case and a set of earphones for listening to music. I repeated the instructions she had given the steward, but the attendant insisted on hearing from Beauty's own lips that she did not want supper either. The steward had to confirm her instructions, and even so he reproached me because Beauty had not hung the little cardboard "Do Not Disturb" sign around her neck.

I ate a solitary supper, telling myself in silence everything I would have told her if she had been awake. Her sleep was so steady that at one point I had the distressing thought that the pills she had taken were not for sleeping but for dying. With each drink I raised my glass and toasted her.

"To your health, Beauty."

When supper was over the lights were dimmed and a movie was shown to no one, and the two of us were alone in the darkness of the world. The biggest storm of the century had ended, and the Atlantic night was immense and limpid, and the plane seemed motionless among the stars. Then I contemplated her, inch by inch, for several hours, and the only sign of life I could detect were the shadows of the dreams that passed along her forehead like clouds over water. Around her neck she wore a chain so fine it was almost invisible against her golden skin, her perfect ears were unpierced, her nails were rosy with good health, and on her left hand was a plain band. Since she looked no older than twenty, I consoled myself with the idea that it was not a wedding ring but the sign of an ephemeral engagement. "To know you are sleeping, certain, secure, faithful channel of renunciation, pure line, so close to my manacled arms," I thought on the foaming crest of champagne, repeating the masterful sonnet by Gerardo Diego.[1] Then I lowered the back of my seat to the level of hers, and we lay together, closer than if we had been in a marriage bed. The climate of her breathing was the same as that of her voice, and her skin exhaled a delicate breath that could only be the scent of her beauty. It seemed incredible: The previous spring I had read a beautiful novel by Yasunari Kawabata[2] about the ancient bourgeois of Kyoto who paid enormous sums to spend the night watching the most beautiful girls in the city, naked and drugged, while they agonized with love in the same bed. They could not wake them, or touch them, and they did not even try, because the essence of their pleasure was to see them sleeping. That night, as I watched over Beauty's sleep, I not only understood that senile refinement but lived it to the full.

"Who would have thought," I said to myself, my vanity exacerbated by champagne, "that I'd become an ancient Japanese at this late date."

I think I slept several hours, conquered by champagne and the mute explosions of the movie, and when I awoke my head was splitting. I went to the bathroom. Two seats behind mine the old woman with the eleven suitcases lay in an awkward sprawl, like a forgotten corpse on a battlefield. Her reading glasses, on a chain of colored beads, were on the floor in the middle of the aisle, and for a moment I enjoyed the malicious pleasure of not picking them up.

After I got rid of the excesses of champagne, I caught sight of myself, contemptible and ugly, in the mirror, and was amazed that the devastation of love could be so terrible. The plane lost altitude without warning, then managed to straighten out and continue full speed ahead. The "Return to Your Seat" sign went on. I hurried

---

1   Gerardo Diego Cendóya (1896-1987): Spanish anthropologist, musicologist, and poet.
2   Yasunari Kawabata (1899-1972): Japanese novelist, among whose works was the novel, *The Sleeping Beauty* (1960); winner of the Nobel Prize for Literature in 1968.

out with the hope that God's turbulence might awaken Beauty and she would have to take refuge in my arms to escape her terror. In my haste I almost stepped on the Dutchwoman's glasses and would have been happy if I had. But I retraced my steps, picked them up, and put them on her lap in sudden gratitude for her not having chosen seat number four before I did.

Beauty's sleep was invincible. When the plane stabilized, I had to resist the temptation to shake her on some pretext, because all I wanted in the last hour of the flight was to see her awake, even if she were furious, so that I could recover my freedom, and perhaps my youth. But I couldn't do it. "Damn it," I said to myself with great scorn. "Why wasn't I born a Taurus!"[1]

She awoke by herself at the moment the landing lights went on, and she was as beautiful and refreshed as if she had slept in a rose garden. That was when I realized that, like old married couples, people who sit next to each other on airplanes do not say good morning to each other when they wake up. Nor did she. She took off her mask, opened her radiant eyes, straightened the back of the seat, moved the blanket aside, shook her hair that fell into place of its own weight, put the cosmetics case back on her knees, and applied rapid, unnecessary makeup, which took just enough time so that she did not look at me until the plane door opened. Then she put on her lynx jacket, almost stepped over me with a conventional excuse in pure Latin American Spanish, left without even saying good-bye or at least thanking me for all I had done to make our night together a happy one, and disappeared into the sun of today in the Amazon jungle of New York.

THE SLEEPING BEAUTY[2]

Wilfred Owen

SOJOURNING THROUGH A SOUTHERN REALM in youth,
I came upon a house by happy chance
Where bode a marvellous Beauty. There, romance
Flew faerily until I lit on truth—
For lo! the fair Child slumbered. Though, forsooth,
She lay not blanketed in drowsy trance,

---

1 Taurus: The astrological sign named for the bull disguise that Zeus used in order to seduce Europa.
2 First published in 1914. From *The Complete Poems and Fragments*, ed. Jon Stallworthy (New York: Norton, 1984).

But leapt alert of limb and keen of glance,
From sun to shower; from gaiety to ruth;
Yet breathed her loveliness asleep in her:
For, when I kissed, her eyelids knew no stir.
So back I drew tiptoe from that Princess,
Because it was too soon, and not my part,
To start voluptuous pulses in her heart,
And kiss her to the world of Consciousness.

CINDERELLA

WE CONCLUDE THE COMPARATIVE SECTIONS with versions of "Cinderella," which, with "Little Red Riding Hood" and "Sleeping Beauty," might be described as the core of the Western fairy-tale canon. As with the two previous tales, the abiding popularity of "Cinderella" raises the inevitable question: what is the explanation behind such success?

Part of the answer lies in the phrase that has entered the vernacular: "hers (or his!) is a real Cinderella story." It signifies that the individual has risen from obscurity and oppression to success and celebrity, perhaps with the implication that the good fortune is well deserved. There can be little doubt that the attraction of this tale has a lot to do with its theme of virtue revealed and rewarded: it invites us to recall times when we felt ourselves unappreciated and rejected and then to share Cinderella's satisfaction at being discovered as a true princess. (Hans Andersen taps into much the same feeling in "The Ugly Duckling.")

At this point, we should not be surprised to discover that Perrault's Cinderella is a rather passive young lady, no stranger to self-denial; she goes out of her way to assist her obnoxious stepsisters in preparing for the ball while denying that she has any right to such pleasures. On their departure, Cinderella collapses in tears, provoking the appearance of a fairy-tale *deus ex machina* in the shape of her fairy godmother, who provides her with all the accoutrements necessary for an impressive entry into high society.

In a number of respects, Perrault's version of this tale is quite unique. In no other tale, for example, do we find a fairy godmother transforming a pumpkin into a coach, mice into horses, or lizards into lackeys—and no other tale contains that famous glass slipper. The Russian tale "Vasilisa the Beautiful" stays much closer to its folk-tale origins in that the heroine receives magical assistance from her dead mother in the form of a tiny doll that Vasilisa carries in her pocket. (This is a motif common to numerous versions of the tale; in the Grimms' version, for instance, the spirit of the dead mother takes the form of a hazel tree and a white bird.) Although Vasilisa is ultimately rewarded with a royal husband, she wins him in rather less glamorous fashion than does Cinderella and only after surviving an encounter with the Baba Yaga, one of the most formidable "bad mothers" in all of fairy tale.

The world of "Cap o' Rushes" is somewhat reminiscent of that in "The Neapolitan Soldier" (from Italo Calvino's *Italian Folktales* in the "Sleeping Beauty" section), in that it shares the same earthy forthrightness, which is made the more obvious by the dialect that Joseph Jacobs (1854-1916) reproduced in his collection *English Fairy Tales* (1890). (One assumes that such was also the case in the original Italian of Calvino's tale; we must not forget the translator's involvement in many of these tales.) Here, too, there is a striking contrast between the bourgeois virtues of forbearance and self-denial displayed by Cinderella and the vigorous practicality of Cap o' Rushes as she deals with the challenges life throws in her path. Jacobs's tale contains some obvious differences from Perrault's, the most immediately apparent being the absence of a wicked stepmother and stepsisters. The opening episode bears a striking resemblance, of course, to the scene in Shakespeare's *King Lear* in which the king's youngest daughter, Cordelia, offers as honest and plain an answer to her father as Cap o' Rushes—with the same consequence. The point here, however, is that in Cap o' Rushes we have a no-nonsense heroine who reacts to her rejection by creating a plan and following it through to a successful conclusion that not only brings her a husband but also reconciles her to her father. Although less well-known, "Cap o' Rushes" is a significant variant of the Cinderella story that can be found in many collections, including those of the Grimm Brothers ("All-Fur") and Charles Perrault ("Donkeyskin"), although it differs from the latter two in omitting the father's incestuous attraction to his daughter.

Although some of the familiar elements in "The Indian Cinderella" may well be attributable to European influence, the fact remains that the flavor of this tale is quite different; it serves to remind us that the term "fairy tale" must have a broad definition if it is to include not only the stories from the Western tradition but also those from other continents and cultures. Unlike the familiar European versions, in which the prince must seek out his elusive bride, here the roles are reversed, although now the seeking becomes a test in itself. Deeply embedded in the natural world, this tale has an impressive mythic quality; the girl's discovery that Strong Wind draws his sled with the Rainbow and uses the Milky Way for his bowstring makes for an impressively large-scale climax to the story. Other unusual elements in this story are the symbolic bathing that transforms the young woman and the fact that, once married to Strong Wind, "she helped him to do great deeds."

There is an explicit religious element in the Hispanic tale "Little Gold Star," expressed both in the fact that the Blessed Mary fills the role of the fairy godmother and also in the symbolism of the gold star with which Teresa is blessed and which remains the focus of her beauty, unlike the splendid gowns and jewels often granted to Cinderella. However, the manner in which the rest of the Holy Family is depicted is unexpectedly down to earth—the contrast between the virtuous Teresa and her unpleasant stepsisters being established largely by the varying treatment meted out to the Holy Infant. And yet redemption is possible, in the shape of the gradual (and therefore convincing) reconciliation of Teresa's stepmother and sisters, which produces a particularly satisfying conclusion. The interweaving in this tale of matters religious and romantic, magical and mundane, surely tells us something of the Spanish-American people among whom it evolved.

In her gothic makeover of the tale, "When the Clock Strikes" (1983), Tanith Lee comes close to turning the story inside out. To convince us of the moral darkness of the world that she is describing, Lee introduces the Cinderella theme in relation to Ashella's mother in that she, too, is the object of a search—but for a purpose very different from marriage. As in previous versions, the close relationship between mother and daughter is emphasized, but now it is a bond of hatred and desire for vengeance that passes from one generation to the next. Here again, there is a stepmother and stepsisters, but this time they are well-meaning and inoffensive. Angela Carter produced her startling revision of "Little Red Riding Hood" essentially by reversing the roles of girl and "wolf"; Lee uses much the same tactic here by creating what amounts to an "anti-fairy tale" in which love becomes hate and marriage turns into murder.

One innovation that contemporary writers have introduced to the fairy tale is variation of the narrative voice. Customarily, the tale is recounted in the third person by a narrator who rarely intervenes in the story (one well-known exception is the rather cryptic ending to the Grimms' "Hansel and Gretel": "My story is done, see the mouse run; if you catch it, you may make yourself a great big fur cap out of it"). By contrast, many recent retellings have made the fairy tale multi-dimensional by giving the reader some new perspectives. Thus, the mystery of Tanith Lee's tale is enhanced by its enigmatic narrator, whose motivation remains in question to the tale's unsettling end—and our orthodox notions about Cinderella are thrown into quite a different light in "The Wicked Stepmother's Lament" (1996), by Sara Maitland. It is a daring synthesis of "once-upon-a-time" and the "here-and-now" (at one point, the stepmother-narrator comments on her reaction to seeing Disney's *Snow White*), but at the core of Maitland's tale is an insight applicable to a world of stories beyond

"Cinderella": that there is a profound gap between the innocence of childhood and the experience of adulthood, a gap made deeper by conventional assumptions about growing up female.

Anne Sexton (1928-74) focuses on much the same perceptual gap in "Cinderella" (1971), but while Maitland's stepmother expresses a not-unfamiliar mixture of resignation and frustration, the tone of the poem is bitterly ironic. It is as if the poet is venting her anger at fairy tales for creating a world so much at odds with our own imperfect existence—in other words, that the gap between the two is ultimately unbridgeable, unforgivable. Indeed, her technique of exposing the fantasy of the tale to her sardonic brand of realism is curiously reminiscent of such puritanical critics as Sarah Trimmer (see Introduction, p. 21)

CINDERELLA: OR THE LITTLE GLASS SLIPPER[1]

Charles Perrault

THERE ONCE LIVED A MAN who married twice, and his second wife was the haughtiest and most stuck-up woman in the world. She already had two daughters of her own and her children took after her in every way. Her new husband's first wife had given him a daughter of his own before she died, but she was a lovely and sweet-natured girl, very like her own natural mother, who had been a kind and gentle woman.

The second wedding was hardly over before the stepmother showed her true colours. Her new daughter was so lovable that she made her own children seem even more unpleasant by contrast; so she found the girl insufferable. She gave her all the rough work about the house to do, washing the pots and pans, cleaning out Madame's bedroom and those of her stepsisters, too. She slept at the top of the house, in a garret, on a thin, lumpy mattress, while her stepsisters had rooms with fitted carpets, soft beds and mirrors in which they could see themselves from head to foot. The poor girl bore everything patiently and dared not complain to her father because he would have lost his temper with her. His new wife ruled him with a rod of iron.

When the housework was all done, she would tuck herself away in the chimney corner to sit quietly among the cinders, the only place of privacy she could find, and so the family nicknamed her Cinderbritches. But the younger sister, who was less

---

1 First published in 1697. This text from *Sleeping Beauty and Other Favourite Fairy Tales*, trans. Angela Carter (London: Gollancz, 1982).

spiteful than the older one, changed her nickname to Cinderella. Yet even in her dirty clothes, Cinderella could not help but be a hundred times more beautiful than her sisters, however magnificently they dressed themselves up.

The king's son decided to hold a ball to which he invited all the aristocracy. Our two young ladies received their invitations, for they were well connected. Busy and happy, they set about choosing the dresses and hairstyles that would suit them best and that made more work for Cinderella, who had to iron her sisters' petticoats and starch their ruffles. They could talk about nothing except what they were going to wear.

"I shall wear my red velvet with the lace trimming," said the eldest. "Well, I shall wear just a simple skirt but put my coat with the golden flowers over it and, of course, there's always my diamond necklace, which is really rather special," said the youngest.

They sent for a good hairdresser to cut and curl their hair and they bought the best cosmetics. They called Cinderella to ask for her advice, because she had excellent taste. Cinderella helped them to look as pretty as they could and they were very glad of her assistance, although they did not show it.

As she was combing their hair, they said to her:

"Cinderella, dear, wouldn't you like to go to the ball yourself?"

"Oh don't make fun of me, my ladies, how could I possibly go to the ball!"

"Quite right, too; everyone would laugh themselves silly to see Cinderbritches at a ball."

Any other girl but Cinderella would have made horrid tangles of their hair after that, out of spite; but she was kind, and resisted the temptation. The stepsisters could not eat for two days, they were so excited. They broke more than a dozen corset-laces because they pulled them in so tightly in order to make themselves look slender and they were always primping in front of the mirror.

At last the great day arrived. When they went off, Cinderella watched them until they were out of sight and then began to cry. Her godmother saw how she was crying and asked her what the matter was.

"I want...I want to..."

But Cinderella was crying so hard she could not get the words out. Her godmother was a fairy. She said: "I think you're crying because you want to go to the ball."

"Yes." said Cinderella, sighing.

"If you are a good girl, I'll send you there," said her godmother.

She took her into her own room and said:

"Go into the garden and pick me a pumpkin."

Cinderella went out to the garden and picked the finest pumpkin she could find. She took it to her godmother, although she could not imagine how a pumpkin was going to help her get to the ball. Her godmother hollowed out the pumpkin until there was nothing left but the shell, struck it with her ring—and instantly the pumpkin changed into a beautiful golden coach.

Then the godmother went to look in the mousetrap, and found six live mice there. She told Cinderella to lift up the lid of the trap enough to let the mice come out one by one and, as each mouse crept out, she struck it lightly with her ring. At the touch of the ring, each mouse changed into a carriage horse. Soon the coach had six dappled greys to draw it.

Then she asked herself what would do for a coachman.

"I'll go and see if there is a rat in the rat-trap," said Cinderella. "A rat would make a splendid coachman."

"Yes, indeed," said her godmother. "Go and see."

There were three fat rats in the rat-trap that Cinderella brought to her. One had particularly fine whiskers, so the godmother chose that one; when she struck him with her ring, he changed into a plump coachman who had the most imposing moustache you could wish to see.

"If you look behind the watering-can in the garden, you'll find six lizards," the godmother told Cinderella. "Bring them to me."

No sooner had Cinderella brought them to her godmother than the lizards were all changed into footmen, who stepped up behind the carriage in their laced uniforms and hung on as if they had done nothing else all their lives.

The fairy said to Cinderella:

"There you are! Now you can go to the ball. Aren't you pleased?"

"Yes, of course. But how can I possibly go to the ball in these wretched rags?"

The godmother had only to touch her with her ring and Cinderella's workaday overalls and apron changed into a dress of cloth of gold and silver, embroidered with precious stones. Then she gave her the prettiest pair of glass slippers. Now Cinderella was ready, she climbed into the coach; but her godmother told her she must be home by midnight because if she stayed at the ball one moment more, her coach would turn back into a pumpkin, her horses to mice, her footmen to lizards and her clothes back into overalls again.

She promised her godmother that she would be sure to return from the ball before midnight. Then she drove off. The king's son had been told that a great princess, hitherto unknown to anyone present, was about to arrive at the ball and ran to receive her. He himself helped her down from her carriage with his royal hand and led her into the ballroom where all the guests were assembled. As soon as they saw her, an enormous silence descended. The dancing ceased, the fiddlers forgot to ply their bows as the entire company gazed at this unknown lady. The only sound in the entire ballroom was a confused murmur:

"Oh, isn't she beautiful!"

Even the king himself, although he was an old man, could not help gazing at her and remarked to the queen that he had not seen such a lovely young lady for a long time. All the women studied her hair and her ball-gown attentively so that they would be able to copy them the next day, provided they could find such a capable hairdresser, such a skillful dressmaker, such magnificent silk.

The king's son seated her in the most honoured place and then led her on to the dance floor; she danced so gracefully, she was still more admired. Then there was a fine supper but the prince could not eat at all, he was too preoccupied with the young lady. She herself went and sat beside her sisters and devoted herself to entertaining them. She shared the oranges and lemons the prince had given her with them and that surprised them very much, for they did not recognise her.

While they were talking, Cinderella heard the chimes of the clock striking a quarter to twelve. She made a deep curtsey and then ran off as quickly as she could. As soon as she got home, she went to find her godmother and thanked her and told her how much she wanted to go to the ball that was to be given the following day, because the king's son had begged her to. While she was telling her godmother everything that had happened, her stepsisters knocked at the door. Cinderella hurried to let them in.

"What a long time you've been!" she said to them yawning, rubbing her eyes and stretching as if she could scarcely keep awake, although she had not wanted to sleep for a single moment since they had left the house.

"If you had come to the ball, you wouldn't have been sleepy!" said one of the sisters. "The most beautiful princess you ever saw arrived unexpectedly and she was so kind to us, she gave us oranges and lemons."

Cinderella asked the name of the princess but they told her nobody knew it, and the king's son was in great distress and would give anything to find out more about her. Cinderella smiled and said:

"Was she really so very beautiful? Goodness me, how lucky you are. And can I never see her for myself? What a shame! Miss Javotte, lend me that old yellow dress you wear around the house so that I can go to the ball tomorrow and see her for myself."

"What?" exclaimed Javotte. "Lend my dress to such a grubby little Cinderbritches as it is—it must think I've lost my reason!"

Cinderella had expected a refusal; and she would have been exceedingly embarrassed if her sister had relented and agreed to lend her a dress and taken her to the ball in it.

Next day, the sisters went off to the ball again. Cinderella went, too, but this time she was even more beautifully dressed than the first time. The king's son did not leave her side and never stopped paying her compliments so that the young girl was utterly absorbed in him and time passed so quickly that she thought it must still be only eleven o'clock when she heard the chimes of midnight. She sprang to her feet and darted off as lightly as a doe. The prince sprang after her but he could not catch her; in her flight, however, she let fall one of her glass slippers and the prince tenderly picked it up. Cinderella arrived home out of breath, without her carriage, without her footmen, in her dirty old clothes again; nothing remained of all her splendour but one of her little slippers, the pair of the one she had dropped. The prince asked the guards at the palace gate if they had seen a princess go out; they replied they had seen nobody leave the castle last night at midnight but a ragged young girl who looked more like a kitchen-maid than a fine lady.

When her sisters came home from the ball, Cinderella asked them if they had enjoyed themselves again; and had the beautiful princess been there? They said, yes; but she had fled at the very stroke of midnight, and so promptly that she had dropped one of her little glass slippers. The king's son had found it and never took his eyes off it for the rest of the evening, so plainly he was very much in love with the beautiful lady to whom it belonged.

They spoke the truth. A few days later, the king's son publicly announced that he would marry whoever possessed the foot for which the glass slipper had been made. They made a start by trying the slipper on the feet of all the princesses; then moved on to the duchesses, then to the rest of the court, but all in vain. At last they brought the slipper to the two sisters, who did all they could to squeeze their feet into the slipper but could not manage it, no matter how hard they tried. Cinderella watched them; she recognised her own slipper at once. She laughed, and said:

"I'd like to try and see if it might not fit me!"

Her sisters giggled and made fun of her but the gentleman who was in charge of the slipper trial looked at Cinderella carefully and saw how beautiful she was. Yes, he said; of course she could try on the slipper. He had received orders to try the slipper on the feet of every girl in the kingdom. He sat Cinderella down and, as soon as he saw her foot, he knew it would fit the slipper perfectly. The two sisters were very much astonished, but not half so astonished as they were when Cinderella took her own glass slipper from her pocket. At that the godmother appeared; she struck Cinderella's overalls with her ring and at once the old clothes were transformed to garments more magnificent than all her ball-dresses.

Then her sisters knew she had been the beautiful lady they had seen at the ball. They threw themselves at her feet to beg her to forgive them for all the bad treatment she had received from them. Cinderella raised them up and kissed them and said she forgave them with all her heart and wanted them only always to love her. Then, dressed in splendour, she was taken to the prince. He thought she was more beautiful than ever and married her a few days later. Cinderella, who was as good as she was beautiful, took her sisters to live in the palace and arranged for both of them to be married, on the same day, to great lords.

Moral

Beauty is a fine thing in a woman; it will always be admired. But charm is beyond price and worth more, in the long run. When her godmother dressed Cinderella up and told her how to behave at the ball, she instructed her in charm. Lovely ladies, this gift is worth more than a fancy hairdo; to win a heart, to reach a happy ending, charm is the true gift of the fairies. Without it, one can achieve nothing; with it, everything.

Another Moral

It is certainly a great advantage to be intelligent, brave, well-born, sensible and have other similar talents given only by heaven. But however great may be your god-given store, they will never help you to get on in the world unless you have either a godfather or a godmother to put them to work for you.

VASILISA THE BEAUTIFUL[1]

Aleksandr Afanas'ev

IN A CERTAIN KINGDOM THERE lived a merchant. Although he had been married for twelve years, he had only one daughter, called Vasilisa the Beautiful. When the girl was eight years old, her mother died. On her deathbed the merchant's wife called her daughter, took a doll from under her coverlet, gave it to the girl, and said: "Listen, Vasilisushka. Remember and heed my last words. I am dying, and together with my maternal blessing I leave you this doll. Always keep it with you and do not show it to anyone; if you get into trouble, give the doll food, and ask its advice. When it has eaten, it will tell you what to do in your trouble." Then the mother kissed her child and died.

After his wife's death the merchant mourned as is proper, and then began to think of marrying again. He was a handsome man and had no difficulty in finding a bride, but he liked best a certain widow. Because she was elderly and had two daughters of her own, of almost the same age as Vasilisa, he thought that she was an experienced

---

1 First published in 1855. This text from *Russian Fairy Tales*, trans. Norbert Guterman (New York: Pantheon, 1945).

housewife and mother. So he married her, but was deceived, for she did not turn out to be a good mother for his Vasilisa. Vasilisa was the most beautiful girl in the village; her stepmother and stepsisters were jealous of her beauty and tormented her by giving her all kinds of work to do, hoping that she would grow thin from toil and tanned from exposure to the wind and sun; in truth, she had a most miserable life. But Vasilisa bore all this without complaint and became lovelier and more buxom, every day, while the stepmother and her daughters grew thin and ugly from spite, although they always sat with folded hands, like ladies.

How did all this come about? Vasilisa was helped by her doll. Without its aid the girl could never have managed all that work. In return, Vasilisa sometimes did not eat, but kept the choicest morsels for her doll. And at night, when everyone was asleep, she would lock herself in the little room in which she lived, and would give the doll a treat, saying: "Now, little doll, eat, and listen to my troubles. I live in my father's house but am deprived of all joy; a wicked stepmother is driving me from the white world. Tell me how I should live and what I should do." The doll would eat, then would give her advice and comfort her in her trouble, and in the morning, she would perform all the chores for Vasilisa, who rested in the shade and picked flowers while the flower beds were weeded, the cabbage sprayed, the water brought in, and the stove fired. The doll even showed Vasilisa an herb that would protect her from sunburn. She led an easy life, thanks to her doll.

Several years went by. Vasilisa grew up and reached the marriage age. She was wooed by all the young men in the village, but no one would even look at the stepmother's daughters. The stepmother was more spiteful than ever, and her answer to all the suitors was: "I will not give the youngest in marriage before the elder ones." And each time she sent a suitor away, she vented her anger on Vasilisa in cruel blows.

One day the merchant had to leave home for a long time in order to trade in distant lands. The stepmother moved to another house; near that house was a thick forest, and in a glade of that forest stood a hut, and in the hut lived Baba Yaga. She never allowed anyone to come near her and ate human beings as if they were chickens. Having moved into the new house, the merchant's wife, hating Vasilisa, repeatedly sent the girl to the woods for one thing or another; but each time Vasilisa returned home safe and sound: her doll had shown her the way and kept her far from Baba Yaga's hut.

Autumn came. The stepmother gave evening work to all three maidens: the oldest had to make lace, the second to knit stockings, and Vasilisa had to spin; and each one had to finish her task. The stepmother put out the lights all over the house, leaving only one candle in the room where the girls worked, and went to bed. The girls worked. The candle began to smoke; one of the stepsisters took up a scissor to trim it, but instead, following her mother's order, she snuffed it out, as though inadvertently. "What shall we do now?" said the girls. "There is no light in the house and our tasks are not finished. Someone must run to Baba Yaga and get some light." "The pins on my lace give me light," said the one who was making lace. "I shall not go." "I shall not go either," said the one who was knitting stockings, "my knitting needles give me light." "Then you must go," both of them cried to their stepsister. "Go to Baba Yaga!" And they pushed Vasilisa out of the room. She went into her own little room, put the supper she had prepared before her doll, and said: "Now dolly, eat, and aid me in my need. They are sending me to Baba Yaga for a light, and she will eat me up." The doll ate the supper and its eyes gleamed like two candles. "Fear not, Vasilisushka," it said. "Go where you are sent, only keep me with you all the time. With me in your pocket you will suffer no harm from Baba Yaga." Vasilisa made ready, put her doll in her pocket, and, having made the sign of the cross, went into the deep forest.

She walked in fear and trembling. Suddenly a horseman galloped past her: his face was white, he was dressed in white, his horse was white, and his horse's trappings were white—daybreak came to the woods.

She walked on farther, and a second horseman galloped past her: he was all red, he was dressed in red, and his horse was red—the sun began to rise.

Vasilisa walked the whole night and the whole day, and only on the following evening did she come to the glade where Baba Yaga's hut stood. The fence around the hut was made of human bones, and on the spikes were human skulls with staring eyes; the doors had human legs for doorposts, human hands for bolts, and a mouth with sharp teeth in place of a lock. Vasilisa was numb with horror and stood rooted to the spot. Suddenly another horseman rode by. He was all black, he was dressed in black, and his horse was black. He galloped up to Baba Yaga's door and vanished, as though the earth had swallowed him up—night came. But the darkness did not last long. The eyes of all the skulls on the fence began to gleam and the glade was as bright as day. Vasilisa shuddered with fear, but not knowing where to run, remained on the spot.

Soon a terrible noise resounded through the woods; the trees crackled, the dry leaves rustled; from the woods Baba Yaga drove out in a mortar, prodding it on with a pestle, and sweeping her traces with a broom. She rode up to the gate, stopped, and sniffing the air around her, cried: "Fie, fie! I smell a Russian smell! Who is here?" Vasilisa came up to the old witch and, trembling with fear, bowed low to her and said: "It is I, grandmother. My stepsisters sent me to get some light." "Very well," said Baba Yaga. "I know them, but before I give you the light you must live with me and work for me; if not, I will eat you up." Then she turned to the gate and cried: "Hey, my strong bolts, unlock! Open up, my wide gate!" The gate opened, and Baba Yaga drove in whistling. Vasilisa followed her, and then everything closed again.

Having entered the room, Baba Yaga stretched herself out in her chair and said to Vasilisa: "Serve me what is in the stove; I am hungry." Vasilisa lit a torch from the skulls on the fence and began to serve Yaga the food from the stove—and enough food had been prepared for ten people. She brought kvass, mead, beer, and wine from the cellar. The old witch ate and drank everything, leaving for Vasilisa only a little cabbage soup, a crust of bread, and a piece of pork. Then Baba Yaga made ready to go to bed and said: "Tomorrow after I go, see to it that you sweep the yard, clean the hut, cook the dinner, wash the linen, and go to the cornbin and sort out a bushel of wheat. And let everything be done, or I will eat you up!" Having given these orders, Baba Yaga began to snore. Vasilisa set the remnants of the old witch's supper before her doll, wept bitter tears, and said: "Here dolly, eat, and aid me in my need! Baba Yaga has given me a hard task to do and threatens to eat me up if I do not do it all. Help me!" The doll answered: "Fear not, Vasilisa the Beautiful! Eat your supper, say your prayers, and go to sleep; the morning is wiser than the evening."

Very early next morning Vasilisa awoke, after Baba Yaga had arisen, and looked out of the window. The eyes of the skulls were going out; then the white horseman flashed by, and it was daybreak. Baba Yaga went out into the yard, whistled, and the mortar, pestle, and broom appeared before her. The red horseman flashed by, and the sun rose. Baba Yaga sat in the mortar, prodded it on with the pestle, and swept her traces with the broom. Vasilisa remained alone, looked about Baba Yaga's hut, was amazed at the abundance of everything, and stopped wondering which work she should do first. For lo and behold, all the work was done; the doll was picking the last shreds of chaff from the wheat. "Ah my savior," said Vasilisa to her doll, "you have delivered me from death." "All you have to do," answered the doll, creeping into Vasilisa's pocket, "is to cook the dinner; cook it with the help of God and then rest, for your health's sake."

When evening came Vasilisa set the table and waited for Baba Yaga. Dusk began to fall, the black horseman flashed by the gate, and night came; only the skulls' eyes were shining. The trees crackled, the leaves rustled; Baba Yaga was coming. Vasilisa met her. "Is everything done?" asked Yaga. "Please see for yourself, grandmother," said Vasilisa. Baba Yaga looked at everything, was annoyed that there was nothing she could complain about, and said: "Very well, then." Then she cried: "My faithful servants, my dear friends, grind my wheat!" Three pairs of hands appeared, took the wheat, and carried it out of sight. Baba Yaga ate her fill, made ready to go to sleep, and again gave her orders to Vasilisa. "Tomorrow," she commanded, "do the same work you have done today, and in addition take the poppy seed from the bin and get rid of the dust, grain by grain; someone threw dust into the bins out of spite." Having said this, the old witch turned to the wall and began to snore, and Vasilisa set about feeding her doll. The doll ate, and spoke as she had spoken the day before: "Pray to

God and go to sleep; the morning is wiser than the evening. Everything will be done, Vasilisushka."

Next morning Baba Yaga again left the yard in her mortar, and Vasilisa and the doll soon had all the work done. The old witch came back, looked at everything, and cried: "My faithful servants, my dear friends, press the oil out of the poppy seed!" Three pairs of hands appeared, took the poppy seed, and carried it out of sight. Baba Yaga sat down to dine; she ate, and Vasilisa stood silent. "Why do you not speak to me?" said Baba Yaga. "You stand there as though you were dumb." "I did not dare to speak," said Vasilisa, "but if you'll give me leave, I'd like to ask you something." "Go ahead. But not every question has a good answer; if you know too much, you will soon grow old." "I want to ask you, grandmother, only about what I have seen. As I was on my way to you, a horseman on a white horse, all white himself and dressed in white, overtook me. Who is he?" "He is my bright day," said Baba Yaga. "Then another horseman overtook me; he had a red horse, was red himself, and was dressed in red. Who is he?" "He is my red sun." "And who is the black horseman whom I met at your very gate, grandmother?" "He is my dark night—and all of them are my faithful servants."

Vasilisa remembered the three pairs of hands, but kept silent. "Why don't you ask me more?" said Baba Yaga. "That will be enough," Vasilisa replied. "You said yourself, grandmother, that one who knows too much will grow old soon." "It is well," said Baba Yaga, "that you ask only about what you have seen outside my house, not inside my house; I do not like to have my dirty linen washed in public, and I eat the over-curious. Now I shall ask you something. How do you manage to do the work I set for you?" "I am helped by the blessing of my mother," said Vasilisa. "So that is what it is," shrieked Baba Yaga. "Get you gone, blessed daughter! I want no blessed ones in my house!" She dragged Vasilisa out of the room and pushed her outside the gate, took a skull with burning eyes from the fence, stuck it on a stick, and gave it to the girl, saying: "Here is your light for your stepsisters. Take it; that is what they sent you for."

Vasilisa ran homeward by the light of the skull, which went out only at daybreak, and by nightfall of the following day she reached the house. As she approached the gate, she was about to throw the skull away, thinking that surely they no longer needed a light in the house. But suddenly a dull voice came from the skull, saying "Do not throw me away, take me to your stepmother." She looked at the stepmother's house and, seeing that there was no light in the windows, decided to enter with her skull. For the first time she was received kindly. Her stepmother and stepsisters told her that since she had left they had had no fire in the house; they were unable to strike a flame themselves, and whatever light was brought by the neighbors went out the moment it was brought into the house. "Perhaps your fire will last," said the stepmother. The skull was brought into the room, and its eyes kept staring at the stepmother and her daughters, and burned them. They tried to hide, but wherever they went the eyes followed them. By morning they were all burned to ashes; only Vasilisa remained untouched by the fire.

In the morning Vasilisa buried the skull in the ground, locked up the house, and went to the town. A certain childless old woman gave her shelter, and there she lived, waiting for her father's return. One day she said to the woman: "I am weary of sitting without work, grandmother. Buy me some flax, the best you can get; at least I shall be spinning." The old woman bought good flax and Vasilisa set to work. She spun as fast as lightning and her threads were even and thin as a hair. She spun a great deal of yarn; it was time to start weaving it, but no comb fine enough for Vasilisa's yarn could be found, and no one would undertake to make one. Vasilisa asked her doll for aid. The doll said: "Bring me an old comb, an old shuttle, and a horse's mane; I will make a loom for you." Vasilisa got everything that was required and went to sleep, and during the night the doll made a wonderful loom for her.

By the end of the winter the linen was woven, and it was so fine that it could be passed through a needle like a thread. In the spring the linen was bleached, and Vasilisa said to the old woman: "Grandmother, sell this linen and keep the money for yourself." The old woman looked at the linen and gasped: "No, my child! No one can wear such linen except the tsar; I shall take it to the palace." The old woman went to the tsar's palace and walked back and forth beneath the windows. The tsar saw her and asked: "What do you want, old woman?" "Your Majesty," she answered, "I have brought rare merchandise; I do not want to show it to anyone but you." The tsar ordered her to be brought before him, and when he saw the linen he was amazed. "What do you want for it?" asked the tsar. "It has no price, little father tsar! I have brought it as a gift to you." The tsar thanked her and rewarded her with gifts.

The tsar ordered shirts to be made of the linen. It was cut, but nowhere could they find a seamstress who was willing to sew them. For a long time they tried to find one, but in the end the tsar summoned the old woman and said: "You have known how to spin and weave such linen, you must know how to sew shirts of it." "It was not I that spun and wove this linen, Your Majesty," said the old woman. "This is the work of a maiden to whom I give shelter." "Then let her sew the shirts," ordered the tsar.

The old woman returned home and told everything to Vasilisa. "I knew all the time," said Vasilisa to her, "that I would have to do this work." She locked herself in her room and set to work; she sewed without rest and soon a dozen shirts were ready. The old woman took them to the tsar, and Vasilisa washed herself, combed her hair, dressed in her finest clothes, and sat at the window. She sat there waiting to see what would happen. She saw a servant of the tsar entering the courtyard. The messenger came into the room and said: "The tsar wishes to see the needlewoman who made his shirts, and wishes to reward her with his own hands." Vasilisa appeared before the tsar. When the tsar saw Vasilisa the Beautiful he fell madly in love with her. "No, my beauty," he said, "I will not separate from you; you shall be my wife." He took Vasilisa by her white hands, seated her by his side, and the wedding was celebrated at once. Soon Vasilisa's father returned, was overjoyed at her good fortune, and came to live in his daughter's house. Vasilisa took the old woman into her home too, and carried her doll in her pocket till the end of her life.

CAP O' RUSHES[1]

Joseph Jacobs

WELL, THERE WAS ONCE A very rich gentleman, and he'd three daughters, and he thought he'd see how fond they were of him. So he says to the first, "How much do you love me, my dear?" "Why," says she, "as I love my life." "That's good," says he.

So he says to the second, "How much do *you* love me, my dear?"

"Why," says she, "better nor all the world."

"That's good," says he. So he says to the third, "How much do *you* love me, my dear?"

"Why, I love you as fresh meat loves salt," says she.

Well, but he was angry. "You don't love me at all," says he, "and in my house you stay no more." So he drove her out there and then, and shut the door in her face.

Well, she went away on and on till she came to a fen,[2] and there she gathered a lot of rushes and made them into a kind of a sort of a cloak with a hood, to cover her from head to foot, and to hide her fine clothes. And then she went on and on till she came to a great house.

"Do you want a maid?" says she.

"No, we don't," said they.

"I haven't nowhere to go," says she; "and I ask no wages, and do any sort of work," says she.

"Well," said they, "if you like to wash the pots and scrape the saucepans you may stay," said they.

So she stayed there and washed the pots and scraped the saucepans and did all the dirty work. And because she gave no name they called her "Cap o' Rushes."

Well, one day there was to be a great dance a little way off, and the servants were

---

1   From *English Fairy Tales*, 1890 (repr. New York: Dover, 1967).
2   fen: Bog or marsh.

allowed to go and look on at the grand people. Cap o' Rushes said she was too tired to go, so she stayed at home.

But when they were gone she offed with her cap o' rushes, and cleaned herself, and went to the dance. And no one there was so finely dressed as she.

Well, who should be there but her master's son, and what should he do but fall in love with her the minute he set eyes on her. He wouldn't dance with any one else.

But before the dance was done Cap o' Rushes slipped off, and away she went home. And when the other maids came back she was pretending to be asleep with her cap o' rushes on.

Well, next morning they said to her, "You did miss a sight, Cap o' Rushes!"

"What was that?" says she.

"Why, the beautifullest lady you ever see, dressed right gay and ga'.[1] The young master, he never took his eyes off her." "Well, I should have liked to have seen her," says Cap o' Rushes. "Well, there's to be another dance this evening, and perhaps she'll be there."

But, come the evening, Cap o' Rushes said she was too tired to go with them. Howsoever, when they were gone she offed with her cap o' rushes and cleaned herself, and away she went to the dance.

The master's son had been reckoning on seeing her, and he danced with no one else, and never took his eyes off her. But, before the dance was over, she slipped off, and home she went, and when the maids came back she pretended to be asleep with her cap o' rushes on.

Next day they said to her again, "Well, Cap o' Rushes, you should ha' been there to see the lady. There she was again, gay and ga', and the young master he never took his eyes off her."

"Well, there," says she, "I should ha' liked to ha' seen her."

"Well," says they, "there's a dance again this evening, and you must go with us, for she's sure to be there."

Well, come this evening, Cap o' Rushes said she was too tired to go, and do what they would she stayed at home. But when they were gone she offed with her cap o' rushes and cleaned herself, and away she went to the dance.

The master's son was rarely glad when he saw her. He danced with none but her and never took his eyes off her. When she wouldn't tell him her name, nor where she came from, he gave her a ring and told her if he didn't see her again he should die.

Well, before the dance was over, off she slipped, and home she went, and when the maids came home she was pretending to be asleep with her cap o' rushes on.

---

1   and ga': And all (colloquial).

Well, next day they says to her, "There, Cap o' Rushes, you didn't come last night, and now you won't see the lady, for there's no more dances."

"Well I should have rarely liked to have seen her," says she.

The master's son he tried every way to find out where the lady was gone, but go where he might, and ask whom he might, he never heard anything about her. And he got worse and worse for the love of her till he had to keep his bed.

"Make some gruel for the young master," they said to the cook. "He's dying for the love of the lady." The cook she set about making it when Cap o' Rushes came in.

"What are you adoing of?" says she.

"I'm going to make some gruel for the young master," says the cook, "for he's dying for love of the lady."

"Let me make it," says Cap o' Rushes.

Well, the cook wouldn't at first, but at last she said yes, and Cap o' Rushes made the gruel. And when she had made it she slipped the ring into it on the sly before the cook took it upstairs.

The young man he drank it and then he saw the ring at the bottom.

"Send for the cook," says he.

So up she comes.

"Who made this gruel here?" says he.

"I did," says the cook, for she was frightened.

And he looked at her.

"No, you didn't," says he. "Say who did it, and you shan't be harmed."

"Well, then, 'twas Cap o' Rushes," says she.

"Send Cap o' Rushes here," says he. So Cap o' Rushes came.

"Did you make my gruel?" says he.

"Yes, I did," says she.

"Where did you get this ring?" says he.

"From him that gave it me," says she.

"Who are you, then?" says the young man.

"I'll show you," says she. And she offed with her cap o' rushes, and there she was in her beautiful clothes.

Well, the master's son he got well very soon, and they were to be married in a little time. It was to be a very grand wedding, and every one was asked far and near. And Cap o' Rushes' father was asked. But she never told anybody who she was.

But before the wedding she went to the cook, and says she:

"I want you to dress every dish without a mite o' salt."

"That'll be rare nasty," says the cook.

"That doesn't signify," says she.

"Very well," says the cook.

Well, the wedding-day came, and they were married. And after they were married all the company sat down to the dinner. When they began to eat the meat, it was so tasteless they couldn't eat it. But Cap o' Rushes' father tried first one dish and then another, and then he burst out crying.

"What is the matter?" said the master's son to him.

"Oh!" says he, "I had a daughter. And I asked her how much she loved me. And she said 'As much as fresh meat loves salt.' And I turned her from my door, for I thought she didn't love me. And now I see she loved me best of all. And she may be dead for aught I know."

"No, father, here she is!" says Cap o' Rushes. And she goes up to him and puts her arms round him. And so they were all happy ever after.

THE INDIAN CINDERELLA[1]

Cyrus Macmillan

ON THE SHORES OF A wide bay on the Atlantic coast there dwelt in old times a great Indian warrior. It was said that he had been one of Glooskap's best helpers and friends, and that he had done for him many wonderful deeds. But that, no man knows. He had, however, a very wonderful and strange power; he could make himself invisible; he could thus mingle unseen with his enemies and listen to their plots. He was known among the people as Strong Wind, the Invisible. He dwelt with his sister in a tent near the sea, and his sister helped him greatly in his work. Many maidens would have been glad to marry him, and he was much sought after because of his mighty deeds; and it was known that Strong Wind would marry the first maiden who could see him as he came home at night. Many made the trial, but it was a long time before one succeeded.

Strong Wind used a clever trick to test the truthfulness of all who sought to win him. Each evening as the day went down, his sister walked on the beach with any girl who wished to make the trial. His sister could always see him, but no one else could see him. And as he came home from work in the twilight, his sister as she saw him drawing near would ask the girl who sought him, "Do you see him?" And each girl would falsely answer, "Yes." And his sister would ask, "With what does he draw his sled?" And each girl would answer, "With the hide of a moose," or "With a pole," or "With a great cord." And then his sister would know that they all had lied, for their

---

1   From *Canadian Wonder Tales* (London: John Lane, the Bodley Head, 1918).

answers were mere guesses. And many tried and lied and failed, for Strong Wind would not marry any who were untruthful.

There lived in the village a great chief who had three daughters. Their mother had been long dead. One of these was much younger than the others. She was very beautiful and gentle and well beloved by all, and for that reason her older sisters were very jealous of her charms and treated her very cruelly. They clothed her in rags that she might be ugly; and they cut off her long black hair; and they burned her face with coals from the fire that she might be scarred and disfigured. And they lied to their father, telling him that she had done these things herself. But the young girl was patient and kept her gentle heart and went gladly about her work.

Like other girls, the chief's two eldest daughters tried to win Strong Wind. One evening, as the day went down, they walked on the shore with Strong Wind's sister and waited for his coming. Soon he came home from his day's work, drawing his sled. And his sister asked as usual, "Do you see him?" And each one, lying, answered, "Yes." And she asked, "Of what is his shoulder strap made?" And each, guessing, said, "Of rawhide." Then they entered the tent where they hoped to see Strong Wind eating his supper; and when he took off his coat and his moccasins they could see them, but more than these they saw nothing. And Strong Wind knew that they had lied, and he kept himself from their sight, and they went home dismayed.

One day the chief's youngest daughter with her rags and her burnt face resolved to seek Strong Wind. She patched her clothes with bits of birch bark from the trees, and put on the few little ornaments she possessed, and went forth to try to see the Invisible One as all the other girls of the village had done before. And her sisters laughed at her and called her "Fool"; and as she passed along the road all the people laughed at her because of her tattered frock and her burnt face, but silently she went her way.

Strong Wind's sister received the little girl kindly, and at twilight she took her to the beach. Soon Strong Wind came home drawing his sled. And his sister asked, "Do you see him?" And the girl answered, "No," and his sister wondered greatly because she spoke the truth. And again she asked, "Do you see him now?" And the girl answered, "Yes, and he is very wonderful." And she asked, "With what does he draw his sled?" And the girl answered, "With the Rainbow," and she was much afraid. And she asked further, "Of what is his bowstring?" And the girl answered, "His bowstring is the Milky Way."

Then Strong Wind's sister knew that because the girl had spoken the truth at first her brother had made himself visible to her. And she said, "Truly, you have seen him." And she took her home and bathed her, and all the scars disappeared from her face and body; and her hair grew long and black again like the raven's wing; and she gave her fine clothes to wear and many rich ornaments. Then she bade her take the wife's seat in the tent. Soon Strong Wind entered and sat beside her, and called her his bride. The very next day she became his wife, and ever afterwards she helped him to do great deeds. The girl's two elder sisters were very cross, and they wondered greatly at what had taken place. But Strong Wind, who knew of their cruelty, resolved to punish them. Using his great power, he changed them both into aspen trees and rooted them in the earth. And since that day the leaves of the aspen have always trembled, and they shiver in fear at the approach of Strong Wind, it matters not how softly he comes, for they are still mindful of his great power and anger because of their lies and their cruelty to their sister long ago.

LITTLE GOLD STAR, A SPANISH AMERICAN CINDERELLA TALE[1]

Robert D. San Souci

Author's Note

This story, well known in New Mexico and the Southwest, is adapted from tales of Spanish origin, though it has roots in such tales as "Cinderella" and narratives collected by the Brothers Grimm and other folklorists.

In addition to working with previously translated versions of the tale from such books as *Literary Folklore of the Hispanic Southwest*, by Aurora Lucero-White Lea, and Jose Manuel Espinosa's *Spanish Folk-Tales from New Mexico*, published in 1937 as Volume XX of the memoirs of the American Folk-Lore Society, I used new translations of several old Spanish-language texts that were reprinted in the American Folk-Lore Society volume.

IN WHAT IS NOW NEW Mexico, there was once a sheepherder named Tomas whose wife had died. He had an only child, Teresa. She kept house while he tended his flocks high in the hills.

Then a widow and her two daughters moved nearby. The woman visited often, and one day she said to Tomas, "Surely you are as lonely as I. Marry me, and make us both happy."

When Tomas refused, the widow began to weep. Not knowing what to do, Tomas agreed to be married.

Teresa cared little for the haughty woman or her vain daughters, Inez and Isabel, but she said nothing.

---

1   Published in 2000 (New York: Harper Collins).

As soon as Tomas's new wife moved into the house, she made life a misery for him and Teresa. She nagged her husband so much, he stayed in the hills longer and longer. And while he was away, Teresa had to do all the chores.

On one rare visit home, Tomas brought his wife and stepdaughters gifts of flowers and oranges. To Teresa he gave a lamb with soft white fleece.

As soon as her husband returned to his flocks, Teresa's stepmother killed the lamb. Handing the heartbroken girl the fleece, she ordered, "Go wash this in the river, so I can make myself a soft pillow."

Teresa had no choice but to obey. As she scrubbed, a fish snatched the wool and swam away. Teresa tried to snatch back the fleece but failed. Fearing her stepmother's anger, she began to weep.

Just then, a woman dressed in blue came by, and asked, "Why are you crying?"

When Teresa told her, the woman said, "Go up to that little shack on the mountain-side. Tend the old man and the child there and sweep the floor, and I will bring the fleece back to you."

Teresa climbed the path to the hut. Inside, an old man with tangled hair and beard dozed while a baby cried in his cradle. Teresa gently rocked the infant and sang a lullaby until he went to sleep. Then she combed the old man's hair and beard. Finally she swept the place clean.

Just as she finished, the woman in blue returned, carrying the snow-white fleece. She gave this to Teresa, saying, "Good child, your kindness carries its own blessing." She touched Teresa's forehead with her finger, and a little gold star appeared there.

Teresa did not know it, but the woman was Blessed Mary. The old man was Saint Joseph, and the baby was the Holy Child, the baby Jesus.

The moment Teresa returned home, her stepmother cried, "Why have you been away so long?"

Teresa told her what had happened, but the woman did not believe her. Then her stepmother tried to scrub off the gold star, but it just shined brighter. And when she touched the fleece, it turned muddy.

The next morning, Isabel was sent to wash the fleece. Again, a fish carried it off, and the woman in blue came. She told the girl to tend the old man and the baby and to take the stewpot off the fire. In return, she would restore the fleece.

But inside the shack, Isabel spanked the Holy Infant because he was crying, pulled Saint Joseph's beard, and dropped the pot, spilling stew all over the floor.

When Blessed Mary returned, she gave Isabel the now-spotless fleece. But as she touched the girl's forehead, she said, "Your unkindness carries its own penance." At this, horns grew out of the sides of Isabel's head.

"What have you done, you silly girl?" her mother asked when she saw Isabel's horns. She tried to twist and tug them off her daughter's head.

"*Ay! Ay! Ay!*" cried the girl.

Her mother pulled harder, but she only made the horns grow longer. She angrily ordered Inez to wash the fleece, because it had become dirtier than ever when the stepmother touched it.

Inez also had the fleece carried off by a fish. She too met the woman in blue, who sent her to care for the old man and the child and to clean the ashes from the fireplace. But Inez scolded the Holy Infant, ignored Saint Joseph, and strewed the hearth ashes all over the floor.

For her punishment, the girl sprouted a pair of donkey's ears.

Yank as she might, Inez's mother only made the ears grow bigger and shaggier. At last she gave up and sewed heavy black *mantillas*, veils, for her daughters to wear.

Because Teresa bore a gold star while her stepsisters wore hideous horns and ears, they taunted her even more. They called her "*Estrellita de Oro*," "Little Gold Star," turning the words into a cruel joke.

About this time, a fiesta was held in honor of the patron saint of the town. The morning of the festival, Isabel and Inez, dressed in fine satins and high *mantillas*, sat in the front pew at mass with their mother. Near them sat Don Miguel, the handsome young man whose mansion overlooked the plaza.

To one side of the altar knelt Teresa. By chance Miguel noticed her, though Isabel and Inez kept fluttering their fans to draw his attention. At one point Teresa's white veil slipped back, and Miguel saw the star shining on her forehead. But before he could speak to her, Teresa left to return to her chores.

That night, Miguel opened his home for feasting and dancing.

Left behind by her stepmother and stepsisters, who went in a carriage, Teresa walked to the party. Her white dress was shabby compared to the elegant gowns that swirled around her, but her gold star outshone the jewels the other women wore.

Seeing the star, Miguel moved through the crowd toward Teresa. He smiled and bowed, and they began to dance. As was the custom, the young couple danced silently and distantly, looking at the floor rather than at each other.

As they danced, Teresa felt her sadness giving way to joy. The tenderness she had seen in Miguel's eyes matched the feeling that was growing in her heart.

Suddenly Teresa's stepmother took her arm and pulled her aside. "You wretched girl," the woman whispered angrily. "How dare you come here and embarrass us? Go home at once!" At these harsh words, Teresa turned and fled.

As the music ended, Miguel finally looked up and discovered his dancing partner was gone. He asked who she was, but because Teresa always kept to herself, no one recognized her. Her stepmother remained silent. Still Miguel vowed to find her, though he did not know her name.

At dawn he rode out, stopping at every house, ranch, and farm to ask about the mysterious young woman. Late in the day he came to Tomas's house.

"*Buenas tardes*," Teresa's stepmother greeted the young man.

"Good afternoon," he responded, then explained the reason for his visit.

"I don't know this stranger you are seeking," the woman said. "But I invite you to take some refreshment with us."

Miguel politely agreed. Isabel and Inez brought hot chocolate and little cakes Teresa had baked that morning. Each tried to catch Miguel's eye and put herself ahead of her sister.

When Teresa's stepmother had seen Miguel approaching, she had locked Teresa in a small room. Now the girl happened to brush her forehead, touching the gold star as she sighed, "I wish I could see Miguel again."

At the same moment, in the parlor, the housecat mewed, "*Narow, narow*." Then, to everyone's surprise, it said, "Little Gold Star *is* here, right in the house."

"Did you hear that?" Miguel exclaimed. "The cat said she is here!"

"You are hearing things," said Teresa's stepmother, kicking at the cat while her daughters jabbed at it with their fans. But the cat clawed away their *mantillas*, revealing their ears and horns. The young women fled in dismay, with their mother running after them. Then the cat led Don Miguel to Teresa.

"Little Gold Star!" he cried joyously.

"My proper name is Teresa, Senor," she replied.

"Senorita Teresa," he said, "I beg you to marry me."

"I would marry you in an instant," answered Teresa, "but you must ask my stepmother's permission first."

"Of course," Miguel agreed. Then he kissed her hand and left.

The next morning, Miguel's servant brought a letter asking for Teresa's hand in marriage. After she had read it, Teresa's stepmother shook with anger. To Isabel and Inez she said, "I will allow Teresa to marry only if she performs three tasks. So help me to choose some impossible challenges."

When they had agreed upon the tasks, the stepmother went to Teresa and said, "You must do three things before we return from market. If you fail, I will refuse Don Miguel's marriage offer."

"First," said Isabel, "you must fill ten bottles with birds' tears."

"Next," said Inez, "you must stuff twelve mattresses with birds' feathers."

"Finally," said Teresa's stepmother, "you must prepare a tableful of fine food." Then the three left.

Though Teresa despaired of completing these tasks, she was determined to try. But she could find only a handful of rice and beans in the house; not a single bird appeared in the sky.

Suddenly, there was a tap at the door. Blessed Mary stood there. "Do not worry," she said. "Touch your gold star and call the birds of heaven to help."

Teresa did, and instantly the sky was filled with birds. They wept until she filled ten bottles with their tears. The second time she touched her star, the birds shed feathers like soft rain, while Teresa stuffed twelve mattresses. When she touched the star a third time, the birds flew away and came back, carrying delicacies of every sort.

Teresa's stepmother and stepsisters gazed in wonder when they returned. Realizing that Teresa had been blessed, the woman sent Miguel a letter agreeing to the marriage.

Tomas returned in time to see his daughter married. And the joy of the bride and groom touched everyone. Gradually, Teresa's stepmother grew less disagreeable and began to treat her as a daughter. Isabel and Inez grew kinder, and the donkey's ears and horns became smaller, then finally disappeared.

Miguel and Teresa lived lovingly all their days. And the little gold star remained a sign of heaven's blessing on them and their children.

WHEN THE CLOCK STRIKES[1]

Tanith Lee

Yes, the great ballroom is filled only with dust now. The slender columns of white marble and the slender columns of rose-red marble are woven together by cobwebs. The vivid frescoes, on which the duke's treasury spent so much, are dimmed by the dust; the faces of the painted goddesses look gray. And the velvet curtains—touch them, they will crumble. Two hundred years, now, since anyone danced in this place on the sea-green floor in the candle gleam. Two hundred years since the wonderful clock struck for the very last time.

I thought you might care to examine the clock. It was considered exceptional in its day. The pedestal is ebony and the face fine porcelain. And these figures, which are of silver, would pass slowly about the circlet of the face. Each figure represents, you understand, an hour. And as the appropriate hours came level with this golden bell, they would strike it the correct number of times. All the figures are unique, you see. Beginning at the first hour, they are, in this order, a girl-child, a dwarf, a maiden, a youth, a lady, and a knight. And here, notice, the figures grow older as the

---

1   From *Red as Blood, or Tales from the Sisters Grimmer* (New York: Daw, 1983).

day declines: a queen and king for the seventh and eighth hours, and after these, an abbess and a magician and next to last, a hag. But the very last is strangest of all. The twelfth figure: do you recognize him? It is Death. Yes, a most curious clock. It was reckoned a marvelous thing then. But it has not struck for two hundred years. Possibly you have been told the story? No? Oh, but I am certain that you have heard it, in another form, perhaps.

However, as you have some while to wait for your carriage, I will recount the tale, if you wish.

I will start with what is said of the clock. In those years, this city was prosperous, a stronghold—not as you see it today. Much was made in the city that was ornamental and unusual. But the clock, on which the twelfth hour was Death, caused something of a stir. It was thought unlucky, foolhardy, to have such a clock. It began to be murmured, jokingly by some, by others in earnest, that one night when the clock struck the twelfth hour, Death would truly strike with it.

Now life has always been a chancy business, and it was more so then. The Great Plague had come but twenty years before and was not yet forgotten. Besides, in the duke's court there was much intrigue, while enemies might be supposed to plot beyond the city walls, as happens even in our present age. But there was another thing.

It was rumored that the duke had obtained both his title and the city treacherously. Rumor declared that he had systematically destroyed those who had stood in line before him, the members of the princely house that formerly ruled here. He had accomplished the task slyly, hiring assassins talented with poisons and daggers. But rumor also declared that the duke had not been sufficiently thorough. For though he had meant to rid himself of all that rival house, a single descendant remained, so obscure he had not traced her—for it was a woman.

Of course, such matters were not spoken of openly. Like the prophecy of the clock, it was a subject for the dark.

Nevertheless, I will tell you at once, there was such a descendant he had missed in his bloody work. And she was a woman. Royal and proud she was, and seething with bitter spite and a hunger for vengeance, and as bloody as the duke, had he known it, in her own way.

For her safety and disguise, she had long ago wed a wealthy merchant in the city and presently bore the man a daughter. The merchant, a dealer in silks, was respected, a good fellow but not wise. He rejoiced in his handsome and aristocratic wife. He never dreamed what she might be about when he was not with her. In fact, she had sworn allegiance to Satanas.[1] In the dead of night she would go up into an old tower adjoining the merchant's house, and there she would say portions of the Black Mass, offer

---

1   Satanas: Satan.

sacrifice, and thereafter practice witchcraft against the duke. This witchery took a common form, the creation of a wax image and the maiming of the image that, by sympathy, the injuries inflicted on the wax be passed on to the living body of the victim. The woman was capable in what she did. The duke fell sick. He lost the use of his limbs and was racked by excruciating pains from which he could get no relief. Thinking himself on the brink of death, the duke named his sixteen-year-old son his heir. This son was dear to the duke, as everyone knew, and be sure the woman knew it too.

She intended sorcerously to murder the young man in his turn, preferably in his father's sight. Thus she let the duke linger in his agony and commenced planning the fate of the prince.

Now all this while she had not been toiling alone. She had one helper. It was her own daughter, a maid of fourteen, that she had recruited to her service nearly as soon as the infant could walk. At six or seven, the child had been lisping the satanic rite along with her mother. At fourteen, you may imagine, the girl was well versed in the black arts, though she did not have her mother's natural genius for them.

Perhaps you would like me to describe the daughter at this point. It has a bearing on the story, for the girl was astonishingly beautiful. Her hair was the rich dark red of antique burnished copper, her eyes were the hue of the reddish-golden amber that traders bring from the East. When she walked, you would say she was dancing. But when she danced, a gate seemed to open in the world, and bright fire spangled inside it, but she was the fire.

The girl and her mother were close as gloves in a box. Their games in the old tower bound them closer. No doubt the woman believed herself clever to have got such a helpmate, but it proved her undoing.

It was in this manner. The silk merchant, who had never suspected his wife for an instant of anything, began to mistrust the daughter. She was not like other girls. Despite her great beauty, she professed no interest in marriage and none in clothes or jewels. She preferred to read in the garden at the foot of the tower. Her mother had taught the girl her letters, though the merchant himself could read but poorly. And often the father peered at the books his daughter read, unable to make head nor tail of them, yet somehow not liking them. One night very late, the silk merchant came home from a guild dinner in the city, and he saw a slim pale shadow gliding up the steps of the old tower, and he knew it for his child. On impulse, he followed her, but quietly. He had not considered any evil so far and did not want to alarm her. At an angle of the stair, the lighted room above, he paused to spy and listen. He had something of a shock when he heard his wife's voice rise up in glad welcome. But what came next drained the blood from his heart. He crept away and went to his cellar for wine to stay himself. After the third glass he ran for neighbors and for the watch.

The woman and her daughter heard the shouts below and saw the torches in the garden. It was no use dissembling. The tower was littered with evidence of vile deeds, besides what the woman kept in a chest beneath her unknowing husband's bed. She understood it was all up with her, and she understood, too, how witchcraft was punished hereabouts. She snatched a knife from the altar.

The girl shrieked when she realized what her mother was at. The woman caught the girl by her red hair and shook her.

"Listen to me, my daughter," she cried, "and listen carefully, for the minutes are short. If you do as I tell you, you can escape their wrath and only I need die. And if you live I am satisfied, for you can carry on my labor after me. My vengeance I shall leave you, and my witchcraft to exact it by. Indeed, I promise you stronger powers than mine. I will beg my lord Satanas for it, and he will not deny me, for he is just, in his fashion, and I have served him well. Now will you attend?"

"I will," said the girl.

So the woman advised her and swore her to the fellowship of Hell. And then the woman forced the knife into her own heart and dropped dead on the floor of the tower.

When the men burst in with their swords and staves and their torches and their madness, the girl was ready for them.

She stood blank-faced, blank-eyed, with her arms hanging at her sides. When one touched her, she dropped down at his feet.

"Surely she is innocent," this man said. She was lovely enough that it was hard to accuse her. Then her father went to her and took her hand and lifted her. At that, the girl opened her eyes, and she said, as if terrified: "How did I come here? I was in my chamber and sleeping ..."

"The woman has bewitched her," her father said.

He desired very much that this be so. And when the girl clung to his hand and wept, he was certain of it. They showed her the body with the knife in it. The girl screamed and seemed to lose her senses totally.

She was put to bed. In the morning, a priest came and questioned her. She answered steadfastly. She remembered nothing, not even of the great books she had been observed reading. When they told her what was in them, she screamed again and apparently would have thrown herself from the narrow window, only the priest stopped her.

Finally, they brought her the holy cross in order that she might kiss it and prove herself blameless.

Then she knelt, and whispered softly, that nobody should hear but one: "Lord Satanas, protect thy handmaid." And either that gentleman has more power than he is credited with or else the symbols of God are only as holy as the men who deal in them, for she embraced the cross and it left her unscathed.

At that, the whole household thanked God. The whole household saving, of course, the woman's daughter. She had another to thank.

The woman's body was burned and the ashes put into unconsecrated ground beyond the city gates. Though they had discovered her to be a witch, they had not discovered the direction her witchcraft had selected. Nor did they find the wax image with its limbs all twisted and stuck through with needles. The girl had taken that up and concealed it. The duke continued in his distress, but he did not die. Sometimes, in the dead of night, the girl would unearth the image from under a loose brick by the hearth and gloat over it, but she did nothing else. Not yet. She was fourteen, and the cloud of her mother's acts still hovered over her. She knew what she must do next.

The period of mourning ended.

"Daughter," said the silk merchant to her, "why do you not remove your black? The woman was malign and led you into wickedness. How long will you mourn her, who deserves no mourning?"

"Oh, my father," she said, "never think I regret my wretched mother. It is my own unwitting sin I mourn," and she grasped his hand and spilled her tears on it. "I would rather live in a convent," said she, "than mingle with proper folk. And I would seek a convent too, if it were not that I cannot bear to be parted from you."

Do you suppose she smiled secretly as she said this? One might suppose it. Presently she donned a robe of sackcloth and poured ashes over her red-copper hair. "It is my penance," she said. "I am glad to atone for my sins."

People forgot her beauty. She was at pains to obscure it. She slunk about like an aged woman, a rag pulled over her head, dirt smeared on her cheeks and brow. She elected to sleep in a cold cramped attic and sat all day by a smoky hearth in the kitchens. When someone came to her and begged her to wash her face and put on suitable clothes and sit in the rooms of the house, she smiled modestly, drawing the rag of a piece of hair over her face. "I swear," she said, "I am glad to be humble before God and men."

They reckoned her pious and they reckoned her simple. Two years passed. They mislaid her beauty altogether and reckoned her ugly. They found it hard to call to mind who she was exactly, as she sat in the ashes or shuffled unattended about the streets like a crone.

At the end of the second year, the silk merchant married again. It was inevitable, for he was not a man who liked to live alone.

On this occasion, his choice was a harmless widow. She already had two daughters, pretty in an unremarkable style. Perhaps the merchant hoped they would comfort him for what had gone before, this normal cheery wife and the two sweet, rather silly daughters, whose chief interests were clothes and weddings. Perhaps he hoped also that his deranged daughter might be drawn out by company. But that hope floundered. Not that the new mother did not try to be pleasant to the girl. And the new sisters, their hearts grieved by her condition, went to great lengths to enlist her friendship. They begged her to come from the kitchens or the attic. Failing in that, they sometimes ventured to join her, their fine silk dresses trailing on the greasy floor. They combed her hair, exclaiming, when some of the ash and dirt were removed, on its color. But no sooner had they turned away than the girl gathered up handfuls of soot and ash and rubbed them into her hair again. Now and then, the sisters attempted to interest their bizarre relative in a bracelet or a gown or a current song. They spoke to her of the young men they had seen at the suppers or the balls which were then given regularly by the rich families of the city. The girl ignored it all. If she ever said anything, it was to do with penance and humility. At last, as must happen, the sisters wearied of her and left her alone. They had no cares and did not want to share in hers. They came to resent her moping grayness, as indeed the merchant's second wife had already done.

"Can you do nothing with that girl?" she demanded of her husband. "People will say that I and my daughters are responsible for her condition and that I ill-treat the maid from jealousy of her dead mother."

"Now how could anyone say that," protested the merchant, "when you are famous as the epitome of generosity and kindness?"

Another year passed, and saw no difference in the household.

A difference there was, but not visible.

The girl who slouched in the corner of the hearth was seventeen. Under the filth and grime she was, impossibly, more beautiful, although no one could see it.

And there was one other invisible item: her power (which all this time she had nurtured, saying her prayers to Satanas in the black of midnight), her power rising like a dark moon in her soul.

Three days after her seventeenth birthday, the girl straggled about the streets, as she frequently did. A few noted her and muttered it was the merchant's ugly simple daughter and paid no more attention. Most did not know her at all. She had made herself appear one with the scores of impoverished flotsam which constantly roamed the city, beggars and starvelings. Just outside the city gates, these persons congregated in large numbers, slumped around fires of burning refuse or else wandering to and fro in search of edible seeds, scraps, the miracle of a dropped coin. Here the girl now came and began to wander about as they did. Dusk gathered and the shadows thickened. The girl sank to her knees in a patch of earth as if she had found something. Two or three of the beggars sneaked over to see if it were worth snatching from her—but the girl was only scrabbling in the empty soil. The beggars, making signs to each other that she was touched by God—mad—left her alone. But very far from mad, the girl presently dug up a stoppered urn. In this urn were the ashes and charred bones of her mother. She had got a clue as to the location of the urn by devious questioning here and there. Her occult power had helped her to be sure of it.

In the twilight, padding along through the narrow streets and alleys of the city, the girl brought the urn homeward. In the garden, at the foot of the old tower, gloom-wrapped, unwitnessed, she unstoppered the urn and buried the ashes freshly. She muttered certain unholy magics over the grave. Then she snapped off the sprig of a young hazel tree and planted it in the newly turned ground.

I hazard you have begun to recognize the story by now. I see you suppose I tell it wrongly. Believe me, this is the truth of the matter. But if you would rather I left off the tale … no doubt your carriage will soon be here—No? Very well. I shall continue.

I think I should speak of the duke's son at this juncture. The prince was nineteen, able, intelligent, and of noble bearing. He was of that rather swarthy type of looks one finds here in the north, but tall and slim and clear-eyed. There is an ancient square where you may see a statue of him, but much eroded by two centuries and the elements. After the city was sacked, no care was lavished on it.

The duke treasured his son. He had constant delight in the sight of the young man and what he said and did. It was the only happiness the invalid had.

Then, one night, the duke screamed out in his bed. Servants came running with candles. The duke moaned that a sword was transfixing his heart, an inch at a time. The prince hurried into the chamber, but in that instant the duke spasmed horribly and died. No mark was on his body. There had never been a mark to show what ailed him.

The prince wept. They were genuine tears. He had nothing to reproach his father with, everything to thank him for. Presently, they brought the young man the seal ring of the city, and he put it on.

It was winter, a cold blue-white weather with snow in the streets and country-side and a hard wizened sun that drove thin sharp blades of light through the sky but gave no warmth. The duke's funeral cortege passed slowly across the snow: the broad open chariots, draped with black and silver; the black-plumed horses; the chanting priests with their glittering robes, their jeweled crucifixes and golden censers. Crowds lined the roadways to watch the spectacle. Among the beggar women stood a girl. No one noticed her. They did not glimpse the expression she veiled in her ragged scarf. She gazed at the bier pitilessly. As the young prince rode by in his sables, the seal ring on his hand, the eyes of the girl burned through her ashy hair, like a red fox through grasses.

The duke was buried in the mausoleum you can visit to this day, on the east side of the city. Several months elapsed. The prince put his grief from him and took up the business of the city competently. Wise and courteous he was, but he rarely smiled. At nineteen, his spirit seemed worn. You might think he guessed the destiny that hung over him.

The winter was a hard one too. The snow had come and, having come, was loath to withdraw. When at last the spring returned, flushing the hills with color, it was no longer sensible to be sad.

The prince's name day fell about this time. A great banquet was planned, a ball. There had been neither in the palace for nigh on three years, not since the duke's fatal illness first claimed him. Now the royal doors were to be thrown open to all men of influence and their families. The prince was liberal, charming, and clever even in this. Aristocrat and rich trader were to mingle in the beautiful dining room, and in this very chamber, among the frescoes, the marble, and the candelabra. Even a merchant's daughter, if the merchant was notable in the city, would get to dance on the sea-green floor, under the white eye of the fearful clock.

The clock. There was some renewed controversy about the clock. They did not dare speak to the young prince. He was a skeptic, as his father had been. But had not a death already occurred? Was the clock not a flying in the jaws of fate? For those disturbed by it, there was a dim writing in their minds, in the dust of the street or the pattern of blossoms. *When the clock strikes*—But people do not positively heed these warnings. Man is afraid of his fears. He ignores the shadow of the wolf thrown on the paving before him, saying: It is only a shadow.

The silk merchant received his invitation to the palace, and to be sure, thought nothing of the clock. His house had been thrown into uproar. The most luscious silks of his workshop were carried into the house and laid before the wife and her two daughters, who chirruped and squealed with excitement. "Oh, Father," cried the two sisters, "may I have this one with the gold piping?" "Oh, Father, this one with the design of pineapples?" Later a jeweler arrived and set out his trays. The merchant was generous. He wanted his women to look their best. It might be the night of their lives. Yet all the while, at the back of his mind, a little dark spot, itching, aching. He tried to ignore the spot, not scratch at it. His true daughter, the mad one. Nobody bothered to tell her about the invitation to the palace. They knew how she would react, mumbling in her hair about her sin and her penance, paddling her hands in the greasy ash to smear her face. Even the servants avoided her, as if she were just the cat seated by the fire. Less than the cat, for the cat saw to the mice— just a block of stone. And yet, how fair she might have looked, decked in the pick of the merchant's wares, jewels at her throat. The prince himself could not have been unaware of her. And though marriage was impossible, other, less holy though equally honorable contracts might have been arranged, to the benefit of all concerned. The merchant sighed. He had scratched the darkness after all. He attempted to comfort himself by watching the two sisters exult over their apparel. He refused to admit that the finery would somehow make them seem but more ordinary than they were by contrast.

The evening of the banquet arrived. The family set off. Most of the servants sidled after. The prince had distributed largess in the city; oxen roasted in the squares, and the wine was free by royal order.

The house grew somber. In the deserted kitchen, the fire went out.

By the hearth, a segment of gloom rose up.

The girl glanced around her, and she laughed softly and shook out her filthy hair. Of course, she knew as much as anyone, and more than most. This was to be her night too.

A few minutes later she was in the garden beneath the old tower, standing over the young hazel tree which had thrust up from the earth. It had become strong, the tree, despite the harsh winter. Now the girl nodded to it. She chanted under her breath. At length a pale light began to glow, far down near where the roots of the tree held to the ground. Out of the pale glow flew a thin black bird, which perched on the girl's shoulder. Together, the girl and the bird passed into the old tower. High up, a fire blazed that no one had lit. A tub steamed with scented water that no one had drawn. Shapes that were not real and barely seen flitted about. Rare perfumes, the rustle of garments, the glint of gems as yet invisible, filled and did not fill the restless air.

Need I describe further? No. You will have seen paintings which depict the attendance upon a witch of her familiar demons. How one bathes her, another anoints her, another brings clothes and ornaments. Perhaps you do not credit such things in any case. Never mind that. I will tell you what happened in the courtyard before the palace.

Many carriages and chariots had driven through the square, avoiding the roasting oxen, the barrels of wine, the cheering drunken citizens, and so through the gates into the courtyard. Just before ten o'clock (the hour, if you recall the clock, of the magician), a solitary carriage drove through the square and into the court. The people in the square gawped at the carriage and pressed forward to see who would step out of it, this latecomer. It was a remarkable vehicle that looked to be fashioned of solid gold, all but the domed roof, that was transparent flashing crystal. Six black horses drew it. The coachman and postilions were clad in crimson, and strangely masked as curious beasts and reptiles. One of these beast-men now hopped down and opened the door of the carriage. Out came a woman's figure in a cloak of white fur, and glided up the palace stair and in at the doors.

There was dancing in the ballroom. The whole chamber was bright and clamorous with music and the voices of men and women. There, between those two pillars, the prince sat in his chair, dark, courteous, seldom smiling. Here the musicians played, the deep-throated viol, the lively mandolin. And there the dancers moved up and down on the sea-green floor. But the music and the dancers had just paused. The figures on the clock were themselves in motion. The hour of the magician was about to strike.

As it struck, through the doorway came the figure in the fur cloak. And as if they must, every eye turned to her.

For an instant she stood there, all white, as though she had brought the winter snow back with her. And then she loosed the cloak from her shoulders, it slipped away, and she was all fire.

She wore a gown of apricot brocade embroidered thickly with gold. Her sleeves and the bodice of her gown were slashed over ivory satin sewn with large rosy pearls. Pearls, too, were wound in her hair, that was the shade of antique burnished copper. She was so beautiful that when the clock was still, nobody spoke. She was so beautiful that it was hard to look at her for very long.

The prince got up from his chair. He did not know he had. Now he started out across the floor, between the dancers, who parted silently to let him through. He went toward the girl in the doorway as if she drew him by a chain.

The prince had hardly ever acted without considering first what he did. Now he did not consider. He bowed to the girl.

"Madam," he said. "You are welcome, Madam," he said. "Tell me who you are."

She smiled.

"My rank," she said. "Would you know that, my lord? It is similar to yours, or would be were I now mistress in my dead mother's palace. But, unfortunately, an unscrupulous man caused the downfall of our house."

"Misfortune indeed," said the prince. "Tell me your name. Let me right the wrong done you."

"You shall," said the girl. "Trust me, you shall. For my name, I would rather keep it secret for the present. But you may call me, if you will, a pet name I have given myself—Ashella."

"Ashella ... But I see no ash about you," said the prince, dazzled by her gleam, laughing a little, stiffly, for laughter was not his habit.

"Ash and cinders from a cold and bitter hearth," said she. But she smiled again. "Now everyone is staring at us, my lord, and the musicians are impatient to begin again. Out of all these ladies, can it be you will lead me in the dance?"

"As long as you will dance," he said. "You shall dance with me."

And that is how it was.

There were many dances, slow and fast, whirling measures and gentle ones. And here and there, the prince and the maiden were parted. Always then he looked eagerly after her, sparing no regard for the other girls whose hands lay in his. It was not like him, he was usually so careful. But the other young men who danced on that floor, who clasped her fingers or her narrow waist in the dance, also gazed after her when she was gone. She danced, as she appeared, like fire. Though if you had asked those young men whether they would rather tie her to themselves, as the prince did, they would have been at a loss. For it is not easy to keep pace with fire.

The hour of the hag struck on the clock.

The prince grew weary of dancing with the girl and losing her in the dance to others and refinding her and losing her again.

Behind the curtains there is a tall window in the east wall that opens on the terrace above the garden. He drew her out there, into the spring night. He gave an order, and small tables were brought with delicacies and sweets and wine. He sat by her, watching every gesture she made, as if he would paint her portrait afterward.

In the ballroom, here, under the clock, the people murmured. But it was not quite the murmur you would expect, the scandalous murmur about a woman come from nowhere that the prince had made so much of. At the periphery of the ballroom, the silk merchant sat, pale as a ghost, thinking of a ghost, the living ghost of his true daughter. No one else recognized her. Only he. Some trick of his heart had enabled him to know her. He said nothing of it. As the stepsisters and wife gossiped with other wives and sisters, an awful foreboding weighed him down, sent him cold and dumb.

And now it is almost midnight, the moment when the page of the night turns over into day. Almost midnight, the hour when the figure of Death strikes the golden bell of the clock. And what will happen when the clock strikes? Your face announces that you know. Be patient; let us see if you do.

"I am being foolish," said the prince to Ashella on the terrace. "But perhaps I am entitled to be foolish, just once in my life. What are you saying?" For the girl was speaking low beside him, and he could not catch her words.

"I am saying a spell to bind you to me," she said.

"But I am already bound."

"Be bound, then. Never go free."

"I do not wish it," he said. He kissed her hands, and he said, "I do not know you, but I will wed you. Is that proof your spell has worked? I will wed you, and get back for you the rights you have lost."

"If it were only so simple," said Ashella, smiling, smiling. "But the debt is too cruel. Justice requires a harsher payment."

And then, in the ballroom, Death struck the first note on the golden bell.

The girl smiled and she said:

"I curse you in my mother's name."

The second stroke.

"I curse you in my own name."

The third stroke.

"And in the name of those that your father slew."

The fourth stroke.

"And in the name of my Master, who rules the world."

As the fifth, the sixth, the seventh strokes pealed out, the prince stood non-plussed. At the eighth and ninth strokes, the strength of the malediction seemed to curdle his blood. He shivered and his brain writhed. At the tenth stroke, he saw a change in the loveliness before him. She grew thinner, taller. At the eleventh stroke, he beheld a thing in a ragged black cowl and robe. It grinned at him. It was all grin below a triangle of sockets of nose and eyes. At the twelfth stroke, the prince saw Death and knew him.

In the ballroom, a hideous grinding noise, as the gears of the clock failed. Followed by a hollow booming, as the mechanism stopped entirely.

The conjuration of Death vanished from the terrace.

Only one thing was left behind. A woman's shoe. A shoe no woman could ever have danced in. It was made of glass.

Did you intend to protest about the shoe? Shall I finish the story, or would you rather I did not? It is not the ending you are familiar with. Yes, I perceive you understand that now.

I will go quickly, then, for your carriage must soon be here. And there is not a great deal more to relate.

The prince lost his mind. Partly from what he had seen, partly from the spells the young witch had netted him in. He could think of nothing but the girl who had named herself Ashella. He raved that Death had borne her away but he would recover her from Death. She had left the glass shoe as token of her love. He must discover her with the aid of the shoe. Whomsoever the shoe fitted would be Ashella. For there was this added complication, that Death might hide her actual appearance. None had seen the girl before. She had disappeared like smoke. The one infallible test was the shoe. That was why she had left it for him.

His ministers would have reasoned with the prince, but he was past reason. His intellect had collapsed totally as only a profound intellect can. A lunatic, he rode about the city. He struck out at those who argued with him. On a particular occasion, drawing a dagger, he killed, not apparently noticing what he did. His demand was explicit. Every woman, young or old, maid or married, must come forth from her home, must put her foot into the shoe of glass. They came. They had no choice. Some approached in terror, some weeping. Even the aged beggar women obliged, and they cackled, enjoying the sight of royalty gone mad. One alone did not come.

Now it is not illogical that out of the hundreds of women whose feet were put into the shoe, a single woman might have been found that the shoe fitted. But this did not happen. Nor did the situation alter, despite a lurid fable that some, tickled by the idea of wedding the prince, cut off their toes that the shoe might fit them. And if they did, it was to no avail, for still the shoe did not.

Is it really surprising? The shoe was sorcerous. It constantly changed itself, its shape, its size, in order that no foot, save one, could ever be got into it.

Summer spread across the land. The city took on its golden summer glaze, its fetid summer spell.

What had been a whisper of intrigue swelled into a steady distant thunder. Plots were hatched.

One day the silk merchant was brought, trembling and gray of face, to the prince. The merchant's dumbness had broken. He had unburdened himself of his fear at confession, but the priest had not proved honest. In the dawn, men had knocked on the door of the merchant's house. Now he stumbled to the chair of the prince.

Both looked twice their years, but if anything, the prince looked the elder. He did not lift his eyes. Over and over in his hands he turned the glass shoe.

The merchant, stumbling, too, in his speech, told the tale of his first wife and his daughter. He told everything, leaving out no detail. He did not even omit the end: that since the night of the banquet the girl had been absent from his house, taking nothing with her—save a young hazel from the garden beneath the tower.

The prince leapt from his chair.

His clothes were filthy and unkempt. His face was smeared with sweat and dust ... it resembled, momentarily, another face.

Without guard or attendant, the prince ran through the city toward the merchant's house, and on the road, the intriguers waylaid and slew him. As he fell, the glass shoe dropped from his hands and shattered in a thousand fragments.

There is little else worth mentioning.

Those who usurped the city were villains and not merely that but fools. Within a year, external enemies were at the gates. A year more, and the city had been sacked, half burned out, ruined. The manner in which you find it now is somewhat better than it was then. And it is not now anything for a man to be proud of. As you were quick to note, many here earn a miserable existence by conducting visitors about the streets, the palace, showing them the dregs of the city's past.

Which was not a request, in fact, for you to give me money. Throw some from your carriage window if your conscience bothers you. My own wants are few.

No, I have no further news of the girl Ashella, the witch. A devotee of Satanas, she has doubtless worked plentiful woe in the world. And a witch is long-lived. Even so, she will die eventually. None escapes Death. Then you may pity her, if you like. Those who serve the gentleman below—who can guess what their final lot will be?

But I am very sorry the story did not please you. It is not, maybe, a happy choice before a journey.

And there is your carriage at last.

What? Ah, no, I shall stay here in the ballroom, where you came on me. I have often paused here through the years. It is the clock. It has a certain—what shall I call it?—power to draw me back.

I am not trying to unnerve you. Why should you suppose that? Because of my knowledge of the city, of the story? You think that I am implying that I myself am Death? Now you laugh. Yes, it is absurd. Observe the twelfth figure on the clock. Is he not as you always heard Death described? And am I in the least like that twelfth figure?

Although, of course, the story was not as you have heard it, either.

THE WICKED STEPMOTHER'S LAMENT[1]

Sara Maitland

THE WIFE OF A RICH man fell sick and, as she felt that her end was drawing near, she called her only daughter to her bedside and said, "Dear child, be good and pious, and then the good God will always protect you, and I will look down from heaven and be near you." Thereupon she closed her eyes and departed. Every day the maiden went out to her mother's grave and wept, and she remained pious and good. When winter came the snow spread a white sheet over the grave and by the time the spring sun had drawn it off again the man had taken another wife …

Now began a bad time for the poor step-child … They took her pretty clothes away, put an old grey bedgown on her and gave her wooden shoes … She had to do hard work from morning to night, get up before daybreak, carry water, light fires, cook and wash … In the evening when she had worked until she was weary she had no bed to go to but had to sleep by the hearth in the cinders. And as on that account she always looked dusty and dirty, they called her Cinderella.

You know the rest I expect. Almost everyone does.

I'm not exactly looking for self-justification. There's this thing going on at the moment where women tell all the old stories again and turn them inside-out and

---

1   From *A Book of Spells* (London: Michael Joseph, 1987).

back-to-front—so the characters you always thought were the goodies turn out to be the baddies, and vice versa, and a whole lot of guilt is laid to rest: or that at least is the theory. I'm not sure myself that the guilt isn't just passed on to the next person, *intacta*, so to speak. Certainly I want to carry and cope with my own guilt, because I want to carry and cope with my own virtue and I really don't see that you can have one without the other. Anyway, it would be hard to find a version of this story where I would come out a shiny new-style heroine: no true version, anyway. All I want to say is that it's more complicated, more complex, than it's told, and the reasons why it's told the way it is are complex too.

But I'm not willing to be a victim. I was not innocent, and I have grown out of innocence now and even out of wanting to be thought innocent. Living is a harsh business, as no one warned us when we were young and carefree under the apple bough, and I feel the weight of that ancient harshness and I want to embrace it, and not opt for some washed-out aseptic, hand-wringing, Disneyland garbage. (Though come to think of it he went none-too-easy on step-mothers, did he? Snow White's scared the socks off me the first time I saw the film—and partly of course because I recognised myself. But I digress.)

Look. It was like this. Or rather it was more like this, or parts of it were like this, or this is one part of it.

She was dead pretty in a Pears soap sort of way, and, honestly, terribly sweet and good. At first all I wanted her to do was concentrate. Concentration is the key to power. You have to concentrate on what is real. Concentration is not good or bad necessarily, but it is powerful. Enough power to change the world, that's all I wanted. (I was younger then, of course; but actually they're starving and killing whales and forests and each other out there; shutting your eyes and pretending they're not doesn't change anything. It does matter.) And what she was not was powerful. She wouldn't look out for herself. She was so sweet and so hopeful; so full of faith and forgiveness and love. You have to touch anger somewhere, rage even; you have to spit and roar and bite and scream and know it before you can be safe. And she never bloody would.

When I first married her father I thought she was so lovely, so good and so sad. And so like her mother. I knew her mother very well, you see; we grew up together. I loved her mother. Really. With so much hope and fondness and awareness of her worth. But—and I don't know how to explain this without sounding like an embittered old bitch which I probably am—she was too good. Too giving. She gave herself away, indiscriminately. She didn't even give herself as a precious gift. She gave herself away as though she wasn't worth hanging on to. Generous to a fault, they said, when she was young, but no one acted as though it were a fault, so she never learned. "Free with Kellogg's cornflakes" was her motto. She equated loving with suffering, I thought at one time, but that wasn't right, it was worse, she equated loving with being; as though she did not exist unless she was denying her existence. I mean, he was not a bad bloke, her husband, indeed I'm married to him myself, and I like him and we have good times together, but he wasn't worth it—no one is—not what she gave him, which was her whole self with no price tag on.

And it was just the same with that child. Yes, yes, one can understand: she had difficulty getting pregnant actually, she had difficulties carrying those babies to term too. Even I can guess how that might hurt. But her little girl was her great reward for suffering, and at the same time was also her handle on a whole new world of self-giving. And yes, of course she looked so lovely, who could have resisted her, propped up in her bed with that tiny lovely child sucking, sucking, sucking? The mother who denied her little one nothing, the good mother, the one we all longed for, pouring herself out into the child. Well, I'll tell you, I've done it too, it is hell caring for a tiny daughter, I know. Everything, everything drags you into hell: the fact that you love and desire her, the fact that she's so needy and vulnerable, the fact that she never leaves you alone until your dreams are smashed in little piles and shabby with neglect, the fact that pleasure and guilt come so precisely together, as so seldom happens, working towards the same end and sucking your very selfhood out of you. It is a perilous time for a woman, that nursing of a daughter, and you can only survive it if you cling to yourself with a fierce and passionate love, *and* you back that up with a trained and militant lust for justice *and* you scream at the people around you to meet your needs and desires *and* you do not let them off, *and* when all is said and done you sit back and laugh at yourself with a well-timed and not unmalicious irony. Well, she could not, of course she could not, so she did not survive. She was never angry, she never asked, she took resignation—that tragic so-called virtue—as a ninth-rate alternative to reality and never even realised she had been short-changed.

So when I first married my husband I only meant to tease her a little, to rile her, to make her fight back. I couldn't bear it, that she was so like her mother and would go the same way. My girls were more like me, less agreeable to have about the house, but tough as old boots and capable of getting what they needed and not worrying too much about what they wanted or oughted, so to speak. I didn't have to worry about them. I just could not believe the sweetness of that little girl and her wide-eyed belief that I would be happy and love her if she would just deny herself and follow me. So of course I exploited her a bit, pushed and tested it, if you understand, because I couldn't believe it. Then I just wanted her to *see*, to see that life is not all sweetness and light, that people are not automatically to be trusted, that fairy godmothers are unreliable and damned thin on the ground, and that even the most silvery of princes soon goes out hunting and fighting and drinking and whoring, and doesn't give one tuppenny-ha'penny curse more for you than you give for yourself. Well, she could have looked at her father and known. He hardly proved himself to be the great romantic lover of all time, even at an age when that would have been appropriate, never mind later. He had after all replaced darling Mummy with me, and pretty damned quick too, and so long as he was getting his end off and his supper on the table he wasn't going to exert himself on her behalf, as I pointed out to her, by no means kindly.

(And, I should like to add, I still don't understand about that. I couldn't believe how little the bastard finally cared when it came to the point. Perhaps he was bored to tears by goodness, perhaps he was too lazy. He was a sentimental old fart about her, of course, his eyes could fill with nostalgic tears every time he looked at her and thought of her dead mother; but he never *did* anything; or even asked me to stop doing anything. She never asked, and he never had eyes to see, or energy or … God knows what went on in his head about her and as far as I'm concerned God's welcome. She loved him and trusted him and served him and he never even bloody noticed. Which sort of makes my point actually because he would never treat me like that, and yet he and I get on very well now; like each other and have good times in bed and out of it. Of course I'd never have let him tell me how to behave, but he might have tried, at least just once.)

Anyway, no, she would not see. She would not blame her father. She would not blame her mother, not even for dying, which is the ultimate outrage from someone you love. And she would not blame me. She just smiled and accepted, smiled and invented castles in the air to which someone, though never herself, would come and take her one day, smiled and loved me. No matter what I did to her, she just smiled.

So, yes, in the end I was cruel. I don't know how to explain it and I do not attempt to justify it. Her *wetness* infuriated me. I could not shake her good will, her hopefulness, her capacity to love and love and love such a pointless and even dangerous object. I could not make her hate me. Not even for a moment. I could not make her hate me. And I cannot explain what that frustration did to me. I hated her insane dog-like devotion where it was so undeserved. She treated me as her mother had treated him. I think I hated her stupidity most of all. I can hear myself almost blaming her for my belly-deep madness; I don't want to do that; I don't want to get into blaming the victim and she was my victim. I was older than her, and stronger than her, and had more power than her; and there was no excuse. No excuse, I thought the first time I ever hit her, but there was an excuse and it was my wild need, and it escalated.

So in the end—and yes I have examined all the motives and reasons why one woman should be cruel to another and I do not find them explanatory—so in the end I was cruel to her. I goaded and humiliated and pushed and bullied her. I used all my powers, my superior strength, my superior age, my superior intelligence, against her. I beat her, in the end, systematically and severely; but more than that I used her and worked her and denied her pleasures and gave her pain. I violated her space, her dignity, her integrity, her privacy, even her humanity and perhaps her physical safety. There was an insane urge in me, not simply to hurt her, but to have her admit that I had hurt her. I would lie awake at night appalled, and scald myself with contempt, with anger and with self-disgust, but I had only to see her in the morning for my temper to rise and I would start again, start again at her with an unreasonable savagery that seemed to upset me more than it upset her. Picking, picking and pecking, endlessly. She tried my patience as no one else had ever done and finally I gave up the struggle and threw it away and entered into the horrible game with all my considerable capacity for concentration.

And nothing worked. I could not make her angry. I could not make her hate me. I could not stop her loving me with a depth and a generosity and a forgivingness that were the final blow. Nothing moved her to more than a simper. Nothing penetrated the fantasies and day-dreams with which her head was stuffed so full I'm surprised she didn't slur her consonants. She was locked into perpetual passivity and gratitude and love. Even when she was beaten she covered her bruises to protect me; even when she was hungry she would not take food from my cupboards to feed herself; even when I mocked her she smiled at me tenderly.

All I wanted was for her to grow up, to grow up and realise that life was not a bed of roses and that she had to take some responsibility for her own life, to take some action on her own behalf, instead of waiting and waiting and waiting for something or someone to come shining out of the dark and force safety on her as I forced pain. What Someone? Another like her father who had done nothing, nothing whatever, to help her and never would? Another like him whom she could love generously and hopelessly and serve touchingly and givingly until weariness and pain killed her too. I couldn't understand it. Even when I beat her, even as I beat her, she loved me, she just loved and smiled and hoped and waited, day-dreamed and night-dreamed, and waited and waited and waited. She was untouchable and infantile. I couldn't save her and I couldn't damage her. God knows, I tried.

And now of course it's just an ancient habit. It has lost its sharp edges, lost the passion in both of us to see it out in conflict, between dream and reality, between hope and cynicism. There is a great weariness in me, and I cannot summon up the fire of conviction. I do not concentrate any more, I do not have enough concentration, enough energy, enough power. Perhaps she has won, because she drained that out of me years and years ago. Sometimes I despair, which wastes still more concentration. We plod on together, because we always have. Sweetly she keeps at it, smile, smile, dream, hope, wait, love, forgive, smile, smile, bloody smile. Tiredly, I keep at it too:

"Sweep that grate." "Tidy your room." "Do your homework." "What can you see in that nerd?" "Take out those damn ear-phones and pay attention." "Life doesn't come free, you have to work on it." "Wake up, hurry up, stop day-dreaming, no you can't, yes you must, get a move on, don't be so stupid," and "You're not going to the ball, or party, or disco, or over your Nan's, dressed like *that*."

She calls it nagging.
She calls me Mummy.

CINDERELLA[1]

Anne Sexton

YOU ALWAYS READ ABOUT IT:
the plumber with twelve children
who wins the Irish Sweepstakes.
From toilets to riches.
That story.

Or the nursemaid,
some luscious sweet from Denmark
who captures the oldest son's heart.
From diapers to Dior.
That story.

Or a milkman who serves the wealthy,
eggs, cream, butter, yogurt, milk,
the white truck like an ambulance
who goes into real estate
and makes a pile.
From homogenized to martinis at lunch.

Or the charwoman
who is on the bus when it cracks up
and collects enough from the insurance.
From mops to Bonwit Teller.

---

1   From *Transformations* (Boston, MA: Houghton Mifflin, 1971).

That story.

Once
the wife of a rich man was on her deathbed
and she said to her daughter Cinderella:
Be devout. Be good. Then I will smile
down from heaven in the seam of a cloud.
The man took another wife who had
two daughters, pretty enough
but with hearts like blackjacks.
Cinderella was their maid.
She slept on the sooty hearth each night
and walked around looking like Al Jolson.[1]
Her father brought presents home from town,
jewels and gowns for the other women
but the twig of a tree for Cinderella.
She planted that twig on her mother's grave
and it grew to a tree where a white dove sat.
Whenever she wished for anything the dove
would drop it like an egg upon the ground.
The bird is important, my dears, so heed him.

Next came the ball, as you all know.
It was a marriage market.
The prince was looking for a wife.
All but Cinderella were preparing
and gussying up for the big event.
Cinderella begged to go too.
Her stepmother threw a dish of lentils
into the cinders and said: Pick them
up in an hour and you shall go.
The white dove brought all his friends;
all the warm wings of the fatherland came,
and picked up the lentils in a jiffy.
No, Cinderella, said the stepmother,
you have no clothes and cannot dance.
That's the way with stepmothers.

---

1   Al Jolson (1886-1950): American entertainer who often performed in black-face.

Cinderella went to the tree at the grave
and cried forth like a gospel singer:
Mama! Mama! My turtledove,
send me to the prince's ball!
The bird dropped down a golden dress
and delicate little gold slippers.
Rather a large package for a simple bird.
So she went. Which is no surprise.
Her stepmother and sisters didn't
recognize her without her cinder face
and the prince took her hand on the spot
and danced with no other the whole day.

As nightfall came she thought she'd better
get home. The prince walked her home
and she disappeared into the pigeon house
and although the prince took an axe and broke
it open she was gone. Back to her cinders.
These events repeated themselves for three days.
However on the third day the prince
covered the palace steps with cobbler's wax
and Cinderella's gold shoe stuck upon it.
Now he would find whom the shoe fit
and find his strange dancing girl for keeps.
He went to their house and the two sisters
were delighted because they had lovely feet.
The eldest went into a room to try the slipper on
but her big toe got in the way so she simply
sliced it off and put on the slipper.
The prince rode away with her until the white dove
told him to look at the blood pouring forth.
That is the way with amputations.
They don't just heal up like a wish.
The other sister cut off her heel
but the blood told as blood will.
The prince was getting tired.
He began to feel like a shoe salesman.
But he gave it one last try.

This time Cinderella fit into the shoe
like a love letter into its envelope.

At the wedding ceremony
the two sisters came to curry favor
and the white dove pecked their eyes out.
Two hollow spots were left
like soup spoons.

Cinderella and the prince
lived, they say, happily ever after,
like two dolls in a museum case
never bothered by diapers or dust,
never arguing over the timing of an egg,
never telling the same story twice,
never getting a middle-aged spread,
their darling smiles pasted on for eternity.
Regular Bobbsey Twins.
That story.

GROWING UP (IS HARD TO DO)

As we have seen, the fairy tale did not begin life as the exclusive property of children, for the simple reason that it was originally told by and for adults—which explains what many would now consider its occasionally unsuitable subject matter. We must remember that the concept of childhood has only emerged over the last three to four hundred years; in earlier times, childhood was simply not perceived as being a distinct entity. The explanation for this is partly economic and partly psychological in nature. Among the peasantry, children represented a natural resource, but of a kind that required years of nurturing before any return could be expected, years during which the child was actually a drain on scarce resources, with no guarantee that he or she would live long enough to repay such an investment. The child was obliged to grow up quickly and fend for him or herself, so in a world where mere survival was so constant a challenge, it is reasonable to speculate that the emotional attachment between parent and child was sometimes less intense than in our own world of relative affluence and leisure. Their social and psychological insignificance make it all the more surprising that children are as well-represented in the fairy tale as they are. However, the point must be made that although many of the tales we have read so far *begin* with childhood, their major emphasis is upon the transition to adulthood. The tales in this section are distinguished by the fact that their focus is specifically upon childhood with little or no reference to later life.

There is a deep-seated ambivalence toward children reflected in fairy tales. These tales are about children not so much because they are perceived as interesting or entertaining characters (as is generally the assumption today) but rather as representatives of the upcoming generation, prospective claimants of adult privilege and status. On the one hand, there are tales in which love and protectiveness toward offspring are expressed—more often, it may be added, in tales about the rich than about the poor—although the overprotectiveness found in such tales as "Little Red

Riding Hood," "Sleeping Beauty," and now "Rapunzel" can be seen as leading to un-happy consequences. On the other hand, there is fear and resentment of the child as a potential rival, memorably depicted in "Snow White."

But why is it that so many of these tales focus upon the girl? The answer, at least in part, is that it has long been more of a challenge to grow up female than to grow up male. The inequality of the sexes runs as a central thread through tale after tale, although there is sometimes an intriguing contrast between the conventional role and the actual behavior of some heroines. One distinction is worthy of note: while the princesses we have encountered thus far all manifest differing degrees of passiv-ity, the peasant girls, such as Gretel, Molly Whuppie, or the unnamed girl in "The Story of Grandmother," seem to be much more willing and able to seize the initia-tive. Is this another indication of how important class is in determining patterns of behavior? Yet given the centuries of social prejudice through which these stories have been filtered, these patterns should not surprise us too much. We were well into the second half of the twentieth century, in fact, before serious efforts were made (in the form of the feminist fairy tale) to challenge the assumptions that are firmly entrenched in many traditional tales. Quite apart from the innate originality and inventiveness of the narratives themselves, the popular success of such tales as "Sleeping Beauty," "Cinderella," and "Snow White" have been equally attribut-able to the preconceptions and values of nineteenth-century readers and fairy-tale collectors.

Curiously enough, the few male children who have gained an equivalent renown are either disadvantaged by their small size (like Tom Thumb) or else delinquent ne'er-do-wells such as Jack (of beanstalk fame) or even Aladdin from *The Arabian Nights*. The point here, of course, is that out of such unpromising beginnings comes a winner, through the exercise of such "masculine" qualities as courage, audacity, determination, and a measure of ruthlessness.

The presence and power of the mother is very much an issue in four of the five tales in this section; in both "Hansel and Gretel" and "Snow White," the Grimms chose in later editions to turn mother into stepmother, no doubt because they did not wish to confront their child-readers with such unnatural maternal behavior. (Al-though the witch in "Rapunzel" has no family connection with the girl, she never-theless represents another example of the "bad mother.") By contrast, the father is either entirely absent or a subservient figure.

Several of these tales begin with a depiction of physical hardship—and that is surely based in historical fact. Poverty and famine are experiences that few of us have suffered at first hand, and so we have little conception of the profound effects they have on those afflicted. So while we may brand the mother of Hansel and Gretel as cold-hearted and cruel, we cannot deny that she is responding to a harsh reality in a pragmatic fashion. Is it possible that the roots of these tales reach back to a time when children were, in such extreme circumstances, seen as expendable? In "Jack and the Beanstalk," the situation is reversed, with the widowed mother at the mercy of her immature, good-for-nothing son; while there is certainly no evil intent here, the prospect is nevertheless the same—imminent starvation.

The similarity of structure continues into the second phase of the tales, wherein the realistic gives way to the fantastic, and the child-characters must learn to fend for themselves or perish in the attempt. That they succeed in overcoming the adult characters who oppose them should be seen as a practical acknowledgement of the way the world works, rather than as a glorification of intrepid youth. Any notion of the child as natural adventurer and hero was simply incompatible with the attitudes toward childhood that prevailed in earlier times.

Not surprisingly, Freudian critics such as Bruno Bettelheim have much to say about these visceral conflicts between child and adult which, by virtue of being played out in the realm of the imaginary, sublimate anxiety-creating aggression and rivalry into a form that the listener/reader can accept and resolve. Hansel and Gretel return home (escaping the fantasy world via an obviously symbolic body of water) to discover that their mother has died in their absence. The link between mother and witch seems obvious, and although the children choose to return home, one senses that they are now more likely to look after their father, rather than the reverse. Thanks in part to the intervention of the dwarves, Snow White survives repeated attempts on her life by her rival (step)mother and, after a Sleeping Beauty-style period of growth, emerges as a woman from her coffin-cocoon. It is Rapunzel who arguably suffers the most in the transition from childhood to adulthood, perhaps because her experience is explicitly sexual.

For his part, Jack comes back to earth the same way he left, but as a dramatically different person: the Jack who kills the giant and bestows wealth and security upon his mother is no longer an aimless, impulsive boy. We must, however, confront the moral question that arises from Jack's thefts from the giant, the last of which seems particularly gratuitous, in that his wealth is assured by his possession of the hen that lays the golden eggs. Some versions of this tale present it as a matter of revenge: Jack's father is absent from the story because he has been killed by the giant, and so Jack is simply reclaiming his own. In the case of *this* version, the explanation must be that we judge motive according to the folk tale's simple—even primitive—moral code: the giant is by nature wicked (as his earlier behavior has amply revealed) and, therefore, his possessions must be ill-gotten. If Jack has the youthful audacity to make the attempt, then to the victor go the spoils. The new generation has passed the test and takes its rightful place, until it in turn finds itself cast in the role of giant or witch, and the struggle begins anew.

The final tale in this section stands apart from the others but is unquestionably about growing up to the extent that its title has entered the language as a description of childhood experience. "The Ugly Duckling," a paradigm of autobiographical fantasy, is arguably Hans Christian Andersen's most famous tale, recounting his struggle to extract himself from the poverty-stricken obscurity of his early years and to make his mark in the artistic world. It is as personal a statement as the others are generalized, reflecting an important difference between the anonymous folk tale and the literary tale. Part of Andersen's genius was in his ability to express everyone's experience in his own: all those feelings of inadequacy, rejection, and loneliness that we suffered (or *imagine* that we suffered) are captured in that single unforgettable image of the duckling.

HANSEL AND GRETEL[1]

Jacob and Wilhelm Grimm

At the edge of a large forest there lived a poor woodcutter with his wife and two children. The little boy's name was Hansel, and the little girl's was Gretel. There was never much to eat in the house, and once, in time of famine, there wasn't even enough bread to go around. One night the woodcutter lay in bed thinking, tossing and turning with worry. All at once he sighed and said to his wife: "What's to become of us? How can we feed our poor children when we haven't even got enough for ourselves?" His wife answered: "Husband, listen to me. Tomorrow at daybreak we'll take the children out to the thickest part of the forest and make a fire for them and give them each a piece of bread. Then we'll leave them and go about our work. They'll never find the way home again and that way we'll be rid of them." "No, Wife," said the man. "I won't do it. How can I bring myself to leave my children alone in the woods? The wild beasts will come and tear them to pieces." "You fool!" she said. "Then all four of us will starve. You may as well start planing the boards for our coffins." And she gave him no peace until he consented. "But I still feel badly about the poor children," he said.

The children were too hungry to sleep, and they heard what their stepmother said to their father. Gretel wept bitter tears and said: "Oh, Hansel, we're lost." "Hush,

---

1 First published in 1812/15, in the first edition of *Kinder- und Hausmärchen*. This text from the second edition (1819), from *Grimms' Tales for Young and Old*, trans. Ralph Manheim (Garden City, NY: Anchor Press, 1977).

Gretel," said Hansel. "Don't worry. I'll find a way." When the old people had fallen asleep, he got up, put on his little jacket, opened the bottom half of the Dutch door, and crept outside. The moon was shining bright, and the pebbles around the house glittered like silver coins. Hansel crouched down and stuffed his pocket full of them. Then he went back and said to Gretel: "Don't worry, little sister. Just go to sleep, God won't forsake us," and went back to bed.

At daybreak, before the sun had risen, the woman came and woke the two children. "Get up, you lazybones. We're going to the forest for wood." Then she gave each a piece of bread and said: "This is for your noonday meal. Don't eat it too soon, because there won't be any more." Gretel put the bread under her apron, because Hansel had pebbles in his pocket. Then they all started out for the forest together. When they had gone a little way, Hansel stopped still and looked back in the direction of their house, and every so often he did it again. His father said: "Hansel, why do you keep looking back and lagging behind? Wake up and don't forget what your legs are for." "Oh, father," said Hansel, "I'm looking for my white kitten; he's sitting on the roof, trying to bid me good-bye." The woman said: "You fool, that's not your white kitten. It's the morning sun shining on the chimney." But Hansel hadn't been looking at his kitten. Each time, he had taken a shiny pebble from his pocket and dropped it on the ground.

When they came to the middle of the forest, the father said: "Start gathering wood, children, and I'll make a fire to keep you warm." Hansel and Gretel gathered brushwood till they had a little pile of it. The brushwood was kindled and when the flames were high enough the woman said: "Now, children, lie down by the fire and rest. We're going into the forest to cut wood. When we're done, we'll come back and get you."

Hansel and Gretel sat by the fire, and at midday they both ate their pieces of bread. They heard the strokes of an ax and thought their father was nearby. But it wasn't an ax, it was a branch he had tied to a withered tree, and the wind was shaking it to and fro. After sitting there for some time, they became so tired that their eyes closed and they fell into a deep sleep. When at last they awoke, it was dark night. Gretel began to cry and said: "How will we ever get out of this forest?" But Hansel comforted her: "Just wait a little while. As soon as the moon rises, we'll find the way." And when the full moon had risen, Hansel took his little sister by the hand and followed the pebbles which glistened like newly minted silver pieces and showed them the way. They walked all night and reached their father's house just as day was breaking. They knocked at the door, and when the woman opened it and saw Hansel and Gretel, she said: "Wicked children! Why did you sleep so long in the forest? We thought you'd never get home." But their father was glad, for he had been very unhappy about deserting them.

A while later the whole country was again stricken with famine, and the children heard their mother[1] talking to their father in bed at night: "Everything has been eaten up. We still have half a loaf of bread, and when that's gone there will be no more. The children must go. We'll take them still deeper into the forest, and this time they won't find their way home; it's our only hope." The husband was heavy-hearted, and he thought: "It would be better if I shared the last bite with my children." But the woman wouldn't listen to anything he said; she only scolded and found fault. Once you've said yes, it's hard to say no, and so it was that the woodcutter gave in again.

But the children were awake; they had heard the conversation. When the old people had fallen asleep, Hansel got up again. He wanted to pick up some more pebbles, but the woman had locked the door and he couldn't get out. But he comforted his little sister and said: "Don't cry, Gretel. Just go to sleep, God will help us."

Early in the morning the woman came and got the children out of bed. She gave them their pieces of bread, but they were smaller than the last time. On the way to the forest, Hansel crumbled his bread in his pocket. From time to time he stopped and dropped a few crumbs on the ground. "Hansel," said his father, "why are you always stopping and looking back? Keep moving." "I'm looking at my little pigeon," said Hansel. "He's sitting on the roof, trying to bid me good-bye." "Fool," said the woman. "That's not your little pigeon, it's the morning sun shining on the chimney." But little by little Hansel strewed all his bread on the ground.

The woman led the children still deeper into the forest, to a place where they had never been in all their lives. Again a big fire was made, and the mother said: "Just sit here, children. If you get tired, you can sleep awhile. We're going into the forest to cut wood, and this evening when we've finished we'll come and get you." At midday Gretel shared her bread with Hansel, who had strewn his on the ground. Then they fell asleep and the afternoon passed, but no one came for the poor children. It was dark night when they woke up, and Hansel comforted his little sister. "Gretel," he said, "just wait till the moon rises; then we'll see the breadcrumbs I strewed and they'll show us the way home." When the moon rose, they started out, but they didn't find any breadcrumbs, because the thousands of birds that fly around in the forests and fields had eaten them all up. Hansel said to Gretel: "Don't worry, we'll find the way," but they didn't find it. They walked all night and then all day from morning to night, but they were still in the forest, and they were very hungry, for they had nothing to eat but the few berries they could pick from the bushes. And when they were so tired their legs could carry them no farther, they lay down under a tree and fell asleep.

---

1   mother: The Grimms were concerned that mothers in folk tale were often depicted as villains, so they made the editorial decision to transform them into stepmothers.

It was already the third morning since they had left their father's house. They started out again, but they were getting deeper and deeper into the forest, and unless help came soon, they were sure to die of hunger and weariness. At midday, they saw a lovely snowbird sitting on a branch. It sang so beautifully that they stood still and listened. When it had done singing, it flapped its wings and flew on ahead, and they followed until the bird came to a little house and perched on the roof. When they came closer, they saw that the house was made of bread, and the roof was made of cake and the windows of sparkling sugar. "Let's eat," said Hansel, "and the Lord bless our food. I'll take a piece of the roof. You, Gretel, had better take some of the window; it's sweet." Hansel reached up and broke off a bit of the roof to see how it tasted, and Gretel pressed against the windowpanes and nibbled at them. And then a soft voice called from inside:

"Nibble nibble, little mouse,
Who's that nibbling at my house?"

The children answered:

"The wind so wild,
The heavenly child,"

and went right on eating. Hansel liked the taste of the roof, so he tore off a big chunk, and Gretel broke out a whole round windowpane and sat down on the ground to enjoy it. All at once the door opened, and an old, old woman with a crutch came hobbling out. Hansel and Gretel were so frightened they dropped what they were eating. But the old woman wagged her head and said: "Oh, what dear children! However did you get here? Don't be afraid, come in and stay with me. You will come to no harm." She took them by the hand and led them into her house. A fine meal of milk and pancakes, sugar, apples, and nuts was set before them. And then two little beds were made up clean and white, and Hansel and Gretel got into them and thought they were in heaven.

But the old woman had only pretended to be so kind. Actually she was a wicked witch, who waylaid children and had built her house out of bread to entice them. She killed, cooked, and ate any child who fell into her hands, and that to her was a feast day. Witches have red eyes and can't see very far, but they have a keen sense of smell like animals, so they know when humans are coming. As Hansel and Gretel approached, she laughed her wicked laugh and said with a jeer: "Here come two who will never get away from me." Early in the morning, when the children were still asleep, she got up, and when she saw them resting so sweetly with their plump red cheeks, she muttered to herself: "What tasty morsels they will be!" She grabbed Hansel with her scrawny hand, carried him to a little shed, and closed the iron-barred door behind him. He screamed for all he was worth, but much good it did him. Then she went back to Gretel, shook her awake, and cried: "Get up, lazybones. You must draw water and cook something nice for your brother. He's out in the shed and we've got to fatten him up. When he's nice and fat, I'm going to eat him." Gretel wept bitterly, but in vain; she had to do what the wicked witch told her.

The best of food was cooked for poor Hansel, but Gretel got nothing but crayfish shells. Every morning the old witch crept to the shed and said: "Hansel, hold out your finger. I want to see if you're getting fat." But Hansel held out a bone. The old woman had weak eyes and couldn't see it; she thought it was Hansel's finger and wondered why he wasn't getting fat. When four weeks had gone by and Hansel was as skinny as ever, her impatience got the better of her and she decided not to wait any longer. "Ho there, Gretel," she cried out. "Go and draw water and don't dawdle. Skinny or fat, I'm going to butcher Hansel tomorrow and cook him." Oh, how the little girl wailed at having to carry the water, and how the tears flowed down her cheeks! "Dear God," she cried, "oh, won't you help us? If only the wild beasts had eaten us in the forest, at least we'd have died together." "Stop that blubbering," said the witch. "It won't do you a bit of good."

Early in the morning Gretel had to fill the kettle with water and light the fire. "First we'll bake," said the old witch. "I've heated the oven and kneaded the dough." And she drove poor Gretel out to the oven, which by now was spitting flames. "Crawl in," said the witch, "and see if it's hot enough for the bread." Once Gretel was inside, she meant to close the door and roast her, so as to eat her too. But Gretel saw what she had in mind and said: "I don't know how. How do I get in?" "Silly goose," said the old woman. "The opening is big enough. Look. Even I can get in." She crept to the opening and stuck her head in, whereupon Gretel gave her a push that sent her sprawling, closed the iron door and fastened the bolt. Eek! How horribly she screeched! But Gretel ran away and the wicked witch burned miserably to death.

Gretel ran straight to Hansel, opened the door of the shed, and cried: "Hansel, we're saved! The old witch is dead." Hansel hopped out like a bird when someone opens the door of its cage. How happy they were! They hugged and kissed each other and danced around. And now that there was nothing to be afraid of, they went into the witch's house and in every corner there were boxes full of pearls and precious stones. Hansel stuffed his pockets full of them and said: "These will be much better than pebbles," and Gretel said: "I'll take some home too," and filled her apron with them. "We'd better leave now," said Hansel, "and get out of this bewitched forest." When they had walked a few hours, they came to a big body of water. "How will we ever get across," said Hansel. "I don't see any bridge." "And there's no boat, either," said Gretel, "but over there I see a white duck. She'll help us across if I ask her." And she cried out:

"Duckling, duckling, here is Gretel,
Duckling, duckling, here is Hansel,
No bridge or ferry far and wide—
Duckling, come and give us a ride."

Sure enough, the duck came over to them and Hansel sat down on her back and told his sister to sit beside him. "No," said Gretel, "that would be too much for the poor thing; let her carry us one at a time." And that's just what the good little duck did. And when they were safely across and had walked a little while, the forest began to look more and more familiar, and finally they saw their father's house in the distance. They began to run, and they flew into the house and threw themselves into their father's arms. The poor man hadn't had a happy hour since he had left the children in the forest, and in the meantime his wife had died. Gretel opened out her little apron, the pearls and precious stones went bouncing around the room, and Hansel reached into his pockets and tossed out handful after handful. All their worries were over, and they lived together in pure happiness. My story is done, see the mouse run; if you catch it, you may make yourself a great big fur cap out of it.

SNOW WHITE[1]

Jacob and Wilhelm Grimm

ONCE IN MIDWINTER WHEN THE snowflakes were falling from the sky like feathers, a queen sat sewing at the window, with an ebony frame. And as she was sewing and looking out at the snowflakes, she pricked her finger with her needle and three drops of blood fell on the snow. The red looked so beautiful on the white snow that she thought to herself: "If only I had a child as white as snow and as red as blood and as black as the wood of my window frame." A little while later she gave birth to a daughter, who was as white as snow and as red as blood, and her hair was as black as ebony. They called her Snow White, and when she was born, the queen died.

A year later the king took a second wife. She was beautiful, but she was proud and

---

1 First published in 1812/15, in the first edition of *Kinder- und Hausmärchen*. This text from the second edition (1819), from *Grimms' Tales for Young and Old*, trans. Ralph Manheim (Garden City, NY: Anchor Press, 1977).

overbearing, and she couldn't bear the thought that anyone might be more beautiful than she. She had a magic mirror, and when she went up to it and looked at herself, she said:

"Mirror, Mirror, here I stand.
 Who is the fairest in the land?"

and the mirror answered:

"You, O Queen, are the fairest in the land."

That set her mind at rest, for she knew the mirror told the truth.

But as Snow White grew, she became more and more beautiful, and by the time she was seven years old she was as beautiful as the day and more beautiful than the queen herself. One day when the queen said to her mirror:

"Mirror, Mirror, here I stand.
 Who is the fairest in the land?"

the mirror replied:

"You, O Queen, are the fairest here,
 But Snow White is a thousand times more fair."

The Queen gasped, and turned yellow and green with envy. Every time she laid eyes on Snow White after that she hated her so much that her heart turned over in her bosom. Envy and pride grew like weeds in her heart, until she knew no peace by day or by night. Finally she sent for a huntsman and said: "Get that child out of my sight. Take her into the forest and kill her and bring me her lungs and her liver to prove you've done it." The huntsman obeyed. He took the child out into the forest, but when he drew his hunting knife and prepared to pierce Snow White's innocent heart, she began to cry and said: "Oh, dear huntsman, let me live. I'll run off through the wild woods and never come home again." Because of her beauty the huntsman took pity on her and said: "All right, you poor child. Run away." To himself, he thought: "The wild beasts will soon eat her," but not having to kill her was a great weight off his mind all the same. Just then a young boar came bounding out of the thicket. The huntsman thrust his knife into it, took the lungs and liver and brought them to the queen as proof that he had done her bidding. The cook was ordered to salt and stew them, and the godless woman ate them, thinking she was eating Snow White's lungs and liver.

Meanwhile the poor child was all alone in the great forest. She was so afraid that she looked at all the leaves on the trees and didn't know what to do. She began to run, she ran over sharp stones and through brambles, and the wild beasts passed by without harming her. She ran as long as her legs would carry her and then, just before nightfall, she saw a little house and went in to rest. Inside the house everything was tiny, but wonderfully neat and clean. There was a table spread with a white cloth, and on the table there were seven little plates, each with its own knife, fork, and spoon, and seven little cups. Over against the wall there were seven little beds all in a row, covered with spotless white sheets. Snow White was very hungry and thirsty, but she didn't want to eat up anyone's entire meal, so she ate a bit of bread and vegetables from each plate and drank a sip of wine from each cup. Then she was so tired that she lay down on one of the beds, but none of the beds quite suited her; some were too long and some were too short, but the seventh was just right. There she stayed and when she had said her prayers she fell asleep.

When it was quite dark, the owners of the little house came home. They were seven dwarfs who went off to the mountains every day with their picks and shovels, to mine silver. They lit their seven little candles, and when the light went up they saw someone had been there, because certain things had been moved. The first said: "Who has been sitting in my chair?" The second: "Who has been eating off my plate?" The third: "Who has taken a bite of my bread?" The fourth: "Who has been eating some of my vegetables?" The fifth: "Who has been using my fork?" The sixth: "Who has been cutting with my knife?" And the seventh: "Who has been drinking out of my cup?" Then the first looked around, saw a little hollow in his bed and said: "Who has been lying in my bed?" The others came running, and cried out: "Somebody has been lying in my bed too." But when the seventh looked at his bed, he saw Snow White lying there asleep. He called the others, who came running. They cried out in amazement, went to get their seven little candles, and held them over Snow White: "Heavens above!" they cried. "Heavens above! What a beautiful child!" They were so delighted they didn't wake her but let her go on sleeping in the little bed. The seventh dwarf slept with his comrades, an hour with each one, and then the night was over.

Next morning Snow White woke up, and when she saw the seven dwarfs she was frightened. But they were friendly and asked: "What's your name?" "My name is Snow White," she said. "How did you get to our house?" the dwarfs asked. And she told them how her stepmother had wanted to kill her, how the huntsman had spared her life, and how she had walked all day until at last she found their little house. The dwarfs said: "If you will keep house for us, and do the cooking and make the beds and wash and sew and knit, and keep everything neat and clean, you can stay with us and you'll want for nothing." "Oh, yes," said Snow White. "I'd love to." So she stayed and kept the house in order, and in the morning they went off to the mountains to look for silver and gold, and in the evening they came home again and dinner had to be ready. But all day Snow White was alone, and the kindly dwarfs warned her, saying: "Watch out for your stepmother. She'll soon find out you're here. Don't let anyone in."

After eating Snow White's lungs and liver, the queen felt sure she was again the most beautiful of all. She went to her mirror and said:

"Mirror, Mirror, here I stand.
Who is the fairest in the land?"

And the mirror replied:

"You, O Queen, are the fairest here,
But Snow White, who has gone to stay
With the seven dwarfs far, far away,
Is a thousand times more fair."

The queen gasped. She knew the mirror told no lies and she realized that the huntsman had deceived her and that Snow White was still alive. She racked her brains for a way to kill her, because she simply had to be the fairest in the land, or envy would leave her no peace. At last she thought up a plan. She stained her face and dressed like an old peddler woman, so that no one could have recognized her. In this disguise she made her way across the seven mountains to the house of the seven dwarfs, knocked at the door and cried out: "Pretty things for sale! For sale!" Snow White looked out of the window and said: "Good day, old woman, what have you got to sell?" "Nice things, nice things!" she replied. "Laces, all colors," and she took out a lace woven of bright-colored silk. "This woman looks so honest," thought Snow White. "It must be all right to let her in." So she unbolted the door and bought the pretty lace. "Child!" said the old woman, "you look a fright. Come, let me lace you up properly." Suspecting nothing, Snow White stepped up and let the old woman put in the new lace. But she did it so quickly and pulled the lace so tight that Snow White's breath was cut off and she fell down as though dead. "Well, well," said the queen, "you're not the fairest in the land now." And she hurried away.

A little while later, at nightfall, the seven dwarfs came home. How horrified they were to see their beloved Snow White lying on the floor! She lay so still they thought she was dead. They lifted her up, and when they saw she was laced too tightly, they cut the lace. She breathed just a little, and then little by little she came to life. When the dwarfs heard what had happened, they said: "That old peddler woman was the wicked queen and no one else. You've got to be careful and never let anyone in when we're away."

When the wicked woman got home, she went to her mirror and asked:

"Mirror, Mirror, here I stand.
Who is the fairest in the land?"

And the mirror answered as usual:

"You, O Queen, are the fairest here,
But Snow White, who has gone to stay
With the seven dwarfs far, far away,
Is a thousand times more fair."

When she heard that, it gave her such a pang that the blood rushed to her heart, for she realized that Snow White had revived. "Never mind," she said. "I'll think up something now that will really destroy you," and with the help of some magic spells she knew she made a poisoned comb. Then she disguised herself and took the form of another old woman. And again she made her way over the seven mountains to the house of the seven dwarfs, knocked at the door and said: "Pretty things for sale! For sale!" Snow White looked out and said: "Go away. I can't let anyone in." "You can look, can't you?" said the old woman, taking out the poisoned comb and holding it up. The child liked it so well that she forgot everything else and opened the door. When they had agreed on the price, the old woman said: "Now I'll give your hair a proper combing." Suspecting nothing, poor Snow White stood still for the old woman, but no sooner had the comb touched her hair than the poison took effect and she fell into a dead faint. "There, my beauty," said the wicked woman. "It's all up with you now." And she went away. But luckily it wasn't long till nightfall. When the seven dwarfs came home and found Snow White lying on the floor as though dead, they immediately suspected the stepmother. They examined Snow White and found the poisoned comb, and no sooner had they pulled it out than she woke up and told them what had happened. Again they warned her to be on her guard and not to open the door to anyone. When the queen got home she went to her mirror and said,

"Mirror, Mirror, here I stand.
Who is the fairest in the land?"

And the mirror answered as before:

"You, O Queen, are the fairest here,
But Snow White, who has gone to stay

With the seven dwarfs far, far away,
Is a thousand times more fair." ·

When she heard the mirror say that, she trembled and shook with rage. "Snow White
must die!" she cried out. "Even if it costs me my own life." Then she went to a secret
room that no one else knew about and made a very poisonous apple. It looked so
nice on the outside, white with red cheeks, that anyone who saw it would want it;
but anyone who ate even the tiniest bit of it would die. When the apple was ready,
she stained her face and disguised herself as a peasant woman. And again she made
her way across the seven mountains to the house of the seven dwarfs. She knocked at
the door and Snow White put her head out of the window. "I can't let anyone in," she
said. "The seven dwarfs won't let me." "It doesn't matter," said the peasant woman.
"I only want to get rid of these apples. Here, I'll make you a present of one." "No,"
said Snow White. "I'm not allowed to take anything." "Are you afraid of poison?" said
the old woman. "Look, I'm cutting it in half. You eat the red cheek and I'll eat the
white cheek." But the apple had been so cleverly made that only the red cheek was
poisoned. Snow White longed for the lovely apple, and when she saw the peasant
woman taking a bite out of it she couldn't resist. She held out her hand and took the
poisonous half. And no sooner had she taken a bite than she fell to the floor dead.
The queen gave her a cruel look, laughed a terrible laugh, and said: "White as snow,
red as blood, black as ebony. The dwarfs won't revive you this time." And when she
got home and questioned the mirror:

"Mirror, Mirror, here I stand.
Who is the fairest in the land?"

The mirror answered at last:

"You, O Queen, are the fairest in the land."

Then her envious heart was at peace, insofar as an envious heart can be at peace.
    When the dwarfs came home at nightfall, they found Snow White lying on the
floor. No breath came out of her mouth and she was really dead. They lifted her up,
looked to see if they could find anything poisonous, unlaced her, combed her hair,
washed her in water and wine, but nothing helped; the dear child was dead, and
dead she remained. They laid her on a bier, and all seven sat down beside it and
mourned, and they wept for three whole days. Then they were going to bury her, but
she still looked fresh and alive, and she still had her beautiful red cheeks. "We can't
lower her into the black earth," they said, and they had a coffin made out of glass, so

that she could be seen from all sides, and they put her into it and wrote her name in gold letters on the coffin, adding that she was a king's daughter. Then they put the coffin on the hilltop, and one of them always stayed there to guard it. And the birds came and wept for Snow White, first an owl, then a raven, and then a dove.

Snow White lay in her coffin for years and years. She didn't rot, but continued to look as if she were asleep, for she was still as white as snow, as red as blood, and as black as ebony. Then one day a prince came to that forest and stopped for the night at the dwarfs' house. He saw the coffin on the hilltop, he saw lovely Snow White inside it, and he read the gold letters on the coffin. He said to the dwarfs: "Let me have the coffin, I'll pay you as much as you like for it." But the dwarfs replied: "We wouldn't part with it for all the money in the world." "Then give it to me," he said, "for I can't go on living unless I look at Snow White. I will honor and cherish her forever." Then the dwarfs took pity on him and gave him the coffin. The prince's servants hoisted it up on their shoulders and as they were carrying it away they stumbled over a root. The jolt shook the poisoned core, which Snow White had bitten off, out of her throat, and soon she opened her eyes, lifted the coffin lid, sat up, and was alive again. "Oh!" she cried. "Where am I?" "With me!" the prince answered joyfully. Then he told her what had happened and said: "I love you more than anything in the world; come with me to my father's castle and be my wife." Snow White loved him and went with him, and arrangements were made for a splendid wedding feast.

Snow White's wicked stepmother was among those invited to the wedding. When she had put on her fine clothes, she went to her mirror and said:

"Mirror, Mirror, here I stand.
Who is the fairest in the land?"

And the mirror answered:

"You, O Queen, are the fairest here.
But the young queen is a thousand times more fair."

At that the wicked woman spat out a curse. She was so horrorstricken she didn't know what to do. At first she didn't want to go to the wedding, but then she couldn't resist; she just had to go and see the young queen. The moment she entered the hall she recognized Snow White, and she was so terrified that she just stood there and couldn't move. But two iron slippers had already been put into glowing coals. Someone took them out with a pair of tongs and set them down in front of her. She was forced to step into the red-hot shoes and dance till she fell to the floor dead.

RAPUNZEL[1]

Jacob and Wilhelm Grimm

ONCE AFTER A MAN AND wife had long wished in vain for a child, the wife had reason to hope that God would grant them their wish. In the back of their house there was a little window that looked out over a wonderful garden, full of beautiful flowers and vegetables. But there was a high wall around the garden, and no one dared enter it because it belonged to a witch, who was very powerful and everyone was afraid of her. One day the wife stood at this window, looking down into the garden, and her eyes lit on a bed of the finest rapunzel, which is a kind of lettuce. And it looked so fresh and green that she longed for it and her mouth watered. Her craving for it grew from day to day, and she began to waste away because she knew she would never get any. Seeing her so pale and wretched, her husband took fright and asked: "What's the matter with you, dear wife?" "Oh," she said, "I shall die unless I get some rapunzel to eat from the garden behind our house." Her husband, who loved her, thought: "Sooner than let my wife die, I shall get her some of that rapunzel, cost what it may." As night was falling, he climbed the wall into the witch's garden, took a handful of rapunzel, and brought it to his wife. She made it into a salad right away and ate it hungrily. But it tasted so good, so very good, that the next day her craving for it was three times as great. Her husband could see she would know no peace unless he paid another visit to the garden. So at nightfall he climbed the wall again, but when he came down on the other side he had an awful fright, for there was the witch right in front of him. "How dare you!" she said with an angry look. "How dare you sneak into my garden like a thief and steal my rapunzel! I'll make you pay dearly for this." "Oh, please," he said, "please temper justice with mercy. I only did it because I had to. My wife was looking out of the window, and when she saw your rapunzel she felt such a craving for it that she would have died if I hadn't got her some." At that the witch's anger died down and she said: "If that's how it is, you may take as much rapunzel as you wish, but on one condition: that you give me the child your wife will bear. It will have a good life and I shall care for it like a mother." In his fright, the man agreed to everything, and the moment his wife was delivered, the witch appeared, gave the child the name of Rapunzel, and took her away.

Rapunzel grew to be the loveliest child under the sun. When she was twelve years old, the witch took her to the middle of the forest and shut her up in a tower that had neither stairs nor door, but only a little window at the very top. When the witch

---

1 First published in 1812/15, in the first edition of *Kinder- und Hausmärchen*. This text from the second edition (1819), from *Grimms' Tales for Young and Old*, trans. Ralph Manheim (Garden City, NY: Anchor Press, 1977).

wanted to come in, she stood down below and called out: "Rapunzel, Rapunzel, Let down your hair for me." Rapunzel had beautiful long hair, as fine as spun gold. When she heard the witch's voice, she undid her braids and fastened them to the window latch. They fell to the ground twenty ells down, and the witch climbed up on them.

A few years later it so happened that the king's son was passing through the forest. When he came to the tower, he heard someone singing, and the singing was so lovely that he stopped and listened. It was Rapunzel, who in her loneliness was singing to pass the time. The prince wanted to go up to her and he looked for a door but found none. He rode away home, but the singing had so touched his heart that he went out into the forest every day and listened. Once as he was standing behind a tree, he saw a witch come to the foot of the tower and heard her call out:

"Rapunzel, Rapunzel,
Let down your hair."

Whereupon Rapunzel let down her braids, and the witch climbed up to her. "Aha," he thought, "if that's the ladder that goes up to her, then I'll try my luck too." And next day, when it was beginning to get dark, he went to the tower and called out:

"Rapunzel, Rapunzel,
Let down your hair."

A moment later her hair fell to the ground and the prince climbed up.

At first Rapunzel was dreadfully frightened, for she had never seen a man before, but the prince spoke gently to her and told her how he had been so moved by her singing that he couldn't rest easy until he had seen her. At that Rapunzel lost her fear, and when he asked if she would have him as her husband and she saw he was young and handsome, she thought: "He will love me better than my old godmother." So she said yes and put her hand in his hand. "I'd gladly go with you," she said, "but how will I ever get down? Every time you come, bring a skein of silk and I'll make a ladder with it. When it's finished, I'll climb down, and you will carry me home on your horse." They agreed that in the meantime he would come every evening, because the old witch came during the day. The witch noticed nothing until one day Rapunzel said to her: "Tell me, Godmother, how is it that you're so much harder to pull up than the young prince? With him it hardly takes a minute." "Wicked child!" cried the witch. "What did you say? I thought I had shut you away from the world, but you've deceived me." In her fury she seized Rapunzel's beautiful hair, wound it several times around her left hand and picked up a pair of scissors in her right hand. Snippety-snap went the scissors, and the lovely braids fell to the floor. Then the heartless witch sent poor Rapunzel to a desert place, where she lived in misery and want.

At dusk on the day she had sent Rapunzel away, she fastened the severed braids to the window latch, and when the prince came and called: "Rapunzel, Rapunzel, Let down your hair." she let the hair down. The prince climbed up, but instead of his dearest Rapunzel, the witch was waiting for him with angry, poisonous looks. "Aha!" she cried. "You've come to take your darling wife away, but the bird is gone from the nest, she won't be singing any more; the cat has taken her away and before she's done she'll scratch your eyes out too. You've lost Rapunzel, you'll never see her again." The prince was beside himself with grief, and in his despair he jumped from the tower. It didn't kill him, but the brambles he fell into scratched his eyes out and he was blind. He wandered through the forest, living on roots and berries and weeping and wailing over the loss of his dearest wife. For several years he wandered wretchedly, until at last he came to the desert place where Rapunzel was living in misery with the twins she had born—a boy and a girl. He heard a voice that seemed familiar, and when he approached Rapunzel recognized him, fell on his neck and wept. Two of her tears dropped on his eyes, which were made clear again, so that he could see as well as ever. He took her to his kingdom, where she was welcomed with rejoicing, and they lived happy and contented for many years to come.

JACK AND THE BEANSTALK[1]

Joseph Jacobs

THERE WAS ONCE UPON A time a poor widow who had an only son named Jack, and a cow named Milky-white. And all they had to live on was the milk the cow gave every morning, which they carried to the market and sold. But one morning Milky-white gave no milk, and they didn't know what to do.

"What shall we do, what shall we do?" said the widow, wringing her hands.

"Cheer up, mother, I'll go and get work somewhere," said Jack.

"We've tried that before, and nobody would take you," said his mother; "we must sell Milky-white and with the money start shop, or something."

"All right, mother," says Jack; "it's market-day today, and I'll soon sell Milky-white, and then we'll see what we can do."

---

1   From *English Fairy Tales*, 1890 (repr. New York: Dover, 1967).

So he took the cow's halter in his hand, and off he started. He hadn't gone far when he met a funny-looking old man, who said to him: "Good morning, Jack."

"Good morning to you," said Jack, and wondered how he knew his name.

"Well, Jack, and where are you off to?" said the man.

"I'm going to market to sell our cow here."

"Oh, you look the proper sort of chap to sell cows," said the man; "I wonder if you know how many beans make five."

"Two in each hand and one in your mouth," says Jack, as sharp as a needle.

"Right you are," says the man, "and here they are, the very beans themselves," he went on, pulling out of his pocket a number of strange-looking beans. "As you are so sharp," says he, "I don't mind doing a swap with you—your cow for these beans."

"Go along," says Jack; "wouldn't you like it?"

"Ah! you don't know what these beans are," said the man; "if you plant them over-night, by morning they grow right up to the sky."

"Really?" said Jack; "you don't say so."

"Yes, that is so, and if it doesn't turn out to be true you can have your cow back."

"Right," says Jack, and hands him over Milky-white's halter and pockets the beans.

Back goes Jack home, and as he hadn't gone very far it wasn't dusk by the time he got to his door.

"Back already, Jack?" said his mother; "I see you haven't got Milky-white, so you've sold her. How much did you get for her?"

"You'll never guess, mother," says Jack.

"No, you don't say so. Good boy! Five pounds, ten, fifteen, no, it can't be twenty."

"I told you you couldn't guess. What do you say to these beans; they're magical, plant them overnight and—"

"What!" says Jack's mother, "have you been such a fool, such a dolt, such an idiot, as to give away my Milky-white, the best milker in the parish, and prime beef to boot, for a set of paltry beans? Take that! Take that! Take that! And as for your precious beans here they go out of the window. And now off with you to bed. Not a sup shall you drink, and not a bit shall you swallow this very night."

So Jack went upstairs to his little room in the attic, and sad and sorry he was, to be sure, as much for his mother's sake, as for the loss of his supper.

At last he dropped off to sleep.

When he woke up, the room looked so funny. The sun was shining into part of it, and yet all the rest was quite dark and shady. So Jack jumped up and dressed himself and went to the window. And what do you think he saw? Why, the beans his mother had thrown out of the window into the garden had sprung up into a big beanstalk which went up and up and up till it reached the sky. So the man spoke truth after all.

The beanstalk grew up quite close past Jack's window, so all he had to do was to open it and give a jump on to the beanstalk which ran up just like a big ladder. So Jack climbed, and he climbed and he climbed and he climbed and he climbed and he climbed and he climbed till at last he reached the sky. And when he got there he found a long broad road going as straight as a dart. So he walked along and he walked along and he walked along till he came to a great big tall house, and on the doorstep there was a great big tall woman.

"Good morning, mum," says Jack, quite polite-like. "Could you be so kind as to give me some breakfast?" For he hadn't had anything to eat, you know, the night before and was as hungry as a hunter.

"It's breakfast you want, is it?" says the great big tall woman, "It's breakfast you'll be if you don't move off from here. My man is an ogre and there's nothing he likes better than boys broiled on toast. You'd better be moving on or he'll soon be coming."

"Oh! please mum, do give me something to eat, mum. I've had nothing to eat since yesterday morning, really and truly, mum," says Jack. "I may as well be broiled as die of hunger."

Well, the ogre's wife was not half so bad after all. So she took Jack into the kitchen, and gave him a hunk of bread and cheese and a jug of milk. But Jack hadn't half finished these when thump! thump! thump! the whole house began to tremble with the noise of some one coming.

"Goodness gracious me! It's my old man," said the ogre's wife, "what on earth shall I do? Come along quick and jump in here." And she bundled Jack into the oven just as the ogre came in.

He was a big one, to be sure. At his belt he had three calves strung up by the heels, and he unhooked them and threw them down on the table and said: "Here, wife, broil me a couple of these for breakfast. Ah! what's this I smell?

Fee-fi-fo-fum,
I smell the blood of an Englishman,
Be he alive, or be he dead
I'll have his bones to grind my bread."

"Nonsense dear," said his wife, "you're dreaming. Or perhaps you smell the scraps of that little boy you liked so much for yesterday's dinner. Here, you go and have a wash and tidy up, and by the time you come back your breakfast'll be ready for you."

So off the ogre went, and Jack was just going to jump out of the oven and run away when the woman told him not. "Wait till he's asleep," says she; "he always has a doze after breakfast."

Well, the ogre had his breakfast, and after that he goes to a big chest and takes out of it a couple of bags of gold, and down he sits and counts till at last his head began to nod and he began to snore till the whole house shook again.

Then Jack crept out on tiptoe from his oven, and as he was passing the ogre he took one of the bags of gold under his arm, and off he pelters till he came to the beanstalk, and then he threw down the bag of gold, which of course fell into his mother's garden, and then he climbed down and climbed down till at last he got home and told his mother and showed her the gold and said: "Well, mother, wasn't I right about the beans? They are really magical, you see."

So they lived on the bag of gold for some time, but at last they came to the end of it, and Jack made up his mind to try his luck once more up at the top of the beanstalk. So one fine morning he rose up early, and got on to the beanstalk, and he climbed and he climbed and he climbed and he climbed and he climbed and he climbed till at last he came out on to the road again and up to the great big tall house he had been to before. There, sure enough, was the great big tall woman standing on the doorstep.

"Good morning, mum," says Jack, as bold as brass, "could you be so good as to give me something to eat?"

"Go away, my boy," said the big tall woman, "or else my man will eat you for breakfast. But aren't you the youngster who came here once before? Do you know, that very day, my man missed one of his bags of gold."

"That's strange, mum," said Jack, "I dare say I could tell you something about that, but I'm so hungry I can't speak till I've had something to eat."

Well the big tall woman was so curious that she took him in and gave him something to eat. But he had scarcely begun munching it as slowly as he could when thump! thump! thump! they heard the giant's footstep, and his wife hid Jack away in the oven.

All happened as it did before. In came the ogre as he did before, said: "Fee-fi-fo-fum," and had his breakfast of three broiled oxen. Then he said: "Wife, bring me the hen that lays the golden eggs." So she brought it, and the ogre said: "Lay," and it laid an egg all of gold. And then the ogre began to nod his head, and to snore till the house shook.

Then Jack crept out of the oven on tiptoe and caught hold of the golden hen, and was off before you could say "Jack Robinson." But this time the hen gave a cackle which woke the ogre, and just as Jack got out of the house he heard him calling: "Wife, wife, what have you done with my golden hen?"

And the wife said: "Why, my dear?"

But that was all Jack heard, for he rushed off to the beanstalk and climbed down like a house on fire. And when he got home he showed his mother the wonderful hen, and said "Lay" to it; and it laid a golden egg every time he said "Lay."

Well, Jack was not content, and it wasn't very long before he determined to have another try at his luck up there at the top of the beanstalk. So one fine morning, he rose up early, and got on to the beanstalk, and he climbed and he climbed and he climbed and he climbed till he got to the top. But this time he knew better than to go straight to the ogre's house. And when he got near it, he waited behind a bush till he saw the ogre's wife come out with a pail to get some water, and then he crept into the house and got into the copper.[1] He hadn't been there long when he heard thump! thump! thump! as before, and in come the ogre and his wife.

"Fee-fi-fo-fum, I smell the blood of an Englishman," cried out the ogre. "I smell him, wife, I smell him."

"Do you, my dearie?" says the ogre's wife. "Then, if it's that little rogue that stole your gold and the hen that laid the golden eggs he's sure to have got into the oven." And they both rushed to the oven. But Jack wasn't there, luckily, and the ogre's wife said: "There you are again with your fee-fi-fo-fum. Why of course it's the boy you caught last night that I've just broiled for your breakfast. How forgetful I am, and how careless you are not to know the difference between live and dead after all these years."

So the ogre sat down to the breakfast and ate it, but every now and then he would mutter: "Well, I could have sworn—" and he'd get up and search the larder and the cupboards and everything, only, luckily, he didn't think of the copper.

After breakfast was over, the ogre called out: "Wife, wife, bring me my golden harp." So she brought it and put it on the table before him. Then he said: "Sing!" and the golden harp sang most beautifully. And it went on singing till the ogre fell asleep, and commenced to snore like thunder.

Then Jack lifted up the copperlid very quietly and got down like a mouse and crept on hands and knees till he came to the table, when up he crawled, caught hold of the golden harp and dashed with it towards the door. But the harp called out quite loud: "Master! Master!" and the ogre woke up just in time to see Jack running off with his harp.

Jack ran as fast as he could, and the ogre came rushing after, and would soon have caught him only Jack had a start and dodged him a bit and knew where he was going. When he got to the beanstalk the ogre was not more than twenty yards away when suddenly he saw Jack disappear like, and when he came to the end of the road he saw Jack underneath climbing down for dear life. Well, the ogre didn't like trusting himself to such a ladder, and he stood and waited, so Jack got another start. But just then the harp cried out: "Master! Master!" and the ogre swung himself down on to the beanstalk, which shook with his weight. Down climbs Jack, and after him climbed

---

1   copper: A large metal pot for boiling laundry.

the ogre. By this time Jack had climbed down and climbed down and climbed down till he was very nearly home. So he called out: "Mother! Mother! bring me an axe, bring me an axe." And his mother came rushing out with the axe in her hand, but when she came to the beanstalk she stood stock still with fright for there she saw the ogre with his legs just through the clouds.

But Jack jumped down and got hold of the axe and gave a chop at the beanstalk which cut it half in two. The ogre felt the beanstalk shake and quiver so he stopped to see what was the matter. Then Jack gave another chop with the axe, and the beanstalk was cut in two and began to topple over. Then the ogre fell down and broke his crown, and the beanstalk came toppling after.

Then Jack showed his mother his golden harp, and what with showing that and selling the golden eggs, Jack and his mother became very rich, and he married a great princess, and they lived happy ever after.

THE UGLY DUCKLING[1]

Hans Christian Andersen

IT WAS SO BEAUTIFUL OUT in the country. It was summer. The oats were still green, but the wheat was turning yellow. Down in the meadow the grass had been cut and made into haystacks; and there the storks walked on their long red legs talking Egyptian, because that was the language they had been taught by their mothers. The fields were enclosed by woods, and hidden among them were little lakes and pools. Yes, it certainly was lovely out there in the country!

The old castle, with its deep moat surrounding it, lay bathed in sunshine. Between the heavy walls and the edge of the moat there was a narrow strip of land covered by a whole forest of burdock plants. Their leaves were large and some of the stalks were so tall that a child could stand upright under them and imagine that he was in the middle of the wild and lonely woods. Here a duck had built her nest. While she sat waiting for the eggs to hatch, she felt a little sorry for herself because it was taking so long and hardly anybody came to visit her. The other ducks preferred swimming in the moat to sitting under a dock leaf and gossiping.

Finally the eggs began to crack. "Peep ... Peep," they said one after another. The egg yolks had become alive and were sticking out their heads.

---

1   First published in 1843. This text from *Hans Christian Andersen: His Classic Fairy Tales*, trans. Erik Haugaard (New York: Doubleday, 1974).

"Quack ... Quack ..." said their mother. "Look around you." And the ducklings did; they glanced at the green world about them, and that was what their mother wanted them to do, for green was good for their eyes.

"How big the world is!" piped the little ones, for they had much more space to move around in now than they had had inside the egg.

"Do you think that this is the whole world?" quacked their mother. "The world is much larger than this. It stretches as far as the minister's wheat fields, though I have not been there.... Are you all here?" The duck got up and turned around to look at her nest. "Oh no, the biggest egg hasn't hatched yet; and I'm so tired of sitting here! I wonder how long it will take?" she wailed, and sat down again.

"What's new?" asked an old duck who had come visiting.

"One of the eggs is taking so long," complained the mother duck. "It won't crack. But take a look at the others. They are the sweetest little ducklings you have ever seen; and every one of them looks exactly like their father. That scoundrel hasn't come to visit me once."

"Let me look at the egg that won't hatch," demanded the old duck. "I am sure that it's a turkey egg! I was fooled that way once. You can't imagine what it's like. Turkeys are afraid of the water. I couldn't get them to go into it. I quacked and I nipped them, but nothing helped. Let me see that egg! ... Yes, it's a turkey egg. Just let it lie there. You go and teach your young ones how to swim, that's my advice."

"I have sat on it so long that I suppose I can sit a little longer, at least until they get the hay in," replied the mother duck.

"Suit yourself," said the older duck, and went on.

At last the big egg cracked too. "Peep ... Peep," said the young one, and tumbled out. He was big and very ugly.

The mother duck looked at him. "He's awfully big for his age," she said. "He doesn't look like any of the others. I wonder if he could be a turkey? Well, we shall soon see. Into the water he will go, even if I have to kick him to make him do it."

The next day the weather was gloriously beautiful. The sun shone on the forest of burdock plants. The mother duck took her whole brood to the moat. "Quack ... Quack ..." she ordered.

One after another, the little ducklings plunged into the water. For a moment their heads disappeared, but then they popped up again and the little ones floated like so many corks. Their legs knew what to do without being told. All of the new brood swam very nicely, even the ugly one.

"He is no turkey," mumbled the mother. "See how beautifully he uses his legs and how straight he holds his neck. He is my own child and, when you look closely at him, he's quite handsome.... Quack! Quack! Follow me and I'll take you to the henyard and introduce you to everyone. But stay close to me, so that no one steps on you, and look out for the cat."

They heard an awful noise when they arrived at the henyard. Two families of ducks had got into a fight over the head of an eel. Neither of them got it, for it was swiped by the cat.

"That is the way of the world," said the mother duck, and licked her bill. She would have liked to have had the eel's head herself. "Walk nicely," she admonished them. "And remember to bow to the old duck over there. She has Spanish blood in her veins and is the most aristocratic fowl here. That is why she is so fat and has a red rag tied around one of her legs. That is the highest mark of distinction a duck can be given. It means so much that she will never be done away with; and all the other fowl and the human beings know who she is. Quack! Quack!... Don't walk, waddle like well-brought-up ducklings. Keep your legs far apart, just as your mother and father have always done. Bow your heads and say, 'Quack'!" And that was what the little ducklings did.

Other ducks gathered about them and said loudly, "What do we want that gang here for? Aren't there enough of us already? Pooh! Look how ugly one of them is! He's the last straw!" And one of the ducks flew over and bit the ugly duckling on the neck.

"Leave him alone!" shouted the mother. "He hasn't done anyone any harm."

"He's big and he doesn't look like everybody else!" replied the duck who had bitten him. "And that's reason enough to beat him."

"Very good-looking children you have," remarked the duck with the red rag around one of her legs. "All of them are beautiful except one. He didn't turn out very well. I wish you could make him over again."

"That's not possible, Your Grace," answered the mother duck. "He may not be handsome, but he has a good character and swims as well as the others, if not a little better. Perhaps he will grow handsomer as he grows older and becomes a bit smaller. He was in the egg too long, and that is why he doesn't have the right shape." She smoothed his neck for a moment and then added, "Besides, he's a drake; and it doesn't matter so much what he looks like. He is strong and I am sure he will be able to take care of himself."

"Well, the others are nice," said the old duck. "Make yourself at home, and if you should find an eel's head, you may bring it to me."

And they were "at home."

The poor little duckling, who had been the last to hatch and was so ugly, was bitten and pushed and made fun of both by the hens and by the other ducks. The turkey cock (who had been born with spurs on, and therefore thought he was an emperor) rustled his feathers as if he were a full-rigged ship under sail, and strutted up to the duckling. He gobbled so loudly at him that his own face got all red.

The poor little duckling did not know where to turn. How he grieved over his own ugliness, and how sad he was! The poor creature was mocked and laughed at by the whole henyard.

That was the first day; and each day that followed was worse than the one before. The poor duckling was chased and mistreated by everyone, even his own sisters and brothers, who quacked again and again, "If only the cat would get you, you ugly thing!"

Even his mother said, "I wish you were far away." The other ducks bit him and the hens pecked at him. The little girl who came to feed the fowls kicked him.

At last the duckling ran away. He flew over the tops of the bushes, frightening all the little birds so that they flew up into the air. "They, too, think I am ugly," thought the duckling, and closed his eyes—but he kept on running.

Finally he came to a great swamp where wild ducks lived; and here he stayed for the night, for he was too tired to go any farther.

In the morning he was discovered by the wild ducks. They looked at him and one of them asked, "What kind of bird are you?"

The ugly duckling bowed in all directions, for he was trying to be as polite as he knew how.

"You are ugly," said the wild ducks, "but that is no concern of ours, as long as you don't try to marry into our family."

The poor duckling wasn't thinking of marriage. All he wanted was to be allowed to swim among the reeds and drink a little water when he was thirsty.

He spent two days in the swamp; then two wild geese came—or rather, two wild ganders, for they were males. They had been hatched not long ago; therefore they were both frank and bold.

"Listen, comrade," they said. "You are so ugly that we like you. Do you want to migrate with us? Not far from here there is a marsh where some beautiful wild geese live. They are all lovely maidens, and you are so ugly that you may seek your fortune among them. Come along."

"Bang! Bang!" Two shots were heard and both ganders fell down dead among the reeds, and the water turned red from their blood.

"Bang! Bang!" Again came the sound of shots, and a flock of wild geese flew up.

The whole swamp was surrounded by hunters; from every direction came the awful noise. Some of the hunters had hidden behind bushes or among the reeds but others, screened from sight by the leaves, sat on the long, low branches of the trees that stretched out over the swamp. The blue smoke from the guns lay like a fog over the water and along the trees. Dogs came splashing through the marsh, and they bent and broke the reeds.

The poor little duckling was terrified. He was about to tuck his head under his wing, in order to hide, when he saw a big dog peering at him through the reeds. The dog's tongue hung out of its mouth and its eyes glistened evilly. It bared its teeth. Splash! It turned away without touching the duckling.

"Oh, thank God!" he sighed. "I am so ugly that even the dog doesn't want to bite me."

The little duckling lay as still as he could while the shots whistled through the reeds. Not until the middle of the afternoon did the shooting stop; but the poor little duckling was still so frightened that he waited several hours longer before taking his head out from under his wing. Then he ran as quickly as he could out of the swamp. Across the fields and the meadows he went, but a wind had come up and he found it hard to make his way against it.

Towards evening he came upon a poor little hut. It was so wretchedly crooked that it looked as if it couldn't make up its mind which way to fall and that was why it was still standing. The wind was blowing so hard that the poor little duckling had to sit down in order not to be blown away. Suddenly he noticed that the door was off its hinges, making a crack; and he squeezed himself through it and was inside.

An old woman lived in the hut with her cat and her hen. The cat was called Sonny and could both arch his back and purr. Oh yes, it could also make sparks if you rubbed its fur the wrong way. The hen had very short legs and that was why she was called Cluck Lowlegs. But she was good at laying eggs, and the old woman loved her as if she were her own child.

In the morning the hen and the cat discovered the duckling. The cat meowed and the hen clucked.

"What is going on?" asked the old woman, and looked around. She couldn't see very well, and when she found the duckling she thought it was a fat, full-grown duck. "What a fine catch!" she exclaimed. "Now we shall have duck eggs, unless it's a drake. We'll give it a try."

So the duckling was allowed to stay for three weeks on probation, but he laid no eggs. The cat was the master of the house and the hen the mistress. They always referred to themselves as "we and the world," for they thought that they were half the world— and the better half at that. The duckling thought that he should be allowed to have a different opinion, but the hen did not agree.

"Can you lay eggs?" she demanded.

"No," answered the duckling.

"Then keep your mouth shut."

And the cat asked, "Can you arch your back? Can you purr? Can you make sparks?"

"No."

"Well, in that case, you have no right to have an opinion when sensible people are talking."

The duckling was sitting in a corner and was in a bad mood. Suddenly he recalled how lovely it could be outside in the fresh air when the sun shone: a great longing to be floating in the water came over the duckling, and he could not help talking about it.

"What is the matter with you?" asked the hen as soon as she had heard what he had to say. "You have nothing to do, that's why you get ideas like that. Lay eggs or purr, and such notions will disappear."

"You have no idea how delightful it is to float in the water, and to dive down to the bottom of a lake and get your head wet," said the duckling.

"Yes, that certainly does sound amusing," said the hen. "You must have gone mad. Ask the cat—he is the most intelligent being I know—ask him whether he likes to swim or dive down to the bottom of a lake. Don't take my word for anything.... Ask the old woman, who is the cleverest person in the world; ask her whether she likes to float and to get her head all wet."

"You don't understand me!" wailed the duckling.

"And if I don't understand you, who will? I hope you don't think that you are wiser than the cat or the old woman—not to mention myself. Don't give yourself airs! Thank your Creator for all He has done for you. Aren't you sitting in a warm room, where you can hear intelligent conversation that you could learn something from? While you, yourself, do nothing but say a lot of nonsense and aren't the least bit amusing! Believe me, that's the truth, and I am only telling it to you for your own good. That's how you recognize a true friend: it's someone who is willing to tell you the truth, no matter how unpleasant it is. Now get to work: lay some eggs, or learn to purr and arch your back."

"I think I'll go out into the wide world," replied the duckling.

"Go right ahead!" said the hen.

And the duckling left. He found a lake where he could float in the water and dive to the bottom. There were other ducks, but they ignored him because he was so ugly.

Autumn came and the leaves turned yellow and brown, then they fell from the trees. The wind caught them and made them dance. The clouds were heavy with hail and snow. A raven sat on a fence and screeched, "Ach! Ach!" because it was so cold. When just thinking of how cold it was is enough to make one shiver, what a terrible time the duckling must have had.

One evening just as the sun was setting gloriously, a flock of beautiful birds came out from among the rushes. Their feathers were so white that they glistened; and they had long, graceful necks. They were swans. They made a very loud cry, then they spread their powerful wings. They were flying south to a warmer climate, where the lakes were not frozen in the winter. Higher and higher they circled. The ugly duckling turned round and round in the water like a wheel and stretched his neck up toward the sky; he felt a strange longing. He screeched so piercingly that he frightened himself.

Oh, he would never forget those beautiful birds, those happy birds. When they were out of sight the duckling dived down under the water to the bottom of the lake; and when he came up again he was beside himself. He did not know the name of those birds or where they were going, and yet he felt he loved them as he had never loved any other creatures. He did not envy them. It did not even occur to him to wish that he were so handsome himself. He would have been happy if the other ducks had let him stay in the henyard: that poor, ugly bird!

The weather grew colder and colder. The duckling had to swim round and round in the water, to keep just a little space for himself that wasn't frozen. Each night his hole became smaller and smaller. On all sides of him the ice creaked and groaned. The little duckling had to keep his feet constantly in motion so that the last bit of open water wouldn't become ice. At last he was too tired to swim any more. He sat still. The ice closed in around him and he was frozen fast.

Early the next morning a farmer saw him and with his clogs broke the ice to free the duckling. The man put the bird under his arm and took it home to his wife, who brought the duckling back to life.

The children wanted to play with him. But the duckling was afraid that they were going to hurt him, so he flapped his wings and flew right into the milk pail. From there he flew into a big bowl of butter and then into a barrel of flour. What a sight he was!

The farmer's wife yelled and chased him with a poker. The children laughed and almost fell on top of each other, trying to catch him; and how they screamed! Luckily for the duckling, the door was open. He got out of the house and found a hiding place beneath some bushes, in the newly fallen snow; and there he lay so still, as though there was hardly any life left in him.

It would be too horrible to tell of all the hardship and suffering the duckling experienced that long winter. It is enough to know that he did survive. When again the sun shone warmly and the larks began to sing, the duckling was lying among the reeds in the swamp. Spring had come!

He spread out his wings to fly. How strong and powerful they were! Before he knew it, he was far from the swamp and flying above a beautiful garden. The apple trees were blooming and the lilac bushes stretched their flower-covered branches over the water of a winding canal. Everything was so beautiful: so fresh and green. Out of a forest of rushes came three swans. They ruffled their feathers and floated so lightly on the water. The ugly duckling recognized the birds and felt again that strange sadness come over him.

"I shall fly over to them, those royal birds! And they can hack me to death because I, who am so ugly, dare to approach them! What difference does it make? It is better to be killed by them than to be bitten by the other ducks, and pecked by the hens, and kicked by the girl who tends the henyard; or to suffer through the winter."

And he lighted on the water and swam towards the magnificent swans. When they saw him they ruffled their feathers and started to swim in his direction. They were coming to meet him.

"Kill me," whispered the poor creature, and bent his head humbly while he waited for death. But what was that he saw in the water? It was his own reflection; and he was no longer an awkward, clumsy, grey bird, so ungainly and so ugly. He was a swan!

It does not matter that one has been born in the henyard as long as one has lain in a swan's egg.

He was thankful that he had known so much want, and gone through so much suffering, for it made him appreciate his present happiness and the loveliness of everything about him all the more. The swans made a circle around him and caressed him with their beaks.

Some children came out into the garden. They had brought bread with them to feed the swans. The youngest child shouted, "Look, there's a new one!" All the children joyfully clapped their hands, and they ran to tell their parents.

Cake and bread were cast on the water for the swans. Everyone agreed that the new swan was the most beautiful of them all. The older swans bowed towards him.

He felt so shy that he hid his head beneath his wing. He was too happy, but not proud, for a kind heart can never be proud. He thought of the time when he had been mocked and persecuted. And now everyone said that he was the most beautiful of the most beautiful birds. And the lilac bushes stretched their branches right down to the water for him. The sun shone so warm and brightly. He ruffled his feathers and raised his slender neck, while out of the joy in his heart, he thought, "Such happiness I did not dream of when I was the ugly duckling."

ENCHANTED BRIDE(GROOM)

A FEATURE OF VIRTUALLY ALL TALES that contain animal characters is the unquestioned acceptance of communication between human and animal (or non-human). One explanation that we have already considered (see "Little Red Riding Hood") is that the animal is often the symbolic representation of a particular aspect of the human character, since the fairy tale is first and foremost about people. The essential quality of an animal is its *otherness*; the ability to communicate notwithstanding, the animal represents the unknown, a representation of the shadowy world of instinct.

For the inexperienced young woman depicted in many fairy tales, marriage represents at best a challenge, at worst a threat. We must remember that the husband was often not of the young woman's choosing, so that the prospect was one very different from what we take for granted today. Whether the marriage was the outcome of economic realities (as in "East of the Sun...") or of suitable bloodlines (which amounted to much the same thing), the fact remains that the young bride-to-be was still the helpless bystander to the negotiations. To say the least, the prospect of sexual union with a male stranger was a step into the disturbing unknown, which explains why in this type of fairy tale the male often takes the form of an animal. While marriage represents elevation into womanhood, it brings with it also all the anxieties and even revulsion often associated with initiation into sexuality. Thus, Beauty is terrified by the prospect of a Beast; the girl in "East of the Sun, West of the Moon" is the victim of her mother's jealous suspicions about the White Bear; and the princess in "The Frog King," in hurling the frog against the wall, is finally responding to her anger and disgust at her importunate suitor.

As we might expect, the theme of love is introduced in all three of these tales, but from some rather unexpected angles. In "Beauty and the Beast," for example, the story deals with the gradual development of a daughter's love to embrace both father and husband, while in the somewhat similar "East of the Sun, West of the Moon," love grows out of the youngest daughter's discovery that an imposed liaison can nevertheless succeed when it is nurtured with trust and determination. By contrast, love in "The Frog King" only becomes possible after the princess's act of violent self-assertion that is also her declaration of independence from her father.

"The Frog King" also differs from the two previous tales in the rapid development of the central character—she goes from child to married woman in three pages. This "accelerated childhood" is in fact not an uncommon occurrence in fairy tale (we see something similar in "Snow White" and "Rapunzel," for instance); we are reminded that this is a world in which children are obliged to grow up fast. Certainly the princess's behavior at the beginning of the tale is childlike, as is her obedience to her father; the ending of the tale is noteworthy, since several well-known alternatives exist that invite quite distinct interpretations. The ending that you will read in this anthology is that preferred by the Grimms, although (as D.L. Ashliman reveals on his excellent website[1]) they altered the tale substantially between first and last editions, in part to make it less sexually explicit. An alternative ending, in which the princess permits the frog to sleep on her pillow for three nights and thus break his enchantment, was made popular by Edgar Taylor's first English translation of the Grimms' tales (1823); no doubt he saw such a display of forbearance and resignation as more befitting a well-brought-up young lady.[2] Also not to be forgotten is the ending wherein the princess is induced to kiss the frog in order to break his enchantment. Although scholars have had difficulty in tracing the origins of this particular climax to the story, it is nevertheless firmly entrenched in popular culture where it has provided considerable scope for those adopting a more irreverent approach to the tale.

In "The White Cat," we have an example of a "salon" tale, written by an aristocratic Frenchwoman, Madame la Comtesse d'Aulnoy (1650-1705), whose upper-class perspective is clearly visible in the self-conscious tone and opulent description that characterizes this tale. At the same time, there is no mistaking her debt to the folk tale in the extensive use she makes of the tale that Basile published as "Petrosinella" and the Grimms would later record as "Rapunzel." Reflective of the role these salons played for their predominantly female adherents, there is an interesting example of role-reversal here, in that the youngest prince's good fortune (not to mention that of his father and brothers) is entirely attributable to the assistance of the White Cat, and in that respect the tale may be seen as a contrast to "Beauty and the Beast." These

---

1   See <http://www.pitt.edu/~dash/frogking.html>.

2   The importance of being aware that a specific tale may have many variants is made clear by Alan Dundes in his essay "Fairy Tales from a Folkloristic Perspective" (p. 335).

two tales leave no doubt that the animal's gender is of major consequence. While the Beast's unfailing graciousness towards Beauty is neutralized by his barely restrained passion, there is no such tension between the prince and the White Cat, whose relationship matures gradually to a moment of supreme trust.

BEAUTY AND THE BEAST[1]

Madame Leprince de Beaumont

ONCE UPON A TIME THERE lived a merchant who was exceedingly rich. He had six children—three boys and three girls—and being a sensible man he spared no expense upon their education, but engaged tutors of every kind for them. All his daughters were pretty, but the youngest especially was admired by everybody. When she was small she was known simply as "the little beauty," and this name stuck to her, causing a great deal of jealousy on the part of her sisters.

This youngest girl was not only prettier than her sisters, but very much nicer. The two elder girls were very arrogant as a result of their wealth; they pretended to be great ladies, declining to receive the daughters of other merchants, and associating only with people of quality. Every day they went off to balls and theatres, and for walks in the park, with many a gibe at their little sister, who spent much of her time in reading good books.

Now these girls were known to be very rich, and in consequence were sought in marriage by many prominent merchants. The two eldest said they would never marry unless they could find a duke, or at least a count. But Beauty—this, as I have mentioned, was the name by which the youngest was known—very politely thanked all who proposed marriage to her, and said that she was too young at present, and that she wished to keep her father company for several years yet.

Suddenly the merchant lost his fortune, the sole property which remained to him being a small house in the country, a long way from the capital. With tears he broke it to his children that they would have to move to this house, where by working like peasants they might just be able to live.

The two elder girls replied that they did not wish to leave the town, and that they had several admirers who would be only too happy to marry them, notwithstanding

---

1   First published in 1756. This text from *Sleeping Beauty and Other Favourite Fairy Tales,* trans. Angela Carter (London: Gollancz, 1982).

their loss of fortune. But the simple maidens were mistaken: their admirers would no longer look at them, now that they were poor. Everybody disliked them on account of their arrogance, and folks declared that they did not deserve pity: in fact, that it was a good thing their pride had had a fall—a turn at minding sheep would teach them how to play the fine lady! "But we are very sorry for Beauty's misfortune," everybody added; "she is such a dear girl, and was always so considerate to poor people: so gentle, and with such charming manners!"

There were even several worthy men who would have married her, despite the fact that she was now penniless; but she told them she could not make up her mind to leave her poor father in his misfortune, and that she intended to go with him to the country, to comfort him and help him to work. Poor Beauty had been very grieved at first over the loss of her fortune, but she said to herself:

"However much I cry, I shall not recover my wealth, so I must try to be happy without it."

When they were established in the country the merchant and his family started working on the land. Beauty used to rise at four o'clock in the morning, and was busy all day looking after the house, and preparing dinner for the family. At first she found it very hard, for she was not accustomed to work like a servant, but at the end of a couple of months she grew stronger, and her health was improved by the work. When she had leisure she read, or played the harpsichord, or sang at her spinning-wheel.

Her two sisters, on the other hand, were bored to death; they did not get up till ten o'clock in the morning, and they idled about all day. Their only diversion was to bemoan the beautiful clothes they used to wear and the company they used to keep. "Look at our little sister," they would say to each other; "her tastes are so low and her mind so stupid that she is quite content with this miserable state of affairs."

The good merchant did not share the opinion of his two daughters, for he knew that Beauty was more fitted to shine in company than her sisters. He was greatly impressed by the girl's good qualities, and especially by her patience—for her sisters, not content with leaving her all the work of the house, never missed an opportunity of insulting her.

They had been living for a year in this seclusion when the merchant received a letter informing him that a ship on which he had some merchandise had just come safely home. The news nearly turned the heads of the two elder girls, for they thought that at last they would be able to quit their dull life in the country. When they saw their father ready to set out they begged him to bring them back dresses, furs, caps, and finery of every kind. Beauty asked for nothing, thinking to herself that all the money which the merchandise might yield would not be enough to satisfy her sisters' demands.

"You have not asked me for anything," said her father.

"As you are so kind as to think of me," she replied, "please bring me a rose, for there are none here."

Beauty had no real craving for a rose, but she was anxious not to seem to disparage the conduct of her sisters. The latter would have declared that she purposely asked for nothing in order to be different from them.

The merchant duly set forth; but when he reached his destination there was a law-suit over his merchandise, and after much trouble he returned poorer than he had been before. With only thirty miles to go before reaching home, he was already looking forward to the pleasure of seeing his children again, when he found he had to pass through a large wood. Here he lost himself. It was snowing horribly; the wind was so strong that twice he was thrown from his horse, and when night came on he made up his mind he must either die of hunger and cold or be eaten by the wolves that he could hear howling all about him.

Suddenly he saw, at the end of a long avenue of trees, a strong light. It seemed to be some distance away, but he walked towards it, and presently discovered that it came from a large palace, which was all lit up.

The merchant thanked heaven for sending him this help, and hastened to the castle. To his surprise, however, he found no one about in the courtyards. His horse, which had followed him, saw a large stable open and went in; and on finding hay and oats in readiness the poor animal, which was dying of hunger, set to with a will. The merchant tied him up in the stable, and approached the house, where he found not a soul. He entered a large room; here there was a good fire, and a table laden with food, but with a place laid for one only. The rain and snow had soaked him to the skin, so he drew near the fire to dry himself. "I am sure," he remarked to himself, "that the master of this house or his servants will forgive the liberty I am taking; doubtless they will be here soon."

He waited some considerable time; but eleven o'clock struck and still he had seen nobody. Being no longer able to resist his hunger he took a chicken and devoured it in two mouthfuls, trembling. Then he drank several glasses of wine, and becoming bolder ventured out of the room. He went through several magnificently furnished apartments, and finally found a room with a very good bed. It was now past midnight, and as he was very tired he decided to shut the door and go to bed.

It was ten o'clock the next morning when he rose, and he was greatly astonished to find a new suit in place of his own, which had been spoilt. "This palace," he said to himself, "must surely belong to some good fairy, who has taken pity on my plight."

He looked out of the window. The snow had vanished, and his eyes rested instead upon arbours of flowers—a charming spectacle. He went back to the room where he had supped the night before, and found there a little table with a cup of chocolate on it. "I thank you, Madam Fairy," he said aloud, "for being so kind as to think of my breakfast."

Having drunk his chocolate the good man went forth to look for his horse. As he passed under a bower of roses he remembered that Beauty had asked for one, and he plucked a spray from a mass of blooms. The very same moment he heard a terrible noise, and saw a beast coming towards him which was so hideous that he came near to fainting.

"Ungrateful wretch!" said the Beast, in a dreadful voice; "I have saved your life by receiving you into my castle, and in return you steal that which I love better than anything in the world—my roses. You shall pay for this with your life! I give you fifteen minutes to make your peace with Heaven."

The merchant threw himself on his knees and wrung his hands. "Pardon, my lord!" he cried; "one of my daughters had asked for a rose, and I did not dream I should be giving offence by picking one."

"I am not called 'my lord,'" answered the monster, "but 'The Beast.' I have no liking for compliments, but prefer people to say what they think. Do not hope therefore to soften me by flattery. You have daughters, you say; well, I am willing to pardon you if one of your daughters will come, of her own choice, to die in your place. Do not argue with me—go! And swear that if your daughters refuse to die in your place, you will come back again in three months."

The good man had no intention of sacrificing one of his daughters to this hideous monster, but he thought that at least he might have the pleasure of kissing them once again. He therefore swore to return, and the Beast told him he could go when he wished. "I do not wish you to go empty-handed," he added; "return to the room where you slept; you will find there a large empty box. Fill it with what you will; I will have it sent home for you."

With these words the Beast withdrew, leaving the merchant to reflect that if he must indeed die, at all events he would have the consolation of providing for his poor children.

He went back to the room where he had slept. He found there a large number of gold pieces, and with these he filled the box the Beast had mentioned. Having closed the latter, he took his horse, which was still in the stable, and set forth from the palace, as melancholy now as he had been joyous when he entered it.

The horse of its own accord took one of the forest roads, and in a few hours the good man reached his own little house. His children crowded round him, but at sight of them, instead of welcoming their caresses, he burst into tears. In his hand was the bunch of roses which he had brought for Beauty, and he gave it to her with these words:

"Take these roses, Beauty; it is dearly that your poor father will have to pay for them."

Thereupon he told his family of the dire adventure which had befallen him. On hearing the tale the two elder girls were in a great commotion, and began to upbraid Beauty for not weeping as they did. "See to what her smugness has brought this young chit," they said; "surely she might strive to find some way out of this trouble, as we do! But oh, dear me, no; her ladyship is so determined to be different that she can speak of her father's death without a tear!"

"It would be quite useless to weep," said Beauty. "Why should I lament my father's death? He is not going to die. Since the monster agrees to accept a daughter instead, I intend to offer myself to appease his fury. It will be a happiness to do so, for in dying I shall have the joy of saving my father, and of proving to him my devotion."

"No, sister," said her three brothers; "you shall not die; we will go in quest of this monster, and will perish under his blows if we cannot kill him."

"Do not entertain any such hopes, my children," said the merchant; "the power of this Beast is so great that I have not the slightest expectation of escaping him. I am touched by the goodness of Beauty's heart, but I will not expose her to death. I am old and have not much longer to live; and I shall merely lose a few years that will be regretted only on account of you, my dear children."

"I can assure you, father," said Beauty, "that you will not go to this palace without me. You cannot prevent me from following you. Although I am young I am not so very deeply in love with life, and I would rather be devoured by this monster than die of the grief which your loss would cause me." Words were useless. Beauty was quite determined to go to this wonderful palace, and her sisters were not sorry, for they regarded her good qualities with deep jealousy.

The merchant was so taken up with the sorrow of losing his daughter that he forgot all about the box which he had filled with gold. To his astonishment, when he had shut the door of his room and was about to retire for the night, there it was at the side of his bed! He decided not to tell his children that he had become so rich, for his elder daughters would have wanted to go back to town, and he had resolved to die in the country. He did confide his secret to Beauty, however, and the latter told him that during his absence they had entertained some visitors, amongst whom were two admirers of her sisters. She begged her father to let them marry; for she was of such a sweet nature that she loved them, and forgave them with all her heart the evil they had done her.

When Beauty set off with her father the two heartless girls rubbed their eyes with an onion, so as to seem tearful; but her brothers wept in reality, as did also the merchant. Beauty alone did not cry, because she did not want to add to their sorrow.

The horse took the road to the palace, and by evening they espied it, all lit up as before. An empty stable awaited the nag, and when the good merchant and his daughter entered the great hall, they found there a table magnificently laid for two people.

The merchant had not the heart to eat, but Beauty, forcing herself to appear calm, sat down and served him. Since the Beast had provided such splendid fare, she thought to herself, he must presumably be anxious to fatten her up before eating her.

When they had finished supper, they heard a terrible noise. With tears the merchant bade farewell to his daughter, for he knew it was the Beast. Beauty herself could not help trembling at the awful apparition, but she did her best to compose herself. The Beast asked her if she had come of her own free will, and she timidly answered that such was the case.

"You are indeed kind," said the Beast, "and I am much obliged to you. You, my good man, will depart tomorrow morning, and you must not think of coming back again. Good-bye, Beauty!"

"Good-bye, Beast!" she answered.

Thereupon the monster suddenly disappeared.

"Daughter," said the merchant, embracing Beauty, "I am nearly dead with fright. Let me be the one to stay here!"

"No, father," said Beauty, firmly, "you must go tomorrow morning, and leave me to the mercy of Heaven. Perhaps pity will be taken on me."

They retired to rest, thinking they would not sleep at all during the night, but they were hardly in bed before their eyes were closed in sleep. In her dreams there appeared to Beauty a lady, who said to her:

"Your virtuous character pleases me, Beauty. In thus undertaking to give your life to save your father you have performed an act of goodness which shall not go unrewarded."

When she woke up Beauty related this dream to her father. He was somewhat consoled by it, but could not refrain from loudly giving vent to his grief when the time came to tear himself away from his beloved child.

As soon as he had gone Beauty sat down in the great hall and began to cry. But she had plenty of courage, and after imploring divine protection she determined to grieve no more during the short time she had yet to live.

She was convinced that the Beast would devour her that night, but made up her mind that in the interval she would walk about and have a look at this beautiful castle, the splendour of which she could not but admire.

Imagine her surprise when she came upon a door on which were the words "Beauty's Room"! She quickly opened this door, and was dazzled by the magnificence of the appointments within. "They are evidently anxious that I should not be dull," she murmured, as she caught sight of a large bookcase, a harpsichord, and several volumes of music. A moment later another thought crossed her mind. "If I had only a day to spend here," she reflected, "such provision would surely not have been made for me."

This notion gave her fresh courage. She opened the bookcase, and found a book in which was written, in letters of gold:

"Ask for anything you wish: you are mistress of all here."

"Alas!" she said with a sigh, "my only wish is to see my poor father, and to know what he is doing."

As she said this to herself she glanced at a large mirror. Imagine her astonishment when she perceived her home reflected in it, and saw her father just approaching. Sorrow was written on his face; but when her sisters came to meet him it was impossible not to detect, despite the grimaces with which they tried to simulate grief, the satisfaction they felt at the loss of their sister. In a moment the vision faded away, yet Beauty could not but think that the Beast was very kind, and that she had nothing much to fear from him.

At midday she found the table laid, and during her meal she enjoyed an excellent concert, though the performers were invisible. But in the evening, as she was about to sit down at the table, she heard the noise made by the Beast, and quaked in spite of herself.

"Beauty," said the monster to her, "may I watch you have your supper?"

"You are master here," said the trembling Beauty.

"Not so," replied the Beast; "it is you who are mistress; you have only to tell me to go, if my presence annoys you, and I will go immediately. Tell me, now, do you not consider me very ugly?"

"I do," said Beauty, "since I must speak the truth; but I think you are also very kind."

"It is as you say," said the monster; "and in addition to being ugly, I lack intelligence. As I am well aware, I am a mere beast."

"It is not the way with stupid people," answered Beauty, "to admit a lack of intelligence. Fools never realise it."

"Sup well, Beauty," said the monster, "and try to banish dullness from your home— for all about you is yours, and I should be sorry to think you were not happy."

"You are indeed kind," said Beauty. "With one thing, I must own, I am well pleased, and that is your kind heart. When I think of that you no longer seem to be ugly."

"Oh yes," answered the Beast, "I have a good heart, right enough, but I am a monster."

"There are many men," said Beauty, "who make worse monsters than you, and I prefer you, notwithstanding your looks, to those who under the semblance of men hide false, corrupt, and ungrateful hearts."

The Beast replied that if only he had a grain of wit he would compliment her in the grand style by way of thanks; but that being so stupid he could only say he was much obliged.

Beauty ate with a good appetite, for she now had scarcely any fear of the Beast. But she nearly died of fright when he put this question to her:

"Beauty, will you be my wife?"

For some time she did not answer, fearing lest she might anger the monster by her refusal. She summoned up courage at last to say, rather fearfully, "No, Beast!"

The poor monster gave forth so terrible a sigh that the noise of it went whistling through the whole palace. But to Beauty's speedy relief the Beast sadly took his leave and left the room, turning several times as he did so to look once more at her. Left alone, Beauty was moved by great compassion for this poor Beast. "What a pity he is so ugly," she said, "for he is so good."

Beauty passed three months in the palace quietly enough. Every evening the Beast paid her a visit, and entertained her at supper by a display of much good sense, if not with what the world calls wit. And every day Beauty was made aware of fresh kindnesses on the part of the monster. Through seeing him often she had become accustomed to his ugliness, and far from dreading the moment of his visit, she frequently looked at her watch to see if it was nine o'clock, the hour when the Beast always appeared.

One thing alone troubled Beauty; every evening, before retiring to bed, the monster asked her if she would be his wife, and seemed overwhelmed with grief when she refused. One day she said to him:

"You distress me, Beast. I wish I could marry you, but I cannot deceive you by allowing you to believe that that can ever be. I will always be your friend—be content with that."

"Needs must," said the Beast. "But let me make the position plain. I know I am very terrible, but I love you very much, and I shall be very happy if you will only remain here. Promise that you will never leave me."

Beauty blushed at these words. She had seen in her mirror that her father was stricken down by the sorrow of having lost her, and she wished very much to see him again. "I would willingly promise to remain with you always," she said to the Beast, "but I have so great a desire to see my father again that I shall die of grief if you refuse me this boon."

"I would rather die myself than cause you grief," said the monster. "I will send you back to your father. You shall stay with him, and your Beast shall die of sorrow at your departure."

"No, no," said Beauty, crying; "I like you too much to wish to cause your death. I promise you I will return in eight days. You have shown me that my sisters are married, and that my brothers have joined the army. My father is all alone; let me stay with him one week."

"You shall be with him tomorrow morning," said the Beast. "But remember your promise. All you have to do when you want to return is to put your ring on a table when you are going to bed. Good-bye, Beauty!"

As usual, the Beast sighed when he said these last words, and Beauty went to bed quite down-hearted at having grieved him.

When she awoke the next morning she found she was in her father's house. She rang a little bell which stood by the side of her bed, and it was answered by their servant, who gave a great cry at sight of her. The good man came running at the noise, and was overwhelmed with joy at the sight of his dear daughter. Their embraces lasted for more than a quarter of an hour. When their transports had subsided, it occurred to Beauty that she had no clothes to put on; but the servant told her that she had just discovered in the next room a chest full of dresses trimmed with gold and studded with diamonds. Beauty felt grateful to the Beast for this attention, and having selected the simplest of the gowns she bade the servant pack up the others, as she wished to send them as presents to her sisters. The words were hardly out of her mouth when the chest disappeared. Her father expressed the opinion that the Beast wished her to keep them all for herself, and in a trice dresses and chest were back again where they were before.

When Beauty had dressed she learned that her sisters, with their husbands, had arrived. Both were very unhappy. The eldest had wedded an exceedingly handsome man, but the latter was so taken up with his own looks that he studied them from morning to night, and despised his wife's beauty. The second had married a man with plenty of brains, but he only used them to pay insults to everybody—his wife first and foremost.

The sisters were greatly mortified when they saw Beauty dressed like a princess, and more beautiful than the dawn. Her caresses were ignored, and the jealousy which they could not stifle only grew worse when she told them how happy she was. Out into the garden went the envious pair, there to vent their spleen to the full.

"Why should this chit be happier than we are?" each demanded of the other; "are we not much nicer than she is?"

"Sister," said the elder, "I have an idea. Let us try to persuade her to stay here longer than the eight days. Her stupid Beast will fly into a rage when he finds she has broken her word, and will very likely devour her."

"You are right, sister," said the other; "but we must make a great fuss of her if we are to make the plan successful."

With this plot decided upon they went upstairs again, and paid such attention to their little sister that Beauty wept for joy. When the eight days had passed the two sisters tore their hair, and showed such grief over her departure that she promised to remain another eight days.

Beauty reproached herself, nevertheless, with the grief she was causing to the poor Beast; moreover, she greatly missed not seeing him. On the tenth night of her stay in her father's house she dreamed that she was in the palace garden, where she saw the Beast lying on the grass nearly dead, and that he upbraided her for her ingratitude. Beauty woke up with a start, and burst into tears.

"I am indeed very wicked," she said, "to cause so much grief to a Beast who has shown me nothing but kindness. Is it his fault that he is so ugly, and has so few wits? He is good, and that makes up for all the rest. Why did I not wish to marry him? I should have been a good deal happier with him than my sisters are with their husbands. It is neither good looks nor brains in a husband that make a woman happy; it is beauty of character, virtue, kindness. All these qualities the Beast has. I admit I have no love for him, but he has my esteem, friendship, and gratitude. At all events I must not make him miserable, or I shall reproach myself all my life."

With these words Beauty rose and placed her ring on the table.

Hardly had she returned to her bed than she was asleep, and when she woke the next morning she saw with joy that she was in the Beast's palace. She dressed in her very best on purpose to please him, and nearly died of impatience all day, waiting for nine o'clock in the evening. But the clock struck in vain: no Beast appeared. Beauty now thought she must have caused his death, and rushed about the palace with loud despairing cries. She looked everywhere, and at last, recalling her dream, dashed into the garden by the canal, where she had seen him in her sleep. There she found the poor Beast lying unconscious, and thought he must be dead. She threw herself on his body, all her horror of his looks forgotten, and feeling his heart still beat, fetched water from the canal and threw it on his face.

The Beast opened his eyes and said to Beauty:

"You forgot your promise. The grief I felt as having lost you made me resolve to die of hunger; but I die content since I have the pleasure of seeing you once more."

"Dear Beast, you shall not die," said Beauty; "you shall live and become my husband. Here and now I offer you my hand, and swear that I will marry none but you. Alas, I fancied I felt only friendship for you, but the sorrow I have experienced clearly proves to me that I cannot live without you."

Beauty had scarce uttered these words when the castle became ablaze with lights before her eyes: fireworks, music—all proclaimed a feast. But these splendours were lost on her: she turned to her dear Beast, still trembling for his danger.

Judge of her surprise now! At her feet she saw no longer the Beast, who had disappeared, but a prince, more beautiful than Love himself, who thanked her for having put an end to his enchantment. With good reason were her eyes riveted upon the prince, but she asked him nevertheless where the Beast had gone.

"You see him at your feet," answered the prince. "A wicked fairy condemned me to retain that form until some beautiful girl should consent to marry me, and she forbade me to betray any sign of intelligence. You alone in all the world could show yourself susceptible to the kindness of my character, and in offering you my crown I do but discharge the obligation that I owe you."

In agreeable surprise Beauty offered her hand to the handsome prince, and assisted him to rise. Together they repaired to the castle, and Beauty was overcome with joy to find, assembled in the hall, her father and her entire family. The lady who had appeared to her in her dream had had them transported to the castle.

"Beauty," said this lady (who was a celebrated fairy), "come and receive the reward of your noble choice. You preferred merit to either beauty or wit, and you certainly deserve to find these qualities combined in one person. It is your destiny to become a great queen, but I hope that the pomp of royalty will not destroy your virtues. As for you, ladies," she continued, turning to Beauty's two sisters, "I know your hearts and the malice they harbour. Your doom is to become statues, and under the stone that wraps you round to retain all your feelings. You will stand at the door of your sister's palace, and I can visit no greater punishment upon you than that you shall be witnesses of her happiness. Only when you recognise your faults can you return to your present shape, and I am very much afraid that you will be statues for ever. Pride, ill-temper, greed, and laziness can all be corrected, but nothing short of a miracle will turn a wicked and envious heart."

In a trice, with a tap of her hand, the fairy transported them all to the prince's realm, where his subjects were delighted to see him again. He married Beauty, and they lived together for a long time in happiness the more perfect because it was founded on virtue.

EAST OF THE SUN AND WEST OF THE MOON[1]

Asbjørnsen and Moe

ONCE UPON A TIME THERE was a poor husbandman who had many children and little to give them in the way either of food or clothing. They were all pretty, but

---

1 First published in 1852. This text from *Popular Tales from the Norse*, trans. George Webbe Dasent (New York: D. Appleton, 1859).

the prettiest of all was the youngest daughter, who was so beautiful that there were no bounds to her beauty.

So once—it was late on a Thursday evening in autumn, and wild weather outside, terribly dark, and raining so heavily and blowing so hard that the walls of the cottage shook again—they were all sitting together by the fireside, each of them busy with something or other, when suddenly someone rapped three times against the window-pane. The man went out to see what could be the matter, and when he got out there stood a great big white bear.

"Good-evening to you," said the White Bear.

"Good-evening," said the man.

"Will you give me your youngest daughter?" said the White Bear; "if you will, you shall be as rich as you are now poor."

Truly the man would have had no objection to being rich, but he thought to himself: "I must first ask my daughter about this," so he went in and told them that there was a great white bear outside who had faithfully promised to make them all rich if he might but have the youngest daughter.

She said no, and would not hear of it; so the man went out again, and settled with the White Bear that he should come again next Thursday evening, and get her answer. Then the man persuaded her, and talked so much to her about the wealth that they would have, and what a good thing it would be for herself, that at last she made up her mind to go, and washed and mended all her rags, made herself as smart as she could, and held herself in readiness to set out. Little enough had she to take away with her.

Next Thursday evening the White Bear came to fetch her. She seated herself on his back with her bundle, and thus they departed. When they had gone a great part of the way, the White Bear said: "Are you afraid?"

"No, that I am not," said she.

"Keep tight hold of my fur, and then there is no danger," said he.

And thus she rode far, far away, until they came to a great mountain. Then the White Bear knocked on it, and a door opened, and they went into a castle where there were many brilliantly lighted rooms which shone with gold and silver, likewise a large hall in which there was a well-spread table, and it was so magnificent that it would be hard to make anyone understand how splendid it was. The White Bear gave her a silver bell, and told her that when she needed anything she had but to ring this bell, and what she wanted would appear. So after she had eaten, and night was drawing near, she grew sleepy after her journey, and thought she would like to go to bed. She rang the bell, and scarcely had she touched it before she found herself in a chamber where a bed stood ready made for her, which was as pretty as anyone could wish to sleep in. It had pillows of silk, and curtains of silk fringed with gold, and everything that was in the room was of gold or silver; but when she had lain down and put out the light, a man came and lay down beside her, and behold it was the White Bear, who cast off the form of a beast during the night. She never saw him, however, for he always came after she had put out her light, and went away before daylight appeared.

So all went well and happily for a time, but then she began to be very sad and sorrowful, for all day long she had to go about alone; and she did so wish to go home to her father and mother and brothers and sisters. Then the White Bear asked what it was that she wanted, and she told him that it was so dull there in the mountain, and that she had to go about all alone, and that in her parents' house at home there were all her brothers and sisters, and it was because she could not go to them that she was so sorrowful.

"There might be a cure for that," said the White Bear, "if you would but promise me never to talk with your mother alone, but only when the others are there too; for she will take hold of your hand," he said, "and will want to lead you into a room to talk with you alone; but that you must by no means do, or you will bring great misery on both of us."

So one Sunday the White Bear came and said that they could now set out to see her father and mother, and they journeyed thither, she sitting on his back, and they went a long, long way, and it took a long, long time; but at last they came to a large white farmhouse, and her brothers and sisters were running outside it, playing, and it was so pretty that it was a pleasure to look at it.

"Your parents dwell here now," said the White Bear; "but do not forget what I said to you, or you will do much harm both to yourself and me."

"No, indeed," said she, "I shall never forget"; and as soon as she was at home the White Bear turned round and went back again.

There were such rejoicings when she went in to her parents that it seemed as if they would never come to an end. Everyone thought that he could never be sufficiently grateful to her for all she had done for them all. Now they had everything that they wanted, and everything was as good as it could be. They all asked her how she was getting on where she was. All was well with her too, she said; and she had everything that she could want. What other answers she gave I cannot say, but I am pretty sure that they did not learn much from her. But in the afternoon, after they had dined at mid-day, all happened just as the White Bear had said. Her mother wanted to talk with her alone in her own chamber. But she remembered what the White Bear had said, and would on no account go. "What we have to say can be said at any time," she answered. But somehow or other her mother at last persuaded her, and she was forced to tell the whole story. So she told how every night a man came and lay down beside her when the lights were all put out, and how she never saw him, because he always went away before it grew light in the morning, and how she continually went about in sadness, thinking how happy she would be if she could but see him, and how all day long she had to go about alone, and it was so dull and solitary. "Oh!" cried the mother, in horror, "you are very likely sleeping with a troll! But I will teach you a way to see him. You shall have a bit of one of my candles, which you can take away with you hidden in your breast. Look at him with that when he is asleep, but take care not to let any tallow drop upon him."

So she took the candle, and hid it in her breast, and when evening drew near the White Bear came to fetch her away. When they had gone some distance on their way, the White Bear asked her if everything had not happened just as he had foretold, and she could not own but that it had. "Then, if you have done what your mother wished," said he, "you have brought great misery on both of us." "No," she said, "I have not done anything at all." So when she had reached home and had gone to bed, it was just the same as it had been before, and a man came and lay down beside her, and late at night, when she could hear that he was sleeping, she got up and kindled a light, lit her candle, let her light shine on him, and saw him, and he was the handsomest prince that eyes had ever beheld, and she loved him so much that it seemed to her that she must die if she did not kiss him that very moment. So she did kiss him; but while she was doing it she let three drops of hot tallow fall upon his shirt, and he awoke. "What have you done now?" said he; "you have brought misery on both of us. If you had but held out for the space of one year I should have been free. I have a stepmother who has bewitched me so that I am a white bear by day and a man by night; but now all is at an end between you and me, and I must leave you, and go to her. She lives in a castle which lies east of the sun and west of the moon, and there too is a princess with a nose which is three ells long, and she now is the one whom I must marry."

She wept and lamented, but all in vain, for go he must. Then she asked him if she could not go with him. But no, that could not be. "Can you tell me the way then, and I will seek you—that I may surely be allowed to do!"

"Yes, you may do that," said he; "but there is no way thither. It lies east of the sun and west of the moon, and never would you find your way there."

When she awoke in the morning both the Prince and the castle were gone, and she was lying on a small green patch in the midst of a dark, thick wood. By her side lay the self-same bundle of rags which she had brought with her from her own home. So when she had rubbed the sleep out of her eyes, and wept till she was weary, she set out on her way, and thus she walked for many and many a long day, until at last she came to a great mountain. Outside it an aged woman was sitting, playing with a golden apple. The girl asked her if she knew the way to the Prince who lived with his stepmother in the castle which lay east of the sun and west of the moon, and who was to marry a princess with a nose which was three ells long. "How do you happen to know about him?" enquired the old woman; "maybe you are she who ought to have had him." "Yes, indeed, I am," she said. "So it is you, then?" said the old woman; "I know nothing about him but that he dwells in a castle which is east of the sun and west of the moon. You will be a long time in getting to it, if ever you get to it at all; but you shall have the loan of my horse, and then you can ride on it to an old woman who is a neighbor of mine: perhaps she can tell you about him. When you have got there you must just strike the horse beneath the left ear and bid it go home again; but you may take the golden apple with you."

So the girl seated herself on the horse, and rode for a long, long way, and at last she came to the mountain, where an aged woman was sitting outside with a gold carding-comb. The girl asked her if she knew the way to the castle which lay east of the sun and west of the moon; but she said what the first old woman had said: "I know nothing about it, but that it is east of the sun and west of the moon, and that you will be a long time in getting to it, if ever you get there at all; but you may have the loan of my horse, and then you can ride on it to an old woman who lives the nearest to me: perhaps she may know where the castle is, and when you have got to her you may just strike the horse beneath the left ear and bid it go home again." Then she gave her the gold carding-comb, for it might, perhaps, be of use to her, she said.

So the girl seated herself on the horse, and rode a wearisome long way onwards again, and after a very long time she came to a great mountain, where an aged woman was sitting, spinning at a golden spinning-wheel. Of this woman, too, she enquired if she knew the way to the Prince, and where to find the castle which lay east of the sun and west of the moon. But it was only the same thing once again. "Maybe it was you who should have had the Prince," said the old woman. "Yes, indeed, I should have been the one," said the girl. But this old crone knew the way no better than the others—it was east of the sun and west of the moon, she knew that, "and you will be a long time in getting to it, if ever you get to it at all," she said; "but you may have the loan of my horse, and I think you had better ride to the East Wind, and ask him: perhaps he may know where the castle is, and will blow you thither. But when you have got to him you must just strike the horse beneath the left ear, and he will come home again." And then she gave her the golden spinning-wheel, saying: "Perhaps you may find that you have a use for it."

The girl had to ride for a great many days, and for a long and wearisome time, before she got there; but at last she did arrive, and then she asked the East Wind if he could tell her the way to the Prince who dwelt east of the sun and west of the moon. "Well," said the East Wind, "I have heard tell of the Prince, and of his castle, but I do not know the way to it, for I have never blown so far; but, if you like, I will go with you to my brother the West Wind: he may know that, for he is much stronger than

I am. You may sit on my back, and then I can carry you there." So she seated herself on his back, and they did go so swiftly! When they got there, the East Wind went in and said that the girl whom he had brought was the one who ought to have had the Prince up at the castle which lay east of the sun and west of the moon, and that now she was travelling about to find him again, so he had come there with her, and would like to hear if the West Wind knew whereabouts the castle was. "No," said the West Wind; "so far as that have I never blown: but if you like I will go with you to the South Wind, for he is much stronger than either of us, and he has roamed far and wide, and perhaps he can tell you what you want to know. You may seat yourself on my back, and then I will carry you to him."

So she did this, and journeyed to the South Wind, neither was she very long on the way. When they had got there, the West Wind asked him if he could tell her the way to the castle that lay east of the sun and west of the moon, for she was the girl who ought to marry the Prince who lived there. "Oh, indeed!" said the South Wind, "is that she? Well," said he, "I have wandered about a great deal in my time, and in all kinds of places, but I have never blown so far as that. If you like, however, I will go with you to my brother the North Wind; he is the oldest and strongest of all of us, and if he does not know where it is, no one in the whole world will be able to tell you. You may sit upon my back, and then I will carry you there." So she seated herself on his back, and off he went from his house in great haste, and they were not long on the way. When they came near the North Wind's dwelling, he was so wild and frantic that they felt cold gusts a long while before they got there. "What do you want?" he roared out from afar, and they froze as they heard. Said the South Wind: "It is I, and this is she who should have had the Prince who lives in the castle which lies east of the sun and west of the moon. And now she wishes to ask you if you have ever been there, and can tell her the way, for she would gladly find him again."

"Yes," said the North Wind, "I know where it is. I once blew an aspen leaf there, but I was so tired that for many days afterwards I was not able to blow at all. However, if you really are anxious to go there, and are not afraid to go with me, I will take you on my back, and try if I can blow you there."

"Get there I must," said she; "and if there is any way of going I will; and I have no fear, no matter how fast you go."

"Very well then," said the North Wind; "but you must sleep here tonight, for if we are ever to get there we must have the day before us."

The North Wind woke her betimes next morning, and puffed himself up, and made himself so big and so strong that it was frightful to see him, and away they went, high up through the air, as if they would not stop until they had reached the very end of the world. Down below there was such a storm! It blew down woods and houses, and when they were above the sea the ships were wrecked by hundreds. And thus they tore on and on, and a long time went by, and then yet more time passed, and still they were above the sea, and the North Wind grew tired, and more tired, and at last so utterly weary that he was scarcely able to blow any longer, and he sank and sank, lower and lower, until at last he went so low that the crests of the waves dashed against the heels of the poor girl he was carrying. "Art thou afraid?" said the North Wind. "I have no fear," said she; and it was true. But they were not very, very far from land, and there was just enough strength left in the North Wind to enable him to throw her on to the shore, immediately under the windows of a castle which lay east of the sun and west of the moon; but then he was so weary and worn out that he was forced to rest for several days before he could go to his own home again.

Next morning she sat down beneath the walls of the castle to play with the golden apple, and the first person she saw was the maiden with the long nose, who was to have the Prince. "How much do you want for that gold apple of yours, girl?" said she, opening the window. "It can't be bought either for gold or money," answered the girl. "If it cannot be bought either for gold or money, what will buy it? You may say what you please," said the Princess.

"Well, if I may go to the Prince who is here, and be with him tonight, you shall have it," said the girl who had come with the North Wind. "You may do that," said the Princess, for she had made up her mind what she would do. So the Princess got the golden apple, but when the girl went up to the Prince's apartment that night he was asleep, for the Princess had so contrived it. The poor girl called to him, and shook him, and between whiles she wept; but she could not wake him. In the morning, as soon as day dawned, in came the Princess with the long nose, and drove her out again. In the daytime she sat down once more beneath the windows of the castle, and began to card with her golden carding-comb; and then all happened as it had happened before. The princess asked her what she wanted for it, and she replied that it was not for sale, either for gold or money, but that if she could get leave to go to the Prince, and be with him during the night, she should have it. But when she went up to the Prince's room he was again asleep, and, let her call him; or shake him, or weep as she would, he still slept on, and she could not put any life in him. When daylight came in the morning, the Princess with the long nose came too, and once more drove her away. When day had quite come, the girl seated herself under the castle windows, to spin with her golden spinning-wheel, and the Princess with the long nose wanted to have that also. So she opened the window, and asked what she would take for it. The girl said what she had said on each of the former occasions—that it was not for sale either for gold or for money, but if she could get leave to go to the Prince who lived there, and be with him during the night, she should have it.

"Yes," said the Princess, "I will gladly consent to that."

But in that place there were some Christian folk who had been carried off, and they had been sitting in the chamber which was next to that of the Prince, and had heard how a woman had been in there who had wept and called on him two nights running, and they told the Prince of this. So that evening, when the Princess came once more with her sleeping-drink, he pretended to drink, but threw it away behind him, for he suspected that it was a sleeping-drink. So, when the girl went into the Prince's room this time he was awake, and she had to tell him how she had come there. "You have come just in time," said the Prince, "for I should have been married tomorrow; but I will not have the long-nosed Princess, and you alone can save me. I will say that I want to see what my bride can do, and bid her wash the shirt which has the three drops of tallow on it. This she will consent to do, for she does not know that it is you who let them fall on it; but no one can wash them out but one born of Christian folk: it cannot be done by one of a pack of trolls; and then I will say that no one shall ever be my bride but the woman who can do this, and I know that you can." There was great joy and gladness between them all that night, but the next day, when the wedding was to take place, the Prince said, "I must see what my bride can do." "That you may do," said the stepmother.

"I have a fine shirt which I want to wear as my wedding shirt, but three drops of tallow have got upon it which I want to have washed off, and I have vowed to marry no one but the woman who is able to do it. If she cannot do that, she is not worth having."

Well, that was a very small matter, they thought, and agreed to do it. The Princess with the long nose began to wash as well as she could, but the more she washed and rubbed, the larger the spots grew. "Ah! you can't wash at all," said the old troll-hag, who was her mother. "Give it to me." But she too had not had the shirt very long in her hands before it looked worse still, and the more she washed it and rubbed it, the larger and blacker grew the spots.

So the other trolls had to come and wash, but, the more they did, the blacker and uglier grew the shirt, until at length it was as black as if it had been up the chimney. "Oh," cried the Prince, "not one of you is good for anything at all! There is a beggar-girl sitting outside the window, and I'll be bound that she can wash better than any of you! Come in, you girl there!" he cried. So she came in. "Can you wash this shirt clean?" he cried. "Oh! I don't know," she said; "but I will try." And no sooner had she taken the shirt and dipped it in the water than it was white as driven snow, and even whiter than that. "I will marry you," said the Prince.

Then the old troll-hag flew into such a rage that she burst, and the Princess with the long nose and all the little trolls must have burst too, for they have never been heard of since. The Prince and his bride set free all the Christian folk who were imprisoned there, and took away with them all the gold and silver that they could carry, and moved far away from the castle which lay east of the sun and west of the moon.

THE FROG KING, OR IRON HEINRICH[1]

Jacob and Wilhelm Grimm

IN OLDEN TIMES, WHEN WISHING still helped, there lived a king, whose daughters were all beautiful, but the youngest was so beautiful that even the sun, who had seen many things, was filled with wonder every time he shone upon her face. Not far from the king's palace there was a great, dark forest, and under an old lime tree in the forest there was a spring. When the weather was very hot, the princess went out to the forest and sat near the edge of the cool spring. And when the time hung heavy on her hands, she took a golden ball, threw it into the air and caught it. It was her favorite plaything.

One day it so happened that when she held out her little hand to catch the golden ball, the ball passed it by, fell to the ground, and rolled straight into the water. The princess followed the ball with her eyes, but it disappeared, and the spring was deep, so deep that you couldn't see the bottom. She began to cry; she cried louder and louder, she was inconsolable. As she was lamenting, someone called out to her: "What's the matter, princess? Why, to hear you wailing, a stone would take pity." She looked to see where the voice came from and saw a frog sticking his big ugly head out of the water. "Oh, it's you, you old splasher," she said. "I'm crying because my ball has fallen into the spring." "Stop crying," said the frog. "I believe I can help you, but what will you give me if I bring you your plaything?" "Anything you like, dear frog," she said. "My clothes, my beads, my jewels, even the golden crown I'm wearing." The frog replied: "I don't want your clothes, your beads and jewels, or your golden crown. But if you will love me, if you will let me be your companion and playmate, and sit at your table and eat from your golden plate and drink from your golden cup and sleep in your bed, if you promise me that, I'll go down and fetch you your golden ball." "Oh yes," she said, "I promise you anything you want, if only you'll bring me my ball." But she thought: "What nonsense that silly frog talks; he lives in the water with other frogs and croaks; how can he be a companion to anybody?"

Once the frog had her promise, he put his head down and dived, and in a little while he came swimming back to the surface. He had her golden ball in his mouth and he tossed it onto the grass. When she saw her beautiful plaything, the princess was very happy. She picked it up and ran off with it. "Wait, wait," cried the frog. "Take me with you, I can't run like you." He croaked and he croaked at the top of his lungs, but it did him no good. The princess didn't listen. She hurried home and soon forgot

---

1 First published in 1812/15, in the first edition of *Kinder- und Hausmärchen*. This text from the second edition (1819), from *Grimms' Tales for Young and Old*, trans. Ralph Manheim (Garden City, NY: Anchor Press, 1977).

the poor frog. There was nothing he could do but go back down into his spring.

The next day, when she had sat down to table with the king and all his courtiers and was eating from her golden plate, something came hopping *plip plop, plip plop,* up the marble steps. When it reached the top, it knocked at the door and cried out: "Princess, youngest princess, let me in." She ran to see who was there, and when she opened the door, she saw the frog. She closed the door as fast as she could and went back to the table. She was frightened to death. The king saw that her heart was going pit-a-pat and said: "What are you afraid of, my child? Is there a giant outside come to take you away?" "Oh no," she said. "It's not a giant, but only a nasty frog." "What does a frog want of you?" "O father dear, yesterday when I was playing beside the spring in the forest, my golden ball fell in the water. And because I was crying so, the frog got it for me, and because he insisted, I promised he could be my companion. I never thought he'd get out of his spring. And now he's outside and he wants to come in after me." Then the frog knocked a second time and cried out:

"Princess, youngest princess,
  Let me in.
  Don't you remember what
  You promised yesterday
  By the cool spring?
  Princess, youngest princess,
  Let me in."

Then the king said: "When you make a promise, you must keep it; just go and let him in." She went and opened the door; the frog hopped in and followed close at her heels. There he sat and cried out: "Lift me up beside you." She didn't know what to do, but the king ordered her to obey. Once the frog was on the chair, he wanted to be on the table, and once he was on the table, he said: "Now push your golden plate up closer to me, so we can eat together." She did as he asked, but anyone could see she wasn't happy about it. The frog enjoyed his meal, but almost every bite stuck in the princess's throat. Finally he said: "I've had enough to eat and now I'm tired, so carry me to your room and prepare your silken bed. Then we'll lie down and sleep." The princess began to cry. She was afraid of the cold frog; she didn't dare touch him and now he wanted to sleep in her lovely clean bed. But the king grew angry and said: "He helped you when you were in trouble and you mustn't despise him now." Then she picked him up between thumb and forefinger, carried him upstairs, and put him down in a corner. But when she lay down in the bed, he came crawling over and said: "I'm tired. I want to sleep as much as you do; pick me up or I'll tell your father." At that she grew very angry, picked him up and dashed him against the wall with all her might. "Now you'll get your rest, you nasty frog."

But when he fell to the floor, he wasn't a frog any longer; he was a king's son with beautiful smiling eyes. At her father's bidding, he became her dear companion and husband. He told her that a wicked witch had put a spell on him and that no one but she alone could have freed him from the spring, and that they would go to his kingdom together the next day. Then they fell asleep and in the morning when the sun woke them a carriage drove up, drawn by eight white horses in golden harness, with white ostrich plumes on their heads, and behind it stood the young king's servant, the faithful Heinrich. Faithful Heinrich had been so sad when his master was turned into a frog that he had had three iron bands forged around his heart, to keep it from bursting with grief and sadness. The carriage had come to take the young king back to his kingdom. Faithful Heinrich lifted the two of them in and sat down again in back, overjoyed that his master had been set free. When they had gone a bit of the way, the prince heard a cracking sound behind him, as though something had broken. He turned around and cried out:

"Heinrich, the carriage is falling apart."

"No, master, it's only an iron ring.
I had it forged around my heart
For fear that it would break in two
When, struck by cruel magic, you
Were turned to a frog in a forest spring."

Once again and yet once again, the cracking was heard, and each time the king's son thought the carriage was falling to pieces, but it was only the bands snapping and falling away from faithful Heinrich's heart, because his master had been set free and was happy.

THE WHITE CAT[1]

Madame la Comtesse d'Aulnoy

ONCE UPON A TIME THERE was a king who had three sons, who were all so clever and brave that he began to be afraid that they would want to reign over the kingdom before he was dead. Now the King, though he felt that he was growing old, did not at all wish to give up the government of his kingdom while he could still manage it very well, so he thought the best way to live in peace would be to divert the minds of his sons by promises which he could always get out of when the time came for keeping them.

So he sent for them all, and, after speaking to them kindly, he added:

"You will quite agree with me, my dear children, that my great age makes it impossible for me to look after my affairs of state as carefully as I once did. I begin to fear that this may affect the welfare of my subjects, therefore I wish that one of you should succeed to my crown; but in return for such a gift as this it is only right that you should do something for me. Now, as I think of retiring into the country, it seems to me that a pretty, lively, faithful little dog would be very good company for me; so, without any regard for your ages, I promise that the one who brings me the most beautiful little dog shall succeed me at once."

The three Princes were greatly surprised by their father's sudden fancy for a little dog, but as it gave the two younger ones a chance they would not otherwise have had of being king, and as the eldest was too polite to make any objection, they accepted the commission with pleasure. They bade farewell to the King, who gave them presents of silver and precious stones, and appointed to meet them at the same hour, in the same place, after a year had passed, to see the little dogs they had brought for him.

Then they went together to a castle which was about a league from the city, accompanied by all their particular friends, to whom they gave a grand banquet, and the three brothers promised to be friends always, to share whatever good fortune befell them, and not to be parted by any envy or jealousy; and so they set out, agreeing to meet at the same castle at the appointed time, to present themselves before the King together. Each one took a different road, and the two eldest met with many adventures; but it is about the youngest that you are going to hear. He was young, and gay, and handsome, and knew everything that a prince ought to know; and as for his courage, there was simply no end to it.

---

1   First published in 1698. This text from *The Blue Fairy Book*, adapted by Minnie Wright, comp. Andrew Lang, 1889 (repr. New York: Dover, 1974).

Hardly a day passed without his buying several dogs—big and little, greyhounds, mastiffs, spaniels, and lapdogs. As soon as he had bought a pretty one, he was sure to see a still prettier, and then he had to get rid of all the others and buy that one, as, being alone, he found it impossible to take thirty or forty thousand dogs about with him. He journeyed from day to day, not knowing where he was going, until at last, just at nightfall, he reached a great, gloomy forest. He did not know his way, and, to make matters worse, it began to thunder, and the rain poured down. He took the first path he could find, and after walking for a long time he fancied he saw a faint light, and began to hope that he was coming to some cottage where he might find shelter for the night. At length, guided by the light, he reached the door of the most splendid castle he could have imagined. This door was of gold covered with carbuncles,[1] and it was the pure red light which shone from them that had shown him the way through the forest. The walls were of the finest porcelain in all the most delicate colours, and the Prince saw that all the stories he had ever read were pictured upon them; but as he was quite terribly wet, and the rain still fell in torrents, he could not stay to look about any more, but came back to the golden door. There he saw a deer's foot hanging by a chain of diamonds, and he began to wonder who could live in this magnificent castle.

"They must feel very secure against robbers," he said to himself. "What is to hinder anyone from cutting off that chain and digging out those carbuncles, and making himself rich for life?"

He pulled the deer's foot, and immediately a silver bell sounded and the door flew open, but the Prince could see nothing but numbers of hands in the air, each holding a torch. He was so much surprised that he stood quite still, until he felt himself pushed forward by other hands, so that, though he was somewhat uneasy, he could not help going on. With his hand on his sword, to be prepared for whatever might happen, he entered a hall paved with lapis-lazuli,[2] while two lovely voices sang:

> "The hands you see floating above
> Will swiftly your bidding obey;
> If your heart dreads not conquering Love,
> In this place you may fearlessly stay."

The Prince could not believe that any danger threatened him when he was welcomed in this way, so, guided by the mysterious hands, he went towards a door of coral, which opened of its own accord, and he found himself in a vast hall of mother-

---

1   carbuncle: A bright red gem.
2   lapis-lazuli: A bright blue mineral.

of-pearl, out of which opened a number of other rooms, glittering with thousands of lights, and full of such beautiful pictures and precious things that the Prince felt quite bewildered. After passing through sixty rooms, the hands that conducted him stopped, and the Prince saw a most comfortable-looking arm-chair drawn up close to the chimney-corner; at the same moment the fire lighted itself, and the pretty, soft, clever hands took off the Prince's wet, muddy clothes, and presented him with fresh ones made of the richest stuffs, all embroidered with gold and emeralds. He could not help admiring everything he saw, and the deft way in which the hands waited on him, though they sometimes appeared so suddenly that they made him jump.

When he was quite ready—and I can assure you that he looked very different from the wet and weary Prince who had stood outside in the rain, and pulled the deer's foot—the hands led him to a splendid room, upon the walls of which were painted the histories of Puss in Boots and a number of other famous cats. The table was laid for supper with two golden plates, and golden spoons and forks, and the sideboard was covered with dishes and glasses of crystal set with precious stones. The Prince was wondering who the second place could be for, when suddenly in came about a dozen cats carrying guitars and rolls of music, who took their places at one end of the room, and under the direction of a cat who beat time with a roll of paper began to mew in every imaginable key, and to draw their claws across the strings of the guitars, making the strangest kind of music that could be heard. The Prince hastily stopped up his ears, but even then the sight of these comical musicians sent him into fits of laughter.

"What funny thing shall I see next?" he said to himself, and instantly the door opened, and in came a tiny figure covered by a long black veil. It was conducted by two cats wearing black mantles and carrying swords, and a large party of cats followed, who brought in cages full of rats and mice.

The Prince was so much astonished that he thought he must be dreaming, but the little figure came up to him and threw back its veil, and he saw that it was the loveliest little white cat it is possible to imagine. She looked very young and very sad, and in a sweet little voice that went straight to his heart she said to the Prince:

"King's son, you are welcome; the Queen of the Cats is glad to see you."

"Lady Cat," replied the Prince, "I thank you for receiving me so kindly, but surely you are no ordinary pussy-cat? Indeed, the way you speak and the magnificence of your castle prove it plainly."

"King's son," said the White Cat, "I beg you to spare me these compliments, for I am not used to them. But now," she added, "let supper be served, and let the musicians be silent, as the Prince does not understand what they are saying."

So the mysterious hands began to bring in the supper, and first they put on the table two dishes, one containing stewed pigeons and the other a fricassée of fat mice.

The sight of the latter made the Prince feel as if he could not enjoy his supper at all; but the White Cat seeing this assured him that the dishes intended for him were prepared in a separate kitchen, and he might be quite certain that they contained neither rats nor mice; and the Prince felt so sure that she would not deceive him that he had no more hesitation in beginning. Presently he noticed that on the little paw that was next him the White Cat wore a bracelet containing a portrait, and he begged to be allowed to look at it. To his great surprise he found it represented an extremely handsome young man, who was so like himself that it might have been his own portrait! The White Cat sighed as he looked at it, and seemed sadder than ever, and the Prince dared not ask any questions for fear of displeasing her; so he began to talk about other things, and found that she was interested in all the subjects he cared for himself, and seemed to know quite well what was going on in the world. After supper they went into another room, which was fitted up as a theatre, and the cats acted and danced for their amusement, and then the White Cat said good-night to him, and the hands conducted him into a room he had not seen before, hung with tapestry worked with butterflies' wings of every colour; there were mirrors that reached from the ceiling to the floor, and a little white bed with curtains of gauze tied up with ribbons. The Prince went to bed in silence, as he did not quite know how to begin a conversation with the hands that waited on him, and in the morning he was awakened by a noise and confusion outside his window, and the hands came and quickly dressed him in hunting costume. When he looked out, all the cats were assembled in the courtyard, some leading greyhounds, some blowing horns, for the White Cat was going out hunting. The hands led a wooden horse up to the Prince and seemed to expect him to mount it, at which he was very indignant; but it was no use for him to object, for he speedily found himself upon its back, and it pranced gaily off with him.

The White Cat herself was riding a monkey, which climbed even up to the eagles' nests when she had a fancy for the young eaglets. Never was there a pleasanter hunting party, and when they returned to the castle the Prince and the White Cat supped together as before, but when they had finished she offered him a crystal goblet, which must have contained a magic draught, for, as soon as he had swallowed its contents, he forgot everything, even the little dog that he was seeking for the King; and only thought how happy he was to be with the White Cat! And so the days passed, in every kind of amusement, until the year was nearly gone. The Prince had forgotten all about meeting his brothers: he did not even know what country he belonged to; but the White Cat knew when he ought to go back, and one day she said to him:

"Do you know that you have only three days left to look for the little dog for your father, and your brothers have found lovely ones?"

Then the Prince suddenly recovered his memory, and cried:

"What can have made me forget such an important thing? my whole fortune depends upon it; and even if I could in such a short time find a dog pretty enough to gain me a kingdom, where should I find a horse who could carry me all that way in three days?" And he began to be very vexed. But the White Cat said to him: "King's son, do not trouble yourself; I am your friend, and will make everything easy for you. You can still stay here for a day, as the good wooden horse can take you to your country in twelve hours."

"I thank you, beautiful Cat," said the Prince; "but what good will it do me to get back if I have not a dog to take to my father?"

"See here," answered the White Cat, holding up an acorn; "there is a prettier one in this than in the Dog-star!"

"Oh! White Cat dear," said the Prince, "how unkind you are to laugh at me now!"

"Only listen," she said, holding the acorn to his ear.

And inside it he distinctly heard a tiny voice say: "Bow-wow!"

The Prince was delighted, for a dog that can be shut up in an acorn must be very small indeed. He wanted to take it out and look at it, but the White Cat said it would be better not to open the acorn till he was before the King, in case the tiny dog should be cold on the journey. He thanked her a thousand times, and said good-bye quite sadly when the time came for him to set out.

"The days have passed so quickly with you," he said, "I only wish I could take you with me now."

But the White Cat shook her head and sighed deeply in answer.

After all the Prince was the first to arrive at the castle where he had agreed to meet his brothers, but they came soon after, and stared in amazement when they saw the wooden horse in the courtyard jumping like a hunter.

The Prince met them joyfully, and they began to tell him all their adventures; but he managed to hide from them what he had been doing, and even led them to think that a turnspit dog[1] which he had with him was the one he was bringing for the King. Fond as they all were of one another, the two eldest could not help being glad to think that their dogs certainly had a better chance. The next morning they started in the same chariot. The elder brothers carried in baskets two such tiny, fragile dogs that they hardly dared to touch them. As for the turnspit, he ran after the chariot, and got so covered with mud that one could hardly see what he was like at all. When they reached the palace, everyone crowded round to welcome them as they went into the King's great hall; and when the two brothers presented their little dogs, nobody could decide which was the prettier. They were already arranging between

---

1   turnspit dog: A short-legged dog bred to turn a wheel to cook meat.

themselves to share the kingdom equally, when the youngest stepped forward, drawing from his pocket the acorn the White Cat had given him. He opened it quickly,
and there upon a white cushion they saw a dog so small that it could easily have been
put through a ring. The Prince laid it upon the ground, and it got up at once and began to dance. The King did not know what to say, for it was impossible that anything
could be prettier than this little creature. Nevertheless, as he was in no hurry to part
with his crown, he told his sons that, as they had been so successful the first time, he
would ask them to go once again, and seek by land and sea for a piece of muslin so
fine that it could be drawn through the eye of a needle. The brothers were not very
willing to set out again, but the two eldest consented because it gave them another
chance, and.they started as before. The youngest again mounted the wooden horse,
and rode back at full speed to his beloved White Cat. Every door of the castle stood
wide open, and every window and turret was illuminated, so it looked more wonderful than before. The hands hastened to meet him, and led the wooden horse off to
the stable, while he hurried in to find the White Cat. She was asleep in a little basket
on a white satin cushion, but she very soon started up when she heard the Prince,
and was overjoyed at seeing him once more.

"How could I hope that you would come back to me, King's son?" she said. And
then he stroked and petted her, and told her of his successful journey, and how he
had come back to ask her help, as he believed that it was impossible to find what the
King demanded. The White Cat looked serious, and said she must think what was
to be done, but that, luckily, there were some cats in the castle who could spin very
well, and if anybody could manage it they could, and she would set them the task
herself.

And then the hands appeared carrying torches, and conducted the Prince and the
White Cat to a long gallery which overlooked the river, from the windows of which
they saw a magnificent display of fireworks of all sorts; after which they had supper,
which the Prince liked even better than the fireworks, for it was very late, and he was
hungry after his long ride. And so the days passed quickly as before; it was impossible to feel dull with the White Cat, and she had quite a talent for inventing new
amusements—indeed, she was cleverer than a cat has any right to be. But when the
Prince asked her how it was that she was so wise, she only said:

"King's son, do not ask me; guess what you please. I may not tell you anything."

The Prince was so happy that he did not trouble himself at all about the time, but
presently the White Cat told him that the year was gone, and that he need not be at
all anxious about the piece of muslin, as they had made it very well.

"This time," she added, "I can give you a suitable escort"; and on looking out into
the courtyard the Prince saw a superb chariot of burnished gold, enamelled in flame
colour with a thousand different devices. It was drawn by twelve snow-white horses,

harnessed four abreast; their trappings were of flame-coloured velvet, embroidered with diamonds. A hundred chariots followed, each drawn by eight horses, and filled with officers in splendid uniforms, and a thousand guards surrounded the procession. "Go!" said the White Cat, "and when you appear before the King in such state he surely will not refuse you the crown which you deserve. Take this walnut, but do not open it until you are before him, then you will find in it the piece of stuff you asked me for."

"Lovely Blanchette," said the Prince, "how can I thank you properly for all your kindness to me? Only tell me that you wish it, and I will give up for ever all thought of being king, and will stay here with you always."

"King's son," she replied, "it shows the goodness of your heart that you should care so much for a little white cat, who is good for nothing but to catch mice; but you must not stay."

So the Prince kissed her little paw and set out. You can imagine how fast he travelled when I tell you that they reached the King's palace in just half the time it had taken the wooden horse to get there. This time the Prince was so late that he did not try to meet his brothers at their castle, so they thought he could not be coming, and were rather glad of it, and displayed their pieces of muslin to the King proudly, feeling sure of success. And indeed the stuff was very fine, and would go through the eyes of a very large needle; but the King, who was only too glad to make a difficulty, sent for a particular needle, which was kept among the Crown jewels, and had such a small eye that everybody saw at once that it was impossible that the muslin should pass through it.

The Princes were angry, and were beginning to complain that it was a trick, when suddenly the trumpets sounded and the youngest Prince came in. His father and brothers were quite astonished at his magnificence, and after he had greeted them he took the walnut from his pocket and opened it, fully expecting to find the piece of muslin, but instead there was only a hazelnut. He cracked it, and there lay a cherry-stone. Everybody was looking on, and the King was chuckling to himself at the idea of finding the piece of muslin in a nutshell.

However, the Prince cracked the cherrystone, but everyone laughed when he saw it contained only its own kernel. He opened that and found a grain of wheat, and in that was a millet seed. Then he himself began to wonder, and muttered softly:

"White Cat, White Cat, are you making fun of me?"

In an instant he felt a cat's claw give his hand quite a sharp scratch, and hoping that it was meant as an encouragement he opened the millet seed, and drew out of it a piece of muslin four hundred ells long, woven with the loveliest colours and most wonderful patterns; and when the needle was brought it went through the eye six times with the greatest ease! The king turned pale, and the other Princes stood silent and sorrowful, for nobody could deny that this was the most marvellous piece of muslin that was to be found in the world.

Presently the King turned to his sons, and said, with a deep sigh:

"Nothing could console me more in old age than to realise your willingness to gratify my wishes. Go then once more, and whoever at the end of a year can bring back the loveliest princess shall be married to her, and shall, without further delay, receive the crown, for my successor must certainly be married." The Prince considered that he had earned the kingdom fairly twice over, but still he was too well bred to argue about it, so he just went back to his gorgeous chariot, and, surrounded by his escort, returned to the White Cat faster than he had come. This time she was expecting him, the path was strewn with flowers, and a thousand braziers were burning scented woods which perfumed the air. Seated in a gallery from which she could see his arrival, the White Cat waited for him. "Well, King's son," she said, "here you are once more, without a crown." "Madam," said he, "thanks to your generosity I have earned one twice over; but the fact is that my father is so loth to part with it that it would be no pleasure to me to take it."

"Never mind," she answered; "it's just as well to try and deserve it. As you must take back a lovely princess with you next time I will be on the lookout for one for you. In the meantime let us enjoy ourselves; tonight I have ordered a battle between my cats and the river rats, on purpose to amuse you." So this year slipped away even more pleasantly than the preceding ones. Sometimes the Prince could not help asking the White Cat how it was she could talk.

"Perhaps you are a fairy," he said. "Or has some enchanter changed you into a cat?"

But she only gave him answers that told him nothing. Days go by so quickly when one is very happy that it is certain the Prince would never have thought of its being time to go back, when one evening as they sat together the White Cat said to him that if he wanted to take a lovely princess home with him the next day he must be prepared to do as she told him.

"Take this sword," she said, "and cut off my head!"

"I!" cried the Prince, "I cut off your head! Blanchette darling, how could I do it?"

"I entreat you to do as I tell you, King's son," she replied.

The tears came into the Prince's eyes as he begged her to ask him anything but that—to set him any task she pleased as a proof of his devotion, but to spare him the grief of killing his dear Pussy. But nothing he could say altered her determination, and at last he drew his sword, and desperately, with a trembling hand, cut off the little white head. But imagine his astonishment and delight when suddenly a lovely princess stood before him, and, while he was still speechless with amazement, the door opened and a goodly company of knights and ladies entered, each carrying a cat's skin! They hastened with every sign of joy to the Princess, kissing her hand and congratulating her on being once more restored to her natural shape.

She received them graciously, but after a few minutes begged that they would leave her alone with the Prince, to whom she said:

"You see, Prince, that you were right in supposing me to be no ordinary cat. My father reigned over six kingdoms. The Queen, my mother, whom he loved dearly, had a passion for travelling and exploring, and when I was only a few weeks old she obtained his permission to visit a certain mountain of which she had heard many marvellous tales, and set out, taking with her a number of her attendants. On the way they had to pass near an old castle belonging to the fairies. Nobody had ever been into it, but it was reported to be full of the most wonderful things, and my mother remembered to have heard that the fairies had in their garden such fruits as were to be seen and tasted nowhere else. She began to wish to try them for herself, and turned her steps in the direction of the garden. On arriving at the door, which blazed with gold and jewels, she ordered her servants to knock loudly, but it was useless; it seemed as if all the inhabitants of the castle must be asleep or dead. Now the more difficult it became to obtain the fruit, the more the Queen was determined that have it she would. So she ordered that they should bring ladders, and get over the wall into the garden; but though the wall did not look very high, and they tied the ladders together to make them very long, it was quite impossible to get to the top.

"The Queen was in despair, but as night was coming on she ordered that they should encamp just where they were, and went to bed herself, feeling quite ill, she was so disappointed. In the middle of the night she was suddenly awakened, and saw to her surprise a tiny, ugly old woman seated by her bedside, who said to her:

"'I must say that we consider it somewhat troublesome of your Majesty to insist upon tasting our fruit; but, to save you any annoyance, my sisters and I will consent to give you as much as you can carry away, on one condition—that is, that you shall give us your little daughter to bring up as our own.'

"'Ah! my dear madam,' cried the Queen, 'is there nothing else that you will take for the fruit? I will give you my kingdoms willingly.'

"'No,' replied the old fairy, 'we will have nothing but your little daughter. She shall be as happy as the day is long, and we will give her everything that is worth having in fairyland, but you must not see her again until she is married.'

"'Though it is a hard condition,' said the Queen, 'I consent, for I shall certainly die if I do not taste the fruit, and so I should lose my little daughter either way.'

"So the old fairy led her into the castle, and, though it was still the middle of the night, the Queen could see plainly that it was far more beautiful than she had been told, which you can easily believe, Prince," said the White Cat, "when I tell you that it was this castle that we are now in. 'Will you gather the fruit yourself, Queen?' said the old fairy, 'or shall I call it to come to you?'

"'I beg you to let me see it come when it is called,' cried the Queen; 'that will be something quite new.' The old fairy whistled twice, then she cried:

"'Apricots, peaches, nectarines, cherries, plums, pears, melons, grapes, apples, oranges, lemons, gooseberries, strawberries, raspberries, come!'

"And in an instant they came tumbling in, one over another, and yet they were neither dusty nor spoilt, and the Queen found them quite as good as she had fancied them. You see they grew upon fairy trees.

"The old fairy gave her golden baskets in which to take the fruit away, and it was as much as four hundred mules could carry. Then she reminded the Queen of her agreement, and led her back to the camp, and next morning she went back to her kingdom; but before she had gone very far she began to repent of her bargain, and when the King came out to meet her she looked so sad that he guessed that something had happened, and asked what was the matter. At first the Queen was afraid to tell him, but when, as soon as they reached the palace, five frightful little dwarfs were sent by the fairies to fetch me, she was obliged to confess what she had promised. The King was very angry, and had the Queen and myself shut up in a great tower and safely guarded, and drove the little dwarfs out of his kingdom; but the fairies sent a great dragon who ate up all the people he met, and whose breath burnt up everything as he passed through the country; and at last, after trying in vain to rid himself of the monster, the King, to save his subjects, was obliged to consent that I should be given up to the fairies. This time they came themselves to fetch me, in a chariot of pearl drawn by seahorses, followed by the dragon, who was led with chains of diamonds. My cradle was placed between the old fairies, who loaded me with caresses, and away we whirled through the air to a tower which they had built on purpose for me. There I grew up surrounded with everything that was beautiful and rare, and learning everything that is ever taught to a princess, but without any companions but a parrot and a little dog, who could both talk; and receiving every day a visit from one of the old fairies, who came mounted upon the dragon. One day, however, as I sat at my window I saw a handsome young prince, who seemed to have been hunting in the forest which surrounded my prison, and who was standing and looking up at me. When he saw that I observed him he saluted me with great deference. You can imagine that I was delighted to have some one new to talk to, and in spite of the height of my window our conversation was prolonged till night fell, then my prince reluctantly bade me farewell. But after that he came again many times, and at last I consented to marry him, but the question was how I was to escape from my tower. The fairies always supplied me with flax for my spinning, and by great diligence I made enough cord for a ladder that would reach to the foot of the tower; but, alas! just as my prince was helping me to descend it, the crossest and ugliest of the old fairies flew in. Before he had time to defend himself, my unhappy lover was swallowed up by the dragon. As for me, the fairies, furious at having their plans defeated, for they intended me to marry the king of the dwarfs and I utterly refused, changed me into a white cat. When they brought me here, I found all the lords and ladies of my father's court awaiting me under the same enchantment, while the people of lesser rank had been made invisible, all but their hands.

"As they laid me under the enchantment the fairies told me all my history, for until then I had quite believed that I was their child, and warned me that my only chance of regaining my natural form was to win the love of a prince who resembled in every way my unfortunate lover."

"And you have won it, lovely Princess," interrupted the Prince.

"You are indeed wonderfully like him," resumed the Princess—"in voice, in features, and everything; and if you really love me all my troubles will be at an end."

"And mine too," cried the Prince, throwing himself at her feet, "if you will consent to marry me."

"I love you already better than anyone in the world," she said; "but now it is time to go back to your father, and we shall hear what he says about it."

So the Prince gave her his hand and led her out, and they mounted the chariot together; it was even more splendid than before, and so was the whole company. Even the horses' shoes were of rubies with diamond nails, and I suppose that is the first time such a thing was ever seen.

As the Princess was as kind and clever as she was beautiful, you may imagine what a delightful journey the Prince found it, for everything the Princess said seemed to him quite charming.

When they came near the castle where the brothers were to meet, the Princess got into a chair carried by four of the guards; it was hewn out of one splendid crystal, and had silken curtains, which she drew round her that she might not be seen.

The Prince saw his brothers walking upon the terrace, each with a lovely princess, and they came to meet him, asking if he had also found a wife. He said that he had found something much rarer—a little white cat! At which they laughed very much, and asked him if he was afraid of being eaten up by mice in the palace. And then they set out together for the town. Each prince and princess rode in a splendid carriage; the horses were decked with plumes of feathers, and glittered with gold. After them came the youngest prince, and last of all the crystal chair, at which everybody looked with admiration and curiosity. When the courtiers saw them coming they hastened to tell the King.

"Are the ladies beautiful?" he asked anxiously.

And when they answered that nobody had ever before seen such lovely princesses he seemed quite annoyed.

However, he received them graciously, but found it impossible to choose between them.

Then turning to his youngest son he said:

"Have you come back alone, after all?"

"Your Majesty," replied the Prince, "will find in that crystal chair a little white cat, which has such soft paws, and mews so prettily, that I am sure you will be charmed with it."

The King smiled, and went to draw back the curtains himself, but at a touch from the Princess the crystal shivered into a thousand splinters, and there she stood in all her beauty; her fair hair floated over her shoulders and was crowned with flowers, and her softly falling robe was of the purest white. She saluted the King gracefully, while a murmur of admiration rose from all around.

"Sire," she said, "I am not come to deprive you of the throne you fill so worthily. I have already six kingdoms, permit me to bestow one upon you, and upon each of your sons. I ask nothing but your friendship, and your consent to my marriage with your youngest son; we shall still have three kingdoms left for ourselves."

The King and all the courtiers could not conceal their joy and astonishment, and the marriage of the three Princes was celebrated at once. The festivities lasted several months, and then each king and queen departed to their own kingdom and lived happily ever after.

BRAIN OVER BRAWN
(THE TRICKSTER)

O F ALL THE DIFFERENT MOTIFS to be found in fairy tale, few are older or more widespread than trickster tales. Ancient though the tradition may be, it continues to prosper today in such iconic figures as Bugs Bunny and Bart Simpson— presumably because the notions of thumbing our nose at Authority, of beating the odds, of spicing up life with a bit of mischief, are as appealing now as they were a thousand years ago. Although in the Western tradition the trickster has acquired a degree of social acceptance as a sort of Robin Hood figure (robbing the rich to help the poor), we should note that in earlier times, he—the role was more or less exclusively male—was a much more amoral character, seeking to indulge his appetites with little regard for others. There is a narcissistic aspect to his behavior that disturbs us even as we are amused by his audacity and quick-wittedness.

But why is it that these tales have retained such popularity? One explanation is to be found in the fact that they come from the folk: stories in which superior size and strength are rendered impotent by superior cunning must have held an immediate appeal to people who lived with constant reminders of their own political and economic powerlessness. To express discontent with their lot in any direct manner would be to invite swift retribution, and so frustrations had to be released imaginatively rather than actively. In this respect, the tales in this section surely provide a kind of socio-political therapy; the exuberant manner in which the underdog/protagonist sets about the task of exploiting the stupidity of his opponent must have provided a very pointed satisfaction.

One character who matches this profile to a tee is the Grimms' brave little tailor. His profession puts him close to the bottom of the social heap, but what he lacks in status he more than makes up for in *chutzpah*. The story illustrates very cleverly the enormous psychological advantage to be gained from a combination of unshakable self-confidence and cunning; the declaration on his belt tells no less than the truth, but then as now, the devil is in the details. The note of animosity that creeps into the narrative when the tailor pits his wits against the king is predictable, for reasons discussed above; likewise, his marriage to the princess is clearly not one made in heaven, but this story is more about getting even than living happily ever after.

Lest one is tempted to draw the conclusion that "female trickster" is an oxymoron, we offer "Molly Whuppie," from Joseph Jacobs's collection *English Fairy Tales* (1890). We hear echoes here of a variety of tales, but there is an obvious similarity to the Grimms' "Hansel and Gretel," particularly in the circumstances that set the tale in motion; indeed, they are set out here in so offhand a manner as to suggest that such poverty and hardship were once upon a time constant companions (and thus demanded desperate remedies). Still, it is noteworthy that Molly is more pragmatic and reactive in her trickery than her male counterparts, a point borne out in her constructive relationship with the king, no doubt because he doesn't see her as a potential rival. And even a giant has feelings, we discover, when he rather plaintively asks Molly "... if I had done as much ill to you as ye have done to me, what would ye do to me?"

In Perrault's "Puss in Boots" we are confronted with a partnership, although it's significant that the roles of servant and master are reversed. The presence of animals in fairy tale is obviously complex and multi-faceted; suffice to say here that part of the explanation has to do with that same sense of inferiority that was noted above: if Man is ostensibly the master, then subordinate Animal must find the means to assert his sense of his own self-worth. We should also recall here the point made earlier about the Wolf in "Little Red Riding Hood"—that the animal can be seen as a metaphor for some specific aspect of human nature, such as ferocity or mischief. That "human" element is particularly apparent here in the cat's insistence upon a pair of boots that play no role in the story beyond reminding us that this is no ordinary feline! Thus in "Puss in Boots" we meet a miller's youngest son (as socially disadvantaged, therefore, as any tailor) who acquires fame and fortune entirely through the quick wits of his helpful animal/servant, his only contribution (apart from allowing himself to be dissuaded from eating and skinning the cat) being to put some faith in Puss's "cunning tricks."

With the stories of Brer Rabbit we find ourselves in that branch of folk tale known as beast-fable; yet, even in this almost exclusively animal world, what we may term the "power structure" remains as clear as ever, since here too the issue is that of an apparently powerless individual having to find ways to outsmart those who supposedly control his destiny. The elements of "The Three Little Pigs" and "Little Red Riding Hood" to be found in this particular story also leave no doubt as to its close connection to the world of fairy tales. Originating on the West Coast of Africa (where Brer Rabbit is known as *Wakaima*), these tales came to America with the slave trade—and thus the human relevance of these stories is immediately apparent: there is at least a taste of freedom in laughter.

The nature of the protagonists in this section deserves some consideration, in that none of them can accurately be described as good, at least in the conventional sense. There is an ambiguous quality in these tales, which can be traced in part to the strong hint of amorality shown by their central characters as they pursue their various goals. Yet we should not be surprised by these tales' implicit assumption that cunning is a virtue. The people among whom these tales evolved had little reason to expect any material change for the better in their lives; for them, prosperity and success could be no more than dreams when simple survival was more often the issue. Thus, it is easy to understand how the character who has the wit and audacity to seize the main chance when it comes along is not to be censored for a lack of honesty or sensitivity.

THE BRAVE LITTLE TAILOR[1]

Jacob and Wilhelm Grimm

ONE SUMMER MORNING A LITTLE tailor was sitting on his table near the window. He was in high good humor and sewed with all his might. A peasant woman came down the street, crying out: "Good jam—cheap!" That sounded sweet to the tailor's ears. He stuck his shapely little head out of the window and cried: "Up here, my good woman, you'll find a buyer." The woman hauled her heavy baskets up the three flights of stairs to the tailor's and he made her unpack every single pot. He examined them all, lifted them up, sniffed at them, and finally said: "This looks like good jam to me; weigh me out three ounces, my good woman, and if it comes to a quarter of a pound you won't find me complaining." The woman, who had hoped to make a good sale, gave him what he asked for, and went away grumbling and very much out of sorts. "God bless this jam and give me health and strength," cried the little tailor. Whereupon he took bread from the cupboard, cut a slice straight across the loaf, and spread it with jam. "I bet this won't taste bitter," he said, "but before biting into it, I'm going to finish my jacket." He put the bread down beside him and went on with his sewing, taking bigger and bigger stitches in his joy. Meanwhile, the flies that had been sitting on the wall, enticed by the sweet smell, came swarming

---

1   First published in 1812/15, in the first edition of *Kinder- und Hausmärchen*. This text from the second edition (1819), from *Grimms' Tales for Young and Old*, trans. Ralph Manheim (Garden City, NY: Anchor Press, 1977).

down on the jam. "Hey, who invited you?" cried the little tailor and shooed the un-bidden guests away. But the flies, who didn't understand his language, refused to be dismissed and kept coming in greater and greater numbers. Finally, at the end of his patience, the tailor took a rag from the catchall under his table. "Just wait! I'll show you!" he cried, and struck out at them unmercifully. When he stopped and counted, no less than seven flies lay dead with their legs in the air. He couldn't help admiring his bravery. "What a man I am!" he cried. "The whole town must hear of this." And one two three, he cut out a belt for himself, stitched it up, and embroidered on it in big letters: "Seven at one blow!" Then he said: "Town, my foot! The whole world must hear of it!" And for joy his heart wagged like a lamb's tail.

The tailor put on his belt and decided to go out into the world, for clearly his shop was too small for such valor. Before leaving, he ransacked the house for something to take with him, but all he could find was an old cheese, so he put that in his pock-et. Just outside the door, he caught sight of a bird that had got itself caught in the bushes, and the bird joined the cheese in his pocket. Ever so bravely he took to the road, and because he was light and nimble, he never seemed to get tired. Up into the mountains he went, and when he reached the highest peak he found an enormous giant sitting there taking it easy and enjoying the view. The little tailor went right up to him; he wasn't the least bit afraid. "Greetings, friend," he said. "Looking out at the great world, are you? Well, that's just where I'm headed for, to try my luck. Would you care to go with me?" The giant looked at the tailor contemptuously and said: "You little pipsqueak! You miserable nobody!" "Is that so?" said the little tailor, unbutton-ing his coat and showing the giant his belt. "Read that! That'll show you what kind of man I am!" When he had read what was written—"Seven at one blow!"—the giant thought somewhat better of the little man. All the same, he decided to put him to the test, so he picked up a stone and squeezed it until drops of water appeared. "Do that," he said, "if you've got the strength." "That?" said the tailor. "Why, that's child's play for a man like me." Whereupon he reached into his pocket, took out the soft cheese, and squeezed it until the whey ran out. "What do you think of that?" he cried. "Not so bad, eh?" The giant didn't know what to say; he couldn't believe the little man was so strong. So he picked up a stone and threw it so high that the eye could hardly keep up with it: "All right, you little runt, let's see you do that." "Nice throw," said the tailor, "but it fell to the ground in the end. Watch me throw one that won't ever come back." Whereupon he reached into his pocket, took out the bird, and tossed it into the air. Glad to be free, the bird flew up and away and didn't come back. "Well," said the tailor. "What do you think of that?" "I've got to admit you can throw," said the giant, "but now let's see what you can carry." Pointing at a big oak tree that lay felled on the ground, he said: "If you're strong enough, help me carry this tree out of the forest." "Glad to," said the little man. "You take the trunk over your shoulder, and

I'll carry the branches; they're the heaviest part." The giant took the trunk over his shoulder, and the tailor sat down on a branch, so that the giant, who couldn't look around, had to carry the whole tree and the tailor to boot. The tailor felt so chipper in his comfortable back seat that he began to whistle "Three Tailors Went a-Riding," as though hauling trees were child's play to a man of his strength. After carrying the heavy load for quite some distance, the giant was exhausted. "Hey!" he cried out, "I've got to drop it." The tailor jumped nimbly down, put his arms around the tree as if he'd been carrying it, and said to the giant: "I wouldn't have thought a tiny tree would be too much for a big man like you."

They went on together until they came to a cherry tree. The giant grabbed the crown where the cherries ripen soonest, pulled it down, handed it to the tailor, and bade him eat. But the tailor was much too light to hold the tree down. When the giant let go, the crown snapped back into place and the tailor was whisked high into the air. When he had fallen to the ground without hurting himself, the giant cried out: "What's the matter? You mean you're not strong enough to hold that bit of a sapling?" "Not strong enough? How can you say such a thing about a man who did for seven at one blow? I jumped over that tree because the hunters down there were shooting into the thicket. Now you try. See if you can do it." The giant tried, but he couldn't get over the tree and got stuck in the upper branches. Once again the little tailor had won out.

"All right," said the giant. "If you're so brave, let me take you to our cave to spend the night with us." The little tailor was willing and went along with him. When they got to the cave, the other giants were sitting around the fire. Each one was holding a roasted sheep in his hands and eating it. The little tailor looked around and thought: "This place is a good deal roomier than my workshop." The giant showed him a bed and told him to lie down and sleep. But the bed was too big for the little tailor, so instead of getting into it, he crept into a corner. At midnight, when the giant thought the tailor must be sound asleep, he got up, took a big iron bar and split the bed in two with one stroke. That will settle the little runt's hash, he thought. At the crack of dawn the giants started into the forest. They had forgotten all about the little tailor. All at once he came striding along as chipper and bold as you please. The giants were terrified. They thought he would kill them all, and ran away as fast as their legs would carry them.

The little tailor went his way. After following his nose for many days he came to the grounds of a king's palace. Feeling tired, he lay down in the grass and went to sleep, and while he was sleeping some courtiers came along. They examined him from all sides and read the inscription on his belt: "Seven at one blow!" "Goodness," they said, "what can a great war hero like this be doing here in peacetime? He must be some great lord." They went and told the king. "If war should break out," they said, "a man like that would come in very handy. Don't let him leave on any account." This struck the king as good advice, and he sent one of his courtiers to offer the tailor a post in his army. The courtier went back to the sleeper, waited until he stretched his limbs and opened his eyes, and made his offer. "That's just what I came here for," said the tailor. "I'll be glad to enter the king's service." So he was received with honor and given apartments of his own.

But the soldiers, who were taken in by the little tailor, wished him a thousand miles away. "What will become of us?" they asked. "If we quarrel with him and he strikes, seven of us will fall at one blow. We won't last long at that rate." So they took counsel together, went to the king and asked to be released from his service. Because, they said, "we can't hope to keep up with a man who does for seven at one blow." The king was sad to be losing all his faithful servants because of one and wished he had never laid eyes on him. He'd have been glad to get rid of him, but he didn't dare dismiss him for fear the great hero might strike him and all his people dead and seize the throne for himself. He thought and thought, and at last he hit on an idea. He sent word to the little tailor that since he was such a great hero he wanted to make him an offer. There were two giants living in a certain forest, and they were murdering, looting, burning, and laying the country waste. No one dared go near them for fear of his life. If the hero should conquer and kill these two giants, the king would give him his only daughter to wife, with half his kingdom as her dowry. And, moreover, the king would send a hundred knights to back him up. "Sounds like just the thing for me," thought the little tailor. "It's not every day that somebody offers you a beautiful princess and half a kingdom." "It's a deal," he replied. "I'll take care of those giants, and I won't need the hundred knights. You can't expect a man who does for seven at one blow to be afraid of two."

The little tailor started out with the hundred knights at his heels. When they got to the edge of the forest, he said to his companions: "Stay here. I'll attend to the giants by myself." Then he bounded into the woods, peering to the right and to the left. After a while he caught sight of the two giants, who were lying under a tree asleep, snoring so hard that the branches rose and fell. Quick as a flash the little tailor picked up stones, filled both his pockets with them, and climbed the tree. Halfway up, he slid along a branch until he was right over the sleeping giants. Then he picked out one of the giants and dropped stone after stone on his chest. For a long while the giant didn't notice, but in the end he woke up, gave his companion a poke, and said: "Why are you hitting me?" "You're dreaming," said the other. "I'm not hitting you." When they had lain down to sleep again, the tailor dropped a stone on the second giant. "What is this?" he cried. "Why are you pelting me?" "I'm not pelting you!" the first grumbled. They argued awhile, but they were too tired to keep it up and finally their eyes closed again. Then the little tailor took his biggest stone and threw it with all his might at the first giant's chest. "This is too much!" cried the giant, and jumping up like a madman he pushed his companion so hard against the tree that it shook. The other repaid him in kind and they both flew into such a rage that they started pulling up trees and belaboring each other until they both lay dead on the ground. The little tailor jumped down. "Lucky they didn't pull up the tree I was sitting in," he said to himself. "I'd have had to jump into another like a squirrel. But then we tailors are quick." He drew his sword, gave them both good thrusts in the chest, and went back to the knights. "The job is done," he said. "I've settled their hash. But it was a hard fight. They were so desperate they pulled up trees to fight with, but how could that help them against a man who does for seven at one blow!" "Aren't you even wounded?" the knights asked. "I should say not!" said the tailor. "Not so much as a scratch." The knights wouldn't believe him, so they rode into the forest, where they found the giants lying in pools of blood, with uprooted trees all around them.

The little tailor went to the king and demanded the promised reward, but the king regretted his promise and thought up another way to get rid of the hero. "Before I give you my daughter and half my kingdom," he said, "you will have to perform one more task. There's a unicorn loose in the forest and he's doing a good deal of damage. You will have to catch him first." "If the two giants didn't scare me, why would I worry about a unicorn? Seven at one blow is my meat." Taking a rope and an ax, he went into the forest, and again told the knights who had been sent with him to wait on the fringe. He didn't have long to look. In a short while the unicorn came along and rushed at the tailor, meaning to run him straight through with his horn. "Not so fast!" said the tailor. "It's not as easy as all that." He stood still, waited until the unicorn was quite near him, and then jumped nimbly behind a tree. The unicorn charged full force and rammed into the tree. His horn went in and stuck so fast that he hadn't the strength to pull it out. He was caught. "I've got him," said the tailor. He came out from behind the tree, put the rope around the unicorn's neck and, taking his ax, chopped the wood away from the horn. When that was done, he led the beast to the king.

But the king was still unwilling to grant him the promised reward and made a third demand. Before the wedding he wanted the tailor to capture a wild boar which had been ravaging the forest, and said the royal huntsmen would help him. "Gladly," said the little tailor. "It's child's play." He didn't take the huntsmen into the forest with him, and they were just as pleased, for several times the boar had given them such a reception that they had no desire to seek him out. When the boar caught sight of the tailor, he gnashed his teeth, foamed at the mouth, made a dash at him, and would have lain him out flat if the nimble hero hadn't escaped into a nearby chapel. The boar ran in after him, but the tailor jumped out of the window, ran around the chapel and slammed the door. The infuriated beast was much too heavy and clumsy to jump out of the window, and so he was caught. The little tailor ran back to the huntsmen and told them to go and see the captive with their own eyes. He himself went to the king, who had to keep his promise this time, like it or not, and give him his daughter and half the kingdom. If he had known that, far from being a war hero, the bridegroom was only a little tailor, he would have been even unhappier than he was. And so the wedding was celebrated with great splendor and little joy, and a tailor became a king.

One night the young queen heard her husband talking in his sleep. "Boy," he said, "hurry up with that jerkin you're making and get those breeches mended or I'll break my yardstick over your head." Then she knew how he had got his start in life. Next morning she went to her father, told him her tale of woe, and begged him to help her get rid of a husband who had turned out to be a common tailor. The king bade her take comfort and said: "Leave the door of your bedroom unlocked tonight. My servants will be waiting outside. Once he's asleep they'll go in, tie him up, and put him aboard a ship bound for the end of the world." The young queen was pleased, but the armor-bearer, who was devoted to the hero, heard the whole conversation and told him all about the plot. "They won't get away with that!" said the little tailor. That night he went to bed with his wife at the usual hour. When she thought he was asleep, she got up, opened the door, and lay down again. The little tailor, who was only pretending to be asleep, cried out in a loud voice: "Boy, hurry up with that jerkin you're making and get those breeches mended or I'll break my yardstick over your head. I've done for seven at one blow, killed two giants, brought home a unicorn, and captured a wild boar. And now I'm expected to be afraid of these scoundrels at my door." When they heard that, the servants were terrified. Not one of them dared lay hands on him and they ran as if the hosts of hell had been chasing them. And so the little tailor went on being king for the rest of his days.

MOLLY WHUPPIE[1]

Joseph Jacobs

ONCE UPON A TIME THERE was a man and a wife who had too many children, and they could not get meat for them, so they took the three youngest and left them in a wood. They travelled and travelled and could see never a house. It began to be dark, and they were hungry. At last they saw a light and made for it; it turned out to

---

1   From *English Fairy Tales*, 1890 (repr. New York: Dover, 1967).

be a house. They knocked at the door, and a woman came to it, who said: "What do you want?" They said: "Please let us in and give us something to eat." The woman said: "I can't do that, as my man is a giant, and he would kill you if he comes home." They begged hard. "Let us stop for a little while," said they, "and we will go away before he comes." So she took them in, and set them down before the fire, and gave them milk and bread; but just as they had begun to eat, a great knock came to the door, and a dreadful voice said:

"Fee, fie, fo, fum,
I smell the blood of some earthly one.

Who have you there wife?" "Eh," said the wife, "it's three poor lassies cold and hungry, and they will go away. Ye won't touch 'em, man." He said nothing, but ate up a big supper, and ordered them to stay all night. Now he had three lassies of his own, and they were to sleep in the same bed with the three strangers. The youngest of the three strange lassies was called Molly Whuppie, and she was very clever. She noticed that before they went to bed the giant put straw ropes round her neck and her sisters', and round his own lassies' necks he put gold chains. So Molly took care and did not fall asleep, but waited till she was sure every one was sleeping sound. Then she slipped out of the bed, and took the straw ropes off her own and her sisters' necks, and took the gold chains off the giant's lassies. She then put the straw ropes on the giant's lassies and the gold on herself and her sisters, and lay down. And in the middle of the night up rose the giant, armed with a great club, and felt for the necks with the straw. It was dark. He took his own lassies out of bed on to the floor, and battered them until they were dead, and then lay down again, thinking he had managed finely. Molly thought it time she and her sisters were off and away, so she wakened them and told them to be quiet, and they slipped out of the house. They all got out safe, and they ran and ran, and never stopped until morning, when they saw a grand house before them. It turned out to be a king's house: so Molly went in, and told her story to the king. He said: "Well, Molly, you are a clever girl, and you have managed well; but, if you would manage better, and go back, and steal the giant's sword that hangs on the back of his bed, I would give your eldest sister my eldest son to marry." Molly said she would try. So she went back, and managed to slip into the giant's house, and crept in below the bed. The giant came home, and ate up a great supper, and went to bed. Molly waited until he was snoring, and she crept out, and reached over the giant and got down the sword; but just as she got it out over the bed, it gave a rattle, and up jumped the giant, and Molly ran out at the door and the sword with her; and she ran, and he ran, till they came to the "Bridge of one hair;" and she got over, but he couldn't, and he says, "Woe worth ye, Molly Whuppie! never ye come again." And she says: "Twice yet, carle,"[1] quoth she, "I'll come to Spain." [2] So Molly took the sword to the king, and her sister was married to his son.

Well, the king he says: "Ye've managed well, Molly; but if ye would manage better, and steal the purse that lies below the giant's pillow, I would marry your second sister to my second son." And Molly said she would try. So she set out for the giant's house, and slipped in, and hid again below the bed, and waited till the giant had eaten his supper, and was snoring sound asleep. She slipped out, and slipped her hand below the pillow, and got out the purse; but just as she was going out the giant wakened, and ran after her; and she ran, and he ran, till they came to the "Bridge of one hair," and she got over, but he couldn't, and he said, "Woe worth ye, Molly Whuppie! never you come again." "Once yet, carle," quoth she, "I'll come to Spain." So Molly took the purse to the king, and her second sister was married to the king's second son.

After that the king says to Molly: "Molly, you are a clever girl, but if you would do better yet, and steal the giant's ring that he wears on his finger, I will give you my youngest son for yourself." Molly said she would try. So back she goes to the giant's house, and hides herself below the bed. The giant wasn't long ere he came home, and, after he had eaten a great big supper, he went to his bed, and shortly was snoring loud. Molly crept out and reached over the bed, and got hold of the giant's hand, and she pulled and she pulled until she got off the ring; but just as she got it off the giant got up, and gripped her by the hand, and he says: "Now I have caught you, Molly Whuppie, and, if I had done as much ill to you as ye have done to me, what would ye do to me?"

Molly says: "I would put you into a sack, and I'd put the cat inside wi' you, and the dog aside you, and a needle and thread and a shears, and I'd hang you up upon the wall, and I'd go to the wood, and choose the thickest stick I could get, and I would come home, and take you down, and bang you till you were dead."

"Well, Molly," says the giant, "I'll just do that to you."

So he gets a sack, and puts Molly into it, and the cat and the dog beside her, and a needle and thread and shears, and hangs her up upon the wall, and goes to the wood to choose a stick.

Molly she sings out: "Oh, if ye saw what I see."

"Oh," says the giant's wife, "what do ye see, Molly?"

But Molly never said a word but, "Oh, if ye saw what I see!"

The giant's wife begged that Molly would take her up into the sack till she would see what Molly saw. So Molly took the shears and cut a hole in the sack, and took

---

1   carle: man.

2   I'll come to Spain: I'll venture into enemy territory.

out the needle and thread with her, and jumped down and helped the giant's wife up into the sack, and sewed up the hole.

The giant's wife saw nothing, and began to ask to get down again; but Molly never minded, but hid herself at the back of the door. Home came the giant, and a great big tree in his hand, and he took down the sack, and began to batter it. His wife cried, "It's me, man;" but the dog barked and the cat mewed, and he did not know his wife's voice. But Molly came out from the back of the door, and the giant saw her, and he ran after her; and he ran and she ran, till they came to the "Bridge of one hair," and she got over but he couldn't; and he said, "Woe worth you, Molly Whuppie! never you come again." "Never more, carle," quoth she, "will I come again to Spain."

So Molly took the ring to the king, and she was married to his youngest son, and she never saw the giant again.

PUSS IN BOOTS[1]

Charles Perrault

A CERTAIN POOR MILLER HAD ONLY his mill, his ass and his cat to bequeath to his three sons when he died. The children shared out their patrimony and did not bother to call in the lawyers; if they had done so, they would have been stripped quite bare of course. The eldest took the mill, the second the ass, and the youngest had to make do with the cat.

He felt himself very ill used.

"My brothers can earn an honest living with their inheritance, but once I've eaten my cat and made a muff with his pelt, I shall have to die of hunger."

The cat overheard him but decided to pretend he had not done so; he addressed his master gravely.

"Master, don't fret; give me a bag and a pair of boots to protect my little feet from the thorny undergrowth and you'll see that your father hasn't provided for you so badly, after all."

Although the cat's master could not really believe his cat would support him, he had seen him play so many cunning tricks when he went to catch rats and mice—he would hang upside down by his feet; or hide himself in the meal and play at being dead—that he felt a faint hope his cat might think up some helpful scheme.

---

1 First published in 1697. This text from *Sleeping Beauty and Other Favourite Fairy Tales*, trans. by Angela Carter (London: Gollancz, 1982).

When the cat had got what he asked for, he put on his handsome boots and slung the bag round his neck, keeping hold of the draw-strings with his two front paws. He went to a warren where he knew there were a great many rabbits. He put some bran and a selection of juicy weeds at the bottom of the bag and then stretched out quite still, like a corpse, and waited for some ingenuous young rabbit to come and investigate the bag and its appetizing contents.

No sooner had he lain down than a silly bunny jumped into the bag. Instantly, the cat pulled the draw-strings tight and killed the rabbit without mercy.

Proudly bearing his prey, he went to the king and asked to speak to him. He was taken to his majesty's private apartment. As soon as he got inside the door, he made the king a tremendous bow and said:

"Sire, I present you with a delicious young rabbit that my master, the Marquis of Carabas, ordered me to offer you, with his humblest compliments."

Without his master's knowledge or consent, the cat had decided the miller's son should adopt the name of the Marquis of Carabas.

"Tell your master that I thank him with all my heart," said the king.

The next day, the cat hid himself in a cornfield, with his open bag, and two partridges flew into it. He pulled the strings and caught them both. Then he went to present them to the king, just as he had done with the rabbit. The king accepted the partridges with great glee and rewarded the cat with a handsome tip.

The cat kept on taking his master's game to the king for two or three months. One day, he learned that the king planned to take a drive along the riverside with his beautiful daughter. He said to his master:

"If you take my advice, your fortune is made. You just go for a swim in the river at a spot I'll show to you and leave the rest to me."

The Marquis of Carabas obediently went off to swim, although he could not think why the cat should want him to. While he was bathing, the king drove by and the cat cried out with all its might:

"Help! Help! The Marquis of Carabas is drowning!"

The king put his head out of his carriage window when he heard this commotion and recognised the cat who had brought him so much game. He ordered his servants to hurry and save the Marquis of Carabas.

While they were pulling the marquis out of the river, the cat went to the king's carriage and told him how robbers had stolen his master's clothes while he swam in the river even though he'd shouted "Stop thief!" at the top of his voice. In fact, the cunning cat had hidden the miller's son's wretched clothes under a stone.

The king ordered the master of his wardrobe to hurry back to the palace and bring a selection of his own finest garments for the Marquis of Carabas to wear. When the young man put them on, he looked very handsome and the king's daughter thought:

"What an attractive young man!" The Marquis of Carabas treated her with respect mingled with tenderness and she fell madly in love.

The king invited the Marquis of Carabas to join him in his carriage and continue the drive in style. The cat was delighted to see his scheme begin to succeed and busily ran ahead of the procession. He came to a band of peasants who were mowing a meadow and said:

"Good people, if you don't tell the king that this meadow belongs to the Marquis of Carabas, I'll make mincemeat of every one of you."

As soon as he saw the mowers, the king asked them who owned the hayfield. They had been so intimidated by the cat that they dutifully chorused:

"It belongs to the Marquis of Carabas."

"You have a fine estate," remarked the king to the marquis.

"The field crops abundantly every year," improvised the marquis.

The cat was still racing ahead of the party and came to a band of harvesters. He said to them:

"Good harvesters, if you don't say that all these cornfields belong to the Marquis of Carabas, I'll make mincemeat of every one of you."

The king passed by a little later and wanted to know who owned the rolling cornfield.

"The Marquis of Carabas possesses them all," said the harvesters.

The king expressed his increasing admiration of the marquis' estates. The cat ran before the carriage and made the same threats to everyone he met on the way; the king was perfectly astonished at the young man's great possessions.

At last the cat arrived at a castle. In this castle lived an ogre. This ogre was extraordinarily rich; he was the true owner of all the land through which the king had travelled. The cat had taken good care to find out all he could about this ogre, and now he asked the servant who answered the door if he could speak to him; he said he couldn't pass so close by the castle without paying his respects to such an important man as its owner.

The ogre made him as welcome as an ogre can.

"I'm told you can transform yourself into all sorts of animals," said the cat. "That you can change yourself into a lion, for example, or even an elephant."

"Quite right," replied the ogre. "Just to show you, I'll turn myself into a lion."

When he found himself face to face with a lion, even our cat was so scared that he jumped up on to the roof and balanced there precariously because his boots weren't made for walking on tiles.

As soon as the ogre had become himself again, the cat clambered down and confessed how terrified he had been.

"But gossip also has it—though I can scarcely believe it—that you also have the power to take the shapes of the very smallest animals. They say you can even shrink down as small as a rat or a mouse. But I must admit, even if it seems rude, that I think that's quite impossible."

"Impossible?" said the ogre. "Just you see!" He changed into a mouse and began to scamper around on the floor. The cat no sooner saw him than he jumped on him and gobbled him up.

Meanwhile, the king saw the ogre's fine castle as he drove by and decided to pay it a visit. The cat heard the sound of carriage wheels on the drawbridge, ran outside and greeted the king.

"Welcome, your majesty, to the castle of the Marquis of Carabas."

"What sir? Does this fine castle also belong to you? I've never seen anything more splendid than this courtyard and the battlements that surround it; may we be permitted to view the interior?"

The marquis gave his hand to the young princess and followed the king. They entered a grand room where they found a banquet ready prepared; the ogre had invited all his friends to a dinner party, but none of the guests dared enter the castle when they saw the king had arrived. The king was delighted with the good qualities of the Marquis of Carabas and his daughter was beside herself about them. There was also the young man's immense wealth to be taken into account. After his fifth or sixth glass of wine, the king said:

"Say the word, my fine fellow, and you shall become my son-in-law."

The marquis bowed very low, immediately accepted the honour the king bestowed on him and married the princess that very day. The cat was made a great lord and gave up hunting mice, except for pleasure.

Moral
A great inheritance may be a fine thing, but hard work and ingenuity will take a young man further than his father's money.

Another moral
If a miller's son can so quickly win the heart of a princess, that is because clothes, bearing and youth speedily inspire affection; and the means to achieve them are not always entirely commendable.

THE DEATH OF BRER WOLF[1]

Julius Lester

BRER RABBIT HAD TRICKED BRER Wolf and he was four times seven times eleven mad.

One day Brer Rabbit left his house to go to town, and Brer Wolf tore it down and took off one of his children.

Brer Rabbit built a straw house and Brer Wolf tore that down. Then he made one out of pine tops. Brer Wolf tore that one down. He made one out of bark, and that didn't last too much longer than it takes to drink a milk shake. Finally, Brer Rabbit hired some carpenters and built him a house with a stone foundation, two-car garage, and a picture window. After that, he had a little peace and quiet and wasn't scared to leave home and visit his neighbors every now and then.

One afternoon he was at home when he heard a lot of racket outside. Before he could get up to see what was going on, Brer Wolf bust through the front door. "Save me! Save me! Some hunters with dogs are after me. Hide me somewhere so the dogs won't get me."

"Jump in that chest over there," Brer Rabbit said, pointing toward the fireplace.

Brer Wolf jumped in. He figured that when night came, he'd get out and take care of Brer Rabbit once and for all. He was so busy thinking about what he was going to do, he didn't hear what Brer Rabbit did. Brer Rabbit locked the trunk!

Brer Rabbit sat back down in his rocking chair and stuck a big wad of chewing tobacco in his jaw. This here was rabbit-chewing tobacco. From what I hear, it's supposed to be pretty good. So he sat there just rocking, chewing, and spitting.

"Is the dogs gone yet, Brer Rabbit?" Brer Wolf asked after a while.

"No. I think I hear one sniffing around the chimney."

Brer Rabbit got up and filled a great big pot with water and put it on the fire.

Brer Wolf was listening and said, "What you doing, Brer Rabbit?"

"Just fixing to make you a nice cup of elderberry tea."

Brer Rabbit went to his tool chest, got out a drill, and started boring holes in the chest.

"What you doing now, Brer Rabbit?"

"Just making some holes so you can get some air."

Brer Rabbit put some more wood on the fire.

"Now what you doing?"

"Building the fire up so you won't get cold."

---

1 From *The Tales of Uncle Remus: The Adventures of Brer Rabbit* (New York: Dial, 1987).

The water was boiling now. Brer Rabbit took the kettle off the fire and started pouring it on the chest.

"What's that I hear, Brer Rabbit?"

"Just the wind blowing."

The water started splattering through the holes.

"What's that I feel, Brer Rabbit?"

"Must be fleas biting you."

"They biting mighty hard."

"Turn over," suggested Brer Rabbit.

Brer Wolf turned over and Brer Rabbit kept pouring.

"What's that I feel now, Brer Rabbit?"

"Must be more fleas."

"They eating me up, Brer Rabbit." And them was the last words Brer Wolf said, 'cause that scalding water did what it was supposed to.

Next winter all the neighbors admired the nice wolfskin mittens Brer Rabbit and his family had.

VILLAINS

Obviously there is no shortage of villains in the fairy tale, since the black-and-white simplicity of its dramatic structure produces the clearest of distinctions between protagonist and antagonist. We will not find in the fairy tale the kind of psychological analysis typical of the modern omniscient narrator, but once we remind ourselves how concrete the tale often is, we can easily perceive that in many cases the inner self is expressed through action or visual images. In other words, we are very rarely told what a character is thinking, and such editorial comment as Perrault is prone to offer must be seen as extraneous to the tale proper. At the simplest level, then, goodness is equated with beauty and wickedness with ugliness. As we have already observed, however, the equation is often more complex, as in the instance of Snow White's stepmother, whose beauty is all the more disturbing because it conceals her wickedness. Although this externalization reflects a simplistic brand of logic, the two latter tales in this section illustrate very effectively how much subtlety and insight can be conveyed through use of this "simple" convention.

Practically all the villains that we have met to this point have been female, which raises an interesting question: in a patriarchal society, why is it that the older female is so often depicted as strong, ruthless, and malevolent—qualities that have traditionally been identified with the masculine stereotype? Is this in fact part of the answer: that qualities deemed acceptable, perhaps even desirable, in a male can only be an aberration in a woman? Does the frequent occurrence of the witch in Western fairy tale represent a tacit acknowledgment of a power that has been corrupted by repression and denial? It is reasonable to observe that such women often have a motive for their behavior: Snow White's stepmother fears sexual rivalry, the wicked old fairy in "Sleeping Beauty" resents being passed over, and the witch in "Rapunzel" is just pathologically possessive.

A different kind of female villainy is depicted in the Grimms' "The Fisherman and his Wife," where the fisherman's good fortune in catching (and then freeing) an enchanted fish triggers an insatiable ambition and greed in his wife. Once again the woman is the dominant partner, which surely explains the misogynistic tone of the tale and its ending; the tale takes a positively lip-smacking pleasure in detailing the trajectory of her lust for power and glory. (Incidentally, this tale provides an amusing instance of what we might term "euphemistic translation," reminding us of the intervention not only of the translator but of the editor as well; their home may be a "pigsty" here but a more literal translation from the German would be "pisspot"!) This is an unusually visual tale, not only in the various stages of the wife's elevation but in the remarkable descriptions of an increasingly turbulent sea that indicate the extent to which her demands are contrary to nature; the disharmony that she is creating in the natural world (and in her marriage) is the measure of her villainy.

It is perhaps not coincidental that the two tales about male villains make them central characters, if only in the sense that their influence (rather than presence) dominates the story. In both cases they eventually get their comeuppance, although not without leaving behind a certain moral murkiness that characterizes these tales and gives them a distinctly modern "feel." That is particularly true of Perrault's "Bluebeard," in part because the central character is a wealthy businessman (not a common fairy-tale profession!) and also because the theme of this tale strikes as raw a nerve today as it ever may have done in the past, constantly reminded as we are of the primitive forces of psychopathic rage. Consequently, this tale has a realism that sets it apart from other tales (including the others in this section). Some regard it as having an historical origin—in *The Classic Fairy Tales*, the Opies nominate two possible candidates[1]—which suggests that the basis of a fairy tale is to be found in the combustible mixture of reality and imagination. Indeed, our ongoing fascination with the mysteries of the aberrant mind is well documented; from Jack the Ripper to Adolf Hitler, from Lady Macbeth to Hannibal Lecter, we find it difficult to avert our eyes from those who would lead us into the moral abyss.

In its dramatic inevitability, "Bluebeard" may usefully be compared to "Little Red Riding Hood": in each tale the central female character falls victim to a rapacious male, and in each there is the same chilling sense of doom as the trap is sprung. One way in which the tales differ, however, is in the level of symbolism: unlike the "human" wolf, Bluebeard appears to be a normal person in every respect except the color of his beard. The story hinges on our readiness to rationalize away what we would prefer not to see, even when the evidence is, so to speak, staring us in the face:

---

1   Iona and Peter Opie, *The Classic Fairy Tales* (New York: Oxford University Press, 1974) 134-36.

"Everything went so well that the youngest daughter began to think that the beard of the master of the house was not so very blue, after all."

Rumpelstiltskin also seems to have his "human" side, despite clearly being of netherworldly (and thus wicked) origin. We must resist the temptation to interpret his sympathy for the Queen's predicament as evidence of a heart of gold; his name (his English counterpart is called "Spindleshanks") is as clear an indicator as Bluebeard's beard that he is truly a villain. His generosity must be seen in the light of its deceitful and exploitative motive; his "guess-my-name" offer to the Queen is based on the conviction that he is setting her an impossible task.

The ambivalent feelings that both these tales provoke in us suggest that our identification with the characters is more complex than is customary in the fairy tale. In each instance, our sympathies are drawn in different directions at different points in the story. Few of us can, in all honesty, deny the attractiveness of the riches with which Bluebeard seduces his young wife (proof positive of his dastardly scheme) and the irresistibility of the desire to know what lies behind that closet door—she surely acts for us all in opening it. Yet once she has done so, she bears the guilt alone, and we have the luxury of watching in horrified fascination as her disobedience is discovered. Similarly, we can identify with the Queen's acceptance of the bargain offered to her by Rumpelstiltskin since she is left with no alternative; but when the time comes to face the consequences, we again assume the voyeuristic role, torn as we are (an appropriate turn of phrase, considering the story's ending) between the natural desire of the Queen to keep her baby and Rumpelstiltskin's apparent benevolence in granting her another chance.

One aspect that all these tales have in common is their lack of any "heroic" character; neither the fisherman nor Bluebeard's wife nor the Queen in "Rumpelstiltskin" is a very prepossessing figure. The Queen is perhaps more of a victim than the wife, who, the tale implies, is at least partly to blame for her predicament; however, it can be argued how much either character has earned the happy ending and how much sympathy we should feel for the fisherman back in his pigsty. Be that as it may, justice demands that the villains be punished and their victims compensated for the suffering to which they have been subjected. One hopes that their experiences result in a new maturity, although evidence of that can only be seen in Bluebeard's wife, whose generosity toward her family and marriage to a worthy gentleman bespeak a very different frame of mind from that in which she entered her first marriage!

BLUEBEARD[1]

Charles Perrault

THERE ONCE LIVED A MAN who owned fine town houses and fine country houses, dinner services of gold and silver, tapestry chairs and gilded coaches; but, alas, God had also given him a blue beard, which made him look so ghastly that women fled at the sight of him.

A certain neighbor of his was the mother of two beautiful daughters. He decided to marry one or other of them, but he left the girls to decide between themselves which of them should become his wife; whoever would take him could have him. But neither of them wanted him; both felt a profound distaste for a man with a blue beard. They were even more suspicious of him because he had been married several times before and nobody knew what had become of his wives.

In order to make friends with the girls, Bluebeard threw a lavish house-party at one of his country mansions for the sisters, their mother, three or four of their closest friends and several neighbors. The party lasted for eight whole days. Every day there were elaborate parties of pleasure—fishing, hunting, dancing, games, feasting. The guests hardly slept at all but spent the night playing practical jokes on one another. Everything went so well that the youngest daughter began to think that the beard of the master of the house was not so very blue, after all; that he was, all in all, a very fine fellow.

As soon as they returned to town, the marriage took place.

After a month had passed, Bluebeard told his wife he must leave her to her own devices for six weeks or so; he had urgent business in the provinces and must attend to it immediately. But he urged her to enjoy herself while he was away; her friends should visit her and, if she wished, she could take them to the country with her. But, above all, she must keep in good spirits.

"Look!" he said to her. "Here are the keys of my two large attics, where the furniture is stored; this is the key to the cabinet in which I keep the dinner services of gold and silver that are too good to use every day; these are the keys of the strong-boxes in which I keep my money; these are the keys of my chests of precious stones; and this is the pass key that will let you into every one of the rooms in my mansion. Use these keys freely. All is yours. But this little key, here, is the key of the room at the end of the long gallery on the ground floor; open everything, go everywhere, but I absolutely forbid you to go into that little room and, if you so much as open the door, I warn you that nothing will spare you from my wrath."

---

1   First published in 1697. This text from *Sleeping Beauty and Other Favourite Fairy Tales,* trans. Angela Carter (London: Gollancz, 1982).

She promised to do as he told her. He kissed her, got into his carriage and drove away.

Her friends and neighbors did not wait until she sent for them to visit her. They were all eager to see the splendours of her house. None of them had dared to call while the master was at home because his blue beard was so offensive. But now they could explore all the rooms at leisure and each one was more sumptuous than the last. They climbed into the attics and were lost for words with which to admire the number and beauty of the tapestries, the beds, the sofas, the cabinets, the tables, and the long mirrors, some of which had frames of glass, others of silver or gilded vermilion—all more magnificent than anything they had ever seen. They never stopped congratulating their friend on her good luck, but she took no pleasure from the sight of all this luxury because she was utterly consumed with the desire to open the door of the forbidden room.

Her curiosity so tormented her that, at last, without stopping to think how rude it was to leave her friends, she ran down the little staircase so fast she almost tripped and broke her neck. When she reached the door of the forbidden room, she stopped for a moment and remembered that her husband had absolutely forbidden her to go inside. She wondered if he would punish her for being disobedient; but the temptation was so strong she could not resist it. She took the little key, and, trembling, opened the door.

The windows were shuttered and at first she could see nothing; but, after a few moments, her eyes grew accustomed to the gloom and she saw that the floor was covered with clotted blood. In the blood lay the corpses of all the women whom Bluebeard had married and then murdered, one after the other. She thought she was going to die of fright and the key fell from her hand. After she came to her senses, she picked up the key, closed the door and climbed back to her room to recover herself.

She saw the key of this forbidden room was stained with blood and washed it. But the blood would not go away, so she washed it again. Still the blood-stain stayed. She washed it, yet again, more carefully, then scrubbed it with soap and sandstone; but the blood-stain would not budge. It was a magic key and nothing could clean it. When the blood was scrubbed from one side of the key, the stain immediately reappeared on the other side.

That same night, Bluebeard returned unexpectedly from his journey; a letter had arrived on the way to tell him that his business had already been satisfactorily settled in his absence. His wife did all she could to show him how delighted she was to have him back with her so quickly.

Next day, he asked her for his keys; she gave them to him but her hand was trembling so badly he guessed what had happened.

"How is it that the key of the little room is no longer with the others?" he asked.

"I must have left it upstairs on my dressing-table," she said, flustered.

"Give it to me," said Bluebeard.

She made excuse after excuse but there was no way out; she must go and fetch the key. Bluebeard examined it carefully and said to his wife:

"Why is there blood on this key?"

"I don't know," quavered the poor woman, paler than death.

"You don't know!" said Bluebeard. "But *I* know, very well! You have opened the door of the forbidden room. Well, madame, now you have opened it, you may step straight inside it and take your place beside the ladies whom you have seen there!"

She threw herself at her husband's feet, weeping and begging his forgiveness; she was truly sorry she had been disobedient. She was so beautiful and so distressed that the sight of her would have melted a heart of stone, but Bluebeard's heart was harder than any stone.

"You must die, madame," he said. "And you must die quickly."

She looked at him with eyes full of tears and pleaded:

"Since I must die, give me a little time to pray."

Bluebeard said: "I'll give you a quarter of an hour, but not one moment more."

As soon as she was alone, she called to her sister, Anne, and said:

"Sister Anne, climb to the top of the tower and see if my brothers are coming; they told me they would come to visit me today and if you see them, signal to them to hurry."

Sister Anne climbed to the top of the tower and the poor girl called out to her every minute or so:

"Sister Anne, Sister Anne, do you see anybody coming?"

And Anne, her sister, would reply:

"I see nothing but the sun shining and the grass growing green."

Bluebeard took an enormous cutlass in his hand and shouted to his wife: "Come down at once, or I'll climb up to you!"

"Oh, please, I beg you—just a moment more!" she implored, and called out, in a lower voice: "Sister Anne, Sister Anne, do you see anybody coming?"

Sister Anne replied:

"I see nothing but the sun shining and the grass growing green."

"Come down at once, or I'll climb up to you!" cried Bluebeard.

"I'll be down directly," his wife assured him; but still she whispered: "Sister Anne, Sister Anne, do you see anything coming?"

"I see a great cloud of dust drawing near from the edge of the horizon."

"Is it the dust my brothers make as they ride towards me?"

"Oh, no—it is the dust raised by a flock of sheep!"

"Will you never come down?" thundered Bluebeard.

"Just one moment more!" begged his wife and once again she demanded: "Sister Anne, Sister Anne, do you see anything coming?"

"I see two horsemen in the distance, still far away. Thank God!" she cried a moment later. "They are our brothers; I shall signal to them to hurry."

Bluebeard now shouted so loudly that all the house trembled. His unfortunate wife went down to him and threw herself in tears at his feet, her dishevelled hair tumbling all around her.

"Nothing you can do will save you," said Bluebeard. "You must die." With one hand, he seized her disordered hair and, with the other, raised his cutlass in the air; he meant to chop off her head with it. The poor woman turned her terrified eyes upon him and begged him for a last moment in which to prepare for death.

"No, no!" he said. "Think of your maker." And so he lifted up his cutlass. At that moment came such a loud banging on the door that Bluebeard stopped short. The door opened and in rushed two horsemen with naked blades in their hands.

He recognised his wife's two brothers; one was a dragoon, the other a musketeer. He fled, to save himself, but the two brothers trapped him before he reached the staircase. They thrust their swords through him and left him for dead. Bluebeard's wife was almost as overcome as her husband and did not have enough strength left to get to her feet and kiss her brothers.

Bluebeard left no heirs, so his wife took possession of all his estate. She used part of it to marry her sister Anne to a young man with whom she had been in love for a long time; she used more of it to buy commissions for her two brothers; and she used the rest to marry herself to an honest man who made her forget her sorrows as the wife of Bluebeard.

Moral

Curiosity is a charming passion but may only be satisfied at the price of a thousand regrets; one sees around one a thousand examples of this sad truth every day. Curiosity is the most fleeting of pleasures; the moment it is satisfied, it ceases to exist and it always proves very, very expensive.

Another Moral

It is easy to see that the events described in this story took place many years ago. No modern husband would dare to be half so terrible, nor to demand of his wife such an impossible thing as to stifle her curiosity. Be he never so quarrelsome or jealous, he'll toe the line as soon as she tells him to. And whatever colour his beard might be, it's easy to see which of the two is the master.

RUMPELSTILTSKIN[1]

Jacob and Wilhelm Grimm

ONCE THERE WAS A MILLER who was poor but had a beautiful daughter. One day he happened to be talking with the king, and wanting to impress him he said: "I've got a daughter who can spin straw into gold." The king said to the miller: "That's just the kind of talent that appeals to me. If your daughter is as clever as you say, bring her to my palace tomorrow and I'll see what she can do." When the girl arrived, he took her to a room that was full of straw, gave her a spinning wheel, and said: "Now get to work. You have the whole night ahead of you, but if you haven't spun this straw into gold by tomorrow morning, you will die." Then he locked the room with his own hands and she was left all alone.

The poor miller's daughter sat there, and for the life of her she didn't know what to do. She hadn't the faintest idea how to spin straw into gold, and she was so frightened that in the end she began to cry. Then suddenly the door opened and in stepped a little man. "Good evening, Mistress Miller," he said. "Why are you crying so?" "Oh," she said. "I'm supposed to spin straw into gold, and I don't know how." The little man asked: "What will you give me if I spin it for you?" "My necklace," said the girl. The little man took the necklace, sat down at the spinning wheel, and whirr, whirr, whirr, three turns, and the spool was full. Then he put on another, and whirr, whirr, whirr, three turns, and the second spool was full. All night he spun, and by sun-up all the straw was spun and the spools were full of gold.

First thing in the morning, the king stepped in. He was amazed and delighted when he saw the gold, but the greed for gold grew in his heart. He had the miller's daughter taken to a larger room full of straw and told her to spin this too into gold if she valued her life. She had no idea what to do and she was crying when the door opened. Again the little man appeared and said: "What will you give me if I spin this straw into gold for you?" "The ring off my finger." The little man took the ring and started the wheel whirring again, and by morning he had spun all the straw into glittering gold. The king was overjoyed at the sight, but his appetite for gold wasn't satisfied yet. He had the miller's daughter taken into a still larger room full of straw and said: "You'll have to spin this into gold tonight, but if you succeed, you shall be my wife." "I know she's only a miller's daughter," he said to himself, "but I'll never find a richer woman anywhere."

When the girl was alone, the little man came for the third time and said: "What

---

1   First published in 1812/15, in the first edition of *Kinder- und Hausmärchen*. This text from the second edition (1819), from *Grimms' Tales for Young and Old*, trans. Ralph Manheim (Garden City, NY: Anchor Press, 1977).

will you give me if I spin the straw into gold for you this time?" "I have nothing more to give you," said the girl. "Then promise to give me your first child if you get to be queen." "Who knows what the future will bring?" thought the miller's daughter. Besides, she had no choice. She gave the required promise, and again the little man spun the straw into gold. When the king arrived in the morning and found everything as he had wished, he married her, and the beautiful miller's daughter became a queen.

A year later she brought a beautiful child into the world. She had forgotten all about the little man. Suddenly he stepped into her room and said: "Now give me what you promised." The queen was horrified; she promised him all the riches in the kingdom if only he let her keep her child, but the little man said: "No. I'd sooner have a living thing than all the treasures in the world." Then the queen began to weep and wail so heartrendingly that the little man took pity on her: "I'll give you three days' time," he said. "If by then you know my name, you can keep your child."

The queen racked her brains all night; she went over all the names she had ever heard, and she sent out a messenger to inquire all over the country what other names there might be. When the little man came next day, she started with Caspar, Melchior, and Balthazar, and reeled off all the names she knew, but at each one the little man said: "That is not my name." The second day she sent servants around the district to ask about names, and she tried the strangest and most unusual of them on the little man: "Could your name be Ribcage or Muttonchop or Lacelegs?" But each time he replied: "That is not my name."

The third day the messenger returned and said: "I haven't discovered a single new name, but as I was walking along the edge of the forest, I rounded a bend and found myself at the foot of a high hill, the kind of place where fox and hare bid each other good night. There I saw a hut, and outside the hut a fire was burning, and a ridiculous little man was dancing around the fire and hopping on one foot and bellowing:

'Brew today, tomorrow bake,
After that the child I'll take,
And sad the queen will be to lose it.
Rumpelstiltskin is my name
But luckily nobody knows it.'

You can imagine how happy the queen was to hear that name. It wasn't long before the little man turned up and asked her: "Well, Your Majesty, what's my name?" She started by asking: "Is it Tom?" "No." "Is it Dick?" "No." "Is it Harry?" "No."

"Could it be Rumpelstiltskin?"

"The Devil told you that! The Devil told you that!" the little man screamed, and in his rage he stamped his right foot so hard that it went into the ground up to his waist. Then in his fury he took his left foot in both hands and tore himself in two.

THE FISHERMAN AND HIS WIFE[1]

Jacob and Wilhelm Grimm

THERE WAS ONCE A FISHERMAN who lived with his wife in a pigsty not far from the sea, and every day the fisherman went fishing. And he fished and he fished.

One day he was sitting with his line, looking into the smooth water. And he sat and he sat.

His line sank to the bottom, deep deep down, and when he pulled it up there was a big flounder on it. And the flounder said: "Look here, fisherman. Why not let me live? I'm not a real flounder, I'm an enchanted prince. What good would it do you to kill me? I wouldn't be much good to eat. Put me back in the water and let me go." "Save your breath," said the fisherman. "Do you think I'd keep a talking flounder?" So he put him back in the smooth water, and the flounder swam down to the bottom, leaving a long trail of blood behind him. Whereupon the fisherman got up and went home to his wife in the pigsty.

"Husband," said the wife, "haven't you caught anything today?" "No," said the fisherman. "I caught a flounder who said he was an enchanted prince, so I let him go." "Didn't you make a wish?" the wife asked. "No," he said. "What should I wish for?" "That's easy," said the wife. "It's so dreadful having to live in this pigsty. It stinks, it's disgusting: you could have wished for a little cottage. Go back and tell him we want a little cottage. He's sure to give us one." "How can I go back again?" said the husband. "Didn't you catch him and let him go?" said the wife. "He's bound to do it. Go right this minute." The husband didn't really want to go, but neither did he want to cross his wife, so he went to the shore.

When he got there, the sea was all green and yellow and not nearly as smooth as before. He stood there and said:

"Little man, whoever you be,
Flounder, flounder in the sea,

---

1   First published in 1812/15, in the first edition of *Kinder- und Hausmärchen*. This text from the second edition (1819), from *Grimms' Tales for Young and Old*, trans. Ralph Manheim (Garden City, NY: Anchor Press, 1977).

My wife, her name is Ilsebil,
Has sent me here against my will."

The flounder came swimming and asked: "Well, what does she want?" "It's like this," said the fisherman. "I caught you, didn't I, and now my wife says I should have wished for something. She's sick of living in a pigsty. She wants a cottage." "Just go home," said the flounder. "She's already got it."

The fisherman went home and his wife wasn't sitting in their pigsty any more. She was sitting on a bench outside a little cottage. She took him by the hand and said: "Come on in; look, it's much nicer." They went in, and there was a little hallway and a lovely little parlor and a bedroom with a bed for each of them, and a kitchen and a pantry, all with the best of furnishings and utensils, tinware and brassware, and everything that was needed. And behind the cottage there was a small barnyard with chickens and ducks in it and a little garden full of vegetables and fruit. "See," said the wife. "Isn't it nice?" "Yes indeed," said the husband. "If only it lasts, we shall live happy and contented." "We'll see about that," said the wife. Then they had something to eat and went to bed.

All went well for a week or two. Then the wife said: "Listen to me, husband. This cottage is too cramped and the garden and barnyard are too small. The flounder could have given us a bigger house. I'd like to live in a big stone castle. Go to the flounder and tell him to give us a castle." "Wife, wife," said the husband, "this cottage is plenty good enough. Why would we want to live in a castle?" "Don't argue," said the wife. "Just get going. The flounder can do that for us." "No, wife," said the husband. "The flounder has just given us a cottage, I don't think I ought to go back so soon, he might not like it." "Get going," said the wife. "It's no trouble at all to him and he'll be glad to do it." The husband's heart was heavy; he didn't want to go. He said to himself: "It's not right." But he went.

When he got to the sea, the water wasn't green and yellow any more, it was purple and dark-blue and gray and murky, but still calm. He stood there and said:

"Little man, whoever you be,
Flounder, flounder in the sea,
My wife, her name is Ilsebil,
Has sent me here against my will."

"Well, what does she want?" said the flounder. "Dear me!" said the fisherman in distress. "Now she wants to live in a big stone castle." "Just go home," said the flounder. "She's standing at the gate."

So the man started off and thought he was going home, but when he got there he found a big stone castle, and his wife was standing at the top of the staircase ready to go in. She took him by the hand and said: "Come on in." He went in with her and inside there was a great hall with a marble floor and lots of servants, who flung the big doors open, and the walls were all bright and covered with beautiful tapestries, and in the rooms all the tables and chairs were of gold. Crystal chandeliers hung from the ceiling, and all the halls and bedchambers had carpets, and the tables were so weighed down with victuals and the very best of wine that you'd have thought they'd collapse. And behind the house there was a big yard with barns and stables, and the very best of carriages, and there was also a wonderful big garden with the loveliest flowers and fruit trees, and a park that must have been half a mile long, with stags and deer and hares in it and everything you could possibly wish for. "Well," said the wife. "Isn't it nice?" "Yes, indeed," said the husband. "If only it lasts! We will live in this beautiful castle and be contented." "We'll see about that," said the wife. "We'll sleep on it." And with that they went to bed.

Next morning the wife woke up first. It was just daybreak, and from her bed she could see the beautiful countryside around her. Her husband was still stretching when she poked him in the side with her elbow and said: "Husband, get up and look out of the window. See here. Couldn't we be king over all that country? Go to the flounder and tell him we want to be king." "Wife, wife," said the husband. "What do we want to be king for? I don't want to be king." "Well," said the wife, "if you don't want to be king, then I'll be king. Go to the flounder. I want to be king." "But wife," said the fisherman, "why do you want to be king? I can't tell him that!" "Why not?" asked the wife. "Get going this minute. I must be king." Then the husband went, and he was very unhappy because of his wife wanting to be king. "It's not right, it's not right at all," he thought. And he didn't want to go, but he went.

When he got to the sea, it was all gray-black, and the water came churning up from the depths and it had a foul smell. And he stood there and said:

"Little man, whoever you be,
Flounder, flounder in the sea,
My wife, her name is Ilsebil,
Has sent me here against my will."

"Well, what does she want?" said the flounder. "Dear me," said the man. "She wants to be king." "Just go home," said the flounder, "she is already."

So the man went home, and when he got there the castle was much larger and had a big tower with marvelous ornaments. A sentry was standing at the gate, and there were lots of soldiers and drums and trumpets. And when the fisherman went inside, everything was made of pure marble and gold, with velvet covers and big golden tassels. The doors of the great hall opened, and there was the whole royal household, and his wife was sitting on a high throne of gold and diamonds, wearing a big golden crown and holding a scepter made of pure gold and precious stones, and on both sides of her ladies-in-waiting were standing in rows, each a head shorter than the last. He went and stood there and said: "My goodness, wife! So now you're king?" "That's right," said his wife. "Now I'm king." So he stood there and looked at her and after he'd looked awhile he said: "Now that you're king, suppose we let well enough alone. Let's stop wishing." "No, husband," she said, and she looked very upset. "Already the time is hanging heavy on my hands. I can't stand it any more. Go to the flounder. I'm king, but I've got to be emperor too." "Wife, wife," said the man, "why do you want to be emperor?" "Husband," she said, "go to the flounder. I want to be emperor." "Good Lord, woman," said the fisherman, "he can't make you emperor. I can't tell the flounder that! There's only one emperor in the empire. The flounder can't make you emperor, he just can't." "Fiddlesticks," said the woman. "I'm the king and you're only my husband, so do as you're told. If he can make a king he can also make an emperor. I want to be emperor and that's that. Get going." So he had to go. But on the way he was frightened, and he thought to himself: "This won't end well. Emperor is too much of a good thing. The flounder must be getting sick of all this."

When he got to the sea, it was all black and murky, the water came churning up from the depths and throwing up bubbles, and the wind was so strong that the sea frothed and foamed. The fisherman was filled with dread. And he stood there and said:

"Little man, whoever you may be,
Flounder, flounder in the sea,
My wife, her name is Ilsebil,
Has sent me here against my will."

"Well, what does she want?" said the flounder. "Oh, flounder," he said, "my wife wants to be emperor." "Just go home," said the flounder. "She is already."

So the fisherman went home, and when he got there, the whole palace was made of polished marble with alabaster figures and golden ornaments. Soldiers were marching and blowing trumpets and beating drums outside, and inside the building barons and counts and dukes were going about the duties of servants. They opened the doors for him and the doors were pure gold. When he went in, his wife was sitting on a throne which was all one block of gold and at least two miles high; and on her head she was wearing a big golden crown that was three ells high and studded with diamonds and rubies. In one hand she was holding the scepter and in the other the Imperial Orb, and on either side of her stood a row of lifeguards, each shorter than the one before him, from the most enormous giant, who was two miles high, to the tiniest dwarf, who was no bigger than my little finger. And before her stood a crowd of princes and dukes. Her husband went and stood among them and said: "Well, wife. It looks like you're emperor now." "That's right," she said. "I'm emperor." He stood there and took a good look at her, and when he'd been looking for a while, he said: "Well, wife, now that you're emperor, suppose we let well enough alone." "Husband," she said, "what are you standing there for? Yes, yes, I'm emperor, but now I want to be pope too, so go to the flounder." "Woman, woman," said the husband, "what won't you be asking next! You can't get to be pope, there's only one pope in all Christendom. He can't make you pope." "Husband," she said, "I want to be pope, so do as you're told. I insist on being pope before the day is out." "No, wife," said the husband, "I can't tell him that, it's too much; the flounder can't make you pope." "Husband," said the woman. "That's poppycock. If he can make an emperor, he can make a pope. Do as you're told. I'm the emperor and you're only my husband, so you'd better get going." At that he was afraid and went, but he felt faint. He shivered and shook and he was wobbly at the knees.

A strong wind was blowing, the clouds were flying fast, and toward evening the sky darkened. The leaves were blowing from the trees, the water roared and foamed as if it were boiling, and the waves pounded against the shore. In the distance he saw ships that were bobbing and bounding in the waves, and firing guns in distress. There was still a bit of blue in the middle of the sky, but there was red all around it as in a terrible storm. He stood there in fear and despair and said:

"Little man, whoever you be,
Flounder, flounder in the sea,
My wife, her name is Ilsebil,
Has sent me here against my will."

"Well, what does she want?" said the flounder. "Dear me!" said the fisherman. "She wants to be pope." "Just go home," said the flounder, "she is already."

So he went home, and when he got there, he found a big church with palaces all around it. He pushed through the crowd. Inside, the whole place was lighted with thousands and thousands of candles, and his wife, dressed in pure gold, was sitting on a throne that was even higher, much higher, and she was wearing three big golden crowns. All around her were church dignitaries, and on both sides of her there were rows of candles, from the biggest, which was as tall and thick as the biggest tower, down to the smallest kitchen candle. And all the emperors and kings were down on their knees to her, kissing her slipper. "Well, wife," said the fisherman, watching her closely, "so now you're pope?" "That's right," she said. "I'm pope." He stood there looking at her, and he felt as if he were looking into the bright sun. Then, after he'd been looking at her for a while, he said: "Well, wife, now that you're pope, suppose we let well enough alone!" But she sat there as stiff as a board, she didn't stir and she didn't move. "Wife," he said to her, "you'd better be satisfied now. You can't get to be anything better than pope." "I'll see about that," said the wife, and then they both went to bed. But she wasn't satisfied, her ambition wouldn't let her sleep, and she kept wondering what more she could get to be.

The fisherman slept soundly, for he had covered a lot of ground that day, but his wife couldn't get to sleep. All night she tossed and turned, wondering what more she could get to be, but she couldn't think of a single thing. Then the sun began to rise, and when she saw the red glow, she sat up in bed and looked out of the window. And when she saw the sun rising, she thought: "Ha! Why couldn't I make the sun and the moon rise? Husband!" she cried, poking him in the ribs. "Wake up. Go and see the flounder. I want to be like God." The fisherman was still half-asleep, but her words gave him such a start that he fell out of bed. He thought he'd heard wrong and he rubbed his eyes. "Wife, wife!" he cried out, "what did you say?" "Husband," she said, "if I can't make the sun and moon rise it will be more than I can bear. If I can't make them rise I'll never have another moment's peace." She gave him a grisly look that sent the cold shivers down his spine and cried: "Get going now. I want to be like God." "Wife, wife!" he cried, falling down on his knees, "the flounder can't do that. He can make an emperor and a pope, but please, please, think it over and just go on being pope." At that she grew angry, her hair flew wildly around her head. She tore her nightgown to shreds, and gave him a kick. "I won't stand for it!" she cried. "I won't stand for it another minute. *Will* you get a move on?" Then he pulled on his trousers and ran out like a madman.

A storm was raging. The wind was blowing so hard he could hardly keep his feet. Trees and houses were falling, the mountains were trembling, great boulders were tumbling into the sea, the sky was as black as pitch, the thunder roared, the lightning flashed, the sea was rising up in great black waves as big as mountains and church towers, and each one had a crown of foam on top. He couldn't hear his own words, but he shouted:

> "Little man, whoever you be,
> Flounder, flounder in the sea,
> My wife, her name is Ilsebil,
> Has sent me here against my will."

"Well, what does she want?" asked the flounder. "Dear me," he said, "she wants to be like God." "Just go home, she's back in the old pigsty already."

And there they are living to this day.

A LESS THAN PERFECT WORLD

In general, the fairy tale concerns itself with the crises that confront the individual, such as the challenges of maturation and relationships with others. One way in which individual writers developed the tale, however, was to use it as a vehicle for social critique. We may speculate that the attraction of this idea had something to do with the simple good-vs.-evil morality of the traditional tale that could bring a sharp focus to bear on the complexity of social problems.

For the most part, Andersen (1805-75) made it more of a priority to write indirectly about himself than about others, although he certainly had no difficulty finding fault with Danish society. For much of his life, he felt that his work was being ignored by a dull and unimaginative public, so we should not be too surprised by the gist of "The Emperor's New Clothes" (1837). The story is a satire on vanity and conformity and exhibits Andersen's characteristic ability to build a story around an incisive central idea—in this case, the trickster-weavers' creation of a fabric that is "...invisible to anyone who [is] unfit for his office or unforgivably stupid." It takes the intervention of one who has yet to be oppressed by the dead weight of social conformity to expose the self-deception that has prevailed throughout the story.

A similar concern is at the heart of "A Toy Princess" (1877), by Mary De Morgan (1850-1907), which is difficult not to see as a pointed satire on the emotional coldness that has long been associated with the English personality. It takes on a startling and poignant relevance if one considers it in the light of the unhappy life of the late Princess Diana—often referred to during her life both as "a fairy-tale princess" and "the people's princess"—who, like Ursula in De Morgan's story, appeared to have difficulty adjusting to the restraints that protocol and tradition placed upon her. Through the good offices of a fairy godmother, Ursula was granted a happy ending; reality was less kind to Princess Di, although the unprecedented outpouring of grief following her death contained a hint of indignation at such an inappropriate ending to her story. We could hardly ask for clearer evidence that fairy tale and real life are intimately interwoven.

The opportunity to pluck at the reader's heartstrings was unquestionably a factor that induced Oscar Wilde (1854-1900) to exploit the fairy-tale form; although it can hardly be claimed that he is remembered for his social idealism, the fact remains that several of his tales are notable for their emotive condemnation of such communal ills as poverty and greed. There is also reason to think that Wilde found some inspiration in the tales of Hans Andersen. References crop up throughout his tales that suggest Wilde was quite familiar with Andersen's work, although not necessarily approving of it; in the case of "The Happy Prince" (1888), however, the allusion appears to be an acknowledgment of the impact of his predecessor's story "The Little Match Girl" (1846). The fact that sentimentality plays a significant part in the impact should come as no surprise; Wilde's son reports his father as saying (of one of his own tales) that "really beautiful things always made him cry."[1]

Wilde's cultivated brilliance as raconteur and man of the world produces a self-conscious quality in his tales that gives them a very different feel from the tales of Perrault, Grimm, and even Andersen. (We must remember, of course, that Wilde wrote in English, so the impact of the translator is not an issue.) The diction of his tales draws attention to itself, to the extent that it becomes a major factor in our response to the story. Wilde is so meticulous in his choice of word and phrase, so attentive to rhythm and balance, that we should read his tale as a prose-poem. Consequently, it is impossible to imagine a retelling of any of his stories in the manner of a folk tale; Wilde's language is so integral to the story that, like poetry, it resists paraphrase.

There was something of a revival of dragons and other mythological beasts in the last decades of the nineteenth century, although they were generally of a rather different disposition than their belligerent predecessors. That was a good part of the problem, in fact, since these latecomers were of a more peaceable nature and were therefore finding their fearsome reputation for death and destruction rather a burden. This is the premise with which Frank Stockton (1834-1902) begins "The Griffin and the Minor Canon" (1885), in which the role of the griffin[2] is to act as a catalyst, turning upside-down the complacent daily life of a small town. Stockton is actually more interested in the behavior of the humans in his story: in the contrast between the mob mentality of the citizenry, who—curiously enough—propose to deal with the griffin either through death or destruction, and the lone voice of the minor canon,[3] whose humility and selflessness eventually bring about a happy

---

1   Vyvyan Holland, *Son of Oscar Wilde* (Westport, CT: Greenwood Press, 1973) 42.
2   griffin: A mythological creature with an eagle's head and wings and the body of a lion.
3   minor canon: A low-ranking priest serving in a cathedral.

ending, although not before Stockton has shown us some of the less attractive aspects of human nature. There is of course an element of parody in this story, particularly in the irascible griffin with his rather touching affection for the minor canon, but it remains firmly in the fairy-tale tradition of using fantasy to illuminate aspects of human reality.

As with the Villains section, there is a stronger sense of the real world in these four literary tales, perhaps because we have in recent times become so much more aware of the fact that we behave very differently in a group than as individuals—and just as there are crises to confront in the family orbit, so too in the wider context of the society of which we are members.

THE EMPEROR'S NEW CLOTHES[1]

Hans Christian Andersen

MANY, MANY YEARS AGO THERE was an emperor who was so terribly fond of beautiful new clothes that he spent all his money on his attire. He did not care about his soldiers, or attending the theatre, or even going for a drive in the park, unless it was to show off his new clothes. He had an outfit for every hour of the day. And just as we say, "The king is in his council chamber," his subjects used to say, "The emperor is in his clothes closet."

In the large town where the emperor's palace was, life was gay and happy; and every day new visitors arrived. One day two swindlers came. They told everybody that they were weavers and that they could weave the most marvellous cloth. Not only were the colours and the patterns of their material extraordinarily beautiful, but the cloth had the strange quality of being invisible to anyone who was unfit for his office or unforgivably stupid.

"This is truly marvellous," thought the emperor. "Now if I had robes cut from that material, I should know which of my councillors was unfit for his office, and I would be able to pick out my clever subjects myself. They must weave some material for me!" And he gave the swindlers a lot of money so they could start working at once.

They set up a loom and acted as if they were weaving, but the loom was empty. The fine silk and gold threads they demanded from the emperor they never used,

---

1 First published in 1837. This text from *Hans Christian Andersen: His Classic Fairy Tales*, trans. Erik Haugaard (New York: Doubleday, 1974).

but hid them in their own knapsacks. Late into the night they would sit before their empty loom, pretending to weave.

"I would like to know how far they've come," thought the emperor; but his heart beat strangely when he remembered that those who were stupid or unfit for their office would not be able to see the material. Not that he was really worried that this would happen to him. Still, it might be better to send someone else the first time and see how he fared. Everybody in town had heard about the cloth's magic quality and most of them could hardly wait to find out how stupid or unworthy their neighbours were.

"I shall send my faithful prime minister to see the weaver," thought the emperor. "He will know how to judge the material, for he is both clever and fit for his office, if any man is."

The good-natured old man stepped into the room where the weavers were working and saw the empty loom. He closed his eyes, and opened them again. "God preserve me!" he thought. "I cannot see a thing!" But he didn't say it out loud.

The swindlers asked him to step a little closer so that he could admire the intricate patterns and marvellous colours of the material they were weaving. They both pointed to the empty loom, and the poor old prime minister opened his eyes as wide as he could; but it didn't help, he still couldn't see anything.

"Am I stupid?" he thought. "I can't believe it, but if it is so, it is best no one finds out about it. But maybe I am not fit for my office. No, that is worse, I'd better not admit that I can't see what they are weaving."

"Tell us what you think of it," demanded one of the swindlers.

"It is beautiful. It is very lovely," mumbled the old prime minister, adjusting his glasses. "What patterns! What colours! I shall tell the emperor that I am greatly pleased."

"And that pleases us," the weavers said; and now they described the patterns and told which shades of colour they had used. The prime minister listened attentively, so that he could repeat their words to the emperor, and that is exactly what he did.

The two swindlers demanded more money, and more silk and gold thread. They said they had to use it for their weaving, but their loom remained as empty as ever.

Soon the emperor sent another of his trusted councillors to see how the work was progressing. He looked and looked just as the prime minister had, but since there was nothing to be seen, he didn't see anything.

"Isn't it a marvellous piece of material?" asked one of the swindlers; and they both began to describe the beauty of their cloth again.

"I am not stupid," thought the emperor's councillor. "I must be unfit for my office. That is strange; but I'd better not admit it to anyone." And he started to praise the material, which he could not see, for the loveliness of its patterns and colours.

"I think it is the most charming piece of material I have ever seen," declared the councillor to the emperor.

Everyone in town was talking about the marvellous cloth that the swindlers were weaving.

At last the emperor himself decided to see it before it was removed from the loom. Attended by the most important people in the empire, among them the prime minister and the councillor who had been there before, the emperor entered the room where the weavers were weaving furiously on their empty loom.

"Isn't it *magnifique*?" asked the prime minister.

"Your Majesty, look at the colours and patterns," said the councillor. And the two old gentlemen pointed to the empty loom, believing that all the rest of the company could see the cloth.

"What!" thought the emperor. "I can't see a thing! Why, this is a disaster! Am I stupid? Am I unfit to be emperor? Oh, it is too horrible!" Aloud he said, "It is very lovely. It has my approval," while he nodded his head and looked at the empty loom.

All the councillors, ministers, and men of great importance who had come with him stared and stared; but they saw no more than the emperor had seen, and they said the same thing that he had said, "It is lovely." And they advised him to have clothes cut and sewn, so that he could wear them in the procession at the next great celebration.

"It is magnificent! Beautiful! Excellent!" All of their mouths agreed, though none of their eyes had seen anything. The two swindlers were decorated and given the title "Royal Knight of the Loom."

The night before the procession, the two swindlers didn't sleep at all. They had sixteen candles lighting up the room where they worked. Everyone could see how busy they were, getting the emperor's new clothes finished. They pretended to take cloth from the loom; they cut the air with their big scissors and sewed with needles without thread. At last they announced: "The emperor's new clothes are ready!"

Together with his courtiers, the emperor came. The swindlers lifted their arms as if they were holding something in their hands, and said, "These are the trousers. This is the robe, and here is the train. They are all as light as if they were made of spider webs! It will be as if Your Majesty had almost nothing on, but that is their special virtue."

"Oh yes," breathed all the courtiers; but they saw nothing, for there was nothing to be seen.

"Will Your Imperial Majesty be so gracious as to take off your clothes?" asked the swindlers. "Over there by the big mirror, we shall help you put your new ones on."

The emperor did as he was told; and the swindlers acted as if they were dressing him in the clothes they should have made. Finally they tied around his waist the long train which two of his most noble courtiers were to carry.

The emperor stood in front of the mirror admiring the clothes he couldn't see.

"Oh, how they suit you! A perfect fit!" everyone exclaimed. "What colours! What patterns! The new clothes are magnificent!"

"The crimson canopy, under which Your Imperial Majesty is to walk, is waiting outside," said the imperial master of court ceremony.

"Well, I am dressed. Aren't my clothes becoming?" The emperor turned around once more in front of the mirror, pretending to study his finery.

The two gentlemen of the imperial bedchamber fumbled on the floor trying to find the train which they were supposed to carry. They didn't dare admit that they didn't see anything, so they pretended to pick up the train and held their hands as if they were carrying it.

The emperor walked in the procession under his crimson canopy. And all the people of the town, who had lined the streets or were looking down from the windows, said that the emperor's new clothes were beautiful. "What a magnificent robe! And the train! How well the emperor's clothes suit him!"

None of them were willing to admit that they hadn't seen a thing; for if anyone did, then he was either stupid or unfit for the job he held. Never before had the emperor's clothes been such a success.

"But he doesn't have anything on!" cried a little child.

"Listen to the innocent one," said the proud father. And the people whispered among each other and repeated what the child had said.

"He doesn't have anything on. There's a little child who says that he has nothing on."

"He has nothing on!" shouted all the people at last.

The emperor shivered, for he was certain that they were right; but he thought, "I must bear it until the procession is over." And he walked even more proudly, and the two gentlemen of the imperial bedchamber went on carrying the train that wasn't there.

A TOY PRINCESS[1]

Mary De Morgan

MORE THAN A THOUSAND YEARS ago, in a country quite on the other side of the world, it fell out that the people all grew so very polite that they hardly ever spoke to each other. And they never said more than was quite necessary, as "Just so," "Yes indeed," "Thank you," and "If you please." And it was thought to be the rudest thing in the world for anyone to say they liked or disliked, or loved or hated, or were happy or miserable. No one ever laughed aloud, and if any one had been seen to cry they would at once have been avoided by their friends.

The King of this country married a Princess from a neighbouring land, who was very good and beautiful, but the people in her own home were as unlike her husband's people as it was possible to be. They laughed, and talked, and were noisy and merry when they were happy, and cried and lamented if they were sad. In fact, whatever they felt they showed at once, and the Princess was just like them.

So when she came to her new home, she could not at all understand her subjects, or make out why there was no shouting and cheering to welcome her, and why everyone was so distant and formal. After a time, when she found they never changed, but were always the same, just as stiff and quiet, she wept, and began to pine for her own old home.

Every day she grew thinner and paler. The courtiers were much too polite to notice how ill their young Queen looked; but she knew it herself, and believed she was going to die. Now she had a fairy godmother, named Taboret, whom she loved very dearly, and who was always kind to her. When she knew her end was drawing near she sent for her godmother, and when she came had a long talk with her quite alone. No one knew what was said, and soon afterwards a little Princess was born, and the Queen died. Of course all the courtiers were sorry for the poor Queen's death, but it would have been thought rude to say so. So, although there was a grand funeral, and the court put on mourning, everything else went on much as it had done before.

The little baby was christened Ursula, and given to some court ladies to be taken charge of. Poor little Princess! She cried hard enough, and nothing could stop her.

All her ladies were frightened, and said that they had not heard such a dreadful noise for a long time. But, till she was about two years old, nothing could stop her crying when she was cold or hungry, or crowing when she was pleased.

After that she began to understand a little what was meant when her nurses told

---

1   From *On a Pincushion and Other Fairy Tales* (London: Fisher Unwin, 1877).

her, in cold, polite tones, that she was being naughty, and she grew much quieter.

She was a pretty little girl, with a round baby face and big merry blue eyes; but as she grew older, her eyes grew less and less merry and bright, and her fat little face grew thin and pale. She was not allowed to play with any other children, lest she might learn bad manners; and she was not taught any games or given any toys. So she passed most of her time, when she was not at her lessons, looking out of the window at the birds flying against the clear blue sky; and sometimes she would give a sad little sigh when her ladies were not listening.

One day the old fairy Taboret made herself invisible and flew over to the King's palace to see how things were going on there. She went straight up to the nursery, where she found poor little Ursula sitting by the window, with her head leaning on her hand.

It was a very grand room, but there were no toys or dolls about, and when the fairy saw this, she frowned to herself and shook her head.

"Your Royal Highness's dinner is now ready," said the head nurse to Ursula.

"I don't want any dinner," said Ursula, without turning her head.

"I think I have told your Royal Highness before that it is not polite to say you don't want anything, or that you don't like it," said the nurse. "We are waiting for your Royal Highness."

So the Princess got up and went to the dinner-table, and Taboret watched them all the time. When she saw how pale little Ursula was, and how little she ate, and that there was no talking or laughing allowed, she sighed and frowned even more than before, and then she flew back to her fairy home, where she sat for some hours in deep thought.

At last she rose, and went out to pay a visit to the largest shop in Fairyland.

It was a queer sort of shop. It was neither a grocer's, nor a draper's, nor a hatter's. Yet it contained sugar, and dresses, and hats. But the sugar was magic sugar, which transformed any liquid into which it was put; the dresses each had some special charm; and the hats were wishing-caps. It was, in fact, a shop where every sort of spell or charm was sold.

Into this shop Taboret flew; and as she was well known there as a good customer, the master of the shop came forward to meet her at once and, bowing, begged to know what he could get for her.

"I want," said Taboret, "a Princess."

"A Princess!" said the shopman, who was in reality an old wizard. "What size do you want it? I have one or two in stock."

"It must look now about six years old. But it must grow."

"I can make you one," said the wizard, "but it'll come rather expensive."

"I don't mind that," said Taboret. "See! I want it to look exactly like this," and so saying she took a portrait of Ursula out of her bosom and gave it to the old man, who examined it carefully.

"I'll get it for you," he said. "When will you want it?"

"As soon as possible," said Taboret. "By tomorrow evening if possible. How much will it cost?"

"It'll come to a good deal," said the wizard, thoughtfully. "I have such difficulty in getting these things properly made in these days. What sort of a voice is it to have?"

"It need not be at all talkative," said Taboret, "so that won't add much to the price. It need only say, 'If you please,' 'No, thank you,' 'Certainly,' and 'Just so.'"

"Well, under those circumstances," said the wizard, "I will do it for four cats' footfalls, two fish's screams, and two swans' songs."

"It is too much," cried Taboret. "I'll give you the footfalls and the screams, but to ask for swans' songs!"

She did not really think it dear, but she always made a point of trying to beat tradesmen down.

"I can't do it for less," said the wizard, "and if you think it too much, you'd better try another shop."

"As I am really in a hurry for it, and cannot spend time in searching about, I suppose I must have it," said Taboret; "but I consider the price very high. When will it be ready?"

"By tomorrow evening."

"Very well, then, be sure it is ready for me by the time I call for it, and whatever you do, don't make it at all noisy or rough in its ways"; and Taboret swept out of the shop and returned to her home.

Next evening she returned and asked if her job was done.

"I will fetch it, and I am sure you will like it," said the wizard, leaving the shop as he spoke. Presently he came back, leading by the hand a pretty little girl of about six years old—a little girl so like the Princess Ursula that no one could have told them apart.

"Well," said Taboret, "it looks well enough. But are you sure that it's a good piece of workmanship, and won't give way anywhere?"

"It's as good a piece of work as ever was done," said the wizard, proudly, striking the child on the back as he spoke. "Look at it! Examine it all over, and see if you find a flaw anywhere. There's not one fairy in twenty who could tell it from the real thing, and no mortal could."

"It seems to be fairly made," said Taboret, approvingly, as she turned the little girl round. "Now I'll pay you, and then will be off"; with which she raised her wand in the air and waved it three times, and there arose a series of strange sounds. The first was a low tramping, the second shrill and piercing screams, the third voices of wonderful beauty, singing a very sorrowful song.

The wizard caught all the sounds and pocketed them at once and Taboret, without ceremony, picked up the child, took her head downwards under her arm, and flew away.

At court that night the little Princess had been naughty, and had refused to go to bed. It was a long time before her ladies could get her into her crib, and when she was there, she did not really go to sleep, only lay still and pretended, till every one went away; then she got up and stole noiselessly to the window, and sat down on the windowseat all curled up in a little bunch, while she looked out wistfully at the moon. She was such a pretty soft little thing, with all her warm bright hair falling over her shoulders, that it would have been hard for most people to be angry with her. She leaned her chin on her tiny white hands, and as she gazed out, the tears rose to her great blue eyes; but remembering that her ladies would call this naughty, she wiped them hastily away with her nightgown sleeve.

"Ah moon, pretty bright moon!" she said to herself, "I wonder if they let you cry when you want to. I think I'd like to go up there and live with you; I'm sure it would be nicer than being here."

"Would you like to go away with me?" said a voice close beside her; and looking up she saw a funny old woman in a red cloak, standing near to her. She was not frightened, for the old woman had a kind smile and bright black eyes, though her nose was hooked and her chin long.

"Where would you take me?" said the little Princess, sucking her thumb, and staring with all her might.

"I'd take you to the sea-shore, where you'd be able to play about on the sands, and where you'd have some little boys and girls to play with, and no one to tell you not to make a noise."

"I'll go," cried Ursula, springing up at once.

"Come along," said the old woman, taking her tenderly in her arms and folding her in her warm red cloak. Then they rose up in the air and flew out of the window, right away over the tops of the houses.

The night air was sharp, and Ursula soon fell asleep; but still they kept flying on, on, over hill and dale, for miles and miles, away from the palace, towards the sea.

Far away from the court and the palace, in a tiny fishing village, on the sea, was a little hut where a fisherman named Mark lived with his wife and three children. He was a poor man, and lived on the fish he caught in his little boat. The children, Oliver, Philip, and little Bell, were rosy-cheeked and bright-eyed. They played all day long on the shore, and shouted till they were hoarse. To this village the fairy bore the still sleeping Ursula, and gently placed her on the doorstep of Mark's cottage; then she kissed her cheeks, and with one gust blew the door open, and disappeared before any one could come to see who it was.

The fisherman and his wife were sitting quietly within. She was making children's clothes, and he was mending his net, when without any noise the door opened and the cold night air blew in.

"Wife," said the fisherman, "just see who's at the door."

The wife got up and went to the door, and there lay Ursula, still sleeping soundly, in her little white nightdress.

The woman gave a little scream at sight of the child, and called to her husband.

"Husband, see, here's a little girl!" and so saying she lifted her in her arms, and carried her into the cottage. When she was brought into the warmth and light, Ursula awoke, and sitting up, stared about her in fright. She did not cry, as another child might have done, but she trembled very much, and was almost too frightened to speak.

Oddly enough, she had forgotten all about her strange flight through the air, and could remember nothing to tell the fisherman and his wife, but that she was the Princess Ursula; and, on hearing this, the good man and woman thought the poor little girl must be a trifle mad. However, when they examined her little nightdress, made of white fine linen and embroidery, with a crown worked in one corner, they agreed that she must belong to very grand people. They said it would be cruel to send the poor little thing away on such a cold night, and they must of course keep her till she was claimed. So the woman gave her some warm bread-and-milk and put her to bed with their own little girl.

In the morning, when the court ladies came to wake Princess Ursula, they found her sleeping as usual in her little bed, and little did they think it was not she, but a toy Princess placed there in her stead. Indeed the ladies were much pleased; for, when they said, "It is time for your Royal Highness to arise," she only answered, "Certainly," and let herself be dressed without another word. And as the time passed, and she was never naughty, and scarcely ever spoke, all said she was vastly improved, and she grew to be a great favourite.

The ladies all said that the young Princess bid fair to have the most elegant manners in the country, and the King smiled and noticed her with pleasure.

In the meantime, in the fisherman's cottage far away, the real Ursula grew tall and straight as an alder, and merry and light-hearted as a bird.

No one came to claim her, so the good fisherman and his wife kept her and brought her up among their own little ones. She played with them on the beach, and learned her lessons with them at school, and her old life had become like a dream she barely remembered.

But sometimes the mother would take out the little embroidered nightgown and show it to her, and wonder whence she came, and to whom she belonged.

"I don't care who I belong to," said Ursula; "they won't come and take me from you, and that's all I care about." So she grew tall and fair, and as she grew, the toy Princess, in her place at the court, grew too, and always was just like her, only that whereas Ursula's face was sunburnt and her cheeks red, the face of the toy Princess was pale, with only a very slight tint in her cheeks.

Years passed, and Ursula at the cottage was a tall young woman, and Ursula at the court was thought to be the most beautiful there, and everyone admired her manners, though she never said anything but "If you please," "No, thank you," "Certainly," and "Just so." The King was now an old man, and the fisherman Mark and his wife were grey-headed. Most of their fishing was now done by their eldest son, Oliver, who was their great pride. Ursula waited on them, and cleaned the house, and did the needlework, and was so useful that they could not have done without her. The fairy Taboret had come to the cottage from time to time, unseen by anyone, to see Ursula, and always finding her healthy and merry, was pleased to think of how she had saved her from a dreadful life. But one evening when she paid them a visit, not having been there for some time, she saw something which made her pause and consider. Oliver and Ursula were standing together watching the waves, and Taboret stopped to hear what they said—

"When we are married," said Oliver, softly, "we will live in that little cottage yonder, so that we can come and see them every day. But that will not be till little Bell is old enough to take your place, for how would my mother do without you?"

"And we had better not tell them," said Ursula, "that we mean to marry, or else the thought that they are preventing us will make them unhappy."

When Taboret heard this she became grave, and pondered for a long time. At last she flew back to the court to see how things were going on there. She found the King in the middle of a state council. On seeing this, she at once made herself visible, when the King begged her to be seated near him, as he was always glad of her help and advice.

"You find us," said his Majesty, "just about to resign our sceptre into younger and more vigorous hands; in fact, we think we are growing too old to reign, and mean to abdicate in favour of our dear daughter, who will reign in our stead."

"Before you do any such thing," said Taboret, "just let me have a little private conversation with you"; and she led the King into a corner, much to his surprise and alarm.

In about half an hour he returned to the council, looking very white, and with a dreadful expression on his face, whilst he held a handkerchief to his eyes.

"My lords," he faltered, "pray pardon our apparently extraordinary behaviour. We have just received a dreadful blow; we hear on authority, which we cannot doubt, that our dear, dear daughter"—here sobs choked his voice, and he was almost unable to proceed—"is—is—in fact, not our daughter at all, and only a sham." Here the King sank back in his chair, overpowered with grief, and the fairy Taboret, stepping to the front, told the courtiers the whole story; how she had stolen the real Princess, because she feared they were spoiling her, and how she had placed a toy Princess in her place. The courtiers looked from one to another in surprise, but it was evident they did not believe her.

"The Princess is a truly charming young lady," said the Prime Minister.

"Has your Majesty any reason to complain of her Royal Highness's conduct?" asked the old Chancellor.

"None whatever," sobbed the King; "she was ever an excellent daughter."

"Then I don't see," said the Chancellor, "what reason your Majesty can have for paying any attention to what this—this person says."

"If you don't believe me, you old idiots," cried Taboret, "call the Princess here, and I'll soon prove my words."

"By all means," cried they.

So the King commanded that her Royal Highness should be summoned.

In a few minutes she came, attended by her ladies. She said nothing, but then she never did speak till she was spoken to. So she entered, and stood in the middle of the room silently.

"We have desired that your presence be requested," the King was beginning, but Taboret without any ceremony advanced towards her, and struck her lightly on the head with her wand. In a moment the head rolled on the floor, leaving the body standing motionless as before, and showing that it was but an empty shell. "Just so," said the head, as it rolled towards the King, and he and the courtiers nearly swooned with fear.

When they were a little recovered, the King spoke again. "The fairy tells me," he said, "that there is somewhere a real Princess whom she wishes us to adopt as our daughter. And in the meantime let her Royal Highness be carefully placed in a cupboard, and a general mourning be proclaimed for this dire event."

So saying he glanced tenderly at the body and head, and turned weeping away.

So it was settled that Taboret was to fetch Princess Ursula, and the King and council were to be assembled to meet her.

That evening the fairy flew to Mark's cottage, and told them the whole truth about Ursula, and that they must part from her.

Loud were their lamentations, and great their grief, when they heard she must leave them. Poor Ursula herself sobbed bitterly.

"Never mind," she cried after a time, "if I am really a great Princess, I will have you all to live with me. I am sure the King, my father, will wish it, when he hears how good you have all been to me."

On the appointed day, Taboret came for Ursula in a grand coach and four, and drove her away to the court. It was a long, long drive; and she stopped on the way and had the Princess dressed in a splendid white silk dress trimmed with gold, and put pearls round her neck and in her hair, that she might appear properly at court.

The King and all the council were assembled with great pomp, to greet their new Princess, and all looked grave and anxious. At last the door opened, and Taboret appeared, leading the young girl by the hand.

"That is your father!" said she to Ursula, pointing to the King; and on this, Ursula, needing no other bidding, ran at once to him, and putting her arms round his neck, gave him a resounding kiss.

His Majesty almost swooned, and all the courtiers shut their eyes and shivered.

"This is really!" said one.

"This is truly!" said another.

"What have I done?" cried Ursula, looking from one to another, and seeing that something was wrong, but not knowing what. "Have I kissed the *wrong person*?" On hearing which everyone groaned.

"Come now," cried Taboret, "if you don't like her, I shall take her away to those who do. I'll give you a week, and then I'll come back and see how you're treating her. She's a great deal too good for any of you." So saying she flew away on her wand, leaving Ursula to get on with her new friends as best she might. But Ursula could not get on with them at all, as she soon began to see.

If she spoke or moved they looked shocked, and at last she was so frightened and troubled by them that she burst into tears, at which they were more shocked still.

"This is indeed a change after our sweet Princess," said one lady to another.

"Yes, indeed," was the answer, "when one remembers how even after her head was struck off she behaved so beautifully, and only said, 'Just so.'"

And all the ladies disliked poor Ursula, and soon showed her their dislike. Before the end of the week, when Taboret was to return, she had grown quite thin and pale, and seemed afraid of speaking above a whisper.

"Why, what is wrong?" cried Taboret, when she returned and saw how much poor Ursula had changed. "Don't you like being here? Aren't they kind to you?"

"Take me back, dear Taboret," cried Ursula, weeping. "Take me back to Oliver, and Philip, and Bell. As for these people, I hate them."

And she wept again.

Taboret only smiled and patted her head, and then went into the King and courtiers.

"Now, how is it," she cried, "I find the Princess Ursula in tears? and I am sure you are making her unhappy. When you had that bit of wood-and-leather Princess, you could behave well enough to it, but now that you have a real flesh-and-blood woman, you none of you care for her."

"Our late dear daughter—" began the King, when the fairy interrupted him.

"I do believe," she said, "that you would like to have the doll back again. Now I will give you your choice. Which will you have—my Princess Ursula, the real one, or your Princess Ursula, the sham?"

The King sank back into his chair. "I am not equal to this," he said: "summon the council, and let them settle it by vote." So the council were summoned, and the fairy explained to them why they were wanted.

"Let both Princesses be fetched," she said; and the toy Princess was brought in with great care from her cupboard, and her head stood on the table beside her, and the real Princess came in with her eyes still red from crying and her bosom heaving.

"I should think there could be no doubt which one would prefer," said the Prime Minister to the Chancellor.

"I should think not either," answered the Chancellor.

"Then vote," said Taboret; and they all voted, and every vote was for the sham Ursula, and not one for the real one. Taboret only laughed.

"You are a pack of sillies and idiots," she said, "but you shall have what you want"; and she picked up the head, and with a wave of her wand stuck it on to the body, and it moved round slowly and said, "Certainly," just in its old voice; and on hearing this, all the courtiers gave something as like a cheer as they thought polite, whilst the old King could not speak for joy.

"We will," he cried, "at once make our arrangements for abdicating and leaving the government in the hands of our dear daughter"; and on hearing this the courtiers all applauded again.

But Taboret laughed scornfully, and taking up the real Ursula in her arms, flew back with her to Mark's cottage.

In the evening the city was illuminated, and there were great rejoicings at the recovery of the Princess, but Ursula remained in the cottage and married Oliver, and lived happily with him for the rest of her life.

THE HAPPY PRINCE[1]

Oscar Wilde

HIGH ABOVE THE CITY, ON a tall column, stood the statue of the Happy Prince. He was gilded all over with thin leaves of fine gold, for eyes he had two bright sapphires, and a large red ruby glowed on his sword-hilt.

He was very much admired indeed. "He is as beautiful as a weathercock," remarked one of the Town Councilors who wished to gain a reputation for having artistic tastes; "only not quite so useful," he added, fearing lest people should think him unpractical, which he really was not.

"Why can't you be like the Happy Prince?" asked a sensible mother of her little boy who was crying for the moon. "The Happy Prince never dreams of crying for anything."

"I am glad there is someone in the world who is quite happy," muttered a disappointed man as he gazed at the wonderful statue.

"He looks just like an angel," said the Charity Children as they came out of the cathedral in their bright scarlet cloaks and their clean white pinafores.

"How do you know?" said the Mathematical Master, "you have never seen one."

"Ah! but we have, in our dreams," answered the children, and the Mathematical Master frowned and looked very severe, for he did not approve of children dreaming.

One night there flew over the city a little Swallow. His friends had gone away to Egypt six weeks before, but he had stayed behind, for he was in love with the most beautiful Reed. He had met her early in the spring as he was flying down the river after a big yellow moth, and had been so attracted by her slender waist that he had stopped to talk to her.

"Shall I love you?" said the Swallow, who liked to come to the point at once, and the Reed made him a low bow. So he flew round and round her, touching the water with his wings, and making silver ripples. This was his courtship, and it lasted all through the summer.

"It is a ridiculous attachment," twittered the other Swallows; "she has no money, and far too many relations"; and indeed the river was quite full of Reeds. Then, when the autumn came they all flew away.

After they had gone he felt lonely, and began to tire of his lady-love. "She has no conversation," he said, "and I am afraid that she is a coquette, for she is always flirting with the wind." And certainly, whenever the wind blew, the Reed made the most

---

1   From *The Happy Prince and Other Stories* (London: David Nutt, 1888).

graceful curtsies. "I admit that she is domestic," he continued, "but I love travelling, and my wife, consequently, should love travelling also."

"Will you come away with me?" he said finally to her, but the Reed shook her head, she was so attached to her home.

"You have been trifling with me," he cried. "I am off to the Pyramids. Good-bye!" and he flew away.

All day long he flew, and at nighttime he arrived at the city. "Where shall I put up?" he said; "I hope the town has made preparations."

Then he saw the statue on the tall column.

"I will put up there," he cried; "it is a fine position, with plenty of fresh air." So he alighted just between the feet of the Happy Prince.

"I have a golden bedroom," he said softly to himself as he looked round, and he prepared to go to sleep; but just as he was putting his head under his wing, a large drop of water fell on him. "What a curious thing!" he cried; "there is not a single cloud in the sky, the stars are quite clear and bright, and yet it is raining. The climate in the north of Europe is really dreadful. The Reed used to like the rain, but that was merely her selfishness."

Then another drop fell.

"What is the use of a statue if it cannot keep the rain off?" he said; "I must look for a good chimney-pot," and he determined to fly away.

But before he had opened his wings, a third drop fell, and he looked up, and saw—Ah! what did he see?

The eyes of the Happy Prince were filled with tears, and tears were running down his golden cheeks. His face was so beautiful in the moonlight that the little Swallow was filled with pity.

"Who are you?" he said.

"I am the Happy Prince."

"Why are you weeping then?" asked the Swallow; "you have quite drenched me."

"When I was alive and had a human heart," answered the statue, "I did not know what tears were, for I lived in the Palace of Sans-Souci, where sorrow is not allowed to enter. In the daytime I played with my companions in the garden, and in the evening I led the dance in the Great Hall. Round the garden ran a very lofty wall, but I never cared to ask what lay beyond it, everything about me was so beautiful. My courtiers called me the Happy Prince, and happy indeed I was, if pleasure be happiness. So I lived, and so I died. And now that I am dead they have set me up here so high that I can see all the ugliness and all the misery of my city, and though my heart is made of lead yet I cannot choose but weep."

"What! Is he not solid gold?" said the Swallow to himself. He was too polite to make any personal remarks out loud.

"Far away," continued the statue in a low musical voice, "far away in a little street there is a poor house. One of the windows is open, and through it I can see a woman seated at a table. Her face is thin and worn, and she has coarse, red hands, all pricked by the needle, for she is a seamstress. She is embroidering passion-flowers on a satin gown for the loveliest of the Queen's maids-of-honour to wear at the next Court ball. In a bed in the corner of the room her little boy is lying ill. He has a fever, and is asking for oranges. His mother has nothing to give him but river water, so he is crying. Swallow, Swallow, little Swallow, will you not bring her the ruby out of my sword-hilt? My feet are fastened to this pedestal and I cannot move."

"I am waited for in Egypt," said the Swallow. "My friends are flying up and down the Nile, and talking to the large lotus-flowers. Soon they will go to sleep in the tomb of the great King. The King is there himself in his painted coffin. He is wrapped in yellow linen, and embalmed with spices. Round his neck is a chain of pale green jade, and his hands are like withered leaves."

"Swallow, Swallow, little Swallow," said the Prince, "will you not stay with me for one night, and be my messenger? The boy is so thirsty, and the mother so sad."

"I don't think I like boys," answered the Swallow. "Last summer, when I was staying on the river, there were two rude boys, the miller's sons, who were always throwing stones at me. They never hit me, of course; we swallows fly far too well for that, and besides I come of a family famous for its agility; but still, it was a mark of disrespect."

But the Happy Prince looked so sad that the little Swallow was sorry. "It is very cold here," he said; "but I will stay with you for one night, and be your messenger."

"Thank you, little Swallow," said the Prince.

So the Swallow picked out the great ruby from the Prince's sword, and flew away with it in his beak over the roofs of the town.

He passed by the cathedral tower, where the white marble angels were sculptured. He passed by the palace and heard the sound of dancing. A beautiful girl came out on the balcony with her lover. "How wonderful the stars are," he said to her, "and how wonderful is the power of love!"

"I hope my dress will be ready in time for the State ball," she answered; "I have ordered passion-flowers to be embroidered on it; but the seamstresses are so lazy."

He passed over the river, and saw the lanterns hanging to the masts of the ships. He passed over the Ghetto, and saw the old Jews bargaining with each other, and weighing out money in copper scales. At last he came to the poor house and looked in. The boy was tossing feverishly on his bed, and the mother had fallen asleep, she was so tired. In he hopped, and laid the great ruby on the table beside the woman's thimble. Then he flew gently round the bed, fanning the boy's forehead with his wings. "How cool I feel!" said the boy, "I must be getting better"; and he sank into a delicious slumber.

Then the Swallow flew back to the Happy Prince, and told him what he had done. "It is curious," he remarked, "but I feel quite warm now, although it is so cold."

"That is because you have done a good action," said the Prince. And the little Swallow began to think, and then he fell asleep. Thinking always made him sleepy.

When day broke he flew down to the river and had a bath. "What a remarkable phenomenon!" said the Professor of Ornithology as he was passing over the bridge. "A swallow in winter!" And he wrote a long letter about it to the local newspaper. Everyone quoted it, it was full of so many words that they could not understand.

"Tonight I go to Egypt," said the Swallow, and he was in high spirits at the prospect. He visited all the public monuments, and sat a long time on top of the church steeple. Wherever he went the Sparrows chirruped, and said to each other, "What a distinguished stranger!" so he enjoyed himself very much.

When the moon rose he flew back to the Happy Prince. "Have you any commissions for Egypt?" he cried; "I am just starting."

"Swallow, Swallow, little Swallow," said the Prince, "will you not stay with me one night longer?"

"I am waited for in Egypt," answered the Swallow. "Tomorrow my friends will fly up to the Second Cataract. The river-horse couches there among the bulrushes, and on a great granite throne sits the God Memnon. All night long he watches the stars, and when the morning star shines he utters one cry of joy, and then he is silent. At noon the yellow lions come down to the water's edge to drink. They have eyes like green beryls, and their roar is louder than the roar of the cataract."

"Swallow, Swallow, little Swallow," said the Prince, "far away across the city I see a young man in a garret. He is leaning over a desk covered with papers, and in a tumbler by his side there is a bunch of withered violets. His hair is brown and crisp, and his lips are red as a pomegranate, and he has large and dreamy eyes. He is trying to finish a play for the Director of the Theatre, but he is too cold to write any more. There is no fire in the grate, and hunger has made him faint."

"I will wait with you one night longer," said the Swallow, who really had a good heart. "Shall I take him another ruby?"

"Alas! I have no ruby now," said the Prince: "my eyes are all that I have left. They are made of rare sapphires, which were brought out of India a thousand years ago. Pluck out one of them and take it to him. He will sell it to the jeweller, and buy firewood, and finish his play."

"Dear Prince," said the Swallow, "I cannot do that"; and he began to weep.

"Swallow, Swallow, little Swallow," said the Prince, "do as I command you."

So the Swallow plucked out the Prince's eye, and flew away to the student's garret. It was easy enough to get in, as there was a hole in the roof. Through this he darted, and came into the room. The young man had his head buried in his hands, so he did not hear the flutter of the bird's wings, and when he looked up he found the beautiful sapphire lying on the withered violets.

"I am beginning to be appreciated," he cried; "this is from some great admirer. Now I can finish my play," and he looked quite happy.

The next day the Swallow flew down to the harbour. He sat on the mast of a large vessel and watched the sailors hauling big chests out of the hold with ropes. "Heave ahoy!" they shouted as each chest came up. "I am going to Egypt!" cried the Swallow, but nobody minded, and when the moon rose he flew back to the Happy Prince.

"I am come to bid you good-bye," he cried.

"Swallow, Swallow, little Swallow," said the Prince, "will you not stay with me one night longer?"

"It is winter," answered the Swallow, "and the chill snow will soon be here. In Egypt the sun is warm on the green palm-trees, and the crocodiles lie in the mud and look lazily about them. My companions are building a nest in the Temple of Baalbek, and the pink and white doves are watching them, and cooing to each other. Dear Prince, I must leave you, but I will never forget you, and next spring I will bring you back two beautiful jewels in place of those you have given away. The ruby shall be redder than a red rose, and the sapphire shall be as blue as the great sea."

"In the square below," said the Happy Prince, "there stands a little match-girl. She has let her matches fall in the gutter, and they are all spoiled. Her father will beat her if she does not bring home some money, and she is crying. She has no shoes or stockings, and her little head is bare. Pluck out my other eye, and give it to her, and her father will not beat her."

"I will stay with you one night longer," said the Swallow, "but I cannot pluck out your eye. You would be quite blind then."

"Swallow, Swallow, little Swallow," said the Prince, "do as I command you."

So he plucked out the Prince's other eye, and darted down with it. He swooped past the match-girl, and slipped the jewel into the palm of her hand. "What a lovely bit of glass!" cried the little girl; and she ran home, laughing.

Then the Swallow came back to the Prince. "You are blind now," he said, "so I will stay with you always."

"No little Swallow," said the poor Prince, "you must go away to Egypt."

"I will stay with you always," said the Swallow, and he slept at the Prince's feet.

All the next day he sat on the Prince's shoulder, and told him stories of what he had seen in strange lands. He told him of the red ibises, who stand in long rows on the banks of the Nile, and catch goldfish in their beaks; of the Sphinx, who is as old as the world itself and lives in the desert, and knows everything; of the merchants, who walk slowly by the side of their camels and carry amber beads in their hands; of the King of the Mountains of the Moon, who is as black as ebony, and worships a large crystal; of the great green snake that sleeps in a palm-tree, and has twenty priests to feed it with honey-cakes; and of the pygmies who sail over a big lake on large flat leaves, and are always at war with the butterflies.

"Dear little Swallow," said the Prince, "you tell me of marvelous things, but more marvelous than anything is the suffering of men and of women. There is no Mystery so great as Misery. Fly over my city, little Swallow, and tell me what you see there."

So the Swallow flew over the great city, and saw the rich making merry in their beautiful houses, while the beggars were sitting at the gates. He flew into dark lanes, and saw the white faces of starving children looking out listlessly at the black streets. Under the archway of a bridge two little boys were lying in one another's arms to try and keep themselves warm. "How hungry we are!" they said. "You must not lie here," shouted the watchman, and they wandered out into the rain.

Then he flew back and told the Prince what he had seen.

"I am covered with fine gold," said the Prince, "you must take it off, leaf by leaf, and give it to my poor; the living always think that gold can make them happy."

Leaf after leaf of the fine gold the Swallow picked off, till the Happy Prince looked quite dull and grey. Leaf after leaf of the fine gold he brought to the poor, and the children's faces grew rosier, and they laughed and played games in the street. "We have bread now!" they cried.

Then the snow came, and after the snow came the frost. The streets looked as if they were made of silver, they were so bright and glistening; long icicles like crystal daggers hung down from the eaves of the houses, everybody went about in furs, and the little boys wore scarlet caps and skated on the ice.

The poor little Swallow grew colder and colder, but he would not leave the Prince, he loved him too well. He picked up crumbs outside the baker's door when the baker was not looking, and tried to keep himself warm by flapping his wings.

But at last he knew that he was going to die. He had just enough strength to fly up to the Prince's shoulder once more. "Good-bye, dear Prince!" he murmured, "will you let me kiss your hand?"

"I am glad that you are going to Egypt at last, little Swallow," said the Prince, "you have stayed too long here; but you must kiss me on the lips, for I love you."

"It is not to Egypt that I am going," said the Swallow. "I am going to the House of Death. Death is the brother of Sleep, is he not?"

And he kissed the Happy Prince on the lips, and fell down dead at his feet.

At that moment a curious crack sounded inside the statue, as if something had broken. The fact is that the leaden heart had snapped right in two. It certainly was a dreadfully hard frost.

Early the next morning the Mayor was walking in the square below in company with the Town Councilors. As they passed the column he looked up at the statue: "Dear me! How shabby the Happy Prince looks!" he said.

"How shabby, indeed!" cried the Town Councilors, who always agreed with the Mayor: and they went up to look at it.

"The ruby has fallen out of his sword, his eyes are gone, and he is golden no longer," said the Mayor; "in fact, he is little better than a beggar!"

"Little better than a beggar," said the Town Councilors.

"And here is actually a dead bird at his feet!" continued the Mayor. "We must really issue a proclamation that birds are not to be allowed to die here." And the Town Clerk made a note of the suggestion.

So they pulled down the statue of the Happy Prince. "As he is no longer beautiful he is no longer useful," said the Art Professor at the University.

Then they melted the statue in a furnace, and the Mayor held a meeting of the Corporation to decide what was to be done with the metal. "We must have another statue, of course," he said, "and it shall be a statue of myself."

"Of myself," said each of the Town Councillors, and they quarrelled. When I last heard of them they were quarrelling still.

"What a strange thing!" said the overseer of the workmen at the foundry. "This broken lead heart will not melt in the furnace. We must throw it away." So they threw it on a dust-heap where the dead Swallow was also lying.

"Bring me the two most precious things in the city," said God to one of His Angels; and the Angel brought Him the leaden heart and the dead bird.

"You have rightly chosen," said God, "for in my garden of Paradise this little bird shall sing for evermore, and in my city of gold the Happy Prince shall praise me."

THE GRIFFIN AND THE MINOR CANON[1]

Frank Stockton

OVER THE GREAT DOOR OF an old, old church, which stood in a quiet town of a far-away land, there was carved in stone the figure of a large griffin. The old-time sculptor had done his work with great care, but the image he had made was not a pleasant one to look at. It had a large head, with enormous open mouth and savage teeth. From its back arose great wings, armed with sharp hooks and prongs. It had stout legs in front, with projecting claws, but there were no legs behind, the body running out into a long and powerful tail, finished off at the end with a barbed point. This tail was coiled up under him, the end sticking up just back of his wings.

The sculptor, or the people who had ordered this stone figure, had evidently been very much pleased with it, for little copies of it, also in stone, had been placed here and there along the sides of the church, not very far from the ground, so that people could easily look at them and ponder on their curious forms. There were a great many other sculptures on the outside of this church—saints, martyrs, grotesque heads of men, beasts, and birds, as well as those of other creatures which cannot be named, because nobody knows exactly what they were. But none were so curious and interesting as the great griffin over the door and the little griffins on the sides of the church.

A long, long distance from the town, in the midst of dreadful wilds scarcely known to man, there dwelt the Griffin whose image had been put up over the church door. In some way or other the old-time sculptor had seen him and, afterwards, to the best of his memory, had copied his figure in stone. The Griffin had never known this until, hundreds of years afterwards, he heard from a bird, from a wild animal, or in some manner which it is not easy to find out, that there was a likeness of him on the old church in the distant town.

Now, this Griffin had no idea whatever how he looked. He had never seen a mirror, and the streams where he lived were so turbulent and violent that a quiet piece of water, which would reflect the image of anything looking into it, could not be found. Being, as far as could be ascertained, the very last of his race, he had never seen another griffin. Therefore it was that, when he heard of this stone image of himself, he became very anxious to know what he looked like, and at last he determined to go to the old church and see for himself what manner of being he was. So he started off from the dreadful wilds, and flew on and on until he came to the countries inhabited by men, where his appearance in the air created great consternation. But he alighted nowhere, keeping up a steady flight until he reached the suburbs of the town which

---

1 First published in *St. Nicholas' Magazine*, 1885 (repr. New York: Hyperion, 2005).

had his image on its church. Here, late in the afternoon, he alighted in a green mead-ow by the side of a brook, and stretched himself on the grass to rest. His great wings were tired, for he had not made such a long flight in a century or more.

The news of his coming spread quickly over the town, and the people, frightened nearly out of their wits by the arrival of so extraordinary a visitor, fled into their hous-es and shut themselves up. The Griffin called loudly for some one to come to him; but the more he called, the more afraid the people were to show themselves. At length he saw two laborers hurrying to their homes through the fields, and in a terrible voice he commanded them to stop. Not daring to disobey, the men stood, trembling.

"What is the matter with you all?" cried the Griffin. "Is there not a man in your town who is brave enough to speak to me?"

"I think," said one of the laborers, his voice shaking so that his words could hardly be understood, "that—perhaps—the Minor Canon—would come."

"Go, call him, then!" said the Griffin. "I want to see him."

The Minor Canon, who filled a subordinate position in the old church, had just fin-ished the afternoon service, and was coming out of a side door, with three aged women who had formed the week-day congregation. He was a young man of a kind disposi-tion, and very anxious to do good to the people of the town. Apart from his duties in the church, where he conducted services every weekday, he visited the sick and the poor, counselled and assisted persons who were in trouble, and taught a school com-posed entirely of the bad children in the town, with whom nobody else would have anything to do. Whenever the people wanted something difficult done for them, they always went to the Minor Canon. Thus it was that the laborer thought of the young priest when he found that some one must come and speak to the Griffin.

The Minor Canon had not heard of the strange event, which was known to the whole town except himself and the three old women, and when he was informed of it, and was told that the Griffin had asked to see him, he was greatly amazed and frightened.

"Me!" he exclaimed. "He has never heard of me! What should he want with me?"

"Oh, you must go instantly!" cried the two men. "He is very angry now because he has been kept waiting so long, and nobody knows what may happen if you don't hurry to him."

The poor Minor Canon would rather have had his hand cut off than to go out to meet an angry griffin; but he felt that it was his duty to go, for it would be a woe-ful thing if injury should come to the people of the town because he was not brave enough to obey the summons of the Griffin; so, pale and frightened, he started off.

"Well," said the Griffin, as soon as the young man came near, "I am glad to see that there is someone who has the courage to come to me."

The Minor Canon did not feel very courageous, but he bowed his head.

"Is this the town," said the Griffin, "where there is a church with a likeness of myself over one of the doors?"

The Minor Canon looked at the frightful creature before him, and saw that it was, without doubt, exactly like the stone image on the church. "Yes," he said, "you are right."

"Well, then," said the Griffin, "will you take me to it? I wish very much to see it."

The Minor Canon instantly thought that if the Griffin entered the town without the people knowing what he came for, some of them would probably be frightened to death, and so he sought to gain time to prepare their minds.

"It is growing dark now," he said, very much afraid, as he spoke, that his words might enrage the Griffin, "and objects on the front of the church cannot be seen clearly. It will be better to wait until morning, if you wish to get a good view of the stone image of yourself."

"That will suit me very well," said the Griffin. "I see you are a man of good sense. I am tired, and I will take a nap here on this soft grass, while I cool my tail in the little stream that runs near me. The end of my tail gets red-hot when I am angry or excited, and it is quite warm now. So you may go; but be sure and come early tomorrow morning, and show me the way to the church."

The Minor Canon was glad enough to take his leave, and hurried into the town. In front of the church he found a great many people assembled to hear his report of his interview with the Griffin. When they found that he had not come to spread ruin and devastation, but simply to see his stony likeness on the church, they showed neither relief nor gratification, but began to upbraid the Minor Canon for consenting to conduct the creature into the town.

"What could I do?" cried the young man. "If I should not bring him he would come himself, and perhaps end by setting fire to the town with his red-hot tail."

Still the people were not satisfied, and a great many plans were proposed to prevent the Griffin from coming into the town. Some elderly persons urged that the young men should go out and kill him. But the young men scoffed at such a ridiculous idea. Then someone said that it would be a good thing to destroy the stone image, so that the Griffin would have no excuse for entering the town. This proposal was received with such favor that many of the people ran for hammers, chisels, and crowbars with which to tear down and break up the stone griffin. But the Minor Canon resisted this plan with all the strength of his mind and body. He assured the people that this action would enrage the Griffin beyond measure, for it would be impossible to conceal from him that his image had been destroyed during the night. But they were so determined to break up the stone griffin that the Minor Canon saw that there was nothing for him to do but to stay there and protect it. All night he walked up and down in front of the church door, keeping away the men who brought ladders by which they might mount to the great stone griffin and knock it to pieces with their hammers and crowbars. After many hours the people were obliged to give up their attempts, and went home to sleep. But the Minor Canon remained at his post till early morning, and then he hurried away to the field where he had left the Griffin.

The monster had just awakened, and rising to his fore-legs and shaking himself, he said that he was ready to go into the town. The Minor Canon, therefore, walked back, the Griffin flying slowly through the air at a short distance above the head of his guide. Not a person was to be seen in the streets, and they proceeded directly to the front of the church, where the Minor Canon pointed out the stone griffin.

The real Griffin settled down in the little square before the church and gazed earnestly at his sculptured likeness. For a long time he looked at it. First he put his head on one side, and then he put it on the other. Then he shut his right eye and gazed with his left, after which he shut his left eye and gazed with his right. Then he moved a little to one side and looked at the image, then he moved the other way. After a while he said to the Minor Canon, who had been standing by all this time:

"It is, it must be, an excellent likeness! That breadth between the eyes, that expansive forehead, those massive jaws! I feel that it must resemble me. If there is any fault to find with it, it is that the neck seems a little stiff. But that is nothing. It is an admirable likeness—admirable!"

The Griffin sat looking at his image all the morning and all the afternoon. The Minor Canon had been afraid to go away and leave him, and had hoped all through the day that he would soon be satisfied with his inspection and fly away home. But by evening the poor young man was utterly exhausted and felt that he must eat and sleep. He frankly admitted this fact to the Griffin, and asked him if he would not like something to eat. He said this because he felt obliged in politeness to do so; but as soon as he had spoken the words, he was seized with dread lest the monster should demand half a dozen babies, or some tempting repast of that kind.

"Oh, no," said the Griffin, "I never eat between the equinoxes. At the vernal and at the autumnal equinox I take a good meal, and that lasts me for half a year. I am extremely regular in my habits, and do not think it healthful to eat at odd times. But if you need food, go and get it, and I will return to the soft grass where I slept last night, and take another nap."

The next day the Griffin came again to the little square before the church, and remained there until evening steadfastly regarding the stone griffin over the door. The Minor Canon came once or twice to look at him, and the Griffin seemed very glad to see him. But the young clergyman could not stay as he had done before, for he had many duties to perform. Nobody went to the church, but the people came to the Minor Canon's house, and anxiously asked him how long the Griffin was going to stay.

"I do not know," he answered, "but I think he will soon be satisfied with looking at his stone likeness, and then he will go away."

But the Griffin did not go away. Morning after morning he went to the church, but after a time he did not stay there all day. He seemed to have taken a great fancy to the Minor Canon, and followed him about as he pursued his various avocations. He would wait for him at the side door of the church, for the Minor Canon held services every day, morning and evening, though nobody came now.

"If any one should come," he said to himself, "I must be found at my post."

When the young man came out, the Griffin would accompany him in his visits to the sick and the poor, and would often look into the windows of the school-house where the Minor Canon was teaching his unruly scholars. All the other schools were closed, but the parents of the Minor Canon's scholars forced them to go to school, because they were so bad they could not endure them all day at home—griffin or no griffin. But it must be said they generally behaved very well when that great monster sat up on his tail and looked in at the school-room window.

When it was perceived that the Griffin showed no sign of going away, all the people who were able to do so left the town. The canons and the higher officers of the church had fled away during the first day of the Griffin's visit, leaving behind only the Minor Canon and some of the men who opened the doors and swept the church. All the citizens who could afford it shut up their houses and traveled to distant parts, and only the working-people and the poor were left behind. After some days these ventured to go about and attend to their business, for if they did not work they would starve. They were getting a little used to seeing the Griffin, and having been told that he did not eat between equinoxes, they did not feel so much afraid of him as before.

Day by day the Griffin became more and more attached to the Minor Canon. He kept near him a great part of the time, and often spent the night in front of the little house where the young clergyman lived alone. This strange companionship was often burdensome to the Minor Canon. But, on the other hand, he could not deny that he derived a great deal of benefit and instruction from it. The Griffin had lived for hundreds of years, and had seen much, and he told the Minor Canon many wonderful things.

"It is like reading an old book," said the young clergyman to himself. "But how many books I would have had to read before I would have found out what the Griffin has told me about the earth, the air, the water, about minerals, and metals, and growing things, and all the wonders of the world!"

Thus the summer went on, and drew toward its close. And now the people of the town began to be very much troubled again.

"It will not be long," they said, "before the autumnal equinox is here, and then that monster will want to eat. He will be dreadfully hungry, for he has taken so much exercise since his last meal. He will devour our children. Without doubt, he will eat them all. What is to be done?"

To this question no one could give an answer, but all agreed that the Griffin must not be allowed to remain until the approaching equinox. After talking over the matter a great deal, a crowd of the people went to the Minor Canon, at a time when the Griffin was not with him.

"It is all your fault," they said, "that that monster is among us. You brought him here, and you ought to see that he goes away. It is only on your account that he stays here at all, for, although he visits his image every day, he is with you the greater part of the time. If you were not here he would not stay. It is your duty to go away, and then he will follow you, and we shall be free from the dreadful danger which hangs over us."

"Go away!" cried the Minor Canon, greatly grieved at being spoken to in such a way. "Where shall I go? If I go to some other town, shall I not take this trouble there? Have I a right to do that?"

"No," said the people, "you must not go to any other town. There is no town far enough away. You must go to the dreadful wilds where the Griffin lives, and then he will follow you and stay there."

They did not say whether or not they expected the Minor Canon to stay there also, and he did not ask them anything about it. He bowed his head, and went into his house to think. The more he thought, the more clear it became to his mind that it was his duty to go away, and thus free the town from the presence of the Griffin.

That evening he packed a leather bag full of bread and meat, and early the next morning he set out on his journey to the dreadful wilds. It was a long, weary, and doleful journey, especially after he had gone beyond the habitations of men; but the Minor Canon kept on bravely and never faltered. The way was longer than he had expected, and his provisions soon grew so scanty that he was obliged to eat but a little every day; but he kept up his courage, and pressed on, and after many days of toilsome travel he reached the dreadful wilds.

When the Griffin found that the Minor Canon had left the town, he seemed sorry, but showed no disposition to go and look for him. After a few days had passed, he became much annoyed, and asked some of the people where the Minor Canon had gone. But although the citizens had been so anxious that the young clergyman should go to the dreadful wilds, thinking that the Griffin would immediately follow him, they were now afraid to mention the Minor Canon's destination, for the monster seemed angry already, and if he should suspect their trick, he would doubtless become very much enraged. So everyone said he did not know, and the Griffin wandered about disconsolate. One morning he looked into the Minor Canon's school-house, which was always empty now, and thought that it was a shame that everything should suffer on account of the young man's absence.

"It does not matter so much about the church," he said, "for nobody went there. But it is a pity about the school. I think I will teach it myself until he returns."

It was the hour for opening the school, and the Griffin went inside and pulled the rope which rang the school bell. Some of the children who heard the bell ran in to see what was the matter, supposing it to be a joke of one of their companions. But when they saw the Griffin they stood astonished and scared.

"Go tell the other scholars," said the monster, "that school is about to open, and that if they are not all here in ten minutes I shall come after them."

In seven minutes every scholar was in place.

Never was seen such an orderly school. Not a boy or girl moved or uttered a whisper. The Griffin climbed into the master's seat, his wide wings spread on each side of him, because he could not lean back in his chair while they stuck out behind, and his great tail coiled around in front of the desk, the barbed end sticking up, ready to tap any boy or girl who might misbehave.

The Griffin now addressed the scholars, telling them that he intended to teach them while their master was away. In speaking he endeavored to imitate, as far as possible, the mild and gentle tones of the Minor Canon, but it must be admitted that in this he was not very successful. He had paid a good deal of attention to the studies of the school, and he determined not to attempt to teach them anything new, but to review them in what they had been studying. So he called up the various classes, and questioned them upon their previous lessons. The children racked their brains to remember what they had learned. They were so afraid of the Griffin's displeasure that they recited as they had never recited before. One of the boys, far down in his class, answered so well that the Griffin was astonished.

"I should think you would be at the head," said he. "I am sure you have never been in the habit of reciting so well. Why is this?"

"Because I did not choose to take the trouble," said the boy, trembling in his boots. He felt obliged to speak the truth, for all the children thought that the great eyes of the Griffin could see right through them, and that he would know when they told a falsehood.

"You ought to be ashamed of yourself," said the Griffin. "Go down to the very tail of the class, and if you are not at the head in two days, I shall know the reason why."

The next afternoon this boy was number one.

It was astonishing how much these children now learned of what they had been studying. It was as if they had been educated over again. The Griffin used no severity toward them, but there was a look about him which made them unwilling to go to bed until they were sure they knew their lessons for the next day.

The Griffin now thought that he ought to visit the sick and the poor, and he began to go about the town for this purpose. The effect upon the sick was miraculous. All except those who were very ill indeed, jumped from their beds when they heard he was coming, and declared themselves quite well. To those who could not get up he gave herbs and roots, which none of them had ever before thought of as medicines, but which the Griffin had seen used in various parts of the world, and most of them recovered. But, for all that, they afterwards said that no matter what happened to them, they hoped that they should never again have such a doctor coming to their bedsides, feeling their pulses and looking at their tongues.

As for the poor, they seemed to have utterly disappeared. All those who had depended upon charity for their daily bread were now at work in some way or other, many of them offering to do odd jobs for their neighbors just for the sake of their meals—a thing which before had been seldom heard of in the town. The Griffin could find no one who needed his assistance.

The summer now passed, and the autumnal equinox was rapidly approaching. The citizens were in a state of great alarm and anxiety. The Griffin showed no signs of going away, but seemed to have settled himself permanently among them. In a short time the day for his semi-annual meal would arrive, and then what would happen? The monster would certainly be very hungry, and would devour all their children.

Now they greatly regretted and lamented that they had sent away the Minor Canon. He was the only one on whom they could have depended in this trouble, for he could talk freely with the Griffin, and so find out what could be done. But it would not do to be inactive. Some step must be taken immediately. A meeting of the citizens was called, and two old men were appointed to go and talk to the Griffin. They were instructed to offer to prepare a splendid dinner for him on equinox day—one which would entirely satisfy his hunger. They would offer him the fattest mutton, the most tender beef, fish and game of various sorts, and anything of the kind he might fancy. If none of these suited, they were to mention that there was an orphan asylum in the next town

"Anything would be better," said the citizens, "than to have our dear children devoured."

The old men went to the Griffin, but their propositions were not received with favor.

"From what I have seen of the people of this town," said the monster, "I do not think I could relish anything which was prepared by them. They appear to be all cowards and, therefore, mean and selfish. As for eating one of them, old or young, I could not think of it for a moment. In fact, there was only one creature in the whole place for whom I could have had any appetite, and that is the Minor Canon, who has gone away. He was brave, and good, and honest, and I think I should have relished him."

"Ah!" said one of the old men, very politely, "in that case I wish we had not sent him to the dreadful wilds!"

"What!" cried the Griffin. "What do you mean? Explain instantly what you are talking about!"

The old man, terribly frightened at what he had said, was obliged to tell how the Minor Canon had been sent away by the people, in the hope that the Griffin might be induced to follow him.

When the monster heard this he became furiously angry. He dashed away from the old men and, spreading his wings, flew backward and forward over the town. He was so much excited that his tail became red-hot, and glowed like a meteor against the evening sky. When at last he settled down in the little field where he usually rested, and thrust his tail into the brook, the steam arose like a cloud, and the water of the stream ran hot through the town. The citizens were greatly frightened, and bitterly blamed the old man for telling about the Minor Canon.

"It is plain," they said, "that the Griffin intended at last to go and look for him, and we should have been saved. Now who can tell what misery you have brought upon us?"

The Griffin did not remain long in the little field. As soon as his tail was cool, he flew to the town hall and rang the bell. The citizens knew that they were expected to come there, and although they were afraid to go, they were still more afraid to stay away, and they crowded into the hall. The Griffin was on the platform at one end, flapping his wings and walking up and down, and the end of his tail was still so warm that it slightly scorched the boards as he dragged it after him.

When everybody who was able to come was there, the Griffin stood still and addressed the meeting.

"I have had a contemptible opinion of you," he said, "ever since I discovered what cowards you are, but I had no idea that you were so ungrateful, selfish, and cruel as I now find you to be. Here was your Minor Canon, who labored day and night for your good, and thought of nothing else but how he might benefit you and make you happy; and as soon as you imagine yourselves threatened with a danger—for well I know you are dreadfully afraid of me—you send him off, caring not whether he returns or perishes, hoping thereby to save yourselves. Now, I had conceived a great liking for that young man and had intended, in a day or two, to go and look him up. But I have changed my mind about him. I shall go and find him, but I shall send him back here to live among you, and I intend that he shall enjoy the reward of his labor and his sacrifices. Go, some of you, to the officers of the church, who so cowardly ran away when I first came here, and tell them never to return to this town under penalty of death. And if, when your Minor Canon comes back to you, you do not bow yourselves before him, put him in the highest place among you, and serve and honor him all his life, beware of my terrible vengeance! There were only two good things in this town: the Minor Canon and the stone image of myself over your church door. One of these you have sent away, and the other I shall carry away myself."

With these words he dismissed the meeting; and it was time, for the end of his tail had become so hot that there was danger of its setting fire to the building.

The next morning the Griffin came to the church, and tearing the stone image of himself from its fastenings over the great door, he grasped it with his powerful forelegs and flew up into the air. Then, after hovering over the town for a moment, he gave his tail an angry shake, and took up his flight to the dreadful wilds. When he reached this desolate region, he set the stone griffin upon a ledge of a rock which rose in front of the dismal cave he called his home. There the image occupied a position somewhat similar to that it had had over the church door; and the Griffin, panting with the exertion of carrying such an enormous load to so great a distance, lay down upon the ground, and regarded it with much satisfaction. When he felt somewhat rested he went to look for the Minor Canon. He found the young man, weak and half-starved, lying under the shadow of a rock. After picking him up and carrying him to his cave, the Griffin flew away to a distant marsh, where he procured some roots and herbs which he well knew were strengthening and beneficial to man, though he had never tasted them himself. After eating these the Minor Canon was greatly revived, and sat up and listened while the Griffin told him what had happened in the town.

"Do you know," said the monster, when he had finished, "that I have had, and still have, a great liking for you?"

"I am very glad to hear it," said the Minor Canon, with his usual politeness.

"I am not at all sure that you would be," said the Griffin, "if you thoroughly understood the state of the case, but we will not consider that now. If some things were different, other things would be otherwise. I have been so enraged by discovering the manner in which you have been treated that I have determined that you shall at last enjoy the rewards and honors to which you are entitled. Lie down and have a good sleep, and then I will take you back to the town."

As he heard these words, a look of trouble came over the young man's face.

"You need not give yourself any anxiety," said the Griffin, "about my return to the town. I shall not remain there. Now that I have that admirable likeness of myself in front of my cave, where I can sit at my leisure and gaze upon its noble features and magnificent proportions, I have no wish to see that abode of cowardly and selfish people."

The Minor Canon, relieved from his fears, lay back, and dropped into a doze; and when he was sound asleep, the Griffin took him up and carried him back to the town. He arrived just before daybreak, and putting the young man gently on the grass in the little field where he himself used to rest, the monster, without having been seen by any of the people, flew back to his home.

When the Minor Canon made his appearance in the morning among the citizens, the enthusiasm and cordiality with which he was received were truly wonderful. He was taken to a house which had been occupied by one of the banished high officers of the place, and everyone was anxious to do all that could be done for his health and comfort. The people crowded into the church when he held services, so that the three old women who used to be his weekday congregation could not get to the best seats, which they had always been in the habit of taking; and the parents of the bad children determined to reform them at home, in order that he might be spared the trouble of keeping up his former school. The Minor Canon was appointed to the highest office of the old church, and before he died he became a bishop.

During the first years after his return from the dreadful wilds, the people of the town looked up to him as a man to whom they were bound to do honor and reverence. But they often, also, looked up to the sky to see if there were any signs of the Griffin coming back. However, in the course of time they learned to honor and reverence their former Minor Canon without the fear of being punished if they did not do so.

But they need never have been afraid of the Griffin. The autumnal equinox day came round, and the monster ate nothing. If he could not have the Minor Canon, he did not care for anything. So, lying down with his eyes fixed upon the great stone griffin, he gradually declined, and died. It was a good thing for some of the people of the town that they did not know this.

If you should ever visit the old town, you would still see the little griffins on the sides of the church, but the great stone griffin that was over the door is gone.

JUXTAPOSITIONS

"The Blue Light" (Grimm) and "The Tinderbox" (Andersen)

Hans christian andersen was born in 1805 in a relatively remote part of Denmark and therefore grew up surrounded by a lively oral tradition. In some ways, Andersen proved an ideal transitional figure in the evolution of the European fairy tale, since he was both a recipient of oral folk tales and—later in his life—a writer of original literary tales. His unique position is illustrated in the pair of tales with which we begin this section. The echoes in "The Blue Light" of the story of Aladdin from the *Arabian Nights* must have particularly caught his attention; as a child, he had heard his father read stories from that collection. While Andersen is clearly aiming his version at the child, we may also detect a strong hint of parody.

THE BLUE LIGHT[1]
Jacob and Wilhelm Grimm

There once was a soldier who had served the king faithfully for many years, but when the war was over and he could serve no longer because of his many wounds, the king said to him: "You can go home. I don't need you any more. You won't be getting any more money, because when I pay wages I expect something in return." The soldier was very sad, for he couldn't see how he was going to keep

---

1 First published in 1812/15, in the first edition of *Kinder- und Hausmärchen*. This text from the second edition (1819), from *Grimms' Tales for Young and Old*, trans. Ralph Manheim (Garden City, NY: Anchor Press, 1977).

body and soul together. With a heavy heart he left the king and walked all day until he came to a forest. As night was falling, he saw a light and headed for it. Soon he came to a house that belonged to a witch. "Give me a night's lodging and something to eat and drink," he said, "or I shall die." "Oho!" said she. "Who gives a runaway soldier anything? But I'll be merciful and take you in, if you'll do what I tell you." "And what may that be?" "To spade up my garden tomorrow." The soldier accepted her proposition and worked hard all the next day, but by the time he had finished, night was falling. "Hmm," said the witch, "I see that you can't start out today. I'll keep you another night, but in turn you must chop and split a cord of wood for me." And that took the soldier all day and at nightfall the witch asked him to stay the night. "I have only a little thing to ask of you tomorrow," she said. "There's an old dry well behind the house. My light has fallen into it. It burns blue and never goes out. I want you to go down and get it for me." Next day the old woman took him to the well and let him down in a basket. He found the blue light and gave the signal for her to pull him up. She pulled him up all right, but when he was just below the rim she held out her hand and wanted him to give her the blue light. "Oh no," he said, for he read her wicked thoughts. "I won't give you the light until I have both my feet on the ground." At that the witch flew into a rage, let him drop to the bottom, and went away.

The ground at the bottom was moist and the poor soldier's fall didn't hurt him. The blue light was still burning, but what was the good of that? He was doomed to die, and he knew it. For a while he just sat there, feeling very dejected. Then he happened to put his hand in his pocket and felt his pipe, which was still half full of tobacco. "My last pleasure on earth!" he said to himself, took out the pipe, lit it with the blue light and began to smoke. The smoke rose in a ring and suddenly a black dwarf stood before him. "Master," said the dwarf, "what do you command?" The soldier was amazed. "What am I supposed to command?" he asked. "I must do whatever you ask," said the dwarf. "That's fine," said the soldier. "Then first of all, help me out of this well." The dwarf took him by the hand and led him through an underground passage, and the soldier didn't forget to take the blue light with him. On the way the dwarf showed him all the treasures which the witch had amassed and hidden there, and the soldier took as much gold as he could carry. When he was back above ground, he said to the dwarf: "Now go and tie up the old witch and take her to jail." A second later bloodcurdling screams were heard. She rode past as quick as the wind on the back of a wildcat, and a short while later the dwarf came back. "Your orders have been carried out," he announced. "She's already hanging on the gallows. What else do you command, master?" "Nothing right now. You can go home, but be ready when I call you." "All you have to do," said the dwarf, "is light your pipe with the blue light. I'll be there before you know it." And at that he vanished.

The soldier went back to the town he had come from. He stopped at the best inn, had fine clothes made, and ordered the innkeeper to furnish his room as splendidly as possible. When the room was ready and the soldier moved in, he called the black dwarf and said: "I served the king faithfully, but he sent me away and let me go hungry. Now I'm going to get even." "What shall I do?" asked the dwarf. "Late tonight, when the king's daughter is asleep in her bed, bring her here without waking her. I'm going to make her work as my slavey." "That will be easy for me, but dangerous for you," said the dwarf. "If you're discovered, you'll be in hot water." At the stroke of twelve the door opened and the dwarf carried the king's daughter in. "Aha!" said the soldier. "So there you are. Well, get to work. Go get the broom and sweep the place out." When she had finished he called her over to where he was sitting, stretched out his legs, and said: "Pull my boots off." When she had pulled them off, he threw them in her face, and she had to pick them up, clean them, and polish them until they shone. Only half-opening her eyes, she obeyed his commands without a murmur. At first cockcrow the dwarf carried her back to her bed in the royal palace.

When the king's daughter got up in the morning, she went to her father and told him she had had a strange dream. "I was carried through the streets with the speed of lightning and taken to the room of a soldier. I had to be his slavey and do all the nasty work and sweep the room and clean his boots. It was only a dream, but I'm as tired as if I'd really done it all." "Your dream may have been true," said the king. "Here's my advice. Fill your pocket with peas and make a little hole in it. If they carry you off again, the peas will fall out and leave a trail on the street." When the king said this, the dwarf, who had made himself invisible, was standing right there and he heard it all. And that night when he carried the king's daughter through the streets, some peas did indeed fall out of her pocket, but they couldn't make a trail, because the crafty dwarf had strewn peas in all the streets beforehand. And again the king's daughter had to do slavey's work until cockcrow.

Next morning the king sent his men out to look for the trail, but they couldn't find it because in every street, all over town, children were picking up peas and saying: "Last night it rained peas." "We'll have to think of something else," said the king. "Keep your shoes on when you go to bed. And before you come back from that place, hide one of them. Never fear, I'll find it." The black dwarf heard the king's plan and that night when the soldier asked him once again to go and get the king's daughter, he advised against it. "I don't know of any way to thwart that scheme. If the shoe is found in your room, you'll really be in for it." "Do as you're told," said the soldier. And for the third time the king's daughter had to work as his slavey. But before the dwarf carried her back to the palace, she hid one of her shoes under the bed.

Next morning the king had the whole town searched for his daughter's shoe, and it was found in the soldier's room. The dwarf had implored the soldier to save himself, and he had left town in haste, but was soon caught and thrown into prison. In his hurry to escape he had forgotten his most precious possessions, the blue light and his gold, and all he had in his pocket was one ducat. As he was standing loaded with chains at the window of his prison cell, he saw an old friend passing, and tapped on the windowpane. When his friend came over to him, he said: "Do me a favor. Get me the little bundle I left at the inn. I'll give you a ducat." His friend ran to the inn and brought him his bundle. As soon as the soldier was alone, he lit his pipe with the light and the dwarf appeared. "Don't be afraid," said the dwarf. "Go where they take you, and let them do as they please. Just be sure to take the blue light with you." The next day the soldier was brought to trial and though he had done no evil, the judge sentenced him to death. When he was led out to die, he asked the king for a last kindness. "What sort of kindness?" the king asked. "Let me smoke one last pipe on the way," said the soldier. "You can smoke three," said the king, "but don't expect me to spare your life." The soldier took out his pipe and lit it with the blue light. When a few rings of smoke had gone up, the dwarf appeared, holding a little cudgel. "What does my master command?" he asked. "Strike down those false judges and their henchmen, and don't spare the king who has treated me so badly." The dwarf raced back and forth like forked lightning and everybody his cudgel so much as touched fell to the ground and didn't dare to move. The king was so terrified that he begged for mercy and to preserve his bare life made over his kingdom to the soldier and gave him his daughter for his wife.

THE TINDERBOX[1]

Hans Christian Andersen

A SOLDIER CAME MARCHING DOWN THE road: Left … right! Left … right! He had a pack on his back and a sword at his side. He had been in the war and he was on his way home. Along the road he met a witch. She was a disgusting sight, with a lower lip that hung all the way down to her chest.

"Good evening, young soldier," she said. "What a handsome sword you have and what a big knapsack. I can see that you are a real soldier! I shall give you all the money that you want."

"Thank you, old witch," he said.

"Do you see that big tree?" asked the witch, and pointed to the one they were

---

1 First published in 1835. This text from *Hans Christian Andersen: His Classic Fairy Tales,* trans. Erik Haugaard (New York: Doubleday, 1974).

standing next to. "The trunk is hollow. You climb up to the top of the tree, crawl into the hole, and slide deep down inside it. I'll tie a rope around your waist, so I can pull you up again when you call me."

"What am I supposed to do down in the tree?" asked the soldier.

"Get money!" answered the witch and laughed. "Now listen to me. When you get down to the very bottom, you'll be in a great passageway where you'll be able to see because there are over a hundred lamps burning. You'll find three doors; and you can open them all because the keys are in the locks. Go into the first one; and there on a chest, in the middle of the room, you'll see a dog with eyes as big as teacups. Don't let that worry you. You will have my blue-checked apron; just spread it out on the floor, put the dog down on top of it, and it won't do you any harm. Open the chest and take as many coins as you wish, they are all copper. If it's silver you're after, then go into the next room. There you'll find a dog with eyes as big as millstones; but don't let that worry you, put him on the apron and take the money. If you'd rather have gold, you can have that too; it's in the third room. Wait till you see that dog, he's got eyes as big as the Round Tower in Copenhagen; but don't let that worry you. Put him down on my apron and he won't hurt you; then you can take as much gold as you wish."

"That doesn't sound bad!" said the soldier. "But what am I to do for you, old witch? I can't help thinking that you must want something too."

"No," replied the witch. "I don't want one single coin. Just bring me the old tin-derbox that my grandmother forgot the last time she was down there."

"I'm ready, tie the rope around my waist!" ordered the soldier.

"There you are, and here is my blue-checked apron," said the witch.

The soldier climbed the tree, let himself fall into the hole, and found that he was in the passageway, where more than a hundred lights burned.

He opened the first door. Oh! There sat the dog with eyes as big as teacups glaring at him.

"You are a handsome fellow!" he exclaimed as he put the dog down on the witch's apron. He filled his pockets with copper coins, closed the chest, and put the dog back on top of it.

He went into the second room. Aha! There sat the dog with eyes as big as millstones. "Don't keep looking at me like that," said the soldier good-naturedly. "It isn't polite and you'll spoil your eyes." He put the dog down on the witch's apron and opened the chest. When he saw all the silver coins, he emptied the copper out of his pockets and filled both them and his knapsack with silver.

Now he entered the third room. That dog was big enough to frighten anyone, even a soldier. His eyes were as large as the Round Tower in Copenhagen and they turned around like wheels.

"Good evening," said the soldier politely and saluted, for such a dog he had never seen before. For a while he just stood looking at it; but finally he said to himself, "Enough of this!" Then he put the dog down on the witch's apron and opened up the chest.

"God preserve me!" he cried. There was so much gold that there was enough to buy the whole city of Copenhagen, and all the gingerbread men, rocking horses, riding whips, and tin soldiers in the whole world. Quickly the soldier threw away all the silver coins that he had in his pockets and knapsack and put gold in them instead. He also filled his cap, and he stuffed so many coins in his boots he could hardly walk. Then he put the dog back on the chest, and slammed the door behind him.

"Pull me up, you old witch!" he shouted up through the hollow tree.

"Have you got the tinderbox?" she called back.

"Right you are, I have forgotten it," he replied honestly, and went back to get it. The witch hoisted him up and again he stood on the road; but now his pockets, knapsack, cap, and boots were filled with gold and he felt quite differently.

"Why do you want the tinderbox?" he asked.

"Mind your own business," answered the witch crossly. "You have got your money, just give me the tinderbox."

"Rubbish!" said the soldier. "Tell me what you are going to use it for, right now; or I'll draw my sword and cut off your head."

"No!" replied the witch firmly; so he chopped her head off. And when she lay there dead, he put all his gold in her apron, which he tied into a bundle, and threw over his shoulder. The tinderbox he dropped into his pocket; and off to town he went.

The town was nice, and the soldier went to the nicest inn, where he asked to be put up in the finest room and ordered all the things he liked to eat best for his supper, because now he had so much money that he was rich.

The servant who polished his boots thought it was very odd that a man so wealthy should have such worn-out boots. But the soldier hadn't had time to buy anything yet; the next day he bought boots and clothes that fitted his purse. And the soldier became a refined gentleman. People were eager to tell him all about their town and their king, and what a lovely princess his daughter was.

"I would like to see her," said the soldier.

"But no one sees her," explained the townfolk. "She lives in a copper castle, surrounded by walls, and towers, and a moat. The king doesn't dare allow anyone to visit her because it has been foretold that she will marry a common soldier, and the king doesn't want that to happen."

"If only I could see her," thought the soldier, though it was unthinkable.

The soldier lived merrily, went to the theatre, kept a carriage so he could drive in the king's park, and gave lots of money to the poor. He remembered well what it felt like not to have a penny in his purse.

He was rich and well dressed. He had many friends, and they all said that he was kind and a real cavalier; and such things he liked to hear. But since he used money every day and never received any, he soon had only two copper coins left.

He had to move out of the beautiful room downstairs, up to a tiny one in the garret, where he not only polished his boots himself but also mended them with a large needle. None of his friends came to see him, for they said there were too many stairs to climb.

It was a very dark evening and he could not even buy a candle. Suddenly he remembered that he had seen the stub of a candle in the tinderbox that he had brought up from the bottom of the hollow tree. He found the tinderbox and took out the candle. He struck the flint. There was a spark, and in through the door came the dog with eyes as big as teacups.

"What does my master command?" asked the dog.

"What's this all about?" exclaimed the soldier. "That certainly was an interesting tinderbox. Can I have whatever I want? Bring me some money," he ordered. In less time than it takes to say thank you, the dog was gone and back with a big sack of copper coins in his mouth.

Now the soldier understood why the witch had thought the tinderbox so valuable. If he struck it once, the dog appeared who sat on the chest full of copper coins; if he struck it twice, then the dog came who guarded the silver money; and if he struck it three times, then came the one who had the gold.

The soldier moved downstairs again, wore fine clothes again, and had fine friends, for now they all remembered him and cared for him as they had before.

One night, when he was sitting alone after his friends had gone, he thought, "It is a pity that no one can see that beautiful princess. What is the good of her beauty if she must always remain behind the high walls and towers of a copper castle? Will I never see her? ...Where is my tinderbox?"

He made the sparks fly, and the dog with eyes as big as teacups came. "I know it's very late at night," he said, "but I would so like to see the beautiful princess, if only for a minute."

Away went the dog; and faster than thought he returned with the sleeping princess on his back. She was so lovely that anyone would have known that she was a real princess. The soldier could not help kissing her, for he was a true soldier.

The dog brought the princess back to her copper castle; but in the morning while she was having tea with her father and mother, the king and queen, she told them that she had had a very strange dream that night. A large dog had come and carried her away to a soldier who kissed her.

"That's a nice story," said the queen, but she didn't mean it.

The next night one of the older ladies-in-waiting was sent to watch over the princess while she slept, to find out whether it had only been a dream, and not something worse.

The soldier longed to see the princess so much that he couldn't bear it, so at night he sent the dog to fetch her. The dog ran as fast as he could, but the lady-in-waiting had her boots on and she kept up with him all the way. When she saw which house he had entered, she took out a piece of chalk and made a big white cross on the door.

"Now we'll be able to find it in the morning," she thought, and went home to get some sleep.

When the dog returned the princess to the castle, he noticed the cross on the door of the house where his master lived; so he took a piece of white chalk and put crosses on all the doors of all the houses in the whole town. It was a very clever thing to do, for now the lady-in-waiting would never know which was the right door.

The next morning the king and queen, the old lady-in-waiting, and all the royal officers went out into town to find the house where the princess had been.

"Here it is!" exclaimed the king, when he saw the first door with a cross on it.

"No, my sweet husband, it is here," said his wife, who had seen the second door with a cross on it.

"Here's one!"

"There's one!"

Everyone shouted at once, for it didn't matter where anyone looked: there he would find a door with a cross on it; and so they all gave up.

Now the queen was so clever, she could do more than ride in a golden carriage. She took out her golden scissors and cut out a large piece of silk and sewed it into a pretty little bag. This she filled with the fine grain of buckwheat, and tied the bag around the princess' waist. When this was done, she cut a little hole in the bag just big enough for the little grains of buckwheat to fall out, one at a time, and show the way to the house where the princess was taken by the dog.

During the night the dog came to fetch the princess and carry her on his back to the soldier, who loved her so much that now he had only one desire, and that was to be a prince so that he could marry her.

The dog neither saw nor felt the grains of buckwheat that made a little trail all the way from the copper castle to the soldier's room at the inn. In the morning the king and queen had no difficulty in finding where the princess had been, and the soldier was thrown into jail.

There he sat in the dark with nothing to do; and what made matters worse was that everyone said, "Tomorrow you are going to be hanged!"

That was not amusing to hear. If only he had had his tinder-box, but he had forgotten it in his room. When the sun rose, he watched the people, through the bars of his window, as they hurried toward the gates of the city, for the hanging was to take place outside the walls. He heard the drums and the royal soldiers marching. Everyone was running. He saw a shoemaker's apprentice, who had not bothered to take off his leather apron and was wearing slippers. The boy lifted his legs so high, it looked as though he were galloping. One of his slippers flew off and landed near the window of the soldier's cell.

"Hey!" shouted the soldier. "Listen, shoemaker, wait a minute, nothing much will happen before I get there. But if you will run to the inn and get the tinderbox I left in my room, you can earn four copper coins. But you'd better use your legs or it will be too late."

The shoemaker's apprentice, who didn't have one copper coin, was eager to earn four; and he ran to get the tinderbox as fast as he could, and gave it to the soldier.

And now you shall hear what happened after that!

Outside the gates of the town, a gallows had been built; around it stood the royal soldiers and many hundreds of thousands of people. The king and the queen sat on their lovely throne, and opposite them sat the judge and the royal council.

The soldier was standing on the platform, but as the noose was put around his neck, he declared that it was an ancient custom to grant a condemned man his last innocent wish. The only thing he wanted was to be allowed to smoke a pipe of tobacco.

The king couldn't refuse; and the soldier took out his tinderbox and struck it: once, twice, three times! Instantly, the three dogs were before him: the one with eyes as big as teacups, the one with eyes as big as millstones, and the one with eyes as big as the Round Tower in Copenhagen.

"Help me! I don't want to be hanged!" cried the soldier.

The dogs ran toward the judge and the royal council. They took one man by the leg and another by the nose, and threw them up in the air, so high that when they hit the earth again they broke into little pieces.

"Not me!" screamed the king; but the biggest dog took both the king and the queen and sent them flying up as high as all the others had been.

The royal guards got frightened; and the people began to shout: "Little soldier, you shall be our king and marry the princess!"

The soldier rode in the king's golden carriage; and the three dogs danced in front of it and barked: "Hurrah!"

The little boys whistled and the royal guards presented arms. The princess came out of her copper castle and became queen, which she liked very much. The wedding feast lasted a week; and the three dogs sat at the table and made eyes at everyone.

"The Goose Girl" (Grimm) and "The Tale of the Handkerchief" (Donoghue)

EMMA DONOGHUE IS FAR FROM the first to retell a well-known fairy tale from a first-person perspective, but she is certainly one of the most insightful in her exploration of the nature of social rather than sexual inequality, as the dark, bitter servant-girl imposes her will on the fair, compliant princess. Donoghue's revisionist perspective (1997) achieves its effect by frustrating our expectations at the critical moment, when we anticipate the servant-girl's exposure as an impostor. Instead, Donoghue's goose-girl princess acknowledges that temperament is destiny by willingly ceding her royal position to her ambitious servant.

THE GOOSE GIRL[1]
Jacob and Wilhelm Grimm

THERE WAS ONCE AN OLD queen, whose husband had long been dead, and she had a beautiful daughter. When the princess was old enough, she was betrothed to a king's son who lived far away, and soon it was time for the marriage. The princess prepared to set out for the distant kingdom, and the queen packed all manner of precious things, jewels and goblets and gold and silver plate, in short, everything required for a royal dowry, for she loved her child with all her heart. And she also gave her a waiting maid to keep her company on the way and see to it that she reached her bridegroom safely. They were both given horses for the journey, and the princess's horse, whose name was Fallada, could talk. When it was time for them to go, the old mother went to her bedchamber, took a knife, and cut her finger till it bled. She let three drops of blood fall on a snippet of white cloth, which she gave her daughter, saying: "Take good care of this. You will need it on your journey."

After a sorrowful leavetaking the princess put the snippet of cloth in her bodice, mounted her horse, and rode away to her betrothed. When they had ridden an hour, she was thirsty and said to her waiting maid: "I'm thirsty. Get down from your horse, take the golden cup you've brought and bring me some water from the brook." The waiting maid answered: "If you're thirsty, go and serve yourself. Lie down over the brook and drink. I don't choose to wait on you." The princess was so thirsty that she dismounted, bent over the brook and drank. The maid wouldn't even let her use her

---

1 First published in 1812/15, in the first edition of *Kinder- und Hausmärchen*. This text from the second edition (1819), from *Grimms' Tales for Young and Old*, trans. Ralph Manheim (Garden City, NY: Anchor Press, 1977).

golden cup. "Poor me!" she sighed. And the three drops of blood replied: "If your mother knew of this, it would break her heart." But the princess was meek. She said nothing and remounted. They rode on for a few miles, but it was a hot day, the sun was scorching, and soon she was thirsty again. They came to a stream and again she said to her waiting maid: "Get down and bring me some water in my golden cup," for she had long forgotten the girl's wicked words. But the waiting maid answered even more haughtily than before: "If you're thirsty, go and drink. I don't choose to wait on you." And again the princess was so thirsty that she dismounted. She lay down over the flowing water, wept, and said: "Poor me!" And again the drops of blood replied: "If your mother knew of this, it would break her heart." As she bent over the stream, drinking, the snippet of cloth with the three drops of blood on it fell out of her bodice and flowed away with the stream. In her great distress she didn't notice, but the waiting maid had seen the cloth fall and gloated, for now she had power over the bride who, without the drops of blood, became weak and helpless. When the princess was going to remount the horse named Fallada, the maid said: "I'll take Fallada. My nag is good enough for you." And the princess had to put up with it. Then the waiting maid spoke harshly to her, saying: "Now give me your royal garments and take these rags for yourself." After that she made her swear under the open sky never to breathe a word of all this to a living soul at court, and if she hadn't sworn, the waiting maid would have killed her on the spot. But Fallada saw it all and took good note.

Then the waiting maid mounted Fallada and the true bride mounted the wretched nag, and on they rode until they reached the royal palace. There was great rejoicing at their arrival. The prince ran out to meet them and, taking the waiting maid for his bride, lifted her down from her saddle and led her up the stairs, while the real princess was left standing down below. The old king looked out of the window and saw how delicate and lovely she was, whereupon he went straight to the royal apartments and asked the bride about the girl in the courtyard, the one who had come with her. "Oh, I picked her up on the way to keep me company. Give her some work to keep her out of mischief." But the old king had no work for her and couldn't think of any, so he said: "There's a little boy who tends the geese, she can help him." So the true bride had to help the little gooseherd, whose name was Conrad.

After a while the false bride said to the young king: "Dearest husband, I beg you, do me a favor." "I shall be glad to," he replied. "Then send for the knacker and make him cut the head off the horse that brought me here. The beast infuriated me on the way." The truth was that she was afraid the horse would tell everyone what she had done to the princess. So it was arranged, and when the true princess heard that the faithful Fallada was to die, she secretly promised the knacker some money in return for a small service. At the edge of the town there was a big dark gateway through which she passed morning and evening with the geese. Would he nail Fallada's head to the wall of the gateway, so that she could see it every day? The knacker promised to do it, and after cutting the head off, he nailed it to the wall of the dark gateway.

Early in the morning when she and little Conrad drove the geese through the gateway, she said as she passed by:

"Oh, poor Fallada, hanging there,"

and the head answered:

"Oh, poor princess in despair,
If your dear mother knew,
Her heart would break in two."

After that she didn't open her mouth, and they drove the geese out into the country. When they reached a certain meadow, she sat down and undid her hair, which was pure gold, and little Conrad looked on. He loved the way her hair glistened in the sun and tried to pull some out for himself. Whereupon she said:

"Blow, wind, blow,
Take Conrad's hat and make it go
Flying here and flying there.
And make him run until I've done
Combing and braiding my hair
And putting it up in a bun."

Then a wind came up that sent little Conrad's hat flying far and wide, and he had to run after it. By the time he got back she had finished her combing and braiding, and he couldn't get himself any hair. That made him angry and he stopped talking to her. And so they tended the geese until evening, and then they went home.

Next morning as they drove the geese through the dark gateway, the princess said:

"Oh, poor Fallada, hanging there,"

and Fallada replied:

"Oh, poor princess in despair,
If your dear mother knew,

Her heart would break in two."

When they reached the meadow, she again sat down and combed out her hair. Again Conrad ran and tried to grab at it, and again she said:

"Blow, wind, blow,
Take Conrad's hat and make it go
Flying here and flying there.
And make him run until I've done
Combing and braiding my hair
And putting it up in a bun."

The wind blew and lifted the hat off his head and blew it far away. Little Conrad had to run after it, and by the time he got back, she had put her hair up and he couldn't get hold of it. And so they tended the geese until evening.

When they got home that evening, little Conrad went to the old king and said: "I don't want to tend geese with that girl any more." "Why not?" the old king asked. "Because she aggravates me from morning till night." "Tell me just what she does," said the old king. "Well," said the boy, "in the morning, when we drive the geese through the dark gateway, there's a horse's head on the wall. She always speaks to it and says:

"Oh, poor Fallada, hanging there,"

and the head answers:

"Oh, poor princess in despair,
If your dear mother knew,
Her heart would break in two."

And little Conrad went on to tell the old king what happened in the meadow and how he had to run after his hat in the wind.

The old king ordered him to go out again with the geese next day, and in the morning he himself sat down near the dark gateway and heard the princess talking with Fallada's head. And then he followed her into the meadow and hid behind a bush. With his own eyes he soon saw the goose girl and the little gooseherd coming along with their flock. And after a while he saw her sit down and undo her glistening golden hair. Once again she said:

"Blow, wind, blow,

Take Conrad's hat and make it go
Flying here and flying there.
And make him run until I've done
Combing and braiding my hair
And putting it up in a bun."

Then a gust of wind carried little Conrad's hat away, and he had to run and run, and meanwhile the girl quietly combed and braided her hair. The old king saw it all and went back to the palace unseen, and when the goose girl got home that evening, he called her aside and asked her why she did all those things. "I mustn't tell you that," she said. "I can't pour out my heart to anyone, because under the open sky I swore not to. I'd have been killed if I hadn't." He argued and kept at her, but he couldn't get anything out of her. So finally he said: "If you won't tell me, then pour out your heart to this cast-iron stove." With that he left her and she crawled into the cast-iron stove, and wept and wailed and poured out her heart: "Here I sit, forsaken by the whole world," she said. "And yet I'm a king's daughter. A false waiting maid forced me to give her my royal garments and took my place with my bridegroom, and now I'm a goose girl, obliged to do menial work. If my dear mother knew, her heart would break in two." The old king was standing outside with his ear to the stove-pipe, and he heard everything she said. He came back in and told her to come out of the stove. They dressed her in royal garments, and she was so beautiful that it seemed a miracle. The old king called his son and told him he had the wrong bride, that she was only a waiting maid, and that the one standing there, who had been the goose girl, was the right one. The young king was overjoyed when he saw how beautiful and virtuous she was. A great banquet was made ready, and all the courtiers and good friends were invited. At the head of the table sat the bridegroom. The princess was on one side of him and the waiting maid on the other, but the waiting maid was dazzled by the princess and didn't recognize her in her sparkling jewels. When they had finished eating and drinking and were all in good spirits, the old king put a riddle to the waiting maid: What, he asked, would a woman deserve who had deceived her master in such and such a way? He went on to tell the whole story and ended by asking: "What punishment does such a woman deserve?" The false bride replied: "She deserves no better than to have her clothes taken off and to be shut up stark naked in a barrel studded with sharp nails on the inside. And two white horses should be harnessed to it and made to drag her up street and down until she is dead." "You are that woman!" said the old king. "You have pronounced your own sentence, and that is what will be done to you." When the sentence had been carried out, the young king married the right bride, and they ruled the kingdom together in peace and happiness.

THE TALE OF THE HANDKERCHIEF[1]

Emma Donoghue

THE REASON I WOULD HAVE killed you to stay a queen is that I have no right to be a queen. I have been a fraud from the beginning.

I was born a maid, daughter to a maid, in the court of a widow far across the mountains. How could you, a pampered princess, know what it's like to be a servant, a pair of hands, a household object? To be no one, to own nothing, to owe every last mouthful to those you serve?

All our queen loved in the world was her horse and her daughter.

The horse was white, a magnificent mare with a neck like an oak. The princess was born in the same month of the same year as I was. But where I was dark, with thick brows that overshadowed my bright eyes, the princess was fair. Yellowish, I thought her; slightly transparent, as if the sun had never seen her face. All she liked to do was walk in the garden, up and down the shady paths between the hedges. Once when I was picking nettles for soup, I saw her stumble on the gravel and bruise her knee. The queen ran into the garden at the first cry, lifted her onto her lap and wiped two jeweled tears away with her white handkerchief. Another time I was scrubbing a hearth and stood up to stretch my back, when laughter floated through the open window. I caught sight of the two of them cantering past on the queen's horse, their hands dancing in its snowy mane.

My own mother died young and tired, having made me promise to be a good maid for the rest of my days. I kissed her waxy forehead and knew that I would break my word.

But for the moment I worked hard, kept my head low and my apron clean. At last I was raised to the position of maid to the princess. Telling me of my good fortune, the queen rested her smooth hand for half a moment on my shoulder. If your mother only knew, she said, how it would gladden her heart.

The young princess was a gentle mistress, never having needed to be anything else. The year she came of age, the queen received ambassadors from all the neighboring kingdoms. The prince she chose for her daughter lived a long day's ride away. He was said to be young enough. The girl said neither yes nor no; it was not her question to answer. She stood very still as I tried the bridal dresses on her for size. My hands looked like hen's claws against the shining brocade. The queen told her daughter not to be sad, never to be willful, and always to remember her royal blood. I listened, my mouth full of pins.

---

1   From *Kissing the Witch* (New York: HarperCollins, 1997).

If I had had such a mother I would never have left her to journey into a strange country. I would have fought and screamed and clung to the folds of her cloak. But then, my blood is not royal.

Ahead of her daughter the queen sent gold and silver and a box full of crystals. She took the princess into the chamber where I was packing furs, and there she took out a knife and pressed the point into her own finger. I could hardly believe it; I almost cried out to stop her. The queen let three drops of blood fall onto her lawn handkerchief. She tucked this into the girl's bosom, saying that as long as she kept the handkerchief, she could come to no great harm.

And then the queen led her daughter out into the courtyard, and swung her up onto her own great horse. I would come with you myself, she said, if only my kingdom were secure. In these troubled times you will be safer where you're going. In my place, you will have my own horse to carry you, and your own maid to ride behind you.

This was the first I had heard of it. I went to pack my clean linen. The rest of my bits and pieces I left under the mattress for the next maid; I had nothing worth taking into a far country. In the courtyard, a stableman hoisted me onto a nag weighed down with all the princess's paraphernalia.

I watched the queen and the princess kiss good-bye in the early-morning sunlight. The horse's mane shone like a torch, but where the mother's forehead rested against the daughter's, the sun behind them was blotted out.

We trotted along for some hours without speaking; the princess seemed lost in daydreams, and my mother had taught me never to be the first to break a silence. The day grew hotter as the sun crawled up the sky. Sweat began to break through the princess's white throat, trickling down the neck of her heavy gold dress. My thin smock was scorching through.

Suddenly there was a glint in the trees. The princess brought her great white horse to a halt and said, without looking at me, Please fill my golden cup with some cool water from that stream.

The heat in my head was a hammer on an anvil, pounding a sword into shape. It was the first order I had ever disobeyed in my life. If you're thirsty, I told her, get it yourself.

The princess turned her milky face and stared at me. When my eyes refused to fall she climbed down, a little awkwardly, and untied her cup. She pulled back her veil as she walked to the stream. I was thirsty myself, but I didn't move. The white horse looked round at me with its long eyes that seemed to say, If her mother only knew, it would break her heart. When the princess walked back from the stream, her mouth was wet and her cheeks were pale.

We rode on for several hours until the sun was beginning to sink. The princess reined in at the edge of a river and asked me again, more shyly, if I would fetch her some water. I did mean to say yes this time, now that I had taught her a lesson; I was not plotting anything. But when I opened my mouth, the sound that came out was No. If you want to drink, I said hoarsely, you have to stoop down for it.

I held her gaze until her eyes fell. She got down and stepped through the rushes to the water. The horse tossed its foam-colored head and neighed as if warning of an enemy approach. My lips were cracked; my tongue rasped against them as I watched the princess. She bent over the stream to fill her cup, and something fluttered from the curve of her breast into the water. My handkerchief, she cried, as it slid away. As if saying what it was would bring it back.

With that I leapt down from my knock-kneed horse and waded into the river. I found the square of linen caught in a knot of reeds, mud silting over the three brown drops. I turned and shook it in the princess's face. A drop of water caught on her golden sleeve. You know nothing, I told her. Do you even know how to wash a handkerchief?

She shook her head. Her face was marked with red, like faint lines on a map.

You scrub it on a rock like this, I told her, and scrub again, and scrub harder, and keep scrubbing until your fingers are numb. Look, the spots are coming out. Your mother's royal blood is nearly gone.

The princess made a small moan.

Look, there are only three faint marks left, I said. And then you find somewhere off the ground and leave it to bleach in the sun, I instructed her, tossing the handkerchief up into the high branches of a tree.

The princess's eyes left the handkerchief and came back. Hers was the look of the rabbit, and it brought out all the snake in me. Take off your dress, I told her.

She blinked.

Take off your dress or I'll strip it from your body with my bare hands.

She reached behind to unfasten the hooks. I didn't help. I watched. Then I slipped my own plain dress over my head. The air felt silken on my shoulders. The dresses lay crumpled at our feet like snakeskins. Look, I said. Where is the difference between us now?

The princess had no answer.

I picked up the golden cup and filled it from the stream. I drank until my throat hurt. I splashed my face and arms and breasts until I shivered despite the sun. Then I stepped into the stiff golden dress and turned my back on the girl. After a moment she understood, and began to do up the hooks and eyes. When she was finished, she hesitated, then pulled on the smock I had left in a heap by the rushes. It suited her. Her fair hair hung around her dry lips. I filled the cup again and passed it to her. She drank without a word.

[284]

When I got onto the white horse, it reared under me, and I had to give it a kick to make it stand still. I waited until I could hear the girl settling in the saddle of the old nag, and then I wheeled around. I am the queen's daughter, I told her, and you are my maid, and if you ever say otherwise I will rip your throat open with my bare hands.

Her eyes slid down to my fingers. The skin was angry, with calluses on the thumbs; anyone who saw it would know. I rummaged around in the saddlebag until I found a pair of white gloves and pulled them on. The girl was looking away. I moved my great horse alongside hers, until I was so close I could have struck her. Swear by the open sky, I whispered, that you will never tell anyone what has happened by this river.

I swear by the open sky, she repeated doubtfully, raising her eyes to it.

We rode on. The gold dress was heavier than I could have imagined. My bones felt as if they had been made to bear this burden, as if they had found their one true dress at last.

It was dark by the time we reached the palace. They had lit a double row of torches for us to follow. The prince came to the foot of the steps and lifted me down from my horse. Through the hard brocade I couldn't feel whether he was warm or cold. He was pale with nerves, but he had a kind face. At the top of the steps I made him put me down. I said, The maid I brought with me.

Yes? His voice was thin but not unpleasant.

She does not know anything about waiting on ladies. Could you set her to some simpler task?

Perhaps she could mind the geese, suggested the prince.

I gave a single nod and walked beside him toward the great doors. My back prickled. If the girl was going to denounce me, this would be the moment for it. But I heard nothing except the clinking harnesses as they led the horses away.

I found that I knew how to behave like a princess, from my short lifetime of watching. I snapped my fan; I offered my gloved hand to be kissed; I never bent my back. At times, I forgot for a moment that I was acting.

But I never forgot to be afraid. I had wanted to be married at once, but the pace of royal life is stately. There were pigs to be fattened, spices to wait for, the king and his army to come safely home. I was given a broad chamber with a view of the city arch and all the fields beyond.

The first week slid by. The goose girl seemed to go about her duties without a word. I had never eaten such good food in my life, but my stomach was a knotted rope. Every day I made some excuse to pass by the stables and catch a glimpse of the great white horse in its box. Its eyes grew longer as they fixed on me; If the queen her mother only knew, they seemed to say.

I became convinced that it was the horse who would betray me. It was not scared the way the goose girl was. In the dreams that came to ride me in my gilt feather bed, the horse drew pictures in the mud under the city arch with its hoof, illustrating my crime for all the court to see. Sometimes it spoke aloud in my head, its voice a deep whistle, telling all it knew. I woke with my knees under my chin, as if I were packed in a barrel, as we punish thieves in the mountains. That evening at dinner I said to my pale fiancé, That brute of a horse I rode here tried to throw me on the journey.

Then we will have it destroyed, he assured me.

His eyes were devoted, the shape of almonds. He looked as if he would believe every word that slipped from my mouth.

The next day, I passed by the stableyard, and the box was empty. Back in my chamber, I threw the window open to the delicate air. My eye caught sight of something bright, nailed to the city arch. Something in the shape of a horse's head. Below it stood a girl, geese clacking at her skirts. From this distance I couldn't be sure if her lips were moving.

She must have bribed the knacker to save the horse's head and nail it up where she would pass by. She must have guessed the exact shape of my fears. I watched her make her way through the arch and out into the open fields.

Another week crawled by. Every day I looked out for the girl pausing under the arch with her noisy flock, and tried to read her face. I wore my finest dresses, but my heart was drumming under their weight. I kept my white gloves buttoned, even on the hottest days.

I began to worry that the queen might come to the wedding after all, as a surprise for her daughter, despite the danger of leaving her kingdom unguarded. In the dreams that lined up along my bed, the queen pointed at me across the royal dining table and slapped the crown from my head. She ripped the glove from my hand and held up my finger, pressing it to the point of her knife, till dark drops stained the tablecloth: See, she cried, there is nothing royal about this blood, common as dirt. When I woke, doubled up, I felt as if they were driving long spikes through the sides of the barrel, into my skin.

One day I heard that a messenger had come from the kingdom of my birth. I couldn't get to him before the prince did. I sat in my chamber, waiting for the heavy tramp of the guards. But the step, when it came at last, was soft. The prince said, The queen your mother has fallen in battle.

So she will not be coming to the wedding? I asked, and only then understood his words. I bent over to hide my face from him; his gentle eyes shamed me. I hoped my laughter would sound like tears. And then the tears did come, and I hoped they were for her, a queen dead in her prime, and not just for my own treacherous self.

I don't know who told the goose girl. I hadn't the courage. I suppose she heard it in the kitchen, or from a goose boy. I thought that the moment of hearing might be the moment she would run through the court to denounce me. But the next morning she was standing under the arch in the usual way, her face turned up as if in conversation with the rotting head above her. She paused no longer than usual before walking her flock into the fields.

The day before the wedding, I rode out into the country. I found myself near the river where it all began, this fantastical charade. I stopped beside the bank, and there in the tree above my head was a flash of white.

I had to take off my dress to climb, or I would have got stuck in the branches. The tree left red lashes on my arms and thighs. At last my hand reached the handkerchief. It was washed through by the dew and bleached stiff by the sun, but there were still three faint brown marks.

I saw then that the end was coming. When I had dressed myself, I rode straight for the fields around the castle to find the goose girl. All at once I knew it would be tonight she would tell them; she was waiting till the last minute, so my hopes would be at their highest just before the guards came to take me away to a walled-up, windowless room.

There she was with the breeze blowing her yellow hair out of its bonds and across her sunburnt face. I rode up to her, then jumped down. I held out the handkerchief; my hand was shaking. It still bears the marks of your mother's royal blood, I told her. If I give it to you now, will you let me run away before you tell them?

She tucked the handkerchief into her rough dress and said, Tell what?

I stared at her. Your fear of me will die away, I said. Your need to speak the truth will swell within you. You will be overheard lamenting as you sleep beside the stove; you will confide in the reeds and they will sing it back.

Her eyes flicked upward. She said, By the open sky, I swear I will never tell what is not true.

But you are the royal princess, I reminded her.

A little time passed before she spoke. No, she said, I don't think so, not any more. The horse helped me to understand.

What?

When it was alive, it seemed to be a proud and stern horse, she said. After you had it killed, I could hear it talking in my head, and what it had to say surprised me.

My mouth was hanging open.

I've grown accustomed to this life, the goose girl went on. I have found the fields are wider than any garden. I was always nervous, when I was a princess, in case I would forget what to do. You fit the dresses better; you carry it off.

My mouth was dry; I shut it. I could hardly believe her words, this unlooked-for reprieve. If your mother only knew, I protested, it would break her heart.

My mother is dead, said the girl, and she knows everything now.

As I heard her, the barrel I felt always about my ribs seemed to crack open, its hoops ringing about my feet. I could breathe. I could stretch.

That night at dinner the prince filled my goblet with the best wine, and I gave him a regal smile. He had very clean fingernails, and the blue pallor of true royalty. He was all I needed. Perhaps I would even grow to love him in the end, once I was truly safe; stranger things had happened. Once I had the crown settled on my head and a baby or two on my lap, who knew what kind of woman I might turn out to be? That night I slept deep and dreamless.

During the wedding, my mind wandered. I looked out the chapel window, onto the rooftops. From here I couldn't see the city arch, or the wide yellow fields. I wondered how the goose girl had felt when she heard the wedding bells. I thought of how both of us had refused to follow the paths mapped out for us by our mothers and their mothers before them, but had perversely gone our own ways instead, and I wondered whether this would bring us more or less happiness in the end.

Then I heard a tiny cough. When the prince took his lace handkerchief away from his mouth, there was a spatter of blood on it. I gave my husband a proper, searching look for the first time. I saw the red rims of his eyes, the hollows of his cheeks. Once more I seemed to feel the barrel locked around me, the spikes hammering through. I knew if I was not with child in a month or two, I would have nothing to hold on to. The day after my husband's funeral I would be wandering the world again in search of a crown I could call my own.

"The Story of the Three Little Pigs" (Jacobs) and "The Three Little Pigs" (Garner)

THERE IS NO ESCAPING THE fact that the ingenuous charm of the fairy tale makes it, in our skeptical and sophisticated world, a prime target for parody. Yet even in the garish colors of burlesque, the tale continues to show us to ourselves, albeit more sharply since it now has a satiric edge. The success of James Finn Garner's *Politically Correct Bedtime Stories* (1994) is one more indication that the fairy tale's versatility and appeal are as strong as ever.

THE STORY OF THE THREE LITTLE PIGS[1]

Joseph Jacobs

> *Once upon a time when pigs spoke rhyme*
> *And monkeys chewed tobacco,*
> *And hens took snuff to make them tough,*
> *And ducks went quack, quack, quack, O!*

THERE WAS AN OLD SOW with three little pigs, and as she had not enough to keep them, she sent them out to seek their fortune. The first that went off met a man with a bundle of straw, and said to him:

"Please, man, give me that straw to build me a house."

Which the man did, and the little pig built a house with it. Presently came along a wolf, and knocked at the door, and said:

"Little pig, little pig, let me come in."

To which the pig answered:

"No, no, by the hair of my chinny chin chin."

The wolf then answered to that:

"Then I'll huff, and I'll puff, and I'll blow your house in."

So he huffed, and he puffed, and he blew his house in, and ate up the little pig.

The second little pig met a man with a bundle of furze, and said:

"Please, man, give me that furze to build a house."

Which the man did, and the pig built his house. Then along came the wolf, and said:

---

1 From *English Fairy Tales*, 1890 (repr. New York: Dover, 1967).

"Little pig, little pig, let me come in."

"No, no, by the hair of my chinny chin chin."

"Then I'll puff, and I'll huff, and I'll blow your house in."

So he huffed, and he puffed, and he puffed, and he huffed, and at last he blew the house down, and he ate up the little pig.

The third little pig met a man with a load of bricks, and said:

"Please, man, give me those bricks to build a house with."

So the man gave him the bricks, and he built his house with them. So the wolf came, as he did to the other little pigs, and said:

"Little pig, little pig, let me come in."

"No, no, by the hair of my chinny chin chin."

"Then I'll huff, and I'll puff, and I'll blow your house in."

Well, he huffed, and he puffed, and he huffed and he puffed, and he puffed and huffed, but he could *not* get the house down. When he found that he could not, with all his huffing and puffing, blow the house down, he said:

"Little pig, I know where there is a nice field of turnips."

"Where?" said the little pig.

"Oh, in Mr. Smith's Homefield, and if you will be ready tomorrow morning I will call for you, and we will go together, and get some for dinner."

"Very well," said the little pig, "I will be ready. What time do you mean to go?"

"Oh, at six o'clock."

Well, the little pig got up at five, and got the turnips before the wolf came (which he did about six) and who said:

"Little pig, are you ready?"

The little pig said: "Ready! I have been and come back again, and got a nice potful for dinner."

The wolf felt very angry at this, but thought that he would be up to the little pig somehow or other, so he said:

"Little pig, I know where there is a nice apple-tree."

"Where?" said the pig.

"Down at Merry-garden," replied the wolf, "and if you will not deceive me I will come for you, at five o'clock tomorrow and get some apples."

Well, the little pig bustled up the next morning at four o'clock, and went off for the apples, hoping to get back before the wolf came; but he had further to go, and had to climb the tree, so that just as he was coming down from it, he saw the wolf coming, which, as you may suppose, frightened him very much. When the wolf came up he said:

"Little pig, what! are you here before me? Are they nice apples?"

"Yes, very," said the little pig. "I will throw you down one."

And he threw it so far, that, while the wolf was gone to pick it up, the little pig jumped down and ran home. The next day the wolf came again, and said to the little pig:

"Little pig, there is a fair at Shanklin this afternoon, will you go?"

"Oh yes," said the pig, "I will go; what time shall you be ready?"

"At three," said the wolf. So the little pig went off before the time as usual, and got to the fair, and bought a butter-churn, which he was going home with, when he saw the wolf coming. Then he could not tell what to do. So he got into the churn to hide, and by so doing turned it round, and it rolled down the hill with the pig in it, which frightened the wolf so much, that he ran home without going to the fair. He went to the little pig's house, and told him how frightened he had been by a great round thing which came down the hill past him. Then the little pig said:

"Hah, I frightened you, then. I had been to the fair and bought a butter-churn, and when I saw you, I got into it, and rolled down the hill."

Then the wolf was very angry indeed, and declared he *would* eat up the little pig, and that he would get down the chimney after him. When the little pig saw what he was about, he hung on the pot full of water, and made up a blazing fire, and, just as the wolf was coming down, took off the cover, and in fell the wolf; so the little pig put on the cover again in an instant, boiled him up, and ate him for supper, and lived happy ever afterwards.

THE THREE LITTLE PIGS[1]

James Finn Garner

ONCE THERE WERE THREE LITTLE pigs who lived together in mutual respect and in harmony with their environment. Using materials that were indigenous to the area, they each built a beautiful house. One pig built a house of straw, one a house of sticks, and one a house of dung, clay, and creeper vines shaped into bricks and baked in a small kiln. When they were finished, the pigs were satisfied with their work and settled back to live in peace and self-determination.

But their idyll was soon shattered. One day, along came a big, bad wolf with expansionist ideas. He saw the pigs and grew very hungry, in both a physical and an ideological sense. When the pigs saw the wolf, they ran into the house of straw. The wolf ran up to the house and banged on the door, shouting, "Little pigs, little pigs, let me in!"

---

1   From *Politically Correct Bedtime Stories* (New York: Macmillan, 1994).

The pigs shouted back, "Your gunboat tactics hold no fear for pigs defending their homes and culture."

But the wolf wasn't to be denied what he thought was his manifest destiny. So he huffed and puffed and blew down the house of straw. The frightened pigs ran to the house of sticks, with the wolf in hot pursuit. Where the house of straw had stood, other wolves bought up the land and started a banana plantation.

At the house of sticks, the wolf again banged on the door and shouted, "Little pigs, little pigs, let me in!"

The pigs shouted back, "Go to hell, you carnivorous, imperialistic oppressor!"

At this, the wolf chuckled condescendingly. He thought to himself: "They are so childlike in their ways. It will be a shame to see them go, but progress cannot be stopped."

So the wolf huffed and puffed and blew down the house of sticks. The pigs ran to the house of bricks, with the wolf close at their heels. Where the house of sticks had stood, other wolves built a time-share condo resort complex for vacationing wolves, with each unit a fiberglass reconstruction of the house of sticks, as well as native curio shops, snorkeling, and dolphin shows.

At the house of bricks, the wolf again banged on the door and shouted, "Little pigs, little pigs, let me in!"

This time in response, the pigs sang songs of solidarity and wrote letters of protest to the United Nations.

By now the wolf was getting angry at the pigs' refusal to see the situation from the carnivore's point of view. So he huffed and puffed, and huffed and puffed, then grabbed his chest and fell over dead from a massive heart attack brought on from eating too many fatty foods.

The three little pigs rejoiced that justice had triumphed and did a little dance around the corpse of the wolf. Their next step was to liberate their homeland. They gathered together a band of other pigs who had been forced off their lands. This new brigade of *porcinistas* attacked the resort complex with machine guns and rocket launchers and slaughtered the cruel wolf oppressors, sending a clear signal to the rest of the hemisphere not to meddle in their internal affairs. Then the pigs set up a model socialist democracy with free education, universal health care, and affordable housing for everyone.

Please note: The wolf in this story was a metaphorical construct. No actual wolves were harmed in the writing of the story.

"The Young Slave" (Basile) and "Giant Story" (Scieszka and Smith)

OUR FINAL JUXTAPOSITION OFFERS TWO examples of what the Italian writer Gianni Rodari has referred to as "fairy-tale salads"—that is, tales that make reference to a number of other tales. In recent years, several writers have made use of this idea, but to very different ends: in 1986, Janet and Allan Ahlberg produced a witty and original book in *The Jolly Postman*, which was a collection of unlikely letters written by various well-known fairy-tale characters. The following year, Stephen Sondheim and James Lapine created a successful musical *Into the Woods* (1987) that wove together several famous fairy tales. Jon Scieszka and Lane Smith's "Giant Story" from *The Stinky Cheese Man and Other Fairly Stupid Tales* (1992) arguably takes the "salad" approach to its illogical conclusion; see Figure 17 for this tale. Lest, however, it be assumed that these are simply products of postmodernism, we include a tale by Giambattista Basile, "The Young Slave" (1634), that also shares this characteristic, albeit without the ironic element of the modern tales.

THE YOUNG SLAVE[1]

Giambattista Basile

THERE WAS ONCE UPON A time a baron of Selvascura who had an unmarried sister. This sister always used to go and play in a garden with other girls of her own age. One day they found a lovely rose in full bloom, so they made a compact that whoever jumped clean over it without even touching a single leaf should win something. But although many of the girls jumped leapfrog over it, they all hit it, and not one of them jumped clean over. But when the turn came to Lilla, the Baron's sister, she stood back a little and took such a run at it that she jumped right over to the other side of the rose. Nevertheless, one leaf fell, but she was so quick and ready that she picked it up from the ground without anyone noticing and swallowed it, thereby winning the prize.

Not less than three days later, Lilla felt herself to be pregnant, and nearly died of grief, for she well knew that she had done nothing compromising or dishonest, and could not therefore understand how it was possible for her belly to have swollen. She at once ran to some fairies who were her friends, and when they heard her

---

1 First published in 1634-36. This text from *The Pentamerone*, trans. Benedetto Croce (London: John Lane, the Bodley Head, 1932).

story, they told her not to worry, for the cause of it all was the rose-leaf that she had swallowed.

When Lilla understood this, she took precautions to conceal her condition as much as possible, and when the hour of her deliverance came, she gave birth in hiding to a lovely little girl whom she named Lisa. She sent her to the fairies and they each gave her some charm, but the last one slipped and twisted her foot so badly as she was running to see the child, that in her acute pain she hurled a curse at her, to the effect that when she was seven years old, her mother, whilst combing out the child's hair, would leave the comb in her tresses, stuck into the head, and from this the child would perish.

At the end of seven years the disaster occurred, and the despairing mother, lamenting bitterly, encased the body in seven caskets of crystal, one within the other, and placed her in a distant room of the palace, keeping the key in her pocket. However, after some time her grief brought her to her grave. When she felt the end to be near, she called her brother and said to him, "My brother, I feel death's hook dragging me away inch by inch. I leave you all my belongings for you to have and dispose of as you like; but you must promise me never to open the last room in this house, and always keep the key safely in the casket." The brother, who loved her above all things, gave her his word; at the same moment she breathed, "Adieu, for the beans are ripe."

At the end of some years this lord (who had in the meantime taken a wife) was invited to a hunting-party. He recommended the care of the house to his wife, and begged her above all not to open the room, the key of which he kept in the casket. However, as soon as he had turned his back, she began to feel suspicious, and impelled by jealousy and consumed by curiosity, which is woman's first attribute, took the key and went to open the room. There she saw the young girl, clearly visible through the crystal caskets, so she opened them one by one and found that she seemed to be asleep. Lisa had grown like any other woman, and the caskets had lengthened with her, keeping pace as she grew.

When she beheld this lovely creature, the jealous woman at once thought, "By my life, this is a fine thing! Keys at one's girdle, yet nature makes horns![1] No wonder he never let anyone open the door and see the devil that he worshipped inside the caskets!" Saying this, she seized the girl by the hair, dragged her out, and in so doing caused the comb to drop out, so that the sleeping Lisa awoke, calling out, "Mother, mother!"

"I'll give you mother, and father too!" cried the Baroness, who was as bitter as a slave, as angry as a bitch with a litter of pups, and as venomous as a snake. She

---

1   "Keys ... horns": Even when you think everything's under control, your spouse will find a way to cheat on you.

straightaway cut off the girl's hair and thrashed her with the tresses, dressed her in rags, and every day heaped blows on her head and bruises on her face, blacking her eyes and making her mouth look as if she had eaten raw pigeons.

When her husband came back from his hunting-party, and saw this girl being so hardly used, he asked who she was. His wife answered him that she was a slave sent her by her aunt, only fit for the rope's end, and that one had to be forever beating her.

Now it happened one day, when the Baron had occasion to go to a fair, that he asked everyone in the house, including even the cats, what they would like him to buy for them, and when they had all chosen, one thing and one another, he turned at last to the slave. But his wife flew into a rage and acted unbecomingly to a Christian, saying, "That's right, class her with all the others, this thick-lipped slave, let everyone be brought down to the same level and all use the urinal. Don't pay so much attention to a worthless bitch, let her go to the devil." But the Baron who was kind and courteous insisted that the slave should also ask for something. And she said to him, "I want nothing but a doll, a knife, and a pumice-stone; and if you forget them, may you never be able to cross the first river that you come to on your journey!"

The Baron brought all the other things, but forgot just those for which his niece had asked him; so when he came to a river that carried down stones and trees to the shore to lay foundations of fears and raise walls of wonder, he found it impossible to ford it. Then he remembered the spell put on him by the slave, and turned back and bought the three articles in question. When he arrived home he gave out to each one the thing for which they had asked.

When Lisa had what she wanted, she went into the kitchen, and, putting the doll in front of her, began to weep and lament and recount all the story of her troubles to that bundle of cloth just as if it had been a real person. When it did not reply, she took the knife and sharpened it on the pumice-stone and said, "Mind, if you don't answer me, I will dig this into you, and that will put an end to the game!" And the doll, swelling up like a reed when it has been blown into, answered at last, "All right, I have understood you! I'm not deaf!"

This music had already gone on for a couple of days, when the Baron, who had a little room on the other side of the kitchen, chanced to hear this song, and putting his eye to the keyhole, saw Lisa telling the doll all about her mother's jump over the rose-leaf, how she swallowed it, her own birth, the spell, the curse of the last fairy, the comb left in her hair, her death, how she was shut into the seven caskets and placed in that room, her mother's death, the key entrusted to the brother, his departure for the hunt, the jealousy of his wife, how she opened the room against her husband's commands, how she cut off her hair and treated her like a slave, and the many, many torments she had inflicted on her. And all the while she wept and said, "Answer me, dolly, or I will kill myself with this knife." And sharpening it on the pumice-stone, she would have plunged it into herself had not the Baron kicked down the door and snatched the knife out of her hand.

He made her tell him the story again at greater length and then he embraced his niece and took her away from that house, and left her in the charge of one of his relations in order that she should get better, for the hard usage inflicted on her by that heart of a Medea[1] had made her quite thin and pale. After several months, when she had become as beautiful as a goddess, the Baron brought her home and told everyone that she was his niece. He ordered a great banquet, and when the viands had been cleared away, he asked Lisa to tell the story of the hardships she had undergone and of the cruelty of his wife—a tale which made all the guests weep. Then he drove his wife away, sending her back to her parents, and gave his niece a handsome husband of her own choice. Thus Lisa testified that

Heaven rains favors on us when we least expect it.

---

1   Medea: In the Greek myth, Medea married Jason of the Golden Fleece, but when he left her, she ate their two children.

ILLUSTRATION

No PUBLISHER NOWADAYS WOULD DREAM of trying to sell a volume of fairy tales that was not accompanied by illustrations; indeed, one might be forgiven for thinking that the illustrator is sometimes of greater importance than the tales, which are chosen primarily as suitable vehicles for his or her artistic prowess. The modern fairy-tale book consists, as often as not, of a single tale told primarily in pictures: the text has become a secondary consideration. It's an intriguing question: does the inclusion of illustrations stifle the reader's imagination by imposing a visual representation upon it, or do the pictures actually enhance the reader's imaginative response to the story? Clearly there are many factors involved, such as the age of the reader, the ability of the artist, and the meanings suggested by the illustrations. Yet even if we were able somehow to calculate relative values for such factors, how could we then compare the quality of the reader's response with and without the presence of illustrations? Calculations aside, there can be no question but that pictures add one more dimension to the various imaginative experiences of reading a tale, being read a tale, and being *told* a tale.

The origin of the fairy tale is oral, which accounts for its unique qualities: the emphasis upon action, the lack of physical detail, and the quick movement from one event to another—all ideally suited to the art of the storyteller. Furthermore, a tale can be told in many different ways, its impact upon the audience deriving from the intention, approach, and abilities of the teller. As we have seen, however, the evolution of the oral tale into printed text has all but obliterated the services of the storyteller, leaving room for the intercession of a new intermediary. Although without a teller there is no story, it can reasonably be argued that without an illustrator, the text is still there on the printed page, and yet, as Perry Nodelman points out in his instructive book *Words About Pictures*,[1] our imaginations can rarely achieve the vividness and specificity that can be found in a good illustration. To achieve these qualities, both teller and illustrator must give something of themselves to the tale in order to infuse it with new life, since in its "basic" form the tale leaves ample scope for the inventiveness of both contributors as they work within the familiar framework of the story to create something new.

For example, one significant challenge for the artist is the depiction of characters familiar in name but not in image; he or she presumes thus to make explicit what is vague in the tales (we are told no more than that Little Red Riding Hood is "the prettiest [girl] that had ever been seen" or that Rumpelstiltskin is "a little man"). Alternatively, the artist may choose to concentrate upon the setting of the tale, giving a specificity to time and place that is denied by the traditional beginning of "Once upon a time." Most important, however, is the interpretation of the events an illustration can provide. Indeed, the opportunity to expand and interpret has also been exploited by recorders of the tales for, as we noted earlier, Perrault and the Grimms were quite prepared to leave their mark on the tales in the process of making them more suitable for their respective audiences. There is, of course, no guarantee that the embellishment provided by teller or artist will necessarily enrich the tale: we all know how painful an experience it can be to listen to a flat, indifferent reading of a tale, or how disappointed we feel when confronted by illustrations that do little more than fill space on the page. However, as Nodelman points out, illustrators, like the storytellers before them, have the power to transform the tale into a rich and meaningful tapestry.

We are told that every picture tells a story; an illustration tells at least two, for not only does it provide a visual dimension for the story it accompanies, but it also reveals something of the assumptions and values of the artist and of the culture to which he or she belongs. In this sense, illustrators are no different from the storytellers or the fairy-tale compilers of the past who inevitably kept an eye on their audience, making sure their material was both suitable and satisfying. As a result, the pictures that accompany fairy tales are often as much a mirror as are the tales themselves.

Thus, the encounter between the text and the reader's imagination is made more complex by the contribution of the illustrator, who imposes his or her particular vision and tone upon the narrative. Just how completely the reading of a tale can be influenced by different artists' interpretations will be demonstrated in the following pages: though the words may remain the same, the pictures tell us a different story.

---

1   Perry Nodelman, *Words About Pictures: The Narrative Art of Children's Picture Books* (Athens, GA: University of Georgia Press, 1988).

At the beginning of this chapter we commented that no modern publisher would seriously consider producing a book of fairy tales without illustrations; we might now add that few would publish such a book without illustrations in color. At the same time, the black-and-white originals that are included in our selection provide convincing evidence that the artist's decision not to use color does not signify a lesser commitment to the story. We have chosen examples of illustrative work that range from the last century to the present day. It is admittedly a very partial selection, since the number of illustrated versions of fairy tales has increased so dramatically in recent years. However, it may serve to give some indication of the variety of approaches that certain artists have adopted over the years—and hopefully to provide the student with some stimulus to seek out the work of others.

LITTLE RED RIDING HOOD

As we pointed out in our introduction to this tale, there is more to the story than a simple warning to children not to speak to strangers—and one artist whose work manifests abundant awareness of this aspect is Gustave Doré (1832-83). The fact that Doré's work (published in 1863) is one of the earliest examples of fairy-tale illustration makes his insight into Perrault's tales all the more remarkable, not least because his engravings are of course without the benefit (or is it the distraction?) of color. Like many other artists since, he illustrates a critical moment in this story: the meeting between Little Red Riding Hood and the wolf (Figure 1, 1867). Absent, however, is the anthropomorphic representation of the wolf that many subsequent illustrators have adopted. Nevertheless, Doré provides us with a carefully detailed portrait of the relationship between the two characters, which foreshadows the outcome of their encounter. As is often the case in Doré's work, the eyes are the focal point of the picture, in this instance, the fascinated gaze that binds prey to predator. Doré makes this a claustrophobic picture, as the little girl finds herself hemmed in by the wolf, whose proximity appears at first glance to be protective; its impact is all the more effective because the observer alone knows that deception and malice are at work here. Subtler still is the detail of the girl's unfastened shoe-strap, indicative of her vulnerability, her unpreparedness for harsh experience. As the little girl gazes up at the wolf as if hypnotized, her whole body expresses a naïve trust and uncertainty. Although the wolf is depicted from a highly unusual perspective creating the effect of an upright human stance, Doré still manages to include his penetrating stare. That, together with the half-protective, half-suggestive movement of his hindquarters toward Little Red Riding Hood, reveals to the discerning eye what is to follow.

Sarah Moon focuses on the same fateful moment in her illustration (Figure 2, 1983), only this time in very different surroundings. Locating the tale in a modern urban context and using the "truthful" medium of photography to illustrate the story momentarily frustrate the reader's expectations—but once the associative leap is made, the story's impact is irresistible, so striking and apposite is Moon's imagery. Equally surprising is how similar Moon's treatment is to Doré's, over one hundred years earlier. The girl is a startled creature caught in the glare of the car's headlights, the darkness of the street creates the same claustrophobic effect as Doré's forest, and the menace implicit in the shiny, cold anonymity of the car—a familiar modern symbol of male status and power—is perhaps more meaningful for a contemporary reader than the sight of the "wolf" himself. As in Doré's illustration, the viewer bears the burden of anticipating Perrault's tragic ending. However, Moon's black-and-white photo-journalistic treatment of this very familiar story capitalizes on the ever-increasing currency of the visual medium, rendering the text all but extraneous. It also reminds us how familiar we are with the story that these photographs tell, as a brief glance at today's newspapers or magazines will confirm.

A third visualization of this same scene is to be found in the work of Beni Montresor (1926-2001) who, like Sarah Moon, updates the setting (Figure 3, 1991). Montresor openly acknowledges his debt to Gustave Doré, to the extent of including adaptations of the three Doré illustrations for this tale (two of which are reproduced here). As a review of Figure 1 will indicate, the major change introduced by Montresor (apart from the use of color) is in the appearance of the wolf, which is as urbane as Doré's is feral. What is particularly appealing, at least to the *adult* reader, is the visual pun that the artist (an occasional resident of New York City) makes at the expense of another well-known New Yorker, the writer and man-about-town Tom Wolfe(!). The topicality of this allusion may be compared to the flexibility of the oral tale, as the teller adds a reference to impress and amuse his or her immediate audience. The disadvantage, of course, is that such an addition can only have a temporary appeal: what is familiar today may be forgotten tomorrow.

We return to a Doré illustration (Figure 4, 1867) to demonstrate how, unlike most subsequent illustrators, he did not shy away from the violence inherent in many fairy tales. He chooses to depict Little Red Riding Hood in bed with the Wolf at the moment she realizes the danger of her situation—a scene few illustrators have chosen to dramatize given the association of the story with a child audience. Doré, however, manages to produce another masterpiece of psychological insight. Once again, our attention is drawn to eyes, the windows of the soul. As in Figure 1, we observe the girl's expression of intermingled fear and fascination, not only in her eyes but also in her ambivalent body posture; now, however, the central focus of the image is surely the wolf. He lies inert, paying no attention to the girl, the granny cap pulled absurdly over his ears, apparently lost in his own gloomy thoughts. Is Doré not implying a certain "sympathy for the Devil" here, as the wolf considers the base indignities to which his appetites have brought him? He will fulfill his destiny as a predator, but he will have no illusions about his shame and depravity. Angela Carter expresses a startlingly similar insight in "The Company of Wolves" (see the Little Red Riding Hood section):

There is a vast melancholy in the canticles of the wolves, melancholy infinite as the forest, endless as these long nights of winter, and yet that ghastly sadness, that mourning for their own, irremediable appetites, can never move the heart, for not one phrase in it hints at the possibility of redemption; grace could not come to the wolf from its own despair, only through some external mediator, so that, sometimes, the beast will look as if he half welcomes the knife that dispatches him. (pp. 48-49)

Thus, the imminent catastrophe is rendered all the more disturbing by the psychological depth and intensity that Doré brings to the image.

HANSEL AND GRETEL

Arthur Rackham (1867-1939) was one of the most eminent artists to emerge from what has become known as the Golden Age of children's book illustration (1860-1930). Rackham's wide and lasting popularity rests largely upon the appeal of his extraordinary fantasy worlds, which are believable because they are so firmly rooted in realistic detail. In this sense, Rackham anticipates, in visual terms, J.R.R. Tolkien's creation of a believable "secondary world." Rackham's approach is evident in his illustration from "Hansel and Gretel" (Figure 5, 1903), in which the encounter between the children and the witch reveals a Dickensian combination of the realistic and the grotesque. Although Rackham's focus is clearly on the *human* drama, the observer is equally drawn in by the picturesque setting, the soothing quality of the sepia tones, and the intricate delicacy of the details of wood, leaf, and stone. The attraction of the cottage is certainly not in the sweetness of its candy composition (which Rackham all but ignores) as in its romantic quaintness. We, like the children with whom we identify, long to see what lies beyond the antique bottle panes of the open window— surely a kettle on the boil and cookies in a jar—a welcoming home were it not for the witch who stands at the door. Illustrated is a moment of confrontation with the unexpected and forbidding on the one hand and the welcoming and comforting on the other, which Rackham reveals in the reactions and body postures of both witch and children. So potent is Rackham's mix of fantasy and reality that it imbues his world with an energy that promises a positive outcome to the confrontation.

Kay Nielsen's visualization (Figure 6, 1925) of almost the same moment in the story produces a very different picture. If Rackham is interested in carefully depicting the bare feet of the children and each hair on the witch's chin, Nielsen (1886-1957) is far more attracted by the nightmarish glamor of the scene with its unearthly cottage crouching like a fluorescent spider in the middle of a web composed of sinuous, oppressive trees. Here the children are reduced to observers, sharing our own fascination with the otherworldly oasis of color and light that lies before them. Despite the highly stylized approach, Nielsen's view draws us effectively into the story; the un-individualized children are here cast as our representatives—we too are waiting for that door to open....

Like Sarah Moon in her version of "Little Red Riding Hood" (Figure 2), Anthony Browne takes the step of giving "Hansel and Gretel" a modern setting: this family lives in a brick house containing many of the household items that populate our world also. Both artists, however, have been careful to evoke a contemporary setting that is nevertheless distant enough (vaguely mid-twentieth century) not to be exactly identifiable, thereby combining the open-endedness of "once upon a time" with the here-and-now. In Browne's opening illustration of the parlor (Figure 7, 1981), the familiar look of modern poverty is immediately apparent in the dirty, peeling wallpaper and the threadbare rug, as well as in the father's face and demeanor as he looks in vain through what is clearly the "Employment" section of the newspaper. More arresting, however, is the manner in which Browne manages to underline the crucial aspect of family dynamics and the stepmother's role in the lives of her husband and children. Browne sets her apart from the rest of her family: glamorous and comfortable, she watches a passenger jet take off on television. Through the symbols that permeate the picture—the abandoned "Gretel" doll, the bird mark on the ceiling—Browne paints us a story as meaningful as the words themselves. Illustrators such as Browne and Moon remind us that fairy tales, like Shakespeare's dramas, are as pertinent today as they ever were.

SLEEPING BEAUTY

The sophistication of the work of some modern illustrators once again raises the issue of audience: to whom are these pictures addressed? Do they represent another reminder of the anomaly of fairy tales—that although these tales are commonly perceived as children's literature, the artist intuitively responds to their symbolism, which, as we have already seen, can result in a startlingly different interpretation? Examine, for instance, the illustration by Michael Foreman (Figure 8, 1978) for "Briar Rose; or, The Sleeping Beauty," in which the sexual imagery is, to adult eyes, nothing short of startling. In the tradition of the finest illustrators, Foreman acknowledges the depth of the fairy tale by, in effect, providing two pictures in one, since it contains both a narrative and a symbolic level. As with the tale itself, however, the reader sees what he or she is ready to see. There may well be those who object to such an overtly Freudian interpretation, but it is undeniable that such controversy breathes new life into the fairy tale. It should be noted that this is the only illustration that Foreman provided for the tale (some years later, he illustrated the Perrault version more fully). Thus, his intention was not so much to provide a visual dimension to the tale as an interpretation of it. One may therefore assume that he chose his moment carefully in order to clearly communicate his interpretation of the tale as eloquently and succinctly as possible.

If we turn to Trina Schart Hyman's depiction of the same tale (Figure 9, 1977), we find ourselves at the other end of the illustrative spectrum, so to speak, in that she tells the tale primarily in pictures. As we observed at the outset, this is an instance of the text being given equal if not secondary status, as it is carefully integrated into the design of the double-page spread. There is no single climactic picture, since the intention here is to maintain a continuity of illustration, with the result that setting, characterization, and interpretation are given ample consideration. Thus, while Hyman creates an effective quasi-medieval context for the tale through a rich combination of architectural and costume detail, it is not at the expense of the human drama. Although there is a modern, positively Technicolor glamor to the principal characters depicted here, there is no denying the excitement with which Hyman infuses this courtyard scene, where all is intense action and emotion. As we pointed out in our introduction to "Sleeping Beauty," the fate of the princess has a profound effect on the greater community, a fact that Hyman expresses very effectively in this lively illustration.

BEAUTY AND THE BEAST

Walter Crane (1845-1915) was one of three particularly talented artists (the other two being Kate Greenaway and Randolph Caldecott) who had the good fortune to collaborate with an equally talented and innovative printer, Edmund Evans. Crane was also very much involved—along with such contemporaries as William Morris—in the Arts and Crafts Movement in Britain, which sought to re-assert the role of the craftsman in a world that was quickly succumbing to the new phenomenon of mass production. Consequently, we may find in his illustration of "Beauty and the Beast" (Figure 10, 1900) a greater concern with style than with the substance of the story: the flatness of the picture is reminiscent of a Classical frieze, the Beast's more modern attire notwithstanding. Crane freely acknowledged that the timelessness of fairy tales allowed him an artistic license that he was quite prepared to take advantage of: "I was in the habit of putting in all sorts of subsidiary detail that interested me, and often made them the vehicle for my ideas in furniture and decoration."[1] The preoccupation with decoration and various artistic styles makes this an elegant but at the same time rather detached, even distracting illustration—there is simply no room for the emotional tension that surely fills this encounter.

In strong contrast to the decorous *sang-froid* of Crane's illustration is the ferocity and passion in Alan Barrett's depiction of the Beast (Figure 11, 1972). Over the years, artists have depicted the Beast in a variety of ways, ranging from leonine to monstrous, yet he frequently manifests the kind of savage nobility that we associate with certain large animals. Barrett's intention, on the other hand, is to provoke a more visceral reaction, something closer to the terror inspired by a Beast that appears irrational, alien, and cruel. From our voyeuristic position as reader, we turn the page only to be confronted by the open jaws of the enraged Beast and thus find ourselves cast in Beauty's position. For a moment, our identification with the heroine is complete. Curiously enough, Barrett's illustration bears a striking resemblance to the most memorable image from Steven Spielberg's highly successful movie *Jaws* (1975), which might itself be regarded as an important example of the urban legend phenomenon.

A quite different contrast, this time to all the "subsidiary detail" in Crane's picture, may be found in the work of Barry Moser (Figure 12, 1992), whose minimalist approach produces an illustration as stark as Crane's is elaborate. It is a trademark of Moser's style to look for the key moments in the story and then reduce them to the specific character—or even gesture—that represents the crux of that particular episode. All distractions of color, descriptive detail, and movement are rejected, and out of the darkness an image emerges that arrests our attention: Beauty and the Beast are playing the strategic and intellectual game of chess. Nancy Willard, the author of the text of this version, clearly intends the chess-game as a metaphor for the psychological intricacy and uncertainty of a developing relationship—"She tried not to show her horror as his claws groped for the pieces, and she had to help him make his moves." There may be horror, but Moser's illustration also conveys tenderness and compassion in Beauty's guiding hand.

---

1 Walter Crane, *An Artist's Reminiscences* (1907), quoted in Rodney K. Engen, *Walter Crane as a Book Illustrator* (London: Academy Editions, 1975) 5.

Figure 1: In the woods Little Red Riding Hood met old Father Wolf (1867), Gustav Doré

Figure 2: Little Red Riding Hood (1983), Sarah Moon

Figure 3: Little Red Riding Hood (1991), Beni Montresor

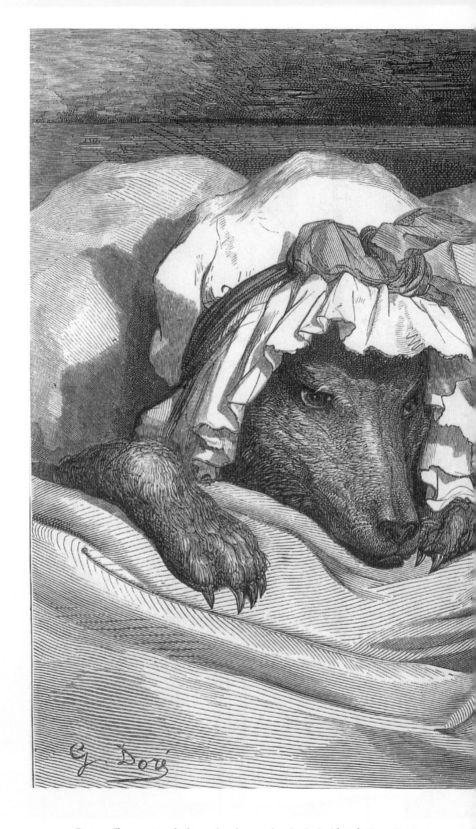

Figure 4: She was astonished to see how her grandmother looked (1867), Gustav Doré

Figure 5: Hansel and Gretel (1903), Arthur Rackham

Figure 6: Hansel and Gretel (1925), Kay Nielsen

Figure 7: Hansel and Gretel (1981), Anthony Browne

Figure 8: Sleeping Beauty (1978), Michael Foreman

Figure 9: The Sleeping Beauty (1977), Trina Schart Hyman

After a little while, they went down from the tower together, hand in hand. Where one drop of blood drains a castle of life, so one kiss can bring it alive again. Then the King and Queen woke up, and so did all their knights and ladies, and everyone looked at each other with astonishment in their sleepy eyes. The horses in the stable stood up and shook themselves, and the grooms scratched their heads and stretched their legs. The hounds began to leap about, barking at nothing and wagging their tails.

Figure 10: Beauty and the Beast (1900), Walter Crane

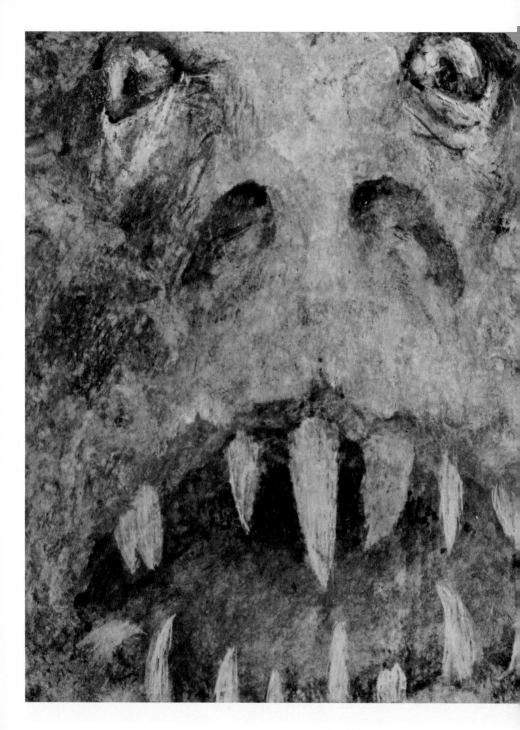

Figure 11: Beauty and the Beast (1972), Alan Barrett

Figure 12: Beauty and the Beast (1992), Barry Moser

Figure 13: Bluebeard (1910), Edmund Dulac

Figure 14: Rapunzel (2003), David Roberts

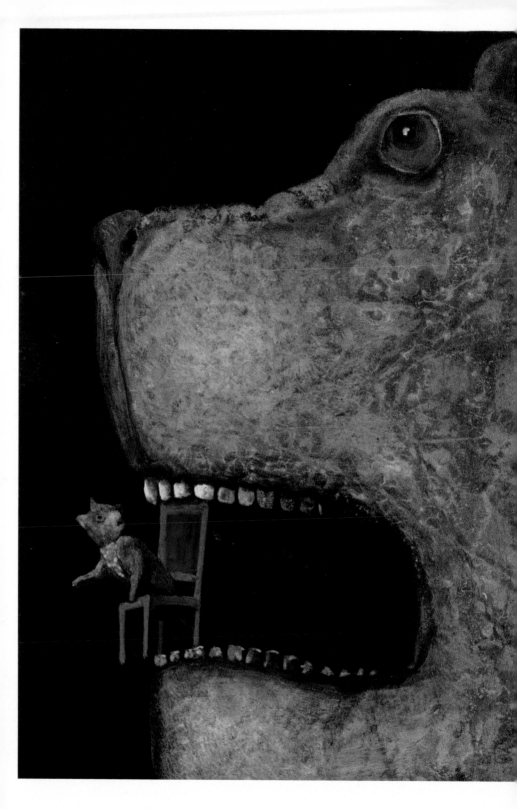

Figure 15: Puss in Boots (1990), Stasys Eidrigevičius

"Never mind," whispered Puss. "I may be able to make your fortune, but first you must buy me some boots." So Jack took him to the boot shop.

Figure 16: Puss in Boots (1981), Tony Ross

THE END

of the evil Stepmother

said "I'll HUFF and SNUFF and

give you three wishes."

The beast changed into

SEVEN DWARVES

HAPPILY EVER AFTER

for a spell had been cast by a Wicked Witch

Once upon a time

"That's your story?" said Jack.
"You've got to be kidding. That's not a
Fairly Stupid Tale. That's an Incredibly Stupid Tale.
That's an Unbelievably Stupid Tale. That is
the Most Stupid Tale I Ever— *awwwk!*"
The Giant grabbed Jack and dragged him to the next page

Figure 17: Giant Story (1992), Jon Scieszka and Lane Smith

Figure 18: The Princess and the Frog (1999), Will Eisner

SETTING: BLUEBEARD AND RAPUNZEL

"Once upon a time...." There can be no doubt that the all-inclusiveness of the fairy tale's opening lines has ensured its endurance and currency across international time zones; nevertheless, it is precisely this vagueness that invites the creativity of the illustrator. As we have already seen, an illustrator has the power to create a world that may be beyond our own imaginings. In the following examples, we will examine in greater depth some of the effects that specific settings can produce.

Along with Arthur Rackham, another eminent artist to emerge during the Golden Age of children's book illustration was Edmund Dulac (1882-1953). It is not surprising that their names continue to be closely associated, as the imaginations of both were drawn to the otherworld of the fairy tale. As we have seen, Rackham's creations are so appealing because despite their fantasy, they seem real. The same can be said for Dulac's: his fabrics have a drape and weight, the woodwork a grain that is almost tactile—how could we doubt the existence of their worlds? Where the artists do differ, however, is in the manner in which they achieved these effects: Rackham through attention to line, Dulac through color.

Dulac's mastery of the technique of watercolor, together with his fascination with Eastern art, particularly Persian miniatures, made him the perfect candidate to illustrate *The Arabian Nights* (1907), an early commission that earned him critical acclaim. Not surprisingly, he would choose a similar setting for his later illustration of "Bluebeard" (Figure 13, 1910). There is no denying the appeal of Dulac's meticulous depiction of this exotic world, with its sensuous colors and textures, rich patterns and decorative details, nor its power—then and now—to take us to a place full of wonder.

Nevertheless, there may be another impulse at work behind the artist's desire and ability to transport us to foreign times and places. As we noted in our discussion of the tale, "Bluebeard" is a frightening story, confronting as it does the anxieties we face in choosing a mate. Here we witness the consequences of an immature marriage-choice to what turns out to be a psychopathic murderer. As Alison Lurie points out in her discussion of children's book illustration,[1] one way to provide some psychological distance from the frightening aspects of a fairy tale is for the illustrator to create an equivalent *physical* separation. The remote and exotic setting of Dulac's "Bluebeard" provides a safe distance from the experience of its horrors. A more disturbing psychological aspect of this setting is the identification of evil in a specific racial stereotype. Thus, Bluebeard's abnormality, so effectively symbolized in the story by the color of his beard, is here represented by his prominent, if not downright

---

1   Alison Lurie, "Louder Than Words: Children's Book Illustrations," in *Boys and Girls Forever: Children's Classics From Cinderella to Harry Potter* (New York: Penguin, 2003) 162.

phallic, turban. Although the inherent prejudice of such an association strikes the modern viewer, the psychological comfort of such distancing cannot be denied; we remain complacent in the belief that such things could not possibly occur in *our* part of the world. Thus, it should not come as a surprise to find other illustrators (Rackham included) adopting a foreign, if not Eastern, setting for "Bluebeard."

This preoccupation with setting is to be found no less among contemporary illustrators. Surely part of the pleasure in viewing (and perhaps illustrating) David Roberts's *Rapunzel: A Groovy Fairy Tale* (Figure 14, 2003) (or his earlier *Cinderella: An Art Deco Love Story*) is in seeing the story unfold at a particular time and in a specific place. Turning the pages is like walking through the galleries of a museum: the viewer is confronted with the artifacts of a bygone time—in this case, the not-so-distant "hippy era" of the late 1960s and early 1970s. We have already seen the desire to bring the fairy tale into the modern world in the work of Sarah Moon and Anthony Browne; now, however, the tendency is for even greater specificity. Rackham and Dulac created believable fantastic visions through the realistic and detailed depiction of texture and atmosphere; Roberts amply displays the recognizable memorabilia of the day. Rapunzel's room contains an assortment of all the icons of the period: posters of rock 'n roll idols, LPs and turntable, rice-paper and lava lamps, white vinyl bed headboard, plants, bell-bottom pants, coffee-house-guitar-playing boyfriend, and, of course, the requisite long hair. We look at these pages and remember our own pasts, or those of our parents or grandparents, with the realization that Rapunzel could have been one of us. In taking us somewhere else, the visions of artists like Rackham and Dulac enlarge our sense of wonder; the closer-to-home settings of some contemporary artists also elicit surprise by showing us that the fairy tale has an immediacy and relevance that is very much our own.

PUSS IN BOOTS

The work of Stasys Eidrigevičius brings us to the post-Freudian world of psychoanalysis. In *Puss in Boots* (Figure 15, 1990), Eidrigevičius represents not so much the events of the story as the visions they might elicit in the dream-world of our unconscious where the facts of daily life mesh with our fears and desires. Such an approach naturally invites controversy, particularly in what is assumed to be a book for children, since the world of dreams is variously perceived as either disturbing or nonsensical. Be that as it may, Eidrigevičius's illustrations obey the rules that govern the workings of the unconscious. Just as our dreams scramble the details of our daily lives, the images are not faithful representations of Perrault's text. For instance, when the ogre transforms himself into a lion, "Puss was so frightened that he leapt onto the roof." The roof, of course, offers some escape, so why is Puss made to perch on a chair that is caught in the jaws of the transformed ogre? The image illustrates the logic of the unconscious, where every character and every situation is an extension of ourselves, our fears and desires, and the boundaries of time and space are not adhered to. It is easier to identify with the frightened Puss perched on a chair; it is where we would seek safety from a rampant mouse—the metamorphosis that Puss intends to invite the ogre to make next. Thus, the image captures the fear inherent in the present moment (although Puss's posture suggests his escape) and also anticipates the next development. Because the transformed ogre bears an unmistakable resemblance to the cat who is in due course planning to devour him, the image represents both moments in the story while, at the same time, suggesting that the ogre is very much Puss's alter ego—which should come as no surprise, given Puss's ruthless behavior. Thus, the starkness and simplicity of this illustration belie its intensity and the complexity of its multiple identifications and levels of meaning. The more one looks, the more one sees and understands.

It takes no more than a glance at the work of Tony Ross (Figure 16, 1981) to realize how different his work is from that of Eidrigevičius and earlier artists. Up until the mid-twentieth century, whatever their individual interests and interpretations, most illustrators represented the fantastic world of the fairy tale in realistic terms. This approach was then challenged by the flatness and simplicity of the comic book and animated cartoon. Ross adopts the garish colors and two-dimensional characterization of this style, which contribute to the slapstick mood of this version. He achieves comic effect more through distortion than accuracy—no cat ever resembled Puss, and yet there is no denying that Ross has created an appropriately anarchic personality. (Not surprisingly, he also rewrites the text, since it's clear that his approach to illustration is incompatible with the serious tone of Perrault's narrative.) Eidrigevičius's picture conveys a mood of silence and introspection; we are invited to contemplate (or to absorb) the meaning of the moment. In Ross's work, however, the moment is fleeting, since he crowds so many separate images onto a single page that the comic energy all but spills out at the reader. The tone is one of detachment, which allows the reader to laugh at the characters and their predicaments. His approach may lack the historical detail or psychological complexity that dignifies other artists' versions of these tales, but his sense of the absurd provides a vivid reminder of the fairy tale's enduring ability to entertain.

MODERN/POSTMODERN WORLD

What should be amply clear by now is that the evolution of the fairy tale, in both text and image, is a dynamic one. We have already seen some evidence, in the shape of James Finn Garner's story from *Politically Correct Bedtime Stories*, to suggest that the fairy tale has entered the postmodern age. If further proof is necessary, it can surely be found in *The Stinky Cheese Man and other Fairly Stupid Tales*, by Jon Scieszka and Lane Smith, from which Figure 17 (1992) is taken. (The cheerful cynicism of these titles tells a story in itself!) The sophistication of both text and illustration is remarkable; "Giant Story" is little short of a deconstruction of the fairy tale, of storytelling, perhaps even of the book itself. It is also an example of the current approach (see Laura Tosi's article in the Criticism section) that favors mixing up the stories to produce what has been termed a "fairy-tale salad." This "tossed" approach, evident in the text and images of "Giant Story," demands, however, an equal sophistication on the part of the reader-viewer: an extensive familiarity with fairy tales and their illustrations is needed to appreciate the numerous allusions found here. A closer examination reveals not only references to "Puss in Boots," "Snow White," and "Cinderella," but also to some of the "classics" of children's literature such as nursery rhymes and, more specifically, Hoffman's "Struwwelpeter" (1848) and Bemelmans's "Madeline" (1939), to name just a couple. Smith's chaotic collage provides a visual representation of Tolkien's seminal image of the Cauldron of Story, suggesting the ever-bubbling, ever-replenished mixture of human experience and imagination that manifests itself in the fairy tale.

Our other example comes from the world of the comic book, a field that has experienced extraordinary growth over the last few years in the development of the graphic novel. Its success marks an intriguing (some might say inevitable) coming together of word and image that has unquestionably caught the popular imagination. Will Eisner (1917-2005), the creator of this version of the Grimms' "The Frog King," was one of the pioneers of this branch of literature, seeing it as an opportunity to reinterpret classic stories for a new readership (he has also re-created *Moby Dick* and *Don Quixote* as graphic novels). This excerpt from *The Princess and the Frog* (Figure 18, 1999) demonstrates how readily the tale can be adapted to the comic-book format; the simple morality, the flatness of character, and the emphasis upon extraordinary incident provide the graphic artist/writer with features remarkably similar to those of the comic book.

This reincarnation of the fairy tale in the comic book demonstrates that its evolution is as much circular as it is linear. Whatever its status among the guardians of culture and education over the centuries, the fairy tale has remained a staple of popular culture. Ignoring the scruples of its critics and any concern for quality, the purveyors of cheap broadsheets and chapbooks of the eighteenth century nevertheless satisfied the appetite for the fairy tale among the common people, many of whom would have been barely literate. Today's lavishly illustrated gift books notwithstanding, the fairy tale's resurgence in the "alternative" medium of the comic book provides ample evidence to support the view that through its versatility, its adaptability, and its universality, the fairy tale is as healthy—and as relevant—today as it was a thousand years ago.

POSTSCRIPT

Nowhere is the role of the visual artist more obvious than in the popular medium of film, synonymous in the world of fairy tale with the work of Walt Disney. Indeed, our familiarity with fairy tales today is attributable almost exclusively to more than half a century of Disney's animated productions.

The transfer from book to screen represents an important qualitative leap in the recipient's experience of the tale. Quality and quantity of the illustrations notwithstanding, the book still provides the reader (or listener) with the text of the story and, thus, imaginative ownership of the material. The reader still has some ability to decide how much of an influence the visual images will have on his or her experience of the narrative. Nevertheless, the number, if not the quality, of pictures is bound to make a difference, and, as we have seen, the growing tendency to illustrate fairy tales ever more profusely can have the effect of relegating the text to secondary importance. This predominance of the visual image at the expense of the text is made complete in the medium of film. The most obvious contrast, of course, is the *total* reliance on the visual image to recreate the story; without any text, each and every detail must be graphically represented—and many more details have to be invented, since the fairy tale leaves much to the imagination.

Not least is the problem of how to make the inherently dark side of fairy tales—their violence and cruelty—visually acceptable to a child audience. In *Snow White* (1937), his first animated tale, Disney had to deal with the stepmother's cannibalism, her three attempts to kill Snow White, and her subsequent horrific death. (Such a gruesome "happy ending" is not untypical of the fairy tale. Much of our satisfaction, in fact, derives from the inexorable working-out of poetic justice in the tales, however harsh it may be.) As with many illustrators confronted with the same issue, Disney's solution was to reduce or eliminate as much of the violent and cruel material as possible. However, the diminution of the stepmother's role and the two-dimensional doll-like portrayal of the characters, the comic characterization of the dwarves, the addition of domestic scenes with cute animal helpers, and the romantic ending—all to the accompaniment of cheerful song and dance—provide a radical departure from the spirit and essence of the original fairy tale. While Disney was quick to recognize and exploit the visually exciting potential of the "scary" scenes he added to the stories—one of the most memorable scenes from *Sleeping Beauty* (1959) is the battle between the Prince and Maleficent during which she transforms herself into a fire-breathing dragon—the effect was to replace the disturbing or complex elements of the tale with the titillation of violence as spectacle, something Hollywood has always excelled at.

As his many critics have pointed out, Disney's shortcomings have less to do with his alteration of the story—the prerogative of every artist—than with his departure from the *spirit* of the fairy tale. As we pointed out at the beginning of this section, in reworking the raw material, the artist's response must be sensitive to its depth of meaning. In the process of translating these stories from book to screen, Disney reduced them to the romantic stereotypes and clichés that have given fairy tales a bad name, especially among feminist critics. Be that as it may, the enormous popularity of his productions makes a statement, which surely reveals more about our own attitudes and aspirations than about fairy tale. In this respect, it can be argued that Walt Disney was as much a man of his time as were the Brothers Grimm and Charles Perrault before him; they too manipulated the fairy tale to suit the tastes and expectations of their audience.

CRITICISM

Serious critical attention to the fairy tale is essentially a phenomenon of the twentieth century. As we have noted in our introduction, discussion prior to that tended to be dismissive, even condemnatory, despite the positive testimonials of various literary figures. In the English-speaking world, a breakthrough of sorts came through the intervention of the eminent scholar and writer Andrew Lang (1844-1912) who, through the publication of his twelve-volume "color" series, was responsible for popularizing the fairy tale well beyond what we might term the classical canon of Perrault and the Grimms. As a folklorist, Lang was a representative of a new field of study that seized upon the folk tale as a repository of valuable information about traditional beliefs, superstitions, and customs. This field of knowledge was gradually absorbed into the larger discipline of anthropology, culminating in the monumental project, initiated in Finland by Antti Aarne (1867-1925) and later taken on by the American Stith Thompson (1885-1976), to produce a comprehensive index of types and motifs to be found in the entire *corpus* of fairy tale.

Since these early years, the critical examination of the fairy tale has proceeded apace, especially in the second half of the last century, and from a variety of different perspectives, as we hope our selection in the following pages illustrates. Given the unique history and evolution of the fairy tale, however, problems can arise if it is subjected to literary criteria that take no account of such matters as multiple national and international variants and inadequate chronological evidence. To clarify this issue more fully, we include the essay "Fairy Tales from a Folkloristic Perspective" (1986) by the distinguished folklorist Alan Dundes, who makes no bones about his concern that many current fairy-tale studies, in favoring the literary approach, tend to build substantial theories upon a single fairy-tale variant or a particular socio-cultural context. From a folkloristic perspective, this is, of course, a flawed methodology.

Fairy-tale scholarship has long prospered in the German-speaking world, in part as the legacy of the Grimm brothers and their Romantic contemporaries. Much of this valuable work remains unavailable in English, but fortunately several works by the Swiss scholar Max Lüthi (1909-91) have been translated, an excerpt from one of which is included here. Lüthi's major concern is to demonstrate the fairy tale's preoccupation with, and relevance for, humanity; drawing upon his knowledge of the European fairy tale, Lüthi tackles such aspects as the central character's gender, isolation, social position, and personal maturation (in this last respect anticipating ideas that would later be more fully explored by Bruno Bettelheim). He was indeed among the first to counter the nineteenth-century view that fairy tales were of interest only to children; on the contrary, "[t]he ease and calm assurance with which [the fairy tale] stylizes, sublimates, and abstracts makes it the quintessence of the poetic process..." (323). Despite the age of this excerpt (first published in 1962), its insights into the purpose and focus of the fairy tale remain as illuminating as ever.

In turning to the work of Bruno Bettelheim, we can observe a contrast to the general perspective of critics such as Lüthi in a more narrowly defined interest in the fairy tale. As a well-known child psychologist, Bettelheim (1903-90) came to write his influential work *The Uses of Enchantment* (1976) in the conviction that "... more can be learned from [fairy tales] about the inner problems of human beings, and of the right solutions to their predicaments in any society, than from any other type of story within a child's comprehension" (325). It has been argued that in his desire to demonstrate the psychic merits of the fairy tale, Bettelheim is selective not only in the tales he chooses to discuss but even in the *versions* thereof: what may hold true for version A may well be contradicted by version B. Certainly since his death in 1990, there have been disturbing accusations aimed at Bettelheim regarding the validity of his work both as a psychologist and as an author. Be that as it may, there is no denying that the publication of his book renewed interest in and appreciation of the fairy tale; as one critic has acknowledged, "Once one has grasped the Bettelheim method, with its unspoken rules—characters can be doublets or triplets of each other, all objects have symbolic meaning—not only do fairy tales become quite easy to interpret, they also provoke and reward interpretation."[1] While such an open-ended prescription may lead to some analytic over-exuberance, it undeniably brings a living relevance to the tales.

There can be little doubt, however, that the most vigorous field of fairy-tale criticism over the last forty years has been the feminist. Debate began with the

---

1   Tom Shippey, "Rewriting the Core: Transformations of the Fairy Tale in Contemporary Writing," in *A Companion to the Fairy Tale*, ed. Hilda Davidson and Anna Chaudri (Cambridge: D.S. Brewer, 2003) 258.

publication in 1970 of "Fairy Tale Liberation,"[1] an essay by Alison Lurie, which in turn provoked a spirited response from Marcia K. Lieberman, "'Some Day My Prince will Come': Female Acculturation through the Fairy Tale."[2] The significance of this initial exchange has recently been defined by Donald Haase: "In the catalytic exchange between Lurie and Lieberman during the early 1970s, we witness simultaneously the inchoate discourse of early feminist fairy-tale research and the advent of modern fairy-tale studies, with its emphases on the genre's socio-political and socio-historical contexts."[3] In exploring the myriad ways in which the female has been taught to accept a subordinate personal and social role, these and other feminist scholars quickly identified the fairy tale in particular as fostering such views. As we have seen, the fairy tale established itself as children's literature in the patriarchal nineteenth century, so it should come as no surprise that many of the most popular tales just happened to reflect and endorse this gender imbalance. First published in 1979 (and updated for this anthology), Karen Rowe's article "Feminism and Fairy Tales" remains a lucid and measured introduction to this important facet of the fairy tale, not least for its exploration of the connection between the fairy tale and the enormously profitable romance industry.

In "What Fairy Tales Tell Us" (2003), Alison Lurie explores the development over the last one hundred and fifty years of the literary tale as successor to the recorded folk tale. She is particularly interested in the differences between the European fairy tale, both traditional and modern, and its American counterpart. Her survey makes clear that these retellings and original stories, like all literary works, have much to say about their authors' preoccupations and their socio-historical contexts.

The desire to write or adapt fairy tales in order to subvert their historically accepted ideology is certainly evident if one examines today's burgeoning juvenile market. Laura Tosi's survey of contemporary fairy-tale publications reveals three particular types: "morally correct," postmodernist, and feminist rewritings. What they all share, however, is a high degree of what has been termed in academic circles "intertextuality"; in other words, their numerous allusions and hybrid composition depend heavily on the reader's familiarity with the fairy-tale canon and narrative structure. However, as Tosi points out, these non-conventional approaches and techniques have revitalized the fairy-tale genre for children.

One medium that has quite simply revolutionized the fairy tale in the modern

---

1   Alison Lurie, "Fairy Tale Liberation," *The New York Review of Books*, 17 December 1970.

2   Marcia K. Lieberman, "Some Day My Prince Will Come: Female Acculturation through the Fairy Tale," *College English* 34 (1972).

3   Donald Haase, "Feminist Fairy Tale Scholarship," in *Fairy Tales and Feminism: New Approaches*, ed. Donald Haase (Detroit, MI: Wayne State University Press, 2004) 2.

world is film—and in that field, the name of Walt Disney has reigned supreme. In the constant ebb and flow of our cultural scene, the Disney product has proved remarkably resilient, although that may be due more to skilful marketing than fidelity to the fairy tale—there is no clearer instance of what Jack Zipes has called the "commodification" of the fairy tale. While in no way excusing Disney for the liberties he (or his team) has taken with his raw material, Betsy Hearne, in her article "Disney Revisited, Or, Jiminy Cricket, It's Musty Down Here!" (1997), is nevertheless concerned that we judge Disney's intervention in the light of what has previously happened in the evolution of the fairy tale. As we have already seen, research has shown conclusively that what such luminaries as Perrault and the Grimms passed on to posterity was sometimes quite different from what they received. Thus, to condemn Disney for his influence is analogous to shooting the messenger, says Hearne. Disney has been successful, at least in part, because he has given us—children and adults alike—what we want.

In recent years, the production of animated fairy tales has been transformed into a competitive and enormously profitable business. The technological refinement in the magic of animation has brought about an extraordinary expansion in its appeal. Fantasy rules—and the fairy tale has continued to adapt (or, more accurately, it has *been* adapted) to changing circumstances. All this has not occurred without consequences, however, as James Poniewozik points out in a perceptive article in *Time* magazine (10 May 2007) anticipating the opening of *Shrek 3*. He makes the point that in our media-dominated world, these sophisticated and elaborate parodies now represent the first exposure that many children have to the world of fairy tale. It is as if amid all the shock and awe of special effects and technological wizardry, the voice (and the companionship) of the storyteller has been all but drowned out; the audience's imagination has been short-circuited by watching the impossible made not just possible but downright easy, with the result that we are in danger of losing our capacity to wonder. Poniewozik finds some cause for optimism in the creative invention that occasionally asserts itself amid all the "riffing on our cartoon patrimony," but there's no denying the strength of the cash-flow current.

THE FAIRY-TALE HERO:
THE IMAGE OF MAN IN THE FAIRY TALE[1]

Max Lüthi

IS IT MERE CHANCE THAT the principal characters we have encountered in our studies are more often female than male: Sleeping Beauty; the Greek princess who kneaded a husband for herself out of groats, sugar, and almonds; good little Anny in the story of the little earth-cow; Rapunzel; the riddle princesses; and the clever peasant girls? The only corresponding male figures we have seen in the European fairy tales are the dragon slayer and that clever poser of riddles, Petit-Jean. Is this preponderance of women typical? Does our sampling reflect the true situation? If we are asked just which fairy-tale figures are generally best known, we immediately think of Sleeping Beauty, Cinderella, Snow White, Little Red Riding Hood, Rapunzel, The Princess in Disguise, and Goldmarie in "Mother Hulda"—all female figures. In "Hansel and Gretel" and in "Brother and Sister," the girl also plays the leading role. We find ourselves nearly at a loss when called upon for the names of male protagonists: Iron Hans and Tom Thumb, perhaps; the Brave Little Tailor, Strong Hans, and Lucky Hans—but here we are already in the realm of the folk-tale jest. How can one explain this peculiar predominance of women and girls? All the names mentioned are taken from the Grimm brothers' collection. Despite the existence of innumerable other collections, this one today is, in German-speaking countries, almost the sole surviving source for the public at large of real contact with the fairy tale. Now the Grimm brothers' informants were predominantly women. And today children learn fairy tales mainly from their mothers, grandmothers, aunts, and female kindergarten and school teachers. Thus, it is natural that the principal figures are mostly women. Moreover, the child—whether boy or girl—is basically closer to the feminine than the masculine, living in the domain of the mother and female teachers and not yet that of the father and male teachers. The fairy tales which grownups remember are those of their childhood. Furthermore, our era, whose character, despite everything, is still determined by men, feels the strong and clear need for a complementary antipole. The woman is assigned a privileged position, not only by social custom; in art and literature, as well, she has occupied a central position since the time of the troubadours and the Mariology[2] of the late Middle Ages. In painting and in the novel, she has been the subject of persistent interest and loving concern.

---

1   From *Once Upon a Time: On the Nature of Fairy Tales*, trans. Lee Chadeayne and Paul Gottwald (New York: Frederick Ungar, 1970).
2   Mariology: The study of the Virgin Mary.

Thus, it comes as no surprise that she also plays a significant role in the fairy tale—which for centuries was one of the most vital and indirectly influential art forms in Europe—the feminine component, that part of man closer to nature, had to come to the forefront to compensate for the technological and economic system created by the masculine spirit, which dominated the external world of reality.

However, that was a peculiarity of the era. Tellers of fairy tales were not always predominantly women, and not always was existence influenced so strongly by the masculine spirit that the antipole asserted itself with such conspicuous force in art. If we go beyond *Grimm's Fairy Tales* and leaf through the many volumes of the *Märchen der Weltliteratur* (Fairy Tales of World Literature), *Das Gesicht der Völker* (The Face of the Peoples), or Richard M. Dorson's *Folktales of the World*, we see that there are at least as many masculine as feminine protagonists, and that, in general, the masculine figures may even predominate, as they do in the myths. But one thing is quite clear: at the focal point in the fairy tale stands *man*. One cannot say this of the local legend and saint's legend: they portray the intrusion of another world upon our own existence; myths tell of gods; and among primitive peoples, animal stories predominate. The hero of the European fairy tale, however, is *man*. In the minds of the ancient Greeks, the earlier animal gods assumed human form. The humanism of the Greek classical period became a basic element of European culture. Thus, a connection no doubt exists between this European or Indo-European attribute and our fairy tales, which, in the main, concern not animals, as in the stories of primitive peoples, but men.

The European fairy tale draws a picture of man and shows him in his confrontation with the world. Since our children are interested in fairy tales in their most receptive years, and since even today almost all children have a considerable number of fairy tales which are told or read to them or which they read themselves, it is worthwhile to ask what sort of picture of man they find there. Can one say that the large number of fairy tales present a coherent picture? In a certain sense, yes. The fairy-tale hero, or heroine, to be sure, is sometimes a rollicking daredevil and sometimes a silent sufferer; at times a lazybones and at times a diligent helper; often sly and wily but just as often open and honest. At times he is a shrewd fellow, an undaunted solver of riddles, a brave fighter; at others, he is a stupid person or one who sits down and begins to cry every time he encounters difficulty. There are friendly and compassionate fairy-tale heroes, but others that are merciless and perfidious. To say nothing of the differences in social class: princess and Cinderella, prince and swineherd. Or must we perhaps say something about them? Are we not perplexed by something we see at just this point? Surprisingly, the difference in social class is often only apparent. The goose girl, in reality, is not at all one of the common folk but a princess forced into her lowly role by her servant girl. And the gardener boy with the mangy hair, whom the beautiful princess observes every morning, is, in reality, a prince who has tied an animal hide over his golden hair.

Thus, in the fairy tale, one and the same person can abruptly change from a mangy-headed youth into one with golden hair, and the despised Cinderella can suddenly turn into a dancer in a radiant gown at whom all gaze in wonder. The one considered to be stupid or loutish often turns out to be the wisest and cleverest of all. In addition, the real swineherd can unexpectedly become the princess's husband, and the poor girl can marry the prince or the king and thus be raised to royal status.

In the fairy tale, all things are possible, not just in the sense that all sorts of miracles occur, but in the sense just mentioned: the lowest can rise to the highest position, and those in the highest position—evil queens, princes, princesses, government ministers—can fall and be destroyed. It has therefore been said that fairy tales derive from the wishful thinking of poor people or those who have been unsuccessful or slighted. But such psychological and sociological interpretations are too limited. Wish dreams and wishful thinking play a part in fairy tales, just as they do in all human matters, and social tensions and yearnings also are reflected in them.

Yet these are only superficial aspects. Fairy-tale figures have an immediate appeal. The king, the princess, a dragon, a witch, gold, crystal, pitch, and ashes—these things are, for the human imagination, age-old symbols for what is high, noble, and pure or dangerous, bestial, and unfathomable; what is genuine and true, or what is sordid and false. The fairy tale often depicts how a penniless wretch becomes wealthy, a maid becomes queen, a disheveled man is changed into a youth with golden hair, or a toad, bear, ape, or dog is transformed into a beautiful maiden or handsome youth. Here, we feel at once the capacity for change of man in general. The focal point is not the rise of the servant to his position of master, not the esteem and recognition accorded the former outcast child; these are images for something more fundamental: man's deliverance from an inauthentic existence and his commencement of a true one. When the real princess lets herself be forced into the role of a goose girl while the lowly maid arrogates to herself the dominant position, this means that a false, ignoble side of the total personality gains control and suppresses that which is truly regal. When the prince marries the witch's ugly daughter instead of his bride-to-be, he has lost the way to his own soul and given himself up to a strange demon. The psychologist views things in this way, assuming that the fairy tale depicts processes within the mind. Although such specialized interpretations are often risky, it is evident that more is involved for both the author and his hearers than mere external action when the fairy tale tells how the hero conquers the dragon, marries the princess, and becomes king.

In general, one can say that the fairy tale depicts processes of development and maturation. Every man has within him an ideal image, and to be king, to wear a crown, is an image for the ascent to the highest attainable realms. And every man has within him his own secret kingdom. The visible kingdom, the figure of the princess and her bridegroom, are fascinating, influential, and oft-cited even in democratic societies because they have a symbolic force. To be king does not mean just to have power; in the modern world, kings and queens have been relieved of almost all their material power. One might say they have been freed of it and by this have acquired even greater symbolic appeal. To be a king is an image for complete self-realization; the crown and royal robe which play such a great role in the fairy tale make visible the splendor and brilliance of the great perfection achieved inwardly. They call to mind an analogous phenomenon in the saint's legend, the halo, which likewise renders visible the inward brilliance. When Goldmarie, after proving herself in the realm of Mother Hulda, is showered with gold, no one doubts that this is an image—one which reveals the girl's good soul. And when other fairy-tale heroines comb golden flowers out of their hair, or when a flower shoots out of the ground at their every step, we likewise immediately take it to be symbolic. Not only alchemists, but people generally feel gold to be a representative for a higher human and cosmic perfection. Kingship, like gold and the royal robe, has symbolic significance and power in the fairy tale. It may well be—as psychologists of the Jungian school assert—that the marriage with the animal bride or animal prince, the union of the king with the armless mute lost in the forest, and the wedding of the princess and the goatherd are images for the union of disparities in the human soul, for the awareness of a hitherto unrecognized spiritual strength, and for the maturation into a complete human personality. In any event, the fairy tale depicts over and over an upward development, the overcoming of mortal dangers and seemingly insoluble problems, the path toward marriage with the prince or princess, toward kingship or gold and jewels. The image of man portrayed in the fairy tale—or, rather, one aspect of this image—is that of one who has the capability to rise above himself, has within him the yearning for the highest things, and is also able to attain them. We can be sure that children, engrossed in the story as it is told to them, do not understand this in all its implications; but, what is more important, they can sense it. The child, at the fairy-tale age, is fascinated not by the upward social movement but by the overcoming of dangers and entry into the realm of glory, whether this is depicted as the realm of the sun and stars or as an earthly kingdom of unearthly splendor.

But the image of man as it appears in the fairy tale can be defined from yet another aspect upon closer examination. The fairy-tale hero is essentially a wanderer. Whereas the events in the local legend usually take place in the hometown or its vicinity, the fairy tale time and again sends its heroes out into the world. Sometimes the parents are too poor to be able to keep their children, at times the hero is forced away by a command or enticed away by a contest, or it may be merely that the hero decides to go out in search of adventure. In a Low German fairy tale, the father sends his two eldest sons out into the world as punishment, but does the same thing to his youngest son as a reward. Nothing shows more clearly that the fairy tale will use any excuse to make its hero a wanderer and lead him far away, often to the stars, to the bottom of the sea, to a region below the earth, or to a kingdom at the end of the world. The female protagonist is also frequently removed to a distant castle or abducted to that place by an animal-husband. This wandering, or soaring, over great distances conveys an impression of freedom and ease that is further strengthened by other characteristics in the fairy tale which also convey a feeling of freedom. Whereas in the local legends man is endowed from the very beginning with something stifling and unfree by stagnation in the ancestral village and dumbfounded gazing at the frightful phenomenon, the fairy-tale hero appears as a free-moving wanderer. In the local legend, man is an impassioned dreamer, a visionary; the fairy-tale hero, however, strides from place to place without much concern or astonishment. The other worldly beings which he encounters interest him only as helpers or opponents and do not inspire him with either curiosity, a thirst for knowledge, or a vague fear of the supernatural. The fairy tale depicts its heroes not as observing and fearful but as moving and active. In the local legend, man is embedded in the society of his village, not only that of the living, but also that of the dead. He is also rooted in the countryside or town in which he lives. The wild people in the forest and the mountains and the water sprites and poltergeists inhabit the general surroundings. The fairy-tale hero, however, breaks away from his home and goes out into the world. He is almost always alone; if there are two brothers, they separate at a certain crossroads and each experiences the decisive adventure alone. Frequently the fairy-tale hero does not return to his home town. When he sets forth to save a king's daughter or accomplish a difficult task, he usually does not know how he will accomplish his purpose. But along the way he meets a little old man, shares his bread with him, and gets from him the advice that will lead him to his goal. Or he meets a wild animal, pulls out a thorn that was hurting it, and thus gains the help of the thankful beast, whose abilities just suffice to solve his problem. In the local legend, people summon the priest or Capuchin to help in conjuring spirits, but the fairy-tale hero enters strange lands all alone and there has the decisive confrontation. The priest or Capuchin is not only a member of the village community, everyone knows the source of his helping powers: the salvation of the Christian church, the grace of God. The helping animals and other supernatural beings in the fairy tale are, however, usually just as isolated as the fairy-tale hero himself. The latter takes their advice and magic gifts nonchalantly, uses them at the decisive moment, and then no longer thinks about them. He doesn't ponder over the mysterious forces or where his helpers have come from; everything he experiences seems natural to him and he is carried along by this help, which he has earned often without his knowledge. The fairy-tale hero quite frequently is the youngest son, an orphan, a despised Cinderella or poor goatherd, and this all contributes to making the hero appear isolated; the prince, princess, and king, as well, at the very pinnacle of society, are in their own way detached, absolute, and isolated.

Local legends and fairy tales, which have existed for centuries side by side among the common folk, complement one another. Local legends originate among the common people half spontaneously and half under the influence of simple traditions and ask, we might say, the anxious question, "What is man, what is the world?" Fairy tales certainly do not originate among simple folk but with great poets, perhaps the so-called "initiated," or religious, poets; and, in a sense, they provide an answer. In the local legend, one senses the anxiety of man, who, though apparently a part of the community of his fellow men, finds himself ultimately confronted with an uncanny world which he finds hard to comprehend and which threatens him with death. The fairy tale, however, presents its hero as one who, though not comprehending ultimate relationships, is led safely through the dangerous, unfamiliar world. The fairy-tale hero is gifted, in the literal sense of the word. Supernatural beings lavish their gifts on him and help him through battles and perils. In the fairy tale, too, the ungifted, the unblessed, appear. Usually, they are the older brothers or sisters of the hero or heroine. They are often deceitful, wicked, envious, coldhearted, or dissolute—though this is by no means always the case. It may be that they just don't come across any helping animal or little man; they are the unblessed. The hearer does not, however, identify with them, but with the hero, who makes his way through the world alone—and for just this reason is free and able to establish contact with essential things. Usually, it is his unconsciously correct behavior that gains him the help of the animal with the magic powers or some other supernatural creature. This behavior, however, need not be moral in the strict sense. The idler is also a favorite of the fairy tale; it may be that he is given the very thing he wants and needs most: that his every wish is fulfilled without his having to move a finger. In the fairy tale about the frog-king, the heroine who repeatedly tries to avoid keeping her promise and finally flings the irksome frog against the wall in order to kill it is neither kind, compassionate, nor even dutiful. But by flinging the frog against the wall, she has, without knowing it, fulfilled the secret conditions for the release of the enchanted prince who had been transformed into a frog.

The hero and heroine in the fairy tale do the right thing, they hit the right key; they are heaven's favorites. The local legend, provided it is not jesting in tone, usually portrays man as unblessed, unsuccessful, and as one who, despite his deep involvement in the community, must face life's ultimate questions alone and uncertain. The fairy tale sees man as one who is essentially isolated but who, for just this reason—because he is not rigidly committed, not tied down—can establish relationships with anything in the world. And the world of the fairy tale includes not just the earth, but the entire cosmos. In the local legend, man is seemingly integrated in the community, but inwardly, essentially, he is alone. The fairy-tale hero is seemingly isolated, but has the capacity for universal relationships. Certainly, we can say that both are true portrayals of man. The local legend expresses a basic human condition: although deeply entrenched in human institutions, man feels abandoned, cast into a threatening world which he can neither understand nor view as a whole. The fairy tale, however, which also knows of failure and depicts it in its secondary characters, shows in its heroes that, despite our ignorance of ultimate things, it is possible to find a secure place in the world. The fairy-tale hero also does not perceive the world as a whole, but he puts his trust in and is accepted by it. As if led by an invisible force and with the confidence of a sleepwalker, he follows the right course. He is isolated and at the same time in touch with all things. The fairy tale is a poetic vision of man and his relationship to the world, a vision that for centuries inspired the fairy tale's hearers with strength and confidence because they sensed the fundamental truth of this vision. Even though man may feel outcast and abandoned in the world, like one groping in the dark, is he not in the course of his life led from step to step and guided safely by a thousand aids? The fairy tale, however, not only inspires trust and confidence; it also provides a sharply defined image of man: isolated, yet capable of universal relationships. It is salutary that in our era, which has experienced the loss of individuality, nationalism, and impending nihilism, our children are presented with just such an image of man in the fairy tales they hear and absorb. This image is all the more effective for having proceeded naturally from the overall style of the fairy tale. The fairy-tale technique—the sharp lines, the two-dimensional, sublimating portrayal we have so often observed as well as the encapsulating of the individual episodes and motifs—this entire technique is isolating, and only for this reason can it interconnect all things so effortlessly. The image of man in the fairy tale, the figure of the hero, grows out of its overall style; this gives it a persuasive power which cannot fail to impress even the realistically minded listener.

Every type of fairy tale portrays events which can safely be interpreted as images for psychological or cosmic processes. Every single fairy tale has a particular message. A beautiful girl's eyes are cruelly torn out and then, one year and a day later, are replaced and can see seven times as clearly as before. Another fairy-tale heroine is locked up in a box by her wicked mother-in-law and hung in the chimney, where she remains without nourishment until her husband returns from the war; yet the smoked woman does not die of hunger—indeed, she emerges from her box younger and more beautiful. Such stories make the listener feel how suffering can purify and strengthen. In speaking of the wisdom in fairy tales, one is usually thinking of similar passages in particular fairy tales. Much more powerful, however, is the overall image of man and the world as portrayed in folk fairy tales generally. This image recurs in a large number of tales and makes a profound impression on the listener—formerly, illiterate grownups; today, children. Is this image in accord with our present-day view of life and the world?

Modern literature, narrative as well as dramatic, is characterized by a strange turning away from the heroic figure. This begins as far back as Naturalism, where the coachman or the cleaning woman takes the place of the tragic hero, the kings and noble ladies, and where the masses—the weavers, for example—can take the place of the individual. In the modern novel, interest centers on impersonal forces, subconscious powers, and processes transcending the individual. If an individual does become the center of attention, he is often an anti-hero, or, as he is sometimes called, the passive or negative hero. The stories of Franz Kafka, which influence so much of present-day literature, have been characterized as out-and-out anti-fairy tales. And yet they have much in common with fairy tales. Their figures, like those of the fairy tale, are not primarily individuals, personalities, characters, but simply figures: doers and receivers of the action. They are no more masters of their destiny than are the figures in the fairy tale. They move through a world which they do not understand but in which they are nevertheless involved. This they have in common with the figures of the fairy tale: they do not perceive their relationship to the world about them. Whereas Kafka's figures stand helpless and despairing amidst the confusion of relationships they do not understand, the fairy-tale hero is happy in his contacts. The fairy tale is the poetic expression of the confidence that we are secure in a world not destitute of sense, that we can adapt ourselves to it and act and live even if we cannot view or comprehend the world as a whole.

The preference of modern literature for the passive hero, the negative hero, is not without parallel in the fairy tale. The simpleton or dejected person who sits down on a stone and cries is not able to help himself, but help comes to him. The fairy tale, too, has a partiality for the negative hero: the insignificant, the neglected, the helpless. But he unexpectedly proves to be strong, noble, and blessed. The spirit of the folk fairy tale parallels that in modern literature to a degree, but then the listener is relieved of his feeling of emptiness and filled with confidence. The grownup, still under the influence of the Enlightenment and realism, quickly turns away from the fairy tale with a feeling of contempt. But in modern art, fascination with the fairy tale is everywhere evident. The turning away from descriptive realism, from the mere description of external reality in itself, implies an approach to the fairy tale. The same can be said of the fantastic mixtures of human, animal, vegetable, and mineral, which, like the fairy tale, bring all things into relationship with one another. Modern architecture has a great preference for what is light, bright, and transparent; one often refers to the dematerialization in architecture, the sublimation of matter. The sublimation of all material things, however, is one of the basic characteristics of fairy-tale style. We find crystal-clear description combined with elusive, mysterious meaning in fairy tales, in modern lyric poetry, and in Ernst Jünger and Franz Kafka, who has said that true reality is always unrealistic. The modern Anglo-American writer W.H. Auden has said, "The sort of pleasure we get from folk fairy tales seems to me similar to that which we derive from Mallarmé's poems or from abstract painting." We are not surprised at such a statement. The fairy tale is a basic form of literature, and of art in general. The ease and calm assurance with which it stylizes, sublimates, and abstracts makes it the quintessence of the poetic process, and art in the twentieth century has again been receptive to it. We no longer view it as mere entertainment for children and those of childlike disposition. The psychologist, the pedagogue, knows that the fairy tale is a fundamental building block and an outstanding aid in development for the child; the art theorist perceives in the fairy tale—in which reality and unreality, freedom and necessity, unite—an archetypal form of literature which helps lay the groundwork for all literature, for all art. We have attempted to show, in addition, that the fairy tale presents an image of man which follows almost automatically from its overall style. The fairy-tale style isolates and unites: its hero is thus isolated and, for this very reason, capable of entering into universal relationships. The style of the fairy tale and its image of man are of timeless validity and, at the same time, of specific significance in our age. Thus, we must hope that despite the one-sided rationalistic outlook of many grownups, it will not be neglected and forgotten by our children and by the arts.

THE STRUGGLE FOR MEANING[1]

Bruno Bettelheim

IF WE HOPE TO LIVE not just from moment to moment, but in true consciousness of our existence, then our greatest need and most difficult achievement is to find meaning in our lives. It is well known how many have lost the will to live, and have stopped trying, because such meaning has evaded them. An understanding of the meaning of one's life is not suddenly acquired at a particular age, not even when one has reached chronological maturity. On the contrary, gaining a secure understanding of what the meaning of one's life may or ought to be—this is what constitutes having attained psychological maturity. And this achievement is the end result

---

1 From *The Uses of Enchantment: The Meaning and Importance of Fairy Tales* (New York: Alfred Knopf, 1976).

of a long development: at each age we seek, and must be able to find, some modicum of meaning congruent with how our minds and understanding have already developed.

Contrary to the ancient myth, wisdom does not burst forth fully developed like Athena out of Zeus's head; it is built up, small step by small step, from most irrational beginnings. Only in adulthood can an intelligent understanding of the meaning of one's existence in this world be gained from one's experiences in it. Unfortunately, too many parents want their children's minds to function as their own do—as if mature understanding of ourselves and the world, and our ideas about the meaning of life, did not have to develop as slowly as our bodies and minds.

Today, as in times past, the most important and also the most difficult task in raising a child is helping him to find meaning in life. Many growth experiences are needed to achieve this. The child, as he develops, must learn step by step to understand himself better; with this he becomes more able to understand others and eventually can relate to them in ways which are mutually satisfying and meaningful.

To find deeper meaning, one must become able to transcend the narrow confines of a self-centered existence and believe that one will make a significant contribution to life—if not right now, then at some future time. This feeling is necessary if a person is to be satisfied with himself and with what he is doing. In order not to be at the mercy of the vagaries of life, one must develop one's inner resources, so that one's emotions, imagination, and intellect mutually support and enrich one another. Our positive feelings give us the strength to develop our rationality; only hope for the future can sustain us in the adversities we unavoidably encounter.

As an educator and therapist of severely disturbed children, my main task was to restore meaning to their lives. This work made it obvious to me that if children were reared so that life was meaningful to them, they would not need special help. I was confronted with the problem of deducing what experiences in a child's life are most suited to promote his ability to find meaning in his life, to endow life in general with more meaning. Regarding this task, nothing is more important than the impact of parents and others who take care of the child; second in importance is our cultural heritage, when transmitted to the child in the right manner. When children are young, it is literature that carries such information best.

Given this fact, I became deeply dissatisfied with much of the literature intended to develop the child's mind and personality, because it fails to stimulate and nurture those resources he needs most in order to cope with his difficult inner problems. The preprimers and primers from which he is taught to read in school are designed to teach the necessary skills, irrespective of meaning. The overwhelming bulk of the rest of so-called "children's literature" attempts to entertain or to inform, or both. But most of these books are so shallow in substance that little of significance can be gained from them. The acquisition of skills, including the ability to read, becomes devalued when what one has learned to read adds nothing of importance to one's life.

We all tend to assess the future merits of an activity on the basis of what it offers now. But this is especially true for the child, who, much more than the adult, lives in the present and, although he has anxieties about his future, has only the vaguest notions of what it may require or be like. The idea that learning to read may enable one later to enrich one's life is experienced as an empty promise when the stories the child listens to, or is reading at the moment, are vacuous. The worst feature of these children's books is that they cheat the child of what he ought to gain from the experience of literature: access to deeper meaning and that which is meaningful to him at his stage of development.

For a story truly to hold the child's attention, it must entertain him and arouse his curiosity. But to enrich his life, it must stimulate his imagination; help him to develop his intellect and to clarify his emotions; be attuned to his anxieties and aspirations; give full recognition to his difficulties, while at the same time suggesting solutions to the problems which perturb him. In short, it must at one and the same time relate to all aspects of his personality—and this without ever belittling but, on the contrary, giving full credence to the seriousness of the child's predicaments, while simultaneously promoting confidence in himself and in his future.

In all these and many other respects, of the entire "children's literature"—with rare exceptions—nothing can be as enriching and satisfying to child and adult alike as the folk fairy tale. True, on an overt level fairy tales teach little about the specific conditions of life in modern mass society; these tales were created long before it came into being. But more can be learned from them about the inner problems of human beings, and of the right solutions to their predicaments in any society, than from any other type of story within a child's comprehension. Since the child at every moment of his life is exposed to the society in which he lives, he will certainly learn to cope with its conditions, provided his inner resources permit him to do so.

Just because his life is often bewildering to him, the child needs even more to be given the chance to understand himself in this complex world with which he must learn to cope. To be able to do so, the child must be helped to make some coherent sense out of the turmoil of his feelings. He needs ideas on how to bring his inner house into order and on that basis be able to create order in his life. He needs—and this hardly requires emphasis at this moment in our history—a moral education which subtly, and by implication only, conveys to him the advantages of moral behavior, not through abstract ethical concepts but through that which seems tangibly right and therefore meaningful to him.

The child finds this kind of meaning through fairy tales. Like many other modern psychological insights, this was anticipated long ago by poets. The German poet Schiller wrote: "Deeper meaning resides in the fairy tales told to me in my childhood than in the truth that is taught by life" (*The Piccolomini*, III, 4).

Through the centuries (if not millennia) during which, in their retelling, fairy tales became ever more refined, they came to convey at the same time overt and covert meanings—came to speak simultaneously to all levels of the human personality, communicating in a manner which reaches the uneducated mind of the child as well as that of the sophisticated adult. Applying the psychoanalytic model of the human personality, fairy tales carry important messages to the conscious, the preconscious, and the unconscious mind, on whatever level each is functioning at the time. By dealing with universal human problems, particularly those which preoccupy the child's mind, these stories speak to his budding ego and encourage its development, while at the same time relieving preconscious and unconscious pressures. As the stories unfold, they give conscious credence and body to id pressures and show ways to satisfy these that are in line with ego and super-ego requirements.

But my interest in fairy tales is not the result of such a technical analysis of their merits. It is, on the contrary, the consequence of asking myself why, in my experience, children—normal and abnormal alike, and at all levels of intelligence—find folk fairy tales more satisfying than all other children's stories.

The more I tried to understand why these stories are so successful at enriching the inner life of the child, the more I realized that these tales, in a much deeper sense than any other reading material, start where the child really is in his psychological and emotional being. They speak about his severe inner pressures in a way that the child unconsciously understands and—without belittling the most serious inner struggles which growing up entails—offer examples of both temporary and permanent solutions to pressing difficulties.

Fairy Tales and the Existential Predicament

In order to master the psychological problems of growing up—overcoming narcissistic disappointments, oedipal dilemmas, sibling rivalries; becoming able to relinquish childhood dependencies; gaining a feeling of selfhood and of self-worth, and a sense of moral obligation—a child needs to understand what is going on within his conscious self so that he can also cope with that which goes on in his unconscious. He can achieve this understanding, and with it the ability to cope, not through rational comprehension of the nature and content of his unconscious, but by becoming familiar with it through spinning out daydreams—ruminating, rearranging, and fantasizing about suitable story elements in response to unconscious pressures. By doing this, the child fits unconscious content into conscious fantasies, which then enable him to deal with that content. It is here that fairy tales have unequaled value, because they offer new dimensions to the child's imagination which would be impossible for him to discover as truly on his own. Even more important, the form and structure of fairy tales suggest images to the child by which he can structure his daydreams and with them give better direction to his life.

In child or adult, the unconscious is a powerful determinant of behavior. When the unconscious is repressed and its content denied entrance into awareness, then eventually the person's conscious mind will be partially overwhelmed by derivatives of these unconscious elements, or else he is forced to keep such rigid, compulsive control over them that his personality may become severely crippled. But when unconscious material *is* to some degree permitted to come to awareness and worked through in imagination, its potential for causing harm—to ourselves or others—is much reduced; some of its forces can then be made to serve positive purposes. However, the prevalent parental belief is that a child must be diverted from what troubles him most: his formless, nameless anxieties, and his chaotic, angry, and even violent fantasies. Many parents believe that only conscious reality or pleasant and wish-fulfilling images should be presented to the child—that he should be exposed only to the sunny side of things. But such one-sided fare nourishes the mind only in a one-sided way, and real life is not all sunny.

There is a widespread refusal to let children know that the source of much that goes wrong in life is due to our very own natures—the propensity of all men for acting aggressively, asocially, selfishly, out of anger and anxiety. Instead, we want our children to believe that, inherently, all men are good. But children know that *they* are not always good; and often, even when they are, they would prefer not to be. This contradicts what they are told by their parents, and therefore makes the child a monster in his own eyes.

The dominant culture wishes to pretend, particularly where children are concerned, that the dark side of man does not exist, and professes a belief in an optimistic meliorism.[1] Psychoanalysis itself is viewed as having the purpose of making life easy—but this is not what its founder intended. Psychoanalysis was created to enable man to accept the problematic nature of life without being defeated by it or giving in to escapism. Freud's prescription is that only by struggling courageously against what seem like overwhelming odds can man succeed in wringing meaning out of his existence.

This is exactly the message that fairy tales get across to the child in manifold form: that a struggle against severe difficulties in life is unavoidable, is an intrinsic part of

---

1   meliorism: A doctrine that the world can be made better by human effort.

human existence—but that if one does not shy away, but steadfastly meets unexpected and often unjust hardships, one masters all obstacles and at the end emerges victorious.

Modern stories written for young children mainly avoid these existential problems, although they are crucial issues for all of us. The child needs most particularly to be given suggestions in symbolic form about how he may deal with these issues and grow safely into maturity. "Safe" stories mention neither death nor aging, the limits to our existence, nor the wish for eternal life. The fairy tale, by contrast, confronts the child squarely with the basic human predicaments.

For example, many fairy stories begin with the death of a mother or father; in these tales the death of the parent creates the most agonizing problems, as it (or the fear of it) does in real life. Other stories tell about an aging parent who decides that the time has come to let the new generation take over. But before this can happen, the successor has to prove himself capable and worthy. The Brothers Grimm's story "The Three Feathers" begins: "There was once upon a time a king who had three sons.... When the king had become old and weak, and was thinking of his end, he did not know which of his sons should inherit the kingdom after him." In order to decide, the king sets all his sons a difficult task; the son who meets it best "shall be king after my death."

It is characteristic of fairy tales to state an existential dilemma briefly and pointedly. This permits the child to come to grips with the problem in its most essential form, where a more complex plot would confuse matters for him. The fairy tale simplifies all situations. Its figures are clearly drawn; and details, unless very important, are eliminated. All characters are typical rather than unique.

Contrary to what takes place in many modern children's stories, in fairy tales evil is as omnipresent as virtue. In practically every fairy tale good and evil are given body in the form of some figures and their actions, as good and evil are omnipresent in life and the propensities for both are present in every man. It is this duality which poses the moral problem and requires the struggle to solve it.

Evil is not without its attractions—symbolized by the mighty giant or dragon, the power of the witch, the cunning queen in "Snow White"—and often it is temporarily in the ascendancy. In many fairy tales a usurper succeeds for a time in seizing the place which rightfully belongs to the hero—as the wicked sisters do in "Cinderella." It is not that the evildoer is punished at the story's end which makes immersing oneself in fairy stories an experience in moral education, although this is part of it. In fairy tales, as in life, punishment or fear of it is only a limited deterrent to crime. The conviction that crime does not pay is a much more effective deterrent, and that is why in fairy tales the bad person always loses out. It is not the fact that virtue wins out at the end which promotes morality, but that the hero is most attractive to the child, who identifies with the hero in all his struggles. Because of this identification the child imagines that he suffers with the hero his trials and tribulations, and triumphs with him as virtue is victorious. The child makes such identifications all on his own, and the inner and outer struggles of the hero imprint morality on him.

The figures in fairy tales are not ambivalent—not good and bad at the same time, as we all are in reality. But since polarization dominates the child's mind, it also dominates fairy tales. A person is either good or bad, nothing in between. One brother is stupid, the other is clever. One sister is virtuous and industrious, the others are vile and lazy. One is beautiful, the others are ugly. One parent is all good, the other evil. The juxtaposition of opposite characters is not for the purpose of stressing right behavior, as would be true for cautionary tales. (There are some amoral fairy tales where goodness or badness, beauty or ugliness, play no role at all.) Presenting the polarities of character permits the child to comprehend easily the difference between the two, which he could not do as readily were the figures drawn more true to life, with all the complexities that characterize real people. Ambiguities must wait until a relatively firm personality has been established on the basis of positive identifications. Then the child has a basis for understanding that there are great differences between people and that therefore one has to make choices about who one wants to be. This basic decision, on which all later personality development will build, is facilitated by the polarizations of the fairy tale.

Furthermore, a child's choices are based, not so much on right versus wrong, as on who arouses his sympathy and who his antipathy. The more simple and straightforward a good character, the easier it is for a child to identify with it and to reject the bad other. The child identifies with the good hero not because of his goodness, but because the hero's condition makes a deep positive appeal to him. The question for the child is not "Do I want to be good?" but "Who do I want to be like?" The child decides this on the basis of projecting himself wholeheartedly into one character. If this fairy-tale figure is a very good person, then the child decides that he wants to be good, too.

Amoral fairy tales show no polarization or juxtaposition of good and bad persons; that is because these amoral stories serve an entirely different purpose. Such tales or type figures as "Puss in Boots," who arranges for the hero's success through trickery, and Jack, who steals the giant's treasure, build character not by promoting choices between good and bad, but by giving the child the hope that even the meekest can succeed in life. After all, what's the use of choosing to become a good person when one feels so insignificant that he fears he will never amount to anything? Morality is not the issue in these tales, but rather, assurance that one can succeed. Whether one meets life with a belief in the possibility of mastering its difficulties or with the expectation of defeat is also a very important existential problem.

The deep inner conflicts originating in our primitive drives and our violent emotions are all denied in much of modern children's literature, and so the child is not helped in coping with them. But the child is subject to desperate feelings of loneliness and isolation, and he often experiences mortal anxiety. More often than not, he is unable to express these feelings in words, or he can do so only by indirection: fear of the dark, of some animal, anxiety about his body. Since it creates discomfort in a parent to recognize these emotions in his child, the parent tends to overlook them, or he belittles these spoken fears out of his own anxiety, believing this will cover over the child's fears.

The fairy tale, by contrast, takes these existential anxieties and dilemmas very seriously and addresses itself directly to them: the need to be loved and the fear that one is thought worthless; the love of life and the fear of death. Further, the fairy tale offers solutions in ways that the child can grasp on his level of understanding. For example, fairy tales pose the dilemma of wishing to live eternally by occasionally concluding: "If they have not died, they are still alive." The other ending—"And they lived happily ever after"—does not for a moment fool the child that eternal life is possible. But it does indicate that which alone can take the sting out of the narrow limits of our time on this earth: forming a truly satisfying bond to another. The tales teach that when one has done this, one has reached the ultimate in emotional security of existence and permanence of relation available to man; and this alone can dissipate the fear of death. If one has found true adult love, the fairy story also tells, one doesn't need to wish for eternal life. This is suggested by another ending found in fairy tales: "They lived for a long time afterward, happy and in pleasure."

An uninformed view of the fairy tale sees in this type of ending an unrealistic wish-fulfillment, missing completely the important message it conveys to the child. These tales tell him that by forming a true interpersonal relation, one escapes the separation anxiety which haunts him (and which sets the stage for many fairy tales, but is always resolved at the story's ending). Furthermore, the story tells, this ending is not made possible, as the child wishes and believes, by holding on to his mother eternally. If we try to escape separation anxiety and death anxiety by desperately keeping our grasp on our parents, we will only be cruelly forced out, like Hansel and Gretel.

Only by going out into the world can the fairy-tale hero (child) find himself there; and as he does, he will also find the other with whom he will be able to live happily ever after, that is, without ever again having to experience separation anxiety. The fairy tale is future-oriented and guides the child—in terms he can understand in both his conscious and his unconscious mind—to relinquish his infantile dependency wishes and achieve a more satisfying independent existence.

Today children no longer grow up within the security of an extended family or of a well-integrated community. Therefore, even more than at the times fairy tales were invented, it is important to provide the modern child with images of heroes who have to go out into the world all by themselves and who, although originally ignorant of the ultimate things, find secure places in the world by following their right way with deep inner confidence.

The fairy-tale hero proceeds for a time in isolation, as the modern child often feels isolated. The hero is helped by being in touch with primitive things—a tree, an animal, nature—as the child feels more in touch with those things than most adults do. The fate of these heroes convinces the child that, like them, he may feel outcast and abandoned in the world, groping in the dark, but, like them, in the course of his life he will be guided step by step, and given help when it is needed. Today, even more than in past times, the child needs the reassurance offered by the image of the isolated man who nevertheless is capable of achieving meaningful and rewarding relations with the world around him.

The Fairy Tale: A Unique Art Form

While it entertains the child, the fairy tale enlightens him about himself and fosters his personality development. It offers meaning on so many different levels, and enriches the child's existence in so many ways, that no one book can do justice to the multitude and diversity of the contributions such tales make to the child's life.

This book [*The Uses of Enchantment*] attempts to show how fairy stories represent in imaginative form what the process of healthy human development consists of and how the tales make such development attractive for the child to engage in. This growth process begins with the resistance against the parents and fear of growing up, and ends when youth has truly found itself, achieved psychological independence and moral maturity, and no longer views the other sex as threatening or demonic, but is able to relate positively to it. In short, this book explicates why fairy tales make such great and positive psychological contributions to the child's inner growth.

If this book had been devoted to only one or two tales, it would have been possible to show many more of their facets, although even then complete probing of their depths would not have been achieved; for this, each story has meanings on too many levels. Which story is most important to a particular child at a particular age depends entirely on his psychological stage of development and the problems which are most pressing to him at the moment. While in writing the book it seemed reasonable to concentrate on a fairy tale's central meanings, this has the shortcoming of neglecting other aspects which might be much more significant to some individual child because of problems he is struggling with at the time. This, then, is another necessary limitation of this presentation.

For example, in discussing "Hansel and Gretel," the child's striving to hold on to his parents even though the time has come for meeting the world on his own is stressed, as well as the need to transcend a primitive orality, symbolized by the children's infatuation with the gingerbread house. Thus, it would seem that this fairy tale has most to offer to the young child ready to make his first steps out into the world. It gives body to his anxieties and offers reassurance about these fears because even in their most exaggerated form—anxieties about being devoured—they prove unwarranted: the children are victorious in the end, and a most threatening enemy—the witch—is utterly defeated. Thus, a good case could be made that this story has its greatest appeal and value for the child at the age when fairy tales begin to exercise their beneficial impact, that is, around the age of four or five.

But separation anxiety—the fear of being deserted—and starvation fear, including oral greediness, are not restricted to a particular period of development. Such fears occur at all ages in the unconscious, and thus this tale also has meaning for, and provides encouragement to, much older children. As a matter of fact, the older person might find it considerably more difficult to admit consciously his fear of being deserted by his parents or to face his oral greed; and this is even more reason to let the fairy tale speak to his unconscious, give body to his unconscious anxieties, and relieve them, without this ever coming to conscious awareness.

Other features of the same story may offer much-needed reassurance and guidance to an older child. In early adolescence a girl had been fascinated by "Hansel and Gretel," and had derived great comfort from reading and rereading it, fantasizing about it. As a child, she had been dominated by a slightly older brother. He had, in a way, shown her the path, as Hansel did when he put down the pebbles which guided his sister and himself back home. As an adolescent, this girl continued to rely on her brother, and this feature of the story felt reassuring. But at the same time she also resented the brother's dominance. Without her being conscious of it at the time, her struggle for independence rotated around the figure of Hansel. The story told her unconscious that to follow Hansel's lead led her back, not forward, and it was also meaningful that although Hansel was the leader at the story's beginning, it was Gretel who in the end achieved freedom and independence for both, because it was she who defeated the witch. As an adult, this woman came to understand that the fairy tale had helped her greatly in throwing off her dependence on her brother, as it had convinced her that an early dependence on him need not interfere with her later ascendancy. Thus, a story which for one reason had been meaningful to her as a young child provided guidance for her at adolescence for a quite different reason.

The central motif of "Snow White" is the pubertal girl's surpassing in every way the evil stepmother who, out of jealousy, denies her an independent existence—symbolically represented by the stepmother's trying to see Snow White destroyed. The story's deepest meaning for one particular five-year-old, however, was far removed from these pubertal problems. Her mother was cold and distant, so much so that she felt lost. The story assured her that she need not despair: Snow White, betrayed by her stepmother, was saved by males—first the dwarfs and later the prince. This child, too, did not despair because of the mother's desertion but trusted that rescue would come from males. Confident that "Snow White" showed her the way, she turned to her father, who responded favorably; the fairy tale's happy ending made it possible for this girl to find a happy solution to the impasse in living into which her mother's lack of interest had projected her. Thus, a fairy tale can have as important a meaning to a five-year-old as to a thirteen-year-old, although the personal meanings they derive from it may be quite different.

In "Rapunzel" we learn that the enchantress locked Rapunzel into the tower when she reached the age of twelve. Thus, hers is likewise the story of a pubertal girl and of a jealous mother who tries to prevent her from gaining independence—a typical adolescent problem, which finds a happy solution when Rapunzel becomes united with her prince. But one five-year-old boy gained quite a different reassurance from this story. When he learned that his grandmother, who took care of him most of the day, would have to go to the hospital because of serious illness—his mother was working all day, and there was no father in the home—he asked to be read the story of Rapunzel. At this critical time in his life, two elements of the tale were important to him. First, there was the security from all dangers in which the substitute mother kept the child, an idea which greatly appealed to him at that moment. So what normally could be viewed as a representation of negative, selfish behavior was capable of having a most reassuring meaning under specific circumstances. And even more important to the boy was another central motif of the story: that Rapunzel found the means of escaping her predicament in her own body—the tresses on which the prince climbed up to her room in the tower. That one's body can provide a lifeline reassured him that, if necessary, he would similarly find in his own body the source of his security. This shows that a fairy tale—because it addresses itself in the most imaginative form to essential human problems and does so in an indirect way—can have much to offer to a little boy even if the story's heroine is an adolescent girl.

These examples may help to counteract any impression made by my concentration here on a story's main motifs, and demonstrate that fairy tales have great psychological meaning for children of all ages, both girls and boys, irrespective of the age and sex of the story's hero. Rich personal meaning is gained from fairy stories because they facilitate changes in identification as the child deals with different problems, one at a time. In the light of her earlier identification with a Gretel who was glad to be led by Hansel, the adolescent girl's later identification with a Gretel who overcame the witch made her growth toward independence more rewarding and secure. The little boy's first finding security in the idea of being kept within the safety of the tower permitted him later on to glory in the realization that a much more dependable security could be found in what his body had to offer him, by way of providing him with a lifeline.

As we cannot know at what age a particular fairy tale will be most important to a particular child, we cannot ourselves decide which of the many tales he should be told at any given time or why. This only the child can determine and reveal by the strength of feeling with which he reacts to what a tale evokes in his conscious and unconscious mind. Naturally a parent will begin by telling or reading to his child a tale the parent himself or herself cared for as a child, or cares for now. If the child does not take to the story, this means that its motifs or themes have failed to evoke a meaningful response at this moment in his life. Then it is best to tell him another fairy tale the next evening. Soon he will indicate that a certain story has become important to him by his immediate response to it, or by his asking to be told this story over and over again. If all goes well, the child's enthusiasm for this story will be contagious, and the story will become important to the parent too, if for no other reason than that it means so much to the child. Finally there will come the time when the child has gained all he can from the preferred story, or the problems which made him respond to it have been replaced by others which find better expression in some other tale. He may then temporarily lose interest in this story and enjoy some other one much more. In the telling of fairy stories it is always best to follow the child's lead.

. Even if a parent should guess correctly why his child has become involved emotionally with a given tale, this is knowledge best kept to oneself. The young child's most important experiences and reactions are largely subconscious and should remain so until he reaches a much more mature age and understanding. It is always intrusive to interpret a person's unconscious thoughts, to make conscious what he wishes to keep preconscious, and this is especially true in the case of a child. Just as important for the child's well-being as feeling that his parent shares his emotions, through enjoying the same fairy tale, is the child's feeling that his inner thoughts are not known to his parent until he decides to reveal them. If the parent indicates that he knows them already, the child is prevented from making the most precious gift to his parent of sharing with him what until then was secret and private to the child. And since, in addition, a parent is so much more powerful than a child, his domination may appear limitless—and hence destructively overwhelming—if he seems able to read the child's secret thoughts, know his most hidden feelings, even before the child himself has begun to become aware of them.

Explaining to a child why a fairy tale is so captivating to him destroys, moreover, the story's enchantment, which depends to a considerable degree on the child's not quite knowing why he is delighted by it. And with the forfeiture of this power to enchant goes also a loss of the story's potential for helping the child struggle on his own and master all by himself the problem which has made the story meaningful to him in the first place. Adult interpretations, as correct as they may be, rob the child of the opportunity to feel that he, on his own, through repeated hearing and ruminating about the story, has coped successfully with a difficult situation. We grow, we find meaning in life and security in ourselves by having understood and solved personal problems on our own, not by having them explained to us by others.

Fairy-tale motifs are not neurotic symptoms, something one is better off understanding rationally so that one can rid oneself of them. Such motifs are experienced as wondrous because the child feels understood and appreciated deep down in his feelings, hopes, and anxieties, without these all having to be dragged up and investigated in the harsh light of a rationality that is still beyond him. Fairy tales enrich the child's life and give it an enchanted quality just because he does not quite know how the stories have worked their wonder on him.

FAIRY TALES FROM A FOLKLORISTIC PERSPECTIVE[1]

Alan Dundes

THE FIRST THING TO SAY about fairy tales is that they are an oral form. Fairy tales, however one may choose ultimately to define them, are a subgenre of the more inclusive category of "folk tale," which exists primarily as a spoken traditional narrative. Once a fairy tale or any other type of folk tale, for that matter, is reduced to written language, one does not have a true fairy tale but instead only a pale and inadequate reflection of what was originally an oral performance complete with raconteur and audience. From this folkloristic perspective, one cannot possibly read fairy tales; one can only properly hear them told.

When one enters into the realm of written-down or transcribed fairy tales, one is involved with a separate order of reality. A vast chasm separates an oral tale with its subtle nuances entailing significant body movements, eye expression, pregnant pauses, and the like from the inevitably flat and fixed written record of what was once a live and often compelling storytelling event. To be sure, there are degrees of authenticity and accuracy with respect to the transcription of fairy tales. In modern

1   From *Fairy Tales and Society: Illusion, Allusion and Paradigm*, ed. Ruth Bottigheimer (Philadelphia, PA: University of Pennsylvania Press, 1986).

times, armed with tape recorders or videotape equipment, a folklorist may be able to capture a live performance in the act, thereby preserving it for enjoyment and study by future audiences. But in the nineteenth century when the formal study of folklore began in Europe, collectors had to do the best they could to take down oral tales verbatim without such advances in technology. Many of them succeeded admirably, such as E. Tang Kristensen (1843-1929), a Danish folklorist who was one of the greatest collectors of fairy tales of all time. Others, including even the celebrated Grimm brothers, failed to live up to the ideal of recording oral tales as they were told. Instead, they altered the oral tales in a misguided effort to "improve" them. The Grimms, for instance, began to conflate different versions of the same tale, and they ended up producing what folklorists now call "composite" texts. A composite text, containing one motif from one version, another motif from another, and so on, exemplifies what folklorists term "fakelore." Fakelore refers to an item which the collector claims is genuine oral tradition but which has been doctored or in some cases entirely fabricated by the purported collector.

The point is that a composite fairy tale has never actually been told in precisely that form by a storyteller operating in the context of oral tradition. It typically appears for the very first time in print. And it is not just a matter of twentieth-century scholars trying to impose twentieth-century standards upon struggling nineteenth-century pioneering collectors. For the Grimms certainly knew better, and they are on record as adamantly opposing the literary reworking of folklore (as had been done in the famous folk song anthology of *Des Knaben Wunderhorn* [1805] which they severely criticized). They specifically called for the collection of fairy tales as they were told—in dialect. In the preface to the first volume of the *Kinder- und Hausmärchen* of 1812, the Grimms bothered to say that they had "endeavored to present these fairy tales as pure as possible.... No circumstance has been added, embellished or changed." Unfortunately, they were later unable or unwilling to adhere to these exemplary criteria. So the Grimms knew what they were doing when they combined different versions of a single folktale and presented it as one of the tales in their *Kinder- und Hausmärchen*.

What this means is that anyone truly interested in the unadulterated fairy tale must study oral texts or as accurate a transcription of oral texts as is humanly possible. The reality of far too much of what passes for fairy tale scholarship, including the majority of essays in this very volume [*Fairy Tales and Society*], is that such fairy tale texts are not considered. Instead, a strong, elitist literary bias prevails and it is the recast and reconstituted fairy tales which serve as the corpus for study. When one analyzes fairy tales as rewritten by Charles Perrault or by the Grimm brothers, one is *not* analyzing fairy tales as they were told by traditional storytellers. One is instead analyzing fairy tale plots as altered by men of letters, often with a nationalistic and romantic axe to grind. The aim was usually to present evidence of an ancient nationalistic patrimony in which the French or German literati could take pride. With such a laudable goal, it was deemed excusable to eliminate any crude or vulgar elements—How many bawdy folk tales does one find in the Grimm canon?—and to polish and refine the oral discourse of "rough" peasant dialects.

This does not mean that versions, composite or not, of tales published by Perrault and the Grimms cannot be studied. They have had an undeniably enormous impact upon popular culture and literature, but they should not be confused with the genuine article—the oral fairy tale.

There is another difficulty with the research carried out by deluded individuals who erroneously believe they are studying fairy tales when they limit themselves to the Grimm or Perrault versions of tales. Any true fairy tale, like all folklore, is characterized by the criteria of "multiple existence" and "variation." An item must exist in at least two versions in order to qualify as authentic folklore. Most items exist in hundreds of versions. Usually, no two versions of an oral fairy tale will be exactly word-for-word the same. That is what is meant by the criteria of multiple existence and variation. When one studies the Perrault or the Grimm text of a fairy tale, one is studying a single text. This may be appropriate for literary scholars who are wont to think in terms of unique, distinctive, individual texts written by a known author or poet. But it is totally inappropriate for the study of folklore wherein there is no such thing as *the* text. There are only texts.

Folklorists have been collecting fairy tales and other forms of folklore for the past several centuries. Not all these versions have been published. In fact, the majority of these tales remain in unpublished form scattered in folklore archives throughout the world. However, one can obtain these versions simply by applying to these archives. Folklorists have carried out extensive comparative studies of various fairy tales in which they have assiduously located and assembled as many as five hundred versions of a single tale type. Ever since the Finnish folklorist Antti Aarne published his *Verzeichnis der Märchen-typen* as Folklore Fellows Communication no. 3 in 1910, folklorists have had an index of folktales (including fairy tales). Twice revised by American folklorist Stith Thompson, in 1928 and again in 1961, *The Types of the Folktale: A Classification and Bibliography* is the standard reference for any serious student of Indo-European folktales. Thompson's revisions took account of the various local, regional, and national tale type indexes which appeared after Aarne's 1910 work. There are more than fifty or sixty national tale-type indexes in print, including several which are not referenced in the Aarne-Thompson 1961 index inasmuch as they were published after that date, for example, for Latvia, China, Korea, Madagascar, Friesland, and Norway.

The Aarne-Thompson tale-type index gives not only a general synopsis of each of some two thousand Indo-European tales but also some sense of how many versions are to be found in the various folklore archives. In addition, if there is a published article or monograph which contains numerous versions of a tale type, it is listed followed by an asterisk. If there has been a substantial, full-fledged comparative study of a particular tale, that bibliographical citation is marked by two asterisks. Thus, if one looked in the Aarne-Thompson tale-type index under tale type 425A, "The Monster (Animal) as Bridegroom (Cupid and Psyche)," one would in a matter of seconds discover no less than five double-asterisked monographs or articles devoted to this tale type. One would also learn that there are eighty-seven Danish versions, twenty-eight Hungarian versions, twenty-nine Rumanian versions, and others located in archives.

The gist of this is that if one is really interested in a particular fairy tale, one has the possibility of considering dozens upon dozens of versions of that tale. Whatever one's particular theoretical interest, the comparative data is essential. If one is concerned with identifying possible national traits in a particular version of a tale, one cannot do so without first ascertaining whether the traits in question are found in versions of the same tale told in other countries. If the same traits are to be found in twenty countries, it would be folly to assume that those traits were somehow typical of German or French culture exclusively.

The sad truth is that most studies of fairy tales are carried out in total ignorance of tale-type indexes (or the related tool, the six volume *Motif-Index of Folk Literature* which first appeared in 1932-36, and was revised in 1955-58). One can say categorically that it is always risky, methodologically speaking, *to limit one's analysis to one single version of a tale*. There is absolutely no need to restrict one's attention to a single version of a tale type when there are literally hundreds of versions of that same tale easily available. The fallacy of using but a single version of a fairy tale is compounded when that one version is a doctored, rewritten composite text, as occurs when one uses the Grimm version alone.

The abysmal lack of knowledge of folktale scholarship among academics in classics, comparative literature, and literature departments generally causes genuine concern among folklorists. Let one example stand for hundreds. Rhys Carpenter publishes a book, *Folk Tale, Fiction and Saga in the Homeric Epics* (Berkeley and Los Angeles: University of California Press, 1958), in which he discusses the story of the Cyclops with absolutely no mention of the fact that it is Aarne-Thompson tale type 1137, "The Ogre Blinded (Polyphemus)." It was in fact collected by the Grimms, and the Homeric version provides a useful *terminus ante quern*[1] for that tale. How can a scholar write a whole book about folk tales without any apparent knowledge of the tale-type index? (And what about the scholars who reviewed the manuscript

---

1   *terminus ante quern*: Latin, meaning "point before which."

for the university press involved?) Despite the existence of a tale-type index since 1910, most of the discussion of fairy tales occurs without the benefit of folkloristic tale typology.

It is hard to document the extent of the parochialism of the bulk of fairy-tale research. There are too few folklorists and too many amateurs. For example, one continues to find essays and books naïvely claiming to extrapolate German national or cultural traits from the Grimm tales. It is not that there could not be any useful data contained in the Grimm versions, it is rather that there are plenty of authentic versions of German fairy tales available which a would-be student of German culture could consult as a check. Psychiatrists writing about fairy tales commit the same error. They typically use only one version of a fairy tale, in most instances the Grimm version, and then they go on to generalize not just about German culture, but all European culture or even all humankind—on the basis of one single (rewritten) version of a fairy tale! This displays a certain arrogance, ethnocentrism, and ignorance.

There is another important question with respect to fairy tales. If one were to read through symposia and books devoted to the fairy tale [such as *Fairy Tales and Society*], one could easily come to the (false) conclusion that the fairy tale, strictly speaking, was a European form. Certainly, if one speaks only of Perrault and the Grimms, one is severely restricted—just to France and Germany, not even considering the fairy-tale traditions of Eastern Europe. But is the fairy tale a subgenre of folk tale limited in distribution to Europe or to the Indo-European (and Semitic) world? Are there fairy tales in Africa? in Polynesia? among North and South American Indians? If one defines fairy tales as consisting of Aarne-Thompson tale types 300 to 749, the so-called tales of magic—as opposed let us say to animal tales (Aarne-Thompson tale types 1-299) or numskull stories (AT 1200-1349) or cumulative (formula) tales (AT 2000-2199)—then one would have a relatively closed corpus. Vladimir Propp, for example, in his pioneering *Morphology of the Folktale*, first published in 1928, tried to define the structure of the "fairy tale," that is, Aarne-Thompson tale types 300-749. The Swedish folklore theorist C.W. von Sydow proposed the term *chimerate*, which included AT 300-749 *and* AT 850-879, which is perhaps a better sampling of the so-called European fairy tale.

The point is that these Aarne-Thompson tale types are *not* universal. They are basically Indo-European (plus Semitic, Chinese, and so on) tale types. "Cinderella," for example, AT 510A, although extremely widespread in the Indo-European world, is not found as an indigenous tale in North and South America, in Africa, or aboriginal Australia. In other words, more than half the peoples of the world do not have a version of "Cinderella" except as borrowed from Indo-European cultures. But they have their own tales. The question is: Are some of their tales fairy tales? Is the tale of Star-Husband which is found throughout native North America a "fairy tale"? An abundant scholarship has been devoted to this American Indian tale type, but the issue of whether or not it is a fairy tale has not been discussed.

The term *fairy tale* is actually a poor one anyway, for fairies rarely appear in fairy tales. The vast majority of stories with fairies in them are classified by folklorists as belonging to the legend genre, not folk tale. So since the term *fairy tale* is so inadequate, it is not clear that there is any advantage in forcing the folk tales of other peoples and cultures into such a Procrustean misnomer. Regardless of whether or not one wants to extend the notion of fairy tale to African and American Indian folk tales, the fact remains that *folk tale* as a folklore genre is a universal one—even if specific tale types do not demonstrate universal distribution. This emphasizes the unduly restrictive nature of treatments of folk tale which in effect ignore the rich folk-tale traditions of so much of the world.

Folklorists who choose to study the folk tales of non-Western cultures enjoy a distinct advantage. In Europe, the study of a particular tale is complicated by the fact that oral and written versions of that tale have existed side-by-side for more than a century. Sometimes the oral tradition influences the written/literary tradition; sometimes (less often) the written tradition influences the oral tradition. (Informants who mean to be helpful will often suppress their own traditional version of a tale, preferring instead to check with the standard literary version, for example, in the Grimm canon, and dutifully parrot the latter to the collector. Much evidence indicates that a number of the Grimms' "German" folk tales actually came from French literary sources—including Perrault.) In non-Western cultures, where literacy may still be relatively rare, storytellers may give oral versions untainted by literary rewritten texts. If one, therefore, is truly interested in studying folk tales, one would do well to consider investigating non-European tales. The study of the interrelationship of oral and printed texts is a legitimate and important one, but it is not the same as the study of a purely oral tradition.

Nowhere is the excessive bias of literary elitism more evident than in the consideration of so-called *Kunstmärchen* and children's book illustrations. The distinction between *Volksmärchen* and *Kunstmärchen* is intended to distinguish true folk tales from artistic or literary tales.[1] The latter are not and were never oral tales but instead are totally artistic imitations of the oral folk-tale genre. The "fairy tales" of Hans Christian Andersen, for example, are *Kunstmärchen*. He wrote them himself—he did not collect them from oral performances from informants. The very distinction between *Volksmärchen* and *Kunstmärchen* becomes virtually meaningless in an oral culture. In a culture which has no written language, there can be no *Kunstmärchen*. So the distinction is once again an example of a strictly Europe-centric view of

---

1   *Volksmärchen*: Folktale; *Kunstmärchen*: Art-fairy tale, or literary fairy tale.

the folk tale. The same holds for children's book illustrations. While the content analysis of the various children's book illustrations of a tale like "Little Red Riding Hood" (AT 333) may be fascinating, it has little to do with the oral tale. There are no picture-book illustrations in an oral tale. Personally, I find children's book illustrations of fairy tales depressingly limiting and stultifying. Why should the audience see the dragon as one particular professional illustrator depicts it? Is not the human imagination far more powerful than anything a single book illustrator could possibly draw? In the oral-tale setting, each member of the audience is free to let his or her imagination create images without limit. So once again, children's book illustrations over and above the fact that versions of fairy tales rewritten for children are often heavily bowdlerized and simplified (in contrast to most societies where children are permitted to hear the same versions of the tales as told to adults) are a peculiar feature of European culture. One should be able to investigate the nature of fairy-tale book illustrations, but one should realize that one is dealing with a derivative, printed art-form, part of a literary and commercial tradition which is at least one full step removed from the original oral tale.

If one were to remove from this volume [Fairy Tales and Society] all the essays which treated literary fairy tales or which treated literary rewritten fairy tales such as by Perrault, the Grimms, or the ones in the Thousand and One Nights, or which were concerned with fairy tale children's book illustrations, one would have very little remaining. This is a pity insofar as the true fairy tale—even if one wished to restrict the subgenre to Europe or the Indo-European world—would essentially not be considered at all. The reader should be cautioned about this bias, especially since no doubt the majority of readers will, like the authors of the other essays, come from the ranks of students of literature, not folklore. The study of Kunstmärchen and literary versions of fairy tales is a legitimate academic enterprise, but it is no substitute for and it ought not to be confused with the study of the oral fairy tale.

Finally, what is even more of an indictment of an overly literary bias in the studies of fairy tale contained in this volume [Fairy Tales and Society] is the narrowness of theoretical approach. A host of alternative theories and methods exist with respect to the analysis of fairy tales, but very few of them are represented in this set of essays. Several essays are totally literal and historical, for example, looking for traces of old German law in the Grimm tales. Fairy tales, oral and literary, are essentially creatures of fantasy. They do not necessarily represent historical reality. The literal approach in folklore includes mythologists who lead expeditions to Mount Ararat searching for remains of Noah's ark or folk-tale scholars who go so far as to suggest that the dragons in fairy tales are primitive man's recollection of prehistoric pterodactyls! The attempt to extrapolate historical features of a culture from fairy tales is admittedly one approach, but it hardly exhausts the content analysis possibilities. Structural, ritual, Jungian, and Freudian interpretations of fairy tales are discussed..., but none of these approaches is applied to any one tale.

The folkloristic approach to fairy tales begins with the oral tale—with literary versions being considered derivative and secondary. It includes a comparative treatment of any particular tale, using the resources of numerous publications and the holdings of folklore archives, as indicated in the standard tale-type indexes. Ideally, the folkloristic approach should incorporate a healthy, eclectic variety of theoretical orientations which would be more likely to reveal the richness of the fairy-tale genre, its symbolic nature, and its enduring fascination.

FEMINISM AND FAIRY TALES [1]

Karen Rowe

To EXAMINE SELECTED POPULAR FOLK tales from the perspective of modern feminism is to revisualize those paradigms which shape our romantic expectations and to illuminate psychic ambiguities which often confound contemporary women. Portrayals of adolescent waiting and dreaming, patterns of double enchantment, and romanticizations of marriage contribute to the potency of fairy tales. Yet, such alluring fantasies gloss the heroine's inability to act self-assertively, her total reliance on external rescues, her willing bondage to father and prince, and her restriction to hearth and nursery. Although many readers discount obvious fantasy elements, they may still fall prey to more subtle paradigms through identification with the heroine. Thus, subconsciously women may transfer from fairy tales into real life cultural norms which exalt passivity, dependency, and self-sacrifice as a female's cardinal virtues. In short, fairy tales perpetuate the patriarchal status quo by making female subordination seem a romantically desirable, indeed an inescapable fate.

Some day my prince will come.[2] With mingled adolescent assurance and anxiety, young girls for many centuries have paid homage to the romantic visions

---

1   First published in 1979 in *Women's Studies: An Interdisciplinary Journal.* This text was newly revised from the original for this anthology.

2   See Marcia R. Lieberman, "'Some Day My Prince Will Come': Female Acculturation Through the Fairy Tale," *College English* 34 (December 1972): 383-95; Kay Stone, "Things Walt Disney Never Told Us," *Journal of American Folklore* 88 (1975): 42-49; Alison Lurie, "Fairy Tale Liberation," *The New York Review of Books,* 17 December 1970: 42-44; and Alison Lurie, "Witches and Fairies: Fitzgerald to Updike," *The New York Review of Books,* 2 December 1971: 6-1.

aroused by this article of faith in fairy tale. Even in modern society where romance co-habits uncomfortably with women's liberation, barely disguised forms of fairy tales transmit romantic conventions through the medium of popular literature. Degenerate offspring of fairy tales, such as *Real Romances, Secret Romances, Intimate Romances*, and *Daring Romances*, capitalize on the allure of romance, but sell instead a grotesque composite of pornography and melodrama ("He Brought My Body to Peaks of Ecstasy on his Water-Bed.... Yet I Knew I Had to Leave Him for Another Lover"[1]). Traditional fairy tales fuse morality with romantic fantasy in order to portray cultural ideals for human relationships. In contrast, pulp romances strip the fantastic machinery and social sanctions to expose, then graphically exploit, the implicit sexuality.

Chaster descendants of fairy tales, the "ladies fictions" of *Good Housekeeping, Redbook,* and *McCalls,* pass on homogenized redactions of romantic conventions. A 1974 version, "The Garlands of Fortune" proffers the predictable narrative, only a shadow away from folklore fantasies of princes: "She was a girl who didn't believe in luck, let alone miracles, or at least she didn't until that fabulous man came along."[2] These "domestic fictions" reduce fairy tales to sentimental clichés, while they continue to glamorize a heroine's traditional yearning for romantic love which culminates in marriage. Distinguished from the pulp magazines' blatant degradation of romance into sexual titillation, women's magazines and "chaste" historical romances, such as Barbara Cartland's, preserve moral strictures and the virtuous heroine from fairy tales, even as they rationalize the fantastic events. They render diminished counterfeits of Victorian novels of sensibility and manners. More conscious imitators of commonplace nineteenth-century fictions and, thereby, of fairy tales, the doyennes Victoria Holt, Mary Stewart, and Phyllis Whitney and their revisionist contemporary successors, Barbara Michaels, Nora Roberts, Colleen Shannon, and newcomer Diane Tyrrel, popularize the modern gothic romance. Tell-tale captions from Holt's *Legend of the Seventh Virgin* (1965) highlight the inherited elements: "It was the most exciting night of my life! Mellyora had wangled an invitation to the masked ball at the Abbas for me, Kerensa Carlee the servant girl!" and "Johnny St. Larnston danced with me out onto the terrace."[3] Virginal dreams of elegant balls, adored princes, and romantic deliverance become captivatingly mysterious when complicated by concealed identities, hints of incest, hidden treasures, ancient curses, supernatural apparitions, and looming mansions. Unlike either sexually exploitative or domesticated

---

1   "He Brought My Body to Peaks of Ecstasy on His Water-Bed," *Real Story,* May 1975: 17-19, 66-68.
2   Leonhard Dowty, "The Garlands of Fortune," *Good Housekeeping,* December 1974: 75, 175-83.
3   Victoria Holt, "Legend of the Seventh Virgin," in *Gothic Tales of Love,* April 1975, 13-33.

romances, these tales of horror maintain historical distance, suppress sexuality, and adhere to rigid social hierarchies. They perpetuate, virtually intact, earlier gothic adaptations of fairy-tale motifs.

The mass popularity of these fictions—erotic, ladies, and gothic—testifies to a pervasive fascination with fairy-tale romance in literature not merely for children but for twentieth-century adults. Moreover, folklorists counter any casual dismissal of folk tales as mere entertainment by arguing that they have always been one of culture's primary mechanisms for inculcating roles and behaviors.[1] The ostensibly innocuous fantasies symbolically portray basic human problems and appropriate social prescriptions. These tales which glorify passivity, dependency, and self-sacrifice as a heroine's cardinal virtues suggest that culture's very survival depends upon a woman's acceptance of roles which relegate her to motherhood and domesticity. Just how potently folklore contributes to cultural stability may be measured by the pressure exerted upon women to emulate fairy-tale prototypes. Few women expect a literally "royal" marriage with Prince Charming; but, subconsciously at least, female readers assimilate more subtle cultural imperatives. They transfer from fairy tales into real life those fantasies which exalt acquiescence to male power and make marriage not simply one ideal, but the only estate toward which women should aspire. The idealizations, which reflect culture's approval, make the female's choice of marriage and maternity seem commendable, indeed predestined. In short, fairy tales are not just entertaining fantasies, but powerful transmitters of romantic myths which encourage women to internalize only aspirations deemed appropriate to our "real" sexual functions within a patriarchy.

As long as fairy-tale paradigms accord closely with cultural norms, women can and have found in romantic fictions satisfying justifications for their conformity. But groundbreaking feminist studies, such as Simone de Beauvoir's *The Second Sex*, Germaine Greer's *The Female Eunuch*, and Betty Friedan's *The Feminine Mystique*, to

---

1   See William Bascom, "Four Functions of Folklore," *Journal of American Folklore* 67 (1954) rpt. in *The Study of Folklore*, ed. Alan Dundes (Englewood Cliffs, NJ: Prentice-Hall, 1965) 279-98. Inheriting his assumptions from anthropologists and folklorists, such as Franz Boas, Ruth Benedict, Melville I. Herskovits, and Bronislaw Malinowski, Bascom succinctly articulates the functional approach to folklore: "Viewed in this light, folklore is an important mechanism for maintaining the stability of culture. It is used to inculcate the customs and ethical standards of the young, and as an adult to reward him with praise when he conforms, to punish him with ridicule or criticism when he deviates, to provide him with rationalizations when the institutions and conventions are challenged or questioned, to suggest that he be content with things as they are, and to provide him with a compensatory escape from 'the hardships, the inequalities, the injustices of everyday life. Here, indeed, is the basic paradox of folklore, that while it plays a vital role in transmitting and maintaining the institutions of a culture and in forcing the individual to conform to them, at the same time it provides socially approved outlets for the repressions which these same institutions impose upon him" (298). See also Bascom's "Folklore and Anthropology," *Journal of American Folklore* 66 (1953), rpt. in *The Study of Folklore* 25-33.

mention only the forerunners, have exposed the historical conditions which subordinate women in all areas from the procreative to the political. With progressive suffrage and liberation movements of the twentieth century and radical redefinitions of sexual and social roles, women are challenging both previous mores and those fairy tales which inculcate romantic ideals. Although lingeringly attracted to fantasies (like Eve to the garden after the Fall), many modern women can no longer blindly accept the promise of connubial bliss with the prince. Indeed, fairy-tale fantasies come to seem more deluding than problem-solving. "Romance" glosses over the heroine's impotence: she is unable to act independently or self-assertively; she relies on external agents for rescue; she binds herself first to the father and then the prince; she restricts her ambitions to hearth and nursery. Fairy tales, therefore, no longer provide mythic validations of desirable female behavior; instead, they seem more purely escapist or nostalgic, having lost their potency because of the widening gap between social practice and romantic idealization.

It is a sign of our conflicted modern times that popular romances nevertheless continue to imitate fairy-tale prototypes, while concurrently path-breaking feminist novels, such as Doris Lessing's *Martha Quest* and *A Proper Marriage*, Erica Jong's *Fear of Flying*, and Alix Kates Shulman's *Memoirs of an Ex-Prom Queen*, portray disillusionments, and later Alice Walker's *The Color Purple*, Margaret Atwood's *The Handmaid's Tale*, and Sandra Cisneros's "Woman Hollering Creek" defiantly subvert heterosexist romantic conventions. An examination of a few popular folk tales from the perspective of modern feminism not only reveals why romantic fantasy exerts such a powerful imaginative allure, but also illuminates how contemporary ambiguities cloud women's attitudes toward men and marriage.

I

Among the classic English tales of romance, "Cinderella," "Sleeping Beauty in the Wood," "Snow-Drop," "The Tale of the Kind and the Unkind Girls," "Beauty and the Beast," and "The Frog-Prince" focus on the crucial period of adolescence, dramatizing archetypal female dilemmas and socially acceptable resolutions.[1] Confronted by the

---

1 Iona and Peter Opie, *The Classic Fairy Tales* (London: Oxford University Press, 1974). All further references to the tales will be to this edition which gives the texts of the "best-known fairy tales as they were first printed in English, or in their earliest surviving or prepotent text" (5) and will be cited parenthetically in the text. The most significant European literary collections appear first in Renaissance Italy (Gianfrancesco Straparola, *Le piacevoli Notti*, 1550-53; and Giambattista Basile, *Lo Cunto de li Cunti*, often called the *Pentamerone*, 5 vols., 1634-36), then in France (Charles Perrault, *Histoires ou Contes du temps passé. Avec des Moralitez*, 1697), and eventually in England with Robert Samber's translation of Perrault (*Histories or Tales of Past Times*, 1729). Comtesse d'Aulnoy contributes the now familiar term by titling her tales *Contes*

trauma of blossoming sexuality, for instance, the young girl subliminally responds to fairy-tale projections of adolescent conflicts.[1] She often achieves comforting release from anxieties by subconsciously perceiving in symbolic tales the commonness of her existential dilemma. Moreover, the equal-handed justice and optimistic endings instil confidence that obstacles can be conquered as she progresses from childhood to maturity. More than alleviating psychic fears associated with the rite of passage, however, tales also prescribe approved cultural paradigms which ease the female's assimilation into the adult community.[2]

The stepmother and bad fairy, who invariably appear odious, embody the major obstacles against this passage to womanhood. Not simply dramatic and moral antagonists to the youthful heroine, they personify predatory female sexuality and the adolescent's negative feelings toward her mother. In Perrault's version of "Cinderella" (AT 510), persecution of the adolescent stems directly from the father's

---

des fées (1697-98), establishes fairy tales as a literary genre through imaginative retellings of older stories in *A Collection of Novels and Tales, Written by that Celebrated Wit of France, The Countess V'Anois* (1721), and introduces "The Story of Finetta the Cinder-Girl" into English (1721). Another Frenchwoman, Madame Marie Le Prince de Beaumont, clearly perceives the value of tales for the engagement and instruction of the young when she publishes her *Magasin des enfans, ou dialogues entre une sage Gouvernante et plusieurs de ses Elèves* (1756), translated as *The Young Misses Magazine* (1759). The eighteenth century tolerates this new vogue of fairy tales, popularly attributed to Mother Goose and Mother Bunch, by relegating them to the nursery. However, such folktales gain a new and lasting respectability with Edgar Taylor's publication of *German Popular Stories* (1823-26), translated from the three volume *Kinder- und Hausmärchen* (1812-22) of the Brothers Grimm. Illustrated by George Cruikshank, this volume provides permissible fantasies for the young, a learned account of the antique origins and diffusions of tales, an inspiration for romantic poets and novelists, and the basis for all future studies of folklore in English. Consult Opie and Opie, "Introduction" 11-23; and Michael Kotzin, *Dickens and the Fairy Tale* (Bowling Green, OH: Bowling Green University Popular Press, 1972) for more complete histories of the fairy tale in English literary tradition.

1 See Bruno Bettelheim, *The Uses of Enchantment: The Meaning and Importance of Fairy Tales* (New York: Knopf, 1976) for a thorough-going Freudian analysis of fairy tales; Marie-Louise Von Franz, *Problems of the Feminine in Fairy Tales*, ed. James Hillman (New York: Spring Publications, 1972) and Hedwig Von Beit, *Das Märchen: Sein Ort in der Geistigen Entwicklung* (Bern: A. Francke, 1965) for Jungian analyses; and Max Lüthi, *Once Upon a Time: On the Nature of Fairy Tales*, trans. Lee Chadeayne and Paul Gottwald (1962; repr., New York: Ungar, 1970). Lüthi reads "Sleeping Beauty," "Cinderella," and particularly "Rapunzel" as representations of maturation processes and acknowledges that "behind many features in our fairy tales there are old customs and beliefs; but in the context of the tale, they have lost their original character. Fairy tales are experienced by their hearers and readers, not as realistic, but as symbolic poetry" (66).

2 See J.L. Fischer, "The Sociopsychological Analysis of Folktales," *Current Anthropology* 4 (1963): 235-95. In this rigorous survey of recent trends, Fischer argues cogently for the complex interaction of psychological, sociological, and structuralist interpretations of tales and formulates a functionalized approach: "For a tale to persist, therefore, some sort of balance must be achieved between two sets of demands: one, the demands of the individual for personal pleasure and the reduction of his anxiety, and the other, the demands of the other members of the society that the individual pursue his personal goals only in ways which will also contribute to, or at least not greatly harm, the welfare of the society" (259).

remarriage and the new stepmother's sexual jealousies.[1] Because "she could not bear the good qualities of this pretty girl; and the less, because they made her own daughters so much the more hated and despised," Cinderella's stepmother displays her "ill humour" by employing the child "in the meanest work of the house" (123: see endnote vi). Similarly proud and vain, Snow-Drop's stepmother in Grimm's recounting plots against the seven-year-old child who "was as bright as the day, and fairer than the queen herself" (177).[2] Although fairy tales carefully displace animosities onto a substitute figure, they in part recreate the fears of a menopausal mother. For the aging stepmother, the young girl's maturation signals her own waning sexual attractiveness and control. In retaliation she jealously torments the more beautiful virginal adolescent who captures the father's affections and threatens the declining queen. Recurrent narrative features make clear this generational conflict, as the stepmothers habitually devise stratagems to retard the heroine's progress. Remanded to the hearth, cursed with one hundred years of sleep, or cast into a death-like trance by a poisoned apple, heroines suffer beneath onslaughts of maternal fear and vengeance. Ironically, both in life and fairy tale, time triumphs, delivering the daughter to inescapable womanhood and the stepmother to aged oblivion or death.

In contrast to persecuting stepmothers, natural mothers provide a counter-pattern of female protection. The christening celebration in Perrault's "Sleeping Beauty" (AT 410) is a jubilant occasion for the "King and a Queen, who were so sorry that they had no children, so sorry that it was beyond expression," and so sorry that they tried "all the waters in the world, vows, pilgrimages, every thing" before successfully conceiving this babe (85).[3] Since the King and Queen do not survive the spell, the

---

1   Tale-type numbers are taken from Antti Aarne, *The Types of the Folktale: A Classification and Bibliography*, trans. and enl. Stith Thompson, 2nd rev., *Folklore Fellows Communications*, no. 184 (Helsinki: Suomalainen Tiedeakatemia, 1961). See Marrian Roalfe Cox, *Cinderella*, Publications of the Folklore Society, vol. 31 (London: D. Nutt, 1893) and Anna Birgitta Rooth, *The Cinderella Cycle* (London: C.W.K. Gleerup, 1951). Although this tale dates back twenty-five hundred years, the earliest recorded version occurs in a Chinese book written about 850 A.D. See Arthur Waley, "The Chinese Cinderella Story," *Folk-Lore: Being the Quarterly Transactions of the Folk-Lore Society* 58 (1947) 226-38.

2   Grimm's "Snow-Drop" is the most well-known modern version, popularized in the United States by Walt Disney's film adaptation, although Basile's variation in the *Pentamerone* makes clearer the oedipal entanglements which give rise to the stepmother's jealousy. See also Stith Thompson, *The Folktale* (New York: Holt, 1946) 23-24; and Ernst Boklen, *Sneewittchenstudien*, Mythologische Bibliothek, vols. 3 and 7 (Leipzig: Hinrichs, 1910 and 1915).

3   Thompson in *The Folktale* notes that stories only slightly variant from the familiar Perrault version of "Sleeping Beauty" appear in Basile's *Pentamerone*, Grimm's *Kinder- und Hausmärchen*, and in outline in the French prose romance of *Perceforest* from the fifteenth century (97). Lüthi uses the three versions by Grimm, Basile, and Perrault for an analysis of differences in literary content and style (21-46), while Bettelheim notes significant psychoanalytic variations (225-36). Consult also Hedwig von Beit, *Symbolik des Märchens; Versuch einer Veutung*, 2 vols. (Bern: A. Francke, 1952-56); Johannes Bolte and George Polivka,

FOLK AND FAIRY TALES

"young Fairy" assumes the role of tutelary spirit and promises that the princess "shall only fall into a profound sleep which shall last a hundred years, at the expiration of which a King's son shall come and awake her" (86). Similarly, Cinderella's deceased mother is lauded only briefly as "the best creature in the world" and the source for the daughter's "unparallelled goodness and sweetness of temper" (123); in her place the fairy godmother acts as guardian. This prominence of contrasting maternal figures offers a paradigm for traumatic ambivalences.[1] As the child matures, she becomes increasingly conscious of conflicting needs for both infantile nurturing and independence and suffers as a result severe ambivalences toward the mother. By splitting the maternal role to envision, however briefly, a protective mother who blesses the heroine with beauty and virtue, romantic tales assuage fears of total separation. Conversely, the stepmother embodies the adolescent's awesome intimations of female rivalry, predatory sexuality, and constrictive authority. As Bruno Bettelheim argues, romantic tales often recreate oedipal tensions, when a mother's early death is followed by the father's rapid remarriage to a cruel stepmother, as in "Cinderella." Kept a child rather than acknowledged as a developing woman and potential recipient of the father's love, a young girl, like Cinderella or Snow-Drop, feels thwarted by her mother's persistent, overpowering intervention. The authoritarian mother becomes the obstacle which seems to stifle natural desires for men, marriage, and hence the achievement of female maturity. Neither heroines nor children rationally explore such deep-rooted feelings; rather, the tales' split depiction of mothers provides a guilt-free enactment of the young female's ambivalences and a means through fantasy for coping with paradoxical impulses of love and hate.

Such traumatic rivalries between young girls and the mother (or heroine and stepmother) comprise, however, only another stage in a progressive cultural as well as psychological pageant. Frequently a good fairy, old woman, or comforting godmother (second substitution for the original mother) releases the heroine from the stepmother's bondage and enables her to adopt appropriate adult roles.

Ammerkungen zu den Kinder- und Hausmärchen der Brüder Grimm, 5 vols. (Leipzig: Dieterich, 1913-32); Fritz Ernst, ed. Dornröschen. In drei Sprachen (Bern: H. Huber, 1949); Karl I. Obenauer, Das Märchens: Dichtung und Deutung (Frankfurt: Klostermann, 1959); and Ian de Vries, "Dornröschen," Fabula: Journal of Folktale Studies 2 (1958): 110-21, for further commentary.

1 Bettelheim, 236-77, focuses upon the sibling rivalry in "Cinderella," but also examines variants of this tale, the "basic trust" between mother and child which asserts itself later with the godmother, the displacements of anger to the stepmother, and the oedipal tensions which the tale dramatizes. Although heavy-handed in his Freudian reading, Bettelheim argues convincingly that "in order to achieve personal identity and gain self-realization on the highest level, the story tells us, both are needed: the original good parents, and later the 'step'-parents who seemed to demand 'cruelly' and 'insensitively.' The two together make up the 'Cinderella' story. If the good mother did not for a time turn into the evil stepmother, there would be no impetus to develop a separate self" (274).

Godmothers or wise women may seem merely fortuitous magical agents who promise transformations to make external circumstances responsive to the heroine's inner virtue. Emancipated from enslavement as a cinderlass, Cinderella, for example, blossoms fully into a marriageable young princess at the ball. Functioning more subtly to exemplify cultural expectations, however, the "dream" figure allows the heroine not only to recall the pattern embedded by the original mother, but also to claim that paradigm of femininity as her own. Aptly, in many versions of "Cinderella" the supernatural helper is not a random apparition, but the natural mother reincarnated into a friendly creature, such as a red calf in the Scottish "Rashin Coatie," or memorialized by a hazel tree and a white bird to grant wishes, as in Grimm's "Aschenputtel."[1] When the heroine gains sexual freedom by repudiating the stepmother, she immediately channels that liberty into social goals epitomized by the primary mother. Fairy tales, therefore, do acknowledge traumatic ambivalences during a female's rite of passage; they respond to the need for both detachment from childish symbioses and a subsequent embracing of adult independence. Yet, this evolution dooms female protagonists (and readers) to pursue adult potentials in one way only: the heroine dreamily anticipates conformity to those predestined roles of wife and mother. As Adrienne Rich so persuasively theorizes in *Of Woman Born*, the unheralded tragedy within Western patriarchies is found in this mother/daughter relationship.[2] If she imitates domestic martyrdom, the daughter may experience a hostile dependency, forever blaming the mother for trapping her within a constricting role. If a daughter rebels, then she risks social denunciations of her femininity; nagging internal doubts about her gender identity; and rejection by a mother who, covertly envying the daughter's courage, must yet overtly defend her own choices. Furthermore, romantic tales point to the complicity of women within a patriarchal culture, since as primary transmitters and models for female attitudes, mothers enforce their daughters' conformity.

By accentuating the young female's struggle with a menacing stepmother, many romantic tales only vaguely suggest the father's role in the complex oedipal and

---

1 Opie and Opie 117-21; Rooth 153-56.
2 Adrienne Rich, *Of Woman Born: Motherhood as Experience and Institution* (New York: Norton, 1973). Defining "matrophobia" as the fear of becoming one's mother, Rich articulates the tension between mothers and daughters: "Thousands of daughters see their mothers as having taught a compromise and self-hatred they are struggling to win free of, the one through whom the restrictions and degradations of a female existence were perforce transmitted.... Matrophobia can be seen as a womanly splitting of the self in the desire to become purged once and for all of our mothers' bondage, to become individuated and free. The mother stands for the victim in ourselves, the unfree woman, the martyr. Our personalities seem dangerously to blur and overlap with our mothers'; and, in a desperate attempt to know where mother ends and daughter begins, we perform radical surgery" (235-36).

[349]

cultural dramas. But in other tales, such as "Beauty and the Beast," the attraction to the father, prohibitions against incest, and the transference of devotion to the prince round out the saga of maturation. In the throes of oedipal ambiguities, a young girl who still desires dependency seizes upon her father's indulgent affection, because it guarantees respite from maternal persecutions and offers a compensating masculine adoration. Many tales implicitly acknowledge the potent attraction between females and the father; but, as purveyors of cultural norms, they often mask latent incest as filial love and displace blatant sexual desires onto a substitute, such as a beast in "The Frog-Prince" (AT 440) or "Snow-White and Rose-Red" (AT 426).[1] Madame de Beaumont's telling of "Beauty and the Beast" (AT 425), for example, focuses on the intimate bonds between father and daughter which impede the heroine's rite of passage. Pursued by suitors, the fifteen-year-old Beauty "civilly thanked them that courted her, and told them she was too young yet to marry, but chose to stay with her father for a few years longer" (139). For a heroine Beauty acts with unusual decisiveness in consigning herself to a passive waiting and in prolonging her allegiance to the father. The abrupt loss of the merchant's wealth casts the family into genteel poverty, which again elicits Beauty's determination: "Nay, several gentlemen would have married her, tho' they knew she had not a penny; but she told them she could not think of leaving her poor father in his misfortunes, but was determined to go along with him into the country to comfort and attend him" (139). She sacrifices individual happiness yet a third time by volunteering to die in her father's stead to satisfy the offended Beast: "Since the monster will accept of one of his daughters, I will deliver myself up to all his fury, and I am very happy in thinking that my death will save my father's life, and be a proof of my tender love for him" (143). Lacking a jealous stepmother to prevent this excessive attachment and to force her into a rebellious search for adult sexuality, Beauty clings childishly to her father. The tale suppresses intimations of incest; nevertheless, it symbolizes the potent, sometimes problematic oedipal dependency of young girls. Well before her encounter with Beast then, Beauty's three decisions—to stay, to serve, finally to sacrifice her life—establish her willing subservience to paternal needs. Complementary to the natural mother's role as model for appropriate female adaptions, the natural father's example of desirable

---

1 Thompson, *The Folktale* 97-102, discusses the variant tale types of the monstrous bridegroom, a theme given its classical form in the story of Cupid and Psyche, recorded in Apuleius' narrative *The Golden Ass* (2nd c. A.D.). Consult also Erich Neumann, *Amor and Psyche; The Psychic Development of the Feminine: A Commentary on the Tale by Apuleius*, trans. Ralph Manheim, Bollingen Series, no. 54 (1952; repr, Princeton, NJ: Princeton University Press, 1956); W.R.S. Ralston, "Beauty and the Beast," *The Nineteenth Century* 4 (1878): 990-1012; Jan Ojvind Swahn, *The Tale of Cupid and Psyche* (Lund: C.W.K. Gleerup, 1955); and Ernst Tegethoff, *Studien zum Märchentypus von Amor und Psyche* (Rhein: Beiträige und Hilfsbucher zur Germ), *Philologie und Volkskunde* 4 (Bonn: K. Schroeder, 1922).

masculine behavior likewise shapes her dreams of a savior and encourages the heroine's later commitment to the prince.

Beauty's apprenticeship in her father's house reveals an early conformity to domestic roles, but her subsequent palatial captivity by Beast symbolizes a further stage in her maturation. Relinquishing filial duties, she must confront male sexuality and transmute initial aversion into romantic commitment.[1] Comparable to the substitution of a stepmother, replacement of Beast for the merchant exemplifies the adolescent's ambivalent yearning for continued paternal protection, yet newly awakened anxieties about masculine desires. Initially horrified by Beast's proposal of marriage, Beauty first ignores his overt ugliness, an act which signifies her repression of sexual fears. When she then discovers his spiritual goodness, her repugnance gradually gives way to compassion, then romantic adoration, and finally marital bliss. Having schooled herself to seek virtue beneath a physically repulsive countenance, she commits herself totally: "No dear Beast, said Beauty, you must not die; live to be my husband; from this moment I give you my hand, and swear to be none but yours. Alas! I thought I had only a friendship for you, but the grief I now feel convinces me that I cannot live without you" (149). The magical transformation of Beast into a dazzling prince makes possible a consummation of this love affair which is no longer grotesque. Not just literally, but psychologically, the beast in the bedroom becomes transmuted into the prince in the palace. Just as Cinderella's prince charming arrives with a glass slipper, or Sleeping Beauty's prince awakens her with a kiss to reward these heroines for patient servitude or dreamy waiting, so too Beast's transformation rewards Beauty for embracing traditional female virtues. She has obligingly reformed sexual reluctance into self-sacrifice to redeem Beast from death. She trades her independent selfhood for subordination. She garners social and moral plaudits by acquiescing to this marriage. While realignment of her passions from father to prince avoids incest and psychologically allays her separation anxieties, still the female remains childlike—subjected to masculine supervision and denied any true independence.

Romantic tales require that the heroine's transference of dependency be not only sexual, but also material. Beneath romantic justifications of "love" lurk actual historical practices which reduce women to marketable commodities. In Perrault's "Diamonds and Toads" (AT 480) the King's son hardly restrains his pecuniary impulses:

The King's son, who was returning from hunting, met her, and seeing her so very pretty, asked her what she did there alone, and why she cry'd! "Alack-a-

---

1   See Bettelheim, 277-310, for a strict Freudian reading of the animal-groom cycle of fairy tales.

day! Sir, my mamma has turned me out of doors." The King's son, who saw five or six pearls and as many diamonds come out of her mouth, desired her to tell him whence this happen'd. She accordingly told him the whole story; upon which the King's son fell in love with her; and considering with himself that such a gift as this was worth more than any marriage portion whatsoever in another, conducted her to the palace of the King, his father, and there married her. (102)

Despite this gallant's empathy for a pathetic story, he computes the monetary profit from such an inexhaustible dowry. Heroines do not so crassly calculate the fortune to be obtained through advantageous marriages, bound as they are by virtue to value love as superior. However, the tales implicitly yoke sexual awakening and surrender to the prince with social elevation and materialistic gain. Originally of regal birth, both Sleeping Beauty and Snow-Drop only regain wealth and a queen's position by marrying a prince. Although Cinderella and little Beauty experience temporary reversals of fortune which lead to servitude or genteel poverty, these heroines also miraculously receive fortunes from their marriages. A strict moral reading would attribute these rewards solely to the heroine's virtue, but the fictional linkage of sexual awakening with the receipt of great wealth implies a more subtle causality. *Because* the heroine adopts conventional female virtues, that is patience, sacrifice, and dependency, and *because* she submits to patriarchal needs, she consequently receives both the prince and a guarantee of social and financial security through marriage. Status and fortune never result from the female's self-exertion but from passive assimilation into her husband's sphere. Allowed no opportunity for discriminating selection, the princess makes a blind commitment to the first prince who happens down the highway, penetrates the thorny barriers, and arrives *deus ex machina* to release her from the charmed captivity of adolescence. Paradoxically this "liberation" symbolizes her absolute capitulation, as she now fulfills the roles of wife and mother imprinted in her memory by the natural mother and re-enters a comfortable world of masculine protection shared earlier with her father.

Not designed to stimulate unilateral actions by aggressive, self-motivated women, romantic tales provide few alternative models for female behavior without criticizing their power. The unfortunate heroines of "The Twelve Dancing Princesses" (AT 306) initially elude marriage by drugging suitors and magically retreating at night to dance with dream princes in an underground kingdom.[1] Apparently unwilling to

---

1   Opie and Opie, 188-89, report that in its current form, "The Twelve Dancing Princesses" is "unlikely to be earlier than the seventeenth century." Recorded first by the Brothers Grimm, it appears in English translation in Edgar Taylor's *German Popular Stories* (1823-26).

forgo romantic fantasies for realistic marriages, the twelve princesses are eventually foiled by a clever soldier, who promptly claims the eldest as reward. Not alone among heroines in this aversion to marriage, nonetheless, most reluctant maidens, including little Beauty, a proud daughter in Grimm's "King Thrushbeard" (AT 900), haughty All-Fair in d'Aulnoy's "The Yellow Dwarf," and the squeamish princess who disdains the frog-prince, ultimately succumb. Romantic tales thus transmit clear warnings to rebellious females: resistance to the cultural imperative to wed constitutes so severe a threat to the social fabric that they will be compelled to submit. Likewise, tales morally censure bad fairies and vain, villainous stepmothers who exhibit manipulative power or cleverness. Allowed momentary triumph over the seemingly dead Snow-White or comatose Sleeping Beauty, eventually these diabolical stepmothers are thwarted by the prince's greater powers. Facing punishment through death, banishment, or disintegration, the most self-disciplined and courageous villainesses execute justice upon themselves, thereby leaving the sterling morality of the prince and princess untarnished. Thus, in Perrault's "Sleeping Beauty" the ogrish mother-in-law voluntarily casts "herself head foremost into the tub" which she had "filled with toads, vipers, snakes, and all kinds of serpents" and where she is now "devoured in an instant by the ugly creatures she had ordered to be thrown into it for others" (92). In condign punishment for jealousy, Snow-White's stepmother dances herself to death on iron-hot shoes, while the witch of "Hansel and Gretel" (AT 327) roasts in her own oven. Because cleverness, willpower, and manipulative skill are allied with vanity, shrewishness, and ugliness, and because of their gruesome fates, odious females hardly recommend themselves as models for young readers. And because they surround alternative roles as life-long maidens or fiendish stepmothers with opprobrium, romantic tales effectively sabotage female assertiveness. By punishing exhibitions of feminine force, tales admonish, moreover, that any disruptive non-conformity will result in annihilation or social ostracism. While readers dissociate from these portraitures of feminine power, defiance, and/or self-expression, they readily identify with the prettily passive heroine whose submission to commendable roles insures her triumphant happiness.

II

Romantic tales exert an awesome imaginative power over the female psyche—a power intensified by formal structures which we perhaps take too much for granted. The pattern of enchantment and disenchantment, the formulaic closing with nuptial rites, and the plot's comic structure seem so conventional that we do not question the implications. Yet, traditional patterns, no less than fantasy characterizations and actions, contribute to the fairy tale's potency as a purveyor of romantic archetypes and, thereby, of cultural precepts for young women. Heroines, for example, habitually spend their adolescence in servitude to an evil stepmother, father, or beast, or in an enchanted sleep, either embalmed in a glass coffin or imprisoned in a castle tower. On one level an "enchantment" serves as a convenient metaphor to characterize the pubertal period during which young women resolve perplexing ambivalences toward both parents, longingly wish and wait for the rescuing prince, and cultivate beauty as well as moral and domestic virtues. Perrault's sixteen-year-old Beauty slumbers blissfully for a hundred years, but retains her capacity to dream, even to plot gambits for her opening conversation with the prince: "He was more at a loss than she, and we need not wonder at it; she had time to think on what to say to him, for it is very probable (tho' history mentions nothing of it) that the good fairy, during so long a sleep, had given her very agreeable dreams" (88). By dramatizing adolescence as an enchanted interlude between childhood and maturity, romantic tales can, however, aggravate the female's psychic helplessness. Led to believe in fairy godmothers, miraculous awakenings, and magical transformations of beasts into lovers, that is, in external powers rather than internal self-initiative as the key which brings release, the reader may feel that maturational traumas will disappear with the wave of a wand or prince's fortuitous arrival. This symbolic use of enchantment can subtly undermine feminine self-confidence. By portraying dream-drenched inactivity and magical redemptions, enchantment makes vulnerability, avoidance, sublimation, and dependency alluringly virtuous.

On another level, tales of romance frequently employ a structure of double enchantment, the stepmother's malevolent spell and the seemingly beneficent countercharm instituted by a guardian spirit. In "Sleeping Beauty," for instance, the double enchantment occurs early: two different fairies bewitch the young princess. The narrator reports that "the old Fairy fancied she was slighted and mutter'd some threats between her teeth. One of the young Fairies, who sat by her, heard her, and judging that she might give the little Princess some unhappy gift, went as soon as they rose from table and hid herself behind the hangings, that she might speak last, and repair as much as possibly she could the evil that the old Fairy might do her" (85). Though the narrative centers on the fulfillment of the old fairy's dire curse, the promises of the young fairy linger in the background, finally to emerge for the denouement. Both the pernicious and felicitous enchantments receive fulfillment: "The princess shall indeed pierce her hand with a spindle; but instead of dying, she shall only fall into a profound sleep which shall last a hundred years, at the expiration of which a King's son shall come and awake her" (86). Likewise, in "Beauty and the Beast" the disenchanted prince attributes his monstrous disguise to the wiles of "a wicked fairy who had condemned me to remain under that shape till a beautiful virgin should consent to marry me" (150).

Appropriately enough, it is a "beautiful lady, that appeared to her in her dream" (150) who reunites Beauty with her family, transforms the envious sisters into statues, rewards Beauty's judicious choice of Beast, and transports everyone to the prince's kingdom. This supernatural lady stage-manages the finale with a "stroke with her wand" (150), counteracting the wicked fairy's earlier enchantment. Double enchantment thus reinforces cultural myths about *both* female adolescence *and* maturity. It suggests that marriage, like the adolescent sleep or servitude, is also an "enchanted" state with the prince or a fairy godmother rather than evil stepmother or bad fairy as charmer. Not really disenchanted into reality or self-reliance, the heroine simply trades one enchanted condition for another; she is subjected in adolescence to anticipatory dreams of rescue and in womanhood to expectations of continuing masculine protection. Romantic tales thus transmit to young women an alarming prophecy that marriage is an *enchantment* which will shield her against harsh realities outside the domestic realm and guarantee everlasting happiness.

Nuptial rites conventionally climax trials through which the heroine passes: separation from the original mother, a stepmother's persecutions, the father's desertion, adolescent waiting and dreaming, and a final awakening by the prince. But marriage stands for more than a single individual's triumph over psychic tribulations. Festive nuptials signify the heroine's conformity to the socially dictated roles of wife and mother and signal her assimilation into the community. Although usually absent from central portions in which the heroine endures her trials *en famille* or alone, a royal court frequently appears at the tale's beginning and end to emphasize the communal context for the individual's passage. For instance in "Sleeping Beauty" the kingdom gathers at the christening, a ritual which auspiciously celebrates the heroine's birth. Then as part of her benevolent charm, the good fairy who thinks that "when the princess should awake she might not know what to do with herself, being all alone in this old palace" (86-87) enchants the household staff. Decorously they remain aloof from the actual bed-chamber in which the princess receives the prince's revivifying kiss. Nevertheless, the palace household comes awake in time to prepare a festive ball in honor of the rebirth and subsequent wedding, when "after supper, without losing any time, the Lord Almoner married them in the chapel of the castle, and the chief lady of honour drew the curtains" (89). Comparable to the christening which acknowledges the birth, the ceremonial wedding here expresses the community's approval of sexuality within marriage. Typically in romantic tales, births, parental remarriages, and the prevalent "debutante" balls mark the preliminary stages in the heroine's progress toward maturity. But as the culminating event in most folk tales and in life, marriage more importantly displays the victory of patriarchal culture itself, since the female receives her reward for tailoring personal behavior to communal norms.

Because it is a major social institution, marriage functions not merely as a comic ending but also as a bridge between the worlds of fantasy and reality. Whereas "once upon a time" draws the reader into a timeless fantasy realm of ogresses, fairies, animistic nature, metamorphoses, and wish-fulfillment, the wedding ceremony catapults her back into contemporary reality. Precisely this close association of romantic fiction with the actuality of marriage as a social institution proves the most influential factor in shaping female expectations. Delivered from the inherent improbability of extreme fantasies, the impressionable young girl falls prey to more subtle fancies, seemingly more real because thought possible. For example, one rarely expects fairy godmothers to transform rags into ball gowns, beasts into men, and the spoken word into diamonds and pearls. Even wealth, beauty, and position may be viewed skeptically as magical accoutrements suitable for princesses, yet hardly accessible to most social classes. But marriage is an estate long sanctioned by culture and theoretically attainable by all women; thus, the female may well expect it to provide a protected existence of happy domesticity, complete with an ever hovering male to rescue her from further dangers. As irrational as this translation of fantasies into ideals for real life may seem, it is often true that romantic myth rather than actual experience governs many women's expectations of men and marriage. If she cannot be a literal princess, she can still hope to become the sheltered mistress of a domestic realm, admired by a "prince of a man" and by children for her self-sacrifices to keep the home fires burning. Certainly marriage need not be a totally unacceptable or self-abnegating goal. Nonetheless, fairy-tale portrayals of matrimony as a woman's *only* option limit female visions to the arena of hearth and cradle, thereby perpetuating a patriarchal *status quo*. Whatever the daily reality of women's wedded or professional life, fairy tales require her *imaginative* assent to the proposition that marriage is the best of all possible worlds. Hence, the comic endings call upon young females to value communal stability over individual needs, because their conformity is the cornerstone for all higher social unities—as moral plaudits and festive celebrations testify. As long as women acquiesce to cultural dicta set forth so mythically in romantic *Märchen*, then the harmonious continuity of civilization will be assured. We cannot ask fairy tales to metamorphosize into Greek tragedies. But we should recognize that the conventional patterns of double enchantment, communal rituals, and nuptial climaxes have serious implications for women's role in society.

III

It is perhaps too easy to ignore the significance of romantic tales in forming female attitudes toward the self, men, marriage, and society by relegating them to the nursery. Or one can dispute their impact by asserting that worldly education enables women to distinguish fantasy promises of bliss from conjugal actualities. Either dismissal of fairy tale implies that adult wisdom is entirely rational, thus negating the potency of cultural myths and personal fantasies in shaping one's experience. Precisely this close relationship between fantasy and reality, art and life, explains why romantic tales have in the past and continue in the present to influence so significantly female expectations of their role in patriarchal cultures. Even in the "liberated" twentieth century, many women internalize romantic patterns from ancient tales. They genuinely hope that their maturation will adhere to traditional prototypes and culminate with predicted felicity—they desperately fear that it won't. Although conscious that all men are not princes and some are unconvertible beasts and that she isn't a princess, even in disguise, still the female dreams of that "fabulous man." But as long as modern women continue to tailor their aspirations and capabilities to conform with romantic paradigms, they will live with deceptions, disillusionments, and/or ambivalences. Dedicated romanticists will reconstruct their reality into tenuous, self-deluding fantasies by suppressing any recognition of a secondary status and defending more vehemently the glories of matrimony and the patriarchy. Witness the contemporary popularity of Laura Doyle's *The Surrendered Wife* and psychologist Laura Schlessinger's *The Proper Care and Feeding of Husbands*; Ann Coulter's ascendance as a conservative polemicist and ideological successor to Phyllis Schafly who battled to defeat the 1970s Equal Rights Amendment by defending marriage, motherhood, and the American family; and, not coincidentally, the soaring corporate profits from the forty-plus percent market share generated by proliferating series of historical, gothic, and Harlequin romances. Grown skeptical by the constant discrepancy between romantic expectations and actual relationships, other women will feel disillusioned and deceived. Consider Anne Sexton's acerbic irony as she dissects fairy tales in *Transformations*, Angela Carter's mockingly gothic refiguring of sadomasochistic sexuality and retributive female vengeance in "The Bloody Chamber," or those fictional heroines who radically renounce all romance and all men, as in Marge Piercy's *Small Changes*. Between these two extremes, other women wallow in confusion, some blaming themselves for failing to actualize their potential as human beings, some assuming a personal guilt for their inability to adapt fully to widespread cultural norms. Think of Jane in Gilman's *The Yellow Wall-Paper*; Edna Pontellier in Chopin's *The Awakening*; Cleófilas in Cisneros's "Woman Hollering Creek," whose *telenovela* fantasies sour with each bloody beating. Marilyn French's *My Summer with George: A Novel of Love* and Lessing's *Love, Again* limn the cultural problematic of erotic desire and bodily aging for autonomous women in their sixties, who indulge in never-to-be consummated "imaginary" fantasies of intoxicating liaisons with younger lovers. Even these feminist authors and their heroines rarely escape unscathed the ensnaring nets of the culturally embedded romantic paradigms they labor to subvert or deconstruct.

While feminist political movements of the last century may seem to signal women's liberation from traditional roles, too often the underlying truth is far more complicated: the liberation of the female psyche has not matured with sufficient strength to sustain a radical assault on the patriarchal culture. Despite an apparent susceptibility to change, modern culture remains itself stubbornly antithetical to ideals of female and male equality. Politically and existentially, women still constitute, to adopt Simon de Beauvoir's classic terms, the Other for the male Subject. Whether expressed in pornographic, domestic, and gothic fictions or enacted in the daily relations of men and women, fairy-tale visions of romance also continue to perpetuate cultural ideals which subordinate women. As a major form of communal or "folk" lore, they preserve rather than challenge the patriarchy. Today women are caught in a dialectic between the cultural *status quo* and the evolving feminist movement, between a need to preserve values and yet to accommodate changing mores, between romantic fantasies and contemporary realities. The capacity of women to achieve equality and of culture to rejuvenate itself depends, I would suggest, upon the metamorphosis of these tensions into balances, of antagonisms into viable cooperations. But one question remains unresolved: Do we have the courageous vision and energy to cultivate a newly fertile ground of psychic and cultural experience from which will grow fairy tales for human beings in the future?

WHAT FAIRY TALES TELL US[1]

Alison Lurie

THE STORIES OF MAGIC AND transformation that we call "fairy tales" (though they usually contain no fairies) are one of the oldest known forms of literature and also one of the most popular and enduring. Even today they are a central part of our imaginative world. We remember and refer to them all our lives; their themes and characters reappear in dreams, in songs, in films, in advertisements, and in casual speech. We say that someone is a giant-killer or that theirs is a Cinderella story.

The fairy tale survives because it presents experience in vivid symbolic form. Sometimes we need to have the truth exaggerated and made more dramatic, even fantastic, in order to comprehend it. (The same sort of thing can occur in other ways, of course, as when at a costume party we suddenly recognize that one of our acquaintances is in fact essentially a six-foot-tall white rabbit, a pirate, or a dancing doll.)

"Hansel and Gretel," for instance, may dramatize the fact that some parents underfeed and neglect their children physically and/or emotionally, while others, like the witch who lives in a house made of cake and candy, overfeed and try to possess and perhaps even devour them. "Beauty and the Beast" may suggest that a good man can seem at first like a dangerous wild animal or that true love has a power to soothe the savage heart. The message may be different for each reader; that is one of the great achievements of the fairy tale, traditional or modern.

For though not everyone knows it, there are modern fairy tales. Though most people think of these stories as having come into existence almost magically long ago, they are in fact still being created and not only in less urbanized parts of the world than our own. Over the last century and a half many famous authors have written tales of wonder and enchantment. In Britain and the United States they have included Nathaniel Hawthorne, Charles Dickens, Robert Louis Stevenson, Oscar Wilde, H.G. Wells, Carl Sandburg, James Thurber, Bernard Malamud, I.B. Singer, T.H. White, Angela Carter, and Louise Erdrich. Like other authors in other countries (especially France and Germany) they have used the characters and settings and events of the fairy tale to create new and marvelous stories—not only for children, but for adults. The traditional fairy tale was not read from a book but passed on orally from one generation to the next, and its audience was not limited to children. Its heroes and heroines most often are not children but young people setting out to make their fortunes or find a mate, or most often both. Many of these stories were written for readers of all ages, or only for adults. But even when they were principally

---

1 From *Boys and Girls Forever: Children's Classics from Cinderella to Harry Potter* (New York: Penguin, 2003).

meant for children, and have child protagonists, these modern tales often contain sophisticated comments and ironic asides directed to the adults who might be reading the story aloud.

The best modern fairy stories, like traditional folk tales, can be understood in many different ways. Like all great literature, they speak to readers of every place and time. They have one message for a seven-year-old and another one, more complex and sometimes more melancholy, for a seventeen-year-old or a seventy-year-old; they may mean one thing to a nineteenth-century reader and another to a twentieth-century one.

George MacDonald's "The Light Princess" (1864), for example, is on the face of it a traditional tale of enchantment. When the princess is born, her parents, in the time-honored manner, fail to invite a wicked witch (who is also the king's sister) to the christening party. As a result, the witch curses the baby with a lack of gravity. This lack manifests itself both physically and psychologically: the princess weighs nothing, and she also is incapable of serious emotions; in contemporary parlance, she is a total airhead. Eventually a prince falls in love with the Light Princess. He is willing to sacrifice his life for her, and when the princess finally realizes it, she too falls in love, and this breaks the enchantment. The prince is restored to life, and they are married and live happily ever after.

A modern reader might come away from this story thinking it says that the best way to grow up fast is to fall in love. To a Victorian reader, however, it would more likely have seemed to be about the proper behavior of women. At the time it was generally considered, as the Light Princess's Queen remarks, a bad thing for a woman to be light-headed and light-minded. Later on the prince who loves her is pleased to discover that when the princess swims in the lake, she is "not so forward in her questions, or pert in her replies.... Neither did she laugh so much, and when she did laugh, it was more gently. She seemed altogether more modest and maidenly." Like the ideal Victorian girl, the princess becomes gentle, quiet, and above all serious.

The earliest attempts to create modern fairy tales were tentative. At first, authors merely rewrote the traditional stories of Grimm and Perrault, sometimes in what now seems a ridiculous manner. In 1853 the Grimms' first English illustrator, George Cruickshank, began to publish revisions of the most popular tales from a teetotal point of view. The Giant in his "Jack and the Beanstalk" turns out to be an alcoholic, and Cinderella's wedding is celebrated by the destruction of all the drink in the Prince's castle.

Meanwhile, other writers were beginning to go beyond revision to compose original tales, often in order to point out an improving moral. The lesson, of course, varied with the convictions of the author. Catherine Sinclair's lighthearted "Uncle David's Nonsensical Story About Giants and Fairies" (1839) suggested that idle and overfed children were apt to be eaten alive, while Juliana Horatia Ewing's "Good

Luck Is Better Than Gold" (1882) and Howard Pyle's "The Apple of Contentment" (1886) punished greed and laziness.

Some writers were concerned with more contemporary issues. John Ruskin's famous ecological fable, "The King of the Golden River" (1851), promotes both his political and his aesthetic beliefs. The two wicked older brothers in this story are shortsighted capitalists who exploit both labor and natural resources, turning a once-fertile and dramatically beautiful valley into a barren wasteland. Their moods are so dark and their hearts so hard that it seems quite appropriate that they should eventually be transformed into two black stones, while little Gluck, who appreciates the sublime natural landscape and relieves the sufferings of the poor and disabled, restores the land to beauty and fruitfulness.

In "A Toy Princess" (1877) Mary De Morgan mounts a scathing attack on the ideal Victorian miss. The courtiers among whom her heroine grows up scold her for expressing her feelings and much prefer the artificial doll-princess who never says anything but "If you please," "No thank you," "Certainly," and "Just so." With the help of a good fairy, the real princess escapes from the palace and finds happiness and love in a fisherman's family.

More unsettling, and with a darker ending, is Lucy Lane Clifford's "The New Mother" (1882), which tells of the awful fate of two innocent children who are repeatedly encouraged in naughty behavior by a strange and charming young woman who may be an evil spirit. Eventually the children try their mother's patience so far that she threatens to leave them and send home a new mother, with glass eyes and a wooden tail. Anyone who has ever seen a harassed parent appear to turn temporarily into a glassy-eyed monster—or done so themselves—will understand this story instinctively, and so will parents who have doubts about the moral qualities of their baby-sitters. The author was a good friend of Henry James, and it is possible that "The New Mother" may be one of the sources of *The Turn of the Screw*.

After Perrault and Grimm the greatest influence on the literary fairy tale was Hans Christian Andersen, whose work was first translated into English in 1846. Andersen's early tales were adaptations of those he had heard from his grandmother, with their commonsense pagan fatality overlaid with Christian morality; later he composed original stories that often celebrated the nineteenth-century virtues of stoicism, piety, and self-sacrifice.

Andersen's romantic, spiritual narratives were echoed in the work of Oscar Wilde and Laurence Housman, among many others. Often their tales seem remarkably modern. In Housman's "The Rooted Lover" (1894) the hero is what my students at Cornell would call a post-feminist man. Like the prince in George MacDonald's "The Light Princess," he does not fight giants and dragons, but shows his courage and virtue through patient endurance for the sake of love.

In Wilde's "The Selfish Giant" (1888) Christian morality and myth dominate. The traditional fairy-tale villain of the title is not slain but reformed by a child who turns out to be Christ. Other writers, following Andersen's example, abandoned the usual happy ending of the fairy tale to create stories with an ambiguous or disturbing conclusion, like Robert Louis Stevenson's "The Song of the Morrow" (1894) in which a series of events is endlessly repeated in an almost Kafka-like manner.

Not all nineteenth-century British fairy tales are this serious: many are quietly or broadly comic. There are good-natured burlesques like Charles Dickens's "The Magic Fishbone" (1868) in which a scatty Micawber-like (or Dickens-like) family is saved by the patience and good sense of the eldest daughter; and there are gentle satires of social conformity and cowardice, like Frances Browne's "The Story of Fairyfoot" (1856), which exposes the arbitrary nature of standards of beauty, imagining a kingdom where the larger your feet are, the better-looking you are thought to be. Perhaps the best known of such stories is Kenneth Grahame's "The Reluctant Dragon" (1898), possibly the first overtly pacifist fairy tale. It features a sentimental dragon who writes sonnets and only wishes to be admired by the villagers whom he has terrified; many readers will recognize a common human type.

The fashion for tales that were humorous and satirical as well as (or instead of) uplifting or improving continued into the early twentieth century. E. Nesbit's "The Book of Beasts" (1900) is a lighthearted fable about the magical power of art. The volume that contains this title has pictures of exotic creatures that come alive when the pages are opened. The boy who finds the book releases first a butterfly, then a Blue Bird of Paradise, and finally a dragon that threatens to destroy the country. If any book is vivid enough, this story seems to say, its content will invade our world for good or evil.

For H.G. Wells, magic was allied with, or a metaphor for, science. His rather spooky Magic Shop, in the story of the same name (1903), contains both traditional supernatural creatures, like a small angry red demon, and the actual inventions of the future, including a train that runs without steam.

Other twentieth-century British writers composed more romantic tales. Some, like Walter de la Mare's "The Lovely My-fawny" (1925) and Sylvia Townsend Warner's witty "Bluebeard's Daughter" (1940), have a traditional fairy-story background of castles and princesses, and rebuke old-fashioned faults—in the former case, possessive paternal love; in the latter, curiosity.

Others are set in the contemporary world. John Collier's "The Chaser" (1941), a very short story with a sting in its tale, takes place in modern London; Naomi Mitchison's "In the Family" (1957) is set in a Scotland complete with buses and parish halls—and a fairy woman who warns the hero of a future highway accident.

Often these twentieth-century tales are interesting variations on earlier classics.

Lord Dunsany's "The Kith of the Elf-Folk" (1910) is a half-poetic, half-satirical version of Andersen's "The Little Mermaid," with a happier, though rather conservative conclusion. In it a Wild Thing from the marshes ends by rejecting both her newly acquired human soul and a singing career in London. She returns to her former life and companions in the depths of the countryside—as other strange wild young women have sometimes done.

More recently the gifted British writer Angela Carter has become famous for her dramatic retellings of well-known fairy tales. Though her stories are as full of mystery and wonder, they are clearly set in modern times: Bluebeard's castle is connected to Paris by telephone, and in "The Courtship of Mr. Lyon" (1979) Beauty returns to her dying Beast from contemporary London on a train. Her characters too have been subtly updated: her Beast is Mr. Lyon, the awkward, lonely, growling owner of a Palladian villa equipped with politely rather than magically invisible servants. Beauty temporarily abandons Mr. Lyon to become a spoiled urban society girl who "smiled at herself in mirrors a little too often," but later she as well as he is transformed by the power of love. In another version of the same story, "The Tiger's Bride," the hero does not become a handsome prince; instead Beauty is transformed into a tigress by his passionate kisses. The implication is that the magical world is not a thing of the past but may coexist with ours. Perhaps, at any moment, we may enter it.

Some modern British authors of fairy tales, like these, revel in descriptions of exotic or luxurious settings. Others, by contrast, sometimes seem deliberately to choose the drabbest and most ordinary backgrounds, as if to remind us that strange and wonderful things can happen anywhere. Joan Aiken's "The Man Who Had Seen the Rope Trick" (1976) takes place in a dreary English seaside boardinghouse, and T.H. White, in "The Troll" (1935), begins with a similarly pedestrian setting, a comfortable railway hotel in northern Sweden where his hero has gone for the fishing. During his first night there he discovers that the professor in the next room is a troll who has eaten his wife. We accept this, and all that follows, not only because of White's great literary skill but because we know that some men, even some professors, are really trolls, and that some husbands do, psychologically at least, devour their wives (and wives their husbands).

In the nineteenth century it was sometimes suggested that Americans didn't need fairy tales, certainly not new ones. Instead of imaginary wonders we had the natural wonders of a new continent: we had Indians and wild animals instead of sprites and dragons; Niagara Falls and the Rockies instead of enchanted lakes and mountains.

However, Americans were already writing new fairy tales. Sometimes these stories featured old-fashioned props and characters: magic potions and spells, dwarves and witches, princes and princesses. But often they also included contemporary objects and figures: hotels and telephones, mayors and gold miners. And even from the beginning the best American stories had a different underlying message than many of those from across the Atlantic.

The standard European fairy tale, both traditional and modern, takes place in a fixed social world. In the usual plot a poor boy or girl, through some combination of luck, courage, beauty, kindness, and supernatural help, becomes rich or marries into royalty. In a variation, a prince or princess who has fallen under an evil enchantment, or been cast out by a cruel relative, regains his or her rightful position. These stories are full of wicked stepmothers and cruel kings and queens, but they seldom attack the institutions of marriage or monarchy. It is assumed that what the heroine or hero wants is to become rich and marry well. Usually the social system is implicitly unquestioned and remains unchanged; what changes is the protagonist, and what he or she hopes for is to succeed within the terms of this system. What makes American fairy tales different is that in many of them this does not happen. Instead, the world within the story alters or is abandoned. In Washington Irving's "Rip Van Winkle" (1820) Rip falls into a twenty-year sleep and wakes to find that a British colony has become a new nation, in which "the very character of the people seemed changed."

Even if the world does not change, its values are often implicitly criticized. The guests who visit "The Rich Man's Place" (1880) in Horace Scudder's story of that name enjoy the palatial house and grounds but don't express any desire to live there. In Frank Stockton's "The Bee-Man of Orn" (1887) a Junior Sorcerer discovers that an old beekeeper has been transformed from his original shape and sets out to dissolve the enchantment. But as it turns out his original shape (like everyone's) was that of a baby. The Junior Sorcerer restores him to infancy, but when he grows up he does not become a prince, but a beekeeper again—and as before he is perfectly contented.

In American fairy tales there is often not much to be said for wealth and high position, or even for good looks. In Nathaniel Hawthorne's "Feathertop" (1854) a New England witch transforms an old scarecrow into a fine gentleman and sends him out into the world, where he exposes the superficiality and snobbery of the well-to-do. In some ways the story is a democratic version of Mary De Morgan's "A Toy Princess." The scarecrow's vocabulary, like that of the Toy Princess, is very limited, consisting only of phrases like "Really! Indeed! Pray tell me! Is it possible! Upon my word! By no means! O! Ah!" and "Hem," but he is taken by the local people for a foreign nobleman and almost succeeds in winning the heart and hand of a good and beautiful girl. Though both these stories end without any real damage having been done, they are full of the unease we feel in the presence of someone with fine clothes and impenetrably bland good manners.

L. Frank Baum's "The Queen of Quok" (1901) contains a castle and royal personages, but Quok is essentially ruled by common sense and small-town American values.

At one point the boy king has to borrow a dime from his chief counselor to buy a ham sandwich. Love of money turns the would-be queen into a haggard old woman, while the insouciant young hero lives happily ever after. And in Baum's "The Glass Dog" (1901) the poor glassblower manages to marry a princess, but she "was very jealous of his beauty and led him a dog's life." The implication of such stories is that an American does not need to become rich or marry up in order to be happy; in fact, one should avoid doing so if possible. Happiness is all around one already, as the boy in Laura Richards's story "The Golden Window" (c. 1904) discovers: his farmhouse already has "windows of gold and diamond" when the setting sun shines on it.

Even further from the traditional pattern are Carl Sandburg's *Rootabaga Stories* (1922), which reflect his love of American tall tales and deadpan humor, as well as his closeness to his pioneer ancestors. The family in his "How They Broke Away to Go to the Rootabaga Country" repeats the experience of many nineteenth-century immigrants to the Midwest. They sell all their possessions and ride to "where the railroad tracks run off into the sky," ending up not in a fairy kingdom but in rich farming country named after a large turnip. "The Story of Blixie Bimber and the Power of the Gold Buckskin Whincher" takes place in what is obviously the early-twentieth-century Midwest, complete with hayrides, band concerts, and steeplejacks. But magic is still potent, and romantic passion is a kind of inexplicable spell. "The first man you meet with an X in his name you must fall head over heels in love with him, said the silent power in the gold buckskin whincher," and Blixie Bimber does, the traditional three times.

Other American fairy tales also take place in a contemporary, unromantic milieu. In Philip K. Dick's "The King of the Elves" (1953), for instance, the future leader of the elves turns out to be an old man in charge of a rundown rural gas station. Anyone, the story says, no matter how mundane his circumstances, may be a magical hero in disguise.

Sometimes American authors used the stock figures of the folktale to criticize contemporary skepticism: James Thurber's famous comic fable "The Unicorn in the Garden" (1939) presents the triumph of a mild visionary over his would-be oppressors: the police, a psychiatrist, and a hostile, suspicious wife who thinks that anyone who sees unicorns is mad.

Some modern American writers have taken the conventions of the folk tale or children's story and turned them upside down, as real life sometimes does. In Richard Kennedy's "The Porcelain Man" (1987) the heroine declines to rescue the enchanted hero, whose only attractive quality is his beauty. Another strange reversal occurs in Ursula Le Guin's "The Wife's Story" (1982), a werewolf tale related by a wolf, which can be read as a brief but terrifying fable about family love, madness, and social prejudice.

Many of the best recent American fairy tales comment on twentieth-century events. In Bernard Malamud's "The Jewbird" (1963) a talking crow flies into the Lower East Side apartment of a frozen-foods salesman and announces that he is fleeing from anti-Semites. To judge by what happens next, he may be one of those immigrant survivors of the Holocaust whom some American Jews, after the Second World War, found burdensome. Donald Bartheleme's experimental "The Glass Mountain" (1970) takes off from a traditional story of the same name in Andrew Lang's *The Yellow Fairy Book*, and manages simultaneously to expose the callous ambition of New Yorkers and the formulaic analysis of literary scholars. The mountain he climbs is a skyscraper, and he rejects the princess because she is only "an enchanted symbol." In the late twentieth century American writers also began to compose tales of magic based upon previously untapped folk traditions. Many of Isaac Bashevis Singer's stories, including "Menaseh's Dream" (1968), draw on Jewish folk beliefs and make wise, if disguised, comments on Jewish life, in this case on the power of memory and of family love. Louise Erdrich, in "Old Man Potchikoo" (1989), uses the Native American trickster tale as a starting point for celebration of Dionysian energy.

Several writers, both British and American, have produced fairy tales with a strong feminist slant. Among them are Tanith Lee's "Prince Amilec" (1972), Jay Williams's "Petronella" (1973), and Jeanne Desy's inventive "The Princess Who Stood on Her Own Two Feet" (1982), in which a well-meaning young woman gives up more and more of her natural abilities in order to make her fiancé feel good about himself—a procedure that unfortunately may still be observed in real life. In the end, of course, she rebels and refuses to marry the prince. And in Angela Carter's "Bluebeard" (1979) the heroine is rescued not by her brothers but by her mother, who has already killed a man-eating tiger.

Another interesting example of the genre is Jane Yolen's "The River Maid" (1982). The protagonists of Yolen's poetic fairy tales are often prefeminist: delicate, passive, and either victimized or self-sacrificing or both. But in "The River Maid," though the eponymous heroine remains frail and helpless, the river of which she is the guardian spirit is strong. A greedy farmer dams and diverts the water to enrich his fields, and abducts and rapes the River Maid. The following spring the river rises, washes away the farm, and drowns the farmer. Afterward it can be heard "playing merrily over [his] bones," with a "high, sweet, bubbling song ... full of freedom and a conquering joy." Women may be imprisoned and abused, the story seems to say, but time and the forces of nature will avenge them.

Today, the fairy tale is often dismissed as old-fashioned, sentimental, and silly: a minor form of literature, appropriate only for children. To readers who have been overexposed to the bowdlerized and prettified cartoon versions of the classic stories, this criticism may seem justified. But any reader who knows the authentic traditional tales, or the many brilliant modern variations on their themes, will realize that fairy tales are not merely childish entertainments set in an unreal and irrelevant universe. Though they can and do entertain children, we will do well to listen seriously to what they tell us about the real world we live in.

DID THEY LIVE HAPPILY EVER AFTER? REWRITING FAIRY TALES FOR A CONTEMPORARY AUDIENCE[1]

Laura Tosi

A long time ago, people used to tell magical stories of wonder and enchantment. Those stories were called Fairy Tales.

Those stories are not in this book. The stories in this book are almost Fairy Tales. But not quite. The stories in this book are Fairly Stupid Tales. [...] In fact, you should definitely go read the stories now, because the rest of this introduction just goes on and on and doesn't really say anything. [...] So stop now. I mean it. Quit reading. Turn the page. If you read this last sentence, it won't tell you anything (Scieszka 1992).

WE HAVE OBVIOUSLY TRAVELLED A long way from the familiar "Once upon a time" opening: a promiscuous anarchic genre which digests high and low elements, the fairy tale has undergone a process of textual and social alteration in the course of the centuries.[2]

The fairy tale, relying on various forms of cultural transmission and ever-changing ideological configuration for its very existence, has pride of place in the system of children's literature. Like many children's genres, it is characterized by a much higher degree of intertextuality than general literature. The term "intertextuality," still relatively recent, may not yet have reached a definitive formulation (see Kristeva 1970; Genette 1982; Worton 1990; Clayton and Rothstein 1991. Among Italian contributors

---

1 From *Hearts of Lightness: The Magic of Children's Literature* (Venice: Universita Ca'Foscari Di Venezia, 2001).

2 By "fairy tales" I mean canonic fairy tales of Western tradition which have always been called by that name even if they do not feature fairy or fairy-tale characters. I am aware of the looseness of the term, which overlaps with very similar genres, like the folk tale, the wonder tale, legends etc.

see Polacco 1998 and Bernardelli 2000), but in its extended sense, it is an essential term, defining the intersection of texts or cultural and ideological discourses (see Segre 1984) within the literature system: as Stephens (1992) has put it succinctly: "intertextuality is concerned with how meaning is produced at points of interaction" (16). No text exists in isolation from other texts or from social and historical contexts (see Lotman 1980). The initiating and socializing function of children's literature, concerned, among other things, with transmitting the cultural inheritance of values, experiences, and prohibitions, makes it necessary to address an audience whose decoding must rely on the reader's recognition of familiar genres and narratives—hence the value of retelling as a strategy to activate the implied child reader's often partial competency and this reader's aesthetic pleasure of recognition and appreciation. Fairy tales in particular—possibly the first examples of poetic form we confront in life—as part of contemporary (even consumer's) culture, are constantly refashioned, restructured, defamiliarized in modern times, so that they resemble, as Marina Warner says,

> [...] an archeological site that has been plundered by tomb robbers, who have turned the strata upside down and inside out and thrown it all back again in any old order. Evidence of conditions from past social and economic arrangements co-exist in the tale with the narrator's innovations: Angela Carter's Beauty is lost to the Beast at cards, a modern variation on the ancient memory, locked into the plot of Beauty and the Beast, that daughters were given in marriage by their fathers without being consulted on the matter. (Warner 1994: xix)

The scholar and common reader alike need a high threshold for tolerance as far as reinterpretation is concerned since even a hasty overview of the rise of the literary fairy tale in Europe reveals further evidence of its hybridity and intertextual nature. As we are often reminded, the fairy tale was not even a genre meant primarily for children. By incorporating oral traditions into a highly literary and aristocratic discourse, the fairy tale dictated and celebrated the standards of *civilité* in the French salons of the seventeenth century (in Italy a century earlier literary fairy tales circulated in the vernacular for an educated audience of upper-class men and women). As Zipes (1983) has written, challenging the assumption that the best fairy tales are universal and timeless:

> The shape of the fairy tale discourse, of the configuration within the tales, was molded and bound by the European civilizing process which was undergoing profound changes in the sixteenth, seventeenth and eighteenth centuries. The profundity of the literary fairy tale for children, its magic, its appeal, is marked

by these changes, for it is one of the cornerstones of our bourgeois heritage. As such, it both revolutionized the institution of literature at that time while abiding by its rules. (10, and see Zipes 1999)

Literary appropriation of oral folk tales also characterizes the Grimms' enterprise of collecting traditional folk tales of German origin (see Kamenetsky 1992), which, in translation, had a powerful influence on further developments of the genre. One of the most common misconceptions about the brothers Grimm's method regards their informants: far from being illiterate peasants, as has often been claimed, the Grimms' storytellers belonged to a cultivated middle class which might have been familiar with written, literary versions of folk tales. Any scholar who handles fairy tales (as the Grimms were perfectly aware) must necessarily abandon the idea of a faithful, "original" tale (for example, the myth of an "Ur-Little Red Riding Hood") and take the plunge in the wide sea of folklore variants in different countries or centuries, with diverse historical perspectives and ideological conformations. In our own time, the younger generation is probably best acquainted with the Disney versions of *Snow White* and *Cinderella*, only loosely based on the Perrault and Grimms' plots and characterization, with much simplification and reinforcement of stereotypes of female passivity (see Zipes 1979 and Stone 1975). The wholesale exploitation of fairy-tale and folklore material by the mass media has only recently been studied by critics and provides one of the latest additions to the abundant and heterogeneous body of criticism on the fairy tale.

As a transitional genre, intended for children and adults alike, the fairy tale has been made the object of several critical approaches. These range from the anthropological (for example, in studies of comparative mythologies and recurrent and cross-cultural folktale themes) to the psychoanalytic, of which Bettelheim's (1977) interpretation of the Grimms' tales as significant instruments in helping the process of maturation in a child is probably the best-known, to the formalistic and structuralist methods of classifying folktales in catalogues, or examining individual structural components as functions (see Propp 1928/1968 and Bremond 1977). When we analyze folk or fairy tales from the vantage point of children's literature, then, it is inevitable that we should use an integrated cross-cultural, interdisciplinary approach. In the last few decades, Jack Zipes has focussed critical attention on the social function of fairy tales, thus providing the basis for an ideological critique of dominant cultural patterns in fairy tales, previously perceived as natural, but "which appear to have been preserved because they reinforce male hegemony in the civilization process" (Zipes 1986: 9). Many contemporary rewritings of fairy tales tend to challenge the conservative norms of social behaviour and the implications of gender roles in fairy tales. Feminist critics and writers have collaborated in the critical exposure of fairy tales as narratives voicing, in the main, patriarchal values, both by providing critical readings which investigate the social construction of gender and by rewriting traditional fairy tales in order to produce non-sexist adult and children's versions.

However, the compulsion to retell or rewrite fairy tales in order to subvert historically inscribed ideological meanings should not be considered exclusively a contemporary practice. One only needs to recall the extraordinary flowering of the fairy tale in Victorian England, a flowering which succeeded the well-documented English resistance to fairy tales in the eighteenth century, born out of a combination of Puritan disapproval and a rationalist distrust of the imagination. Fairy tales, as carriers of reformist ideas and social criticism, not only provided Dickens and Wilde, for example, with a symbolic and imaginative form for their protest against the growing alienation of an increasingly industrialized society, they also questioned stereotypical gender roles and patterns (Zipes 1987 and 1999). Tales like MacDonald's *The Light Princess* (1893), a parody of "Sleeping Beauty," or Mary De Morgan's *A Toy Princess* (1877), the story of an unconventional princess who is rejected by her Court in favour of a more docile toy replica, anticipate feminist issues and concerns in their depiction of strong heroines who refuse to conform to the passive female ideal of the age. In Edith Nesbit's *The Last of the Dragons* (1925/1975), for example, the traditional pattern of "prince rescues princess" is satirically reversed. Though familiar with endless tales where princesses, tied to a pole, patiently wait for a prince to rescue them from the dragon ("such tales are always told in royal nurseries at twilight, so the Princess knew what she had to expect"), the heroine objects to this:

"All the princes I know are such very silly little boys," she told her father. "Why must I be rescued by a prince?"

> "It's always done, my dear," said the King, taking his crown off and putting it on the grass, for they were alone in the garden, and even kings must unbend sometimes. [...]
>
> "Father, darling, couldn't we tie up one of the silly little princes for the dragon to look at—and then I could go and kill the dragon and rescue the prince? I fence much better than any of the princes we know." "What an unladylike idea!" said the King, and put his crown on again, for he saw the Prime Minister coming with a basket of new-laid bills for him to sign.
>
> "Dismiss the thought, my child. I rescued your mother from a dragon, and you don't want to set yourself up above her, I should hope?"
>
> "But this is the last dragon. It is different from all other dragons." (10)

In the end the strong, fencing princess and the pale weak prince "with a head full of mathematics and philosophy" (10) come to an agreement ("he could refuse her nothing," 12) about the way to handle the dragon, who is easily tamed by the princess and becomes a valuable asset to the court as a sort of scaly aeroplane employed to fly children around the kingdom or to the seaside in summer.

The impact of these protofeminist precedents in fairy-tale tradition should not be underestimated: Jay Williams's "The Practical Princess" and "Petronella" (1978) follow a very similar pattern in their depiction of a brave and assertive princess. Williams's ideal audience includes teenagers and adults; in the second half of the twentieth century the fairy tale, once again crossing the boundary between children's and adult literature, was appropriated by postmodernist and feminist writers like Angela Carter, Anne Sexton and Margaret Atwood, as a powerful discourse for the representation of gender (see Bacchilega 1997). Fairy tales have also served as structuring devices for both canonical novels (see the *Cinderella* and the *Beauty and the Beast* subtexts in *Jane Eyre*) and for popular romance. Rewritings both for children and adults assume the reader's knowledge of the original tales, thus encouraging the reader to take note of the formal changes which have led to an ideological reorientation of the tales.

In this essay I intend to give a survey (albeit incomplete and partial, given the ever-growing number of fairy-tale adaptations in the English language) of rewriting practices and techniques, although, as mentioned earlier, it is impossible to trace an archetypal "first telling" or version of a particular fairy tale, nor can the critic expect to fix a fairy tale "hypotext." Genette (1982) in his *Palimpsestes*, defines a hypertextual relationship as "toute relation unissant un texte B (que j'appellerai *hypertexte*) à un texte antérieur A (que j'appellerai, bien sûr, *hypotexte*) sur lequel il se greffe d'une manière qui n'est pas celle du commentaire" (11-12).[1] With reference to fairy tales, Genette's concept of the hypotext as a single and identifiable entity needs to be enlarged and renamed as "hypotextual class," which would include all those versions of a single fairy tale that have combined to create the reader's cultural and diegetic construct of that traditional tale in the canon (the hypotextual class of the *Cinderella* tales, for example). Ironically, the constant restructuring and rewriting of fairy tales' hypotextual classes, in order to adapt them to the new social and moral requirements of contemporary audiences, has had the effect of preserving and encoding traditional fairy tales within the canon so that they are still widely read, alongside more challenging and subversive versions (see Tatar 1992).

In an attempt to classify different practices of fairy-tale adaptations, so as to make this abundant and heterogeneous material easier to analyse, I have chosen to discuss

---

1   *toute relation ... du commentaire*. Translation (from the French): Any relationship uniting a text B (which I will call hypertext) with an earlier text A (which I will call, naturally, hypotext), in which the later text is grafted on the earlier text in a manner that isn't that of a commentary.

three types of fairy-tale rewritings which I have called: a) "morally correct" rewritings; b) postmodernist/metafictional rewritings; c) feminist rewritings. There are several overlappings in the three groups: many adaptations could be grouped indifferently under more than one category as to their ideological orientation and often share formal changes (changes of setting, place and time, focalization—Genette's "transpositions diégétiques,"[1] 341). In the first group, however, I shall discuss primarily rewritings which aim at exposing the presence of an ambiguous morality or a moral gap in the hypotextual class, by superimposing a new ethics of justice and human compassion on traditional tales which reward, for example, acquisitive behaviour. The second group includes tales which emphasise their fictional and conventional status, which leads to a more or less good-natured critique of ideological assumptions about the culture of the child. The third group is probably the most widely studied and includes fairy-tale adaptations which, by breaking established diegetic patterns, like "Princess marries prince," subvert accepted notions of female cultural identity.

Discussions about the ethics or justice of traditional fairy tales are not a recent phenomenon: one only needs to think of the political-ideological appropriation of the Grimms' tales in the Nazi era (Kamenetsky 1992).

Even to the naïve reader it is painfully (or enjoyably) clear that the youngest brother often gets his fortune by chance rather than merit, that valiant little tailors are rewarded for deceit, and that the Giant's seven daughters do not really deserve to die at their father's hand. Many scholarly explanations of fairy or folk-tale ethics have been provided, from the analysis of the Grimms' own moral outlook to the discussion of the peculiar kind of knowledge about life fairy tales were meant to instil: the value of resourcefulness and risk-taking rather than of traditional morality, and the importance of perseverance. Contemporary retellings have challenged the value system of some traditional fairy tales, which, contrary to popular belief, do not always reward good characters and punish evil ones.

This redressing of the moral balance can be effected by means of a change in the narrating voice and the point of view. In the traditional story "Jack and the Beanstalk," the young boy Jack comes into possession of magic beans which allow him to climb a beanstalk and reach the giant's house. He is fed by the giant's wife who takes pity on the starved boy each time he visits their house. As we all remember, Jack first steals the giant's gold, then the magic hen who lays golden eggs, and ultimately the giant's golden harp.[2] By chopping away at the beanstalk on his way home so that

---

1   diegetic transpositions: Rewritten narratives.
2   In the English version of the tale, the giant is the villain of the piece. One only needs to remember his "Fee-fi-fo-fum
     I smell the blood of an Englishman

the giant falls to the ground on his head, Jack secures for his mother and himself a wealthy future, with the giant's gold, hen, and harp.

Alvin Granowsky's *Giants Have Feelings, Too* (1996) exposes the ambiguous morality of the tale, which sets greed as the rewarded virtue, by having the giant's wife retell the story:

> I am sure that the rest of you people living down below are very nice. But that boy, Jack, is something else. After I was so kind to him, he stole from us, and he hurt my husband. All because we are giants! That's no reason to take our treasures or to make my husband fall on his head. See what you think. (3)

The giant couple is reframed as good-natured and middle class, with grown-up children, with savings which are a necessity for their old age, and with an innocent love of food, Mrs. Giant being apparently an exceptional cook:

> Then Herbert came in singing "Fe! Fi! Fo! Fum! My wife's cooking is Yum! Yum! Yum! Be it baked or be it fried, we finish each meal with her tasty pies!" (13)

The reaction to Jack's treachery is a common-sense open-hearted discussion between husband and wife:

> "Oh, dear," Herbert said. "We can only hope that the boy's mother will find out what he has done. Surely, she will make him return our things. Maybe she will even return them herself."
> "You're right, Herbert," I said. "When his mother brings back our gold and our hen, I'll be here to thank her." (18)

Jack, as we all know, only comes back to collect the giant's last treasure, the golden harp:

> "Stop! You're stealing!" Herbert yelled as he ran after Jack. "Don't you know it's wrong to steal?" (22)

The moral at the end of the tale turns into a direct appeal to the reader for sympathy:

Be he alive or be he dead
I'll grind his bones to make my bread."

He had no right to take what was ours or to hurt my husband. Giants have feelings, you know. You wouldn't hurt a giant's feelings, would you? (25)

One interesting aspect of this retelling is that both stories are contained in the same book with a "flip me over" system so that the reader can access both versions of the story at the same time (the series is called "Another Point of View") and question, rather than take passively for granted, Jack's real motives for his actions.

Granowsky's adaptations seem very serious when compared with Dahl's inventive and highly irreverent retellings in *Revolting Rhymes* (1982/1984) and *Rhyme Stew* (1989). His version of the story of *Goldilocks and the Three Bears*, in *Revolting Rhymes*, addresses the issue of Goldilocks' infraction of the basic rules of polite behaviour (i.e., entering a home without an invitation, touching other people's things, breaking an item of furniture in someone else's house) which parental figures teach children in order to ease their assimilation into the adult community. The socializing and cautionary function of fairy tales is generally dependent on the transmission of a code of social behaviour and norms from an older voice of experience to a younger audience badly in need of moral and social guidance.

Goldilocks is called in the course of the story "little toad," "little louse," "a delinquent little tot," "a brazen little crook"—graphic and comic expressions which, rather than celebrating the cuteness of the little blonde girl, convey adult horror at the misbehaved unrestrained child's invasion of one's personal space. One interesting aspect of this retelling is that Dahl is clearly playing with the figure of his ideal reader—not so much the house-proud bourgeois wife who takes pride in "one small children's dining-chair, Elizabethan, very rare" smashed by Goldilocks, as the irreverent and playful reader, to whom he addresses one of his characteristic sadistic endings. In this version Big Bear advises Baby Bear to go upstairs and eat his porridge: "But as it is inside mademoiselle, you'll have to eat her up as well" (39).

Among the various kinds of correspondence that the Ahlbergs' *The Jolly Postman* (1986) delivers to fairy-tale characters, there is a repentant letter by Goldilocks, addressed to Mr. and Mrs. Bear, Three Bears Cottage, the Woods, which says:

Dear Mr and Mrs Bear and Baby Bear,

I am very sorry indeed that I cam into your house and ate Baby Bears porij. Mummy says I am a bad girl. I hardly eat any porij when she cooks it she says. Daddy says he will mend the little chair.

Love from
Goldilocks

In one of the next tableaux among the several fairy-tale characters with whom Goldilocks is celebrating her birthday (a little pig, Humpty Dumpty, the magic goose, etc.) Baby Bear has pride of place near the little girl, who has obviously been forgiven. The Ahlbergs' ingenious toy and picture book, which relies on the reader's knowledge of other children's texts, creates an appealing context for a genial twist in the morality of the tale. It is the heroine herself, in her own tentative and childish writing, who condemns her selfish behaviour and promises to mend her ways.

Not all the protagonists of fairy tales, when allowed to speak and give their side of the story, are as convincing or trustworthy. In Scieszka's *The True Story of the Three Little Pigs* (1989) Mr. Wolf's attempt to rehabilitate his good name is only partly convincing:

> I'm the wolf. Alexander T. Wolf.
> You can call me Al.
> I don't know how this whole Big Bad Wolf thing got started, but it's all wrong.
> Maybe it's because of our diet.
> Hey, it's not my fault wolves eat cute little animals like bunnies and sheep and pigs. That's just the way we are. If cheeseburgers were cute, folks would probably think you were Big and Bad, too.

A contemporary audience, due to environmental awareness, might be willing to concede that wolves eat little pigs as part of the nature food chain and not because they are intrinsically bad. Mr. Wolf's version of the story, however, lays the blame for the destruction of the pigs' houses on the wolf's bad cold and urge to sneeze while he was innocently asking to borrow a cup of sugar for his granny's birthday cake.

Another example of a fairy-tale retelling which, by giving voice to the traditional villain of the piece, attempts to justify his/her actions is Donna Jo Napoli's *The Magic Circle* (1983), marketed to a young adult audience. This prequel, in novel form, to *Hansel and Gretel*, explains the reason for the witch's cannibalistic drive. As the "Ugly One" unfolds the story of her past as a loving mother and blessed healer, the reader learns of the circumstances which led her to be claimed and possessed by devils. The description of her death, which she willingly brings about in order to disobey the demons' order to harm the children, is a tale of liberation and purification from evil.

"A site on which metanarratival and textual processes interact, either to reproduce or contest significance" (Stephens and McCallum 1998: 9), the retold fairy tale on the one hand can distance itself from conventional concepts of morality, perceived as unsuitable or outmoded guidelines for the child's social and moral development, on the other it may suggest a new ethics of compassion and respect for other people's culture and possessions, even extending it, in some cases, to canonically undeserving characters[1] whose motives and actions are defamiliarized in order to be re-encoded in a new system of beliefs.

A second group of fairy tale adaptations includes self-reflexive, often explicitly postmodernist, versions, where make-believe or illusionist conventions are exposed in order to highlight the hypercodification of fairy-tale conventions. In the case of *The Stinky Cheese Man and Other Fairly Stupid Tales*, which opened the present discussion, basic literary conventions are parodied so that the young reader is invited to reflect on what constitutes a book, and the rules that are normally followed by the author, the editor, the publisher etc. In Scieszka's book, essentially postmodernist in its critical and ironic revisiting and disruption of the cultural and literary pattern of the fairy tale, the table of contents falls and squashes all the characters of the first story of the collection ("Chicken Licken"), the dedication is upside down, the "lazy narrator" at some point disappears, leaving a blank page, the little red hen is never given the opportunity to tell her story and the various narratives are constantly interrupted by arguments between the narrator and the characters:

"Now it's time for the best story in the book—my story. Because Once Upon a Time I traded our last cow for three magic beans and ... hey, Giant. What are you doing down here? You're wrecking my whole story."

"I DON'T LIKE THAT STORY," said the Giant.

"YOU ALWAYS TRICK ME."

"That's the best part," said Jack.

"FEE FI FUM FORY I HAVE MADE MY OWN STORY."

"Great rhyme, Giant [...] But there's no room for it. So why don't you climb back up the beanstalk. I'll be up in a few minutes to steal your gold and your singing harp.

"I'LL GRIND YOUR BONES TO MAKE MY BREAD."

"[...] And there's another little thing that's been bugging me. Could you please stop talking in uppercase letters? It really messes up the page."

In such a context of textual and narrative instability a number of fairy-tale retellings are defined by parodic hyperrealism and comic dismissal of the magic and romantic element. "The Really Ugly Duckling" grows up to be just a really ugly duck

---

1   For example, in Robert Coover's retelling of Snow White for an adult audience, "The Dead Queen" (1973), the prince feels sorry for the harsh punishment which is meted out for Snow White's stepmother as he tries, in vain, to kiss her back to life.

instead of a beautiful swan; the frog lies to the princess about being a handsome prince under a spell ("'I was just kidding,' said the frog. He jumped back into the pond and the princess wiped the frog slime off her lips. The End"); the Prince, in order to make sure of marrying the girl of his dreams, places a bowling ball under the one hundred mattresses.

"Cinderrumpelstiltskin" in Scieszka's collection furnishes an example of fairy-tale conflation, or, as the Italian educationalist and children's writer Gianni Rodari would call it, a fairy-tale salad, "una insalata di favole" (Rodari 1973/1997: 72): Cinderella, expecting the customary visit of her fairy godmother to provide her with a dress, glass slippers and a coach to go to the ball, sends Rumpelstiltskin (a character from another Grimms' tale who knows how to spin gold) away ("I am not supposed to talk to strangers," she says), consequently missing the opportunity to become rich ("Please don't cry," he said, "I can help you spin straw into gold." "I don't think that will do me much good [...] If you don't have a dress, it doesn't really matter"). Scieszka's Cinderella, who obviously intends to be faithful to the traditional version, is not rewarded at the end (the ironic subtitle to the tale is "The girl who really blew it").

Fairy-tale salads, based on the comic coexistence of heterogeneous fairy-tale plots and character types, create playful conflations of traditional fairy tales which are easily recognized by the implied child reader who brings his/her knowledge of the character's familiar traits to bear on the new version. These highly intertextual and metafictional versions work within conventions, casting well-known fairy characters in different settings and story lines or, by contrast, combining two or more plots with the same protagonist. An example of the latter kind of procedure is the conflation of *Red Riding Hood* with *The Three Little Pigs*, both based on the powerful and murderous figure of the wolf. In Dahl's *Revolting Rhymes* (1982/1984) Pig number 3, who has built his house of bricks, but is made nervous by the wolf's huffing and puffing, phones Little Red Riding Hood for help. Having already shot a wolf in her own story earlier in the collection, the resourceful girl can now boast a "lovely furry wolfskin coat," but the ending has an unexpected twist, as the pig makes the mistake of trusting Miss Riding Hood. At the end of the story, not only can she boast of two wolfskin coats, "But when she goes from place to place, / She has a PIGSKIN TRAVELLING CASE" (47).

Similarly, in the already quoted Ahlbergs' *Postman* book, the wolf receives a letter from a law-firm representing the interests of both Little Red Riding Hood and the Three Little Pigs:

Dear Mr. Wolf

We are writing to you on behalf of our client, Miss Riding-Hood, concerning her grandma. Miss Hood tells us that you are presently occupying her grandma's cottage and wearing her grandma's clothes without this lady's permission. [...] On a separate matter, we must inform you that Messrs. Three Little Pigs Ltd. are now firmly resolved to sue for damages [...]

Yours sincerely,
Harold Meeney, solicitor

Even in fairy tales which do not deviate from a recognizable story line, characters often show an unusual degree of knowledge of fairy-tale conventions and of their own fictional status. Their awareness of the conventionality of stock situations and the outcome of their expected choices may lead them to question and change the task or the role they are assigned in the story. In Jane Yolen's *Sleeping Ugly* (1997) prince Jojo, who, "being the kind of young man who read fairy tales, [...] knew just what to do" (49), decides to devote special consideration to the issue of kissing and thus awakening the three ladies who lie asleep in the cottage, covered in spiderwebs. The most striking woman is the beautiful, albeit cruel, princess, protagonist of many fairy tales: "But Jojo knew that kind of princess. He had three cousins just like her. Pretty on the outside. Ugly within" (59). Prince Jojo decides to let the beautiful sleeping princess lie, so that she is later used as conversation piece or coat hanger, and kisses (and marries) instead plain Jane, blessed with a kindly disposition, with whom he will attain marital bliss if not social elevation or riches.

Fairy-tale characters who are not well informed regarding fairy-tale conventions are often at a disadvantage in contemporary retellings. In Drew Lamm's *The Prog Frince. A Mixed-Up Tale* (1999) the only chance for the heroine to break the spell, as the reader discovers only at the end of the story, is to learn "The Frog Prince" and behave accordingly towards the talking frog. A sensible girl, Jane dismisses tales of the imagination as untrue:

"Do you read fairy tales?" interrupted the frog, "like the Frog Prince?"
"No," said Jane. "They don't make sense. And they're not true."
"What do you dream about?" he asked.
"I don't," said Jane.
"What do you do?"
"I go to school," she said, glaring at the frog.
"Unfortunate," croaked the frog, and he leapt off Jane's hand.

Only when she is ready to sit and listen to the *The Frog Prince* and therefore begins to grow fond of the frog, does she recover her lost memory and identity as Jaylee, the prince's lover of base descent whom he had to forsake:

Jaylee blinked. The spell was broken. In front of Jaylee stood the prince.
He smiled.
"I thought the princess had to kiss the frog," said Jaylee.
"You're not a princess. You had to miss me."
"Magnificent," said Jaylee. "I'd rather kiss you now, when you are not so green."

In this story the need for familiarity with fairy stories if one is to fulfil one's destiny (even if in a slightly different manner than that suggested in the canonical story) is constantly reasserted.

The comic retelling of *Snow White* in the "Happily Ever Laughter" series (Thaler 1997) has "Schmoe White and the Seven Dorfs" forming a pop group in which Schmoe will play the part of lead singer by virtue of her role in the fairy story:

"We'll call ourselves 'Schmoe White and the Seven Dorfs,'" said Schmoe.
"Why do you get top billing?" asked Grouchy.
"Because if it weren't for me, you wouldn't be in this story," replied Schmoe.

Similarly, in Margaret Atwood's "Unpopular Gals" (1994), the character's self-consciousness as the narrative pivot of the folk tale emerges as the female villain is given a voice:

The thing about those good daughters is, they're so good. Obedient and passive. Sniveling, I might add. No get-up-and-go. What would become of them if it weren't for me? Nothing, that's what. All they'd ever do is the housework, which seems to feature largely in these stories. They'd marry some peasant, have seventeen kids, and get 'A Dutiful Wife' engraved on their tombstones, if any. Big deal. [...] You can wipe your feet on me, twist my motives around all if you like, you can dump millstones on my head and drown me in the river, but you can't get me out of the story. I'm the plot, babe, and don't you ever forget it. (11-12) (See also Gilbert and Gubar's analysis of "Snow White" in *The Madwoman in the Attic* 1979: 38-39.)

A strong narratorial voice (especially when it is intradiegetic) in fairy-tale adaptations (whether directed to an adult or a child reader) obviously implies that the story is a fictional construct which needs to be told (and retold) in order to exist, and relies on a number of diegetic, linguistic, as well as cultural and moral rules in order to be recognizable as such. In metafictional rewritings for children a form of detachment and the surprise following defamiliarization are encouraged, rather than emphatic alignment with the characters. Adaptations of traditional fairy tales continue to awaken the child reader's sense of wonder and humour through the introduction of new narrative incidents, and highly recognizable characters who, by reflecting on their fictional status, engage in playful alliance with the child reader— the aesthetic pleasure of recognition should not be underestimated.

It is to be noted, however, that child readers do not always tolerate retellings or modifications of their favourite stories. Within contemporary retellings experiments of juxtaposing traditional fairy plot-types with unconventional patterns may serve to dramatize the child's resistance to letting go of the stereotypes of the hypotextual class. The adaptation can turn into a hilarious battleground between orthodoxy and innovation, as in Storr's *Little Polly Riding Hood* (1955/1993). In this version the wolf is unable to assimilate the refashioning of the story of which he is a central character:

> "Good afternoon, Polly," said the wolf. "Where are you going, may I ask?"
> "Certainly," said Polly. "I am going to see my grandma."
> "I thought so!" said the wolf, looking very much pleased. "I've been reading about a girl who went to visit her grandmother and it's a very good story."
> "Little Red Riding Hood?" suggested Polly.
> "That's it!" cried the wolf. "I read it out loud to myself as a bedtime story. I did enjoy it. The wolf eats up the grandmother, and Little Red Riding Hood. It's almost the only story where the wolf really gets anything to eat," he added sadly.
> "But in my book he doesn't get Red Riding Hood," said Polly. "Her father comes in just in time to save her."
> "Oh, he doesn't in my book!" said the wolf. "I expect mine is the true story, and yours is just invented. [...] Where does your grandmother live, Polly Riding Hood?"
> "Over the other side of town," answered Polly.
> The wolf frowned.
> "It ought to be 'Through the Wood,'" he said. "But perhaps town will do. How do you get there, Polly Riding Hood?"
> "First I take a train and then I take a bus," said Polly.
> The wolf stamped his foot.
> "No, no, no, no!" he shouted. "That's all wrong. You can't say that. You've got to say, 'By the path winding through the trees,' or something like that. You can't go by trains and buses and things. It isn't fair. [...] it won't work, [...] You just can't say that!" (234-35)

The wolf's unwillingness to adapt to the new story, his blind adherence to the traditional configuration of Little Red Riding Hood, and his refusal to accept major changes in society (like modern means of transport), as well as a more active and assertive version of the tale will lead him to frustration and defeat. The wolf may thus come to embody the young reader's anxiety about unfamiliar retellings of fairy tales, which pose a threat to his/her conventional assumptions and expectations about gender roles and social behaviour.

There is no need to expatiate on the fact that, as educators and psychotherapists have demonstrated, fairy tales do influence the way children conceive the world in terms of power relations, patterns of behaviour, and gender roles.

The third group of fairy-tale adaptations for children I shall be examining shortly, addresses precisely the issue of presenting a non-sexist vision of the world in fairy tales. As Zipes (1986) has remarked: "the political purpose and design of most of the tales are clear: the narratives are symbolical representations of the author's critique of the patriarchal status quo and their desire to change the current socialization process" (xi-xii). In feminist rewritings of canonical fairy tales a tendency to retell princess stories which dispense with marriage-dominated plots and the traditional equation between beauty and goodness can be detected. In both adult and children's modern revisions of princess stories, plots and patterns as well as characterization are subverted and deconstructed in order to reshape female cultural identity into that of an independent, liberated, and self-confident heroine. A new generation of smart princesses can oppose tyrannical or stereotyped role models by assuming active roles or considering alternative options for their self-definition as females: in A. Thompert's *The Clever Princess* (1977) self-fulfilment can be achieved through active involvement in ruling one's kingdom rather than by getting married.

Rewriting *Sleeping Beauty*, the tale that features the most emblematic example of female passivity, can turn into a positive attempt to acculturate women to new rewarding social roles as well as pointing out the value of overcoming ignorance and of intelligent initiative (see Lieberman 1972/1986). Katherine Paterson's *The Wide-Awake Princess* (2000) is given a very precious gift by her judicious fairy godmother, that of being wide-awake all her waking hours in a sleeping world (that is, in a world where greedy and indifferent nobles live in luxury). Throughout the story the value of seeing for oneself (the poverty and unhappiness of the people, for example), the value of being able to assess a situation, and the value of working to spread awareness are constantly reaffirmed. Only by keeping her eyes open while mixing with the people of the kingdom can Princess Miranda form a plan to help her people and regain her rightful place as a queen—a strikingly different model for female behaviour from that of submissive Sleeping Beauty waiting for a brave prince to kiss and wake her (on *Sleeping Beauty* as a literary model for female passivity, see Kolbenschlag 1979).

Cultural autonomy, and a sense of compassion and sisterhood for other girls who embody more conventional prototypes of female passivity, are emphasized in Harriet Herman's *The Forest Princess* (1974), a rewriting of Rapunzel, where the lonely heroine is free to climb up and down the tower by a ladder. After having rescued a prince, she learns of gender differences and spends many happy hours with him. In the neutral setting of the forest they are free to exchange experiences and share the knowledge of the world. Back in the prince's court, however, rigid gender rules are assigned. What is considered praiseworthy in males (reading books, riding horses) is rejected in females, who are forbidden to read and must be suffocated in tight and uncomfortable clothes all day. When the forest princess questions the unfairness of the situation, the Prince defends the status quo:

> "There are so many people here and so many rules. Tell me, prince, why is it that only boys are taught to read in your land?"
> His smile turned into a frown.
> "That is the way it has always been."
> "But you taught me to read."
> "That was in the forest. Things are different here."
> "They don't have to be different. I could teach the girls what you taught me."
> The prince stood up abruptly.
> "Why can't you accept things the way they are?"

As things turn out, because of her outrageous requests, the Princess is forced to leave the castle:

> But if you go to the land of the golden castle today, you will find the boys and girls playing together, reading books together, and riding horses together. For you and I both know that a fairy tale isn't a fairy tale unless everyone lives happily ever after.

The female desire to conform to a pattern of desirability that posits beauty and passivity as the virtues required for marriage is presented as a dilemma in Desy's *The Princess Who Stood On Her Own Two Feet* (1982/1986). The protagonist, in order to subscribe to the prince's patriarchal view of femininity ("haven't you ever heard that women should be seen and not heard?" 42), pretends to be struck mute, as earlier she had feigned not to be able to walk due to a riding accident (the prince seems unable to get over the fact that the princess is much taller than he is). It is through a painful experience of loss that the princess arrives at a new understanding of her self-worth, which results in her meeting a wiser, if shorter, suitor for her hand. Desy's princess story, like *The Forest Princess* and *The Wide-Awake Princess* is aimed at an audience of older children and can therefore explore gender issues in relative depth, but even in some picture books for younger children there is an awareness of sexual stereotyping. In Mike Thaler's *Hanzel and Pretzel* (1997), for example, Pretzel is much more assertive and resourceful than the original Gretel (who, in the Grimms' story displays a worrying tendency to burst into tears at very inappropriate moments). In fact, it is a rejuvenated frightened Hanzel who constantly cries and is jokingly reassured by his cool-tempered sister:

"Hanzel looked out through the bars and began to cry.
"Look on the bright side," joked Pretzel.
"At least we're not lost anymore."

The happy ending is brought about, as in the Grimms' tale, by efficient Pretzel who, after having thrown the witch into a cauldron, flies her brother home on the witch's broom without losing her sense of humour and love for puns.

Babette Cole's *Princess Smartypants* (1986/1996) and *Prince Cinders* (1993) comically reverse fairy-tale plots and culturally determined sexual stereotypes, keeping the text to a minimum and letting pictures convey most of the information regarding the characters. Princess Smartypants, for example, is pictured wearing denim dungarees, and watching horse races with her pet dragons, or brushing her pet giant crocodile with dishevelled hair like a common stable girl. It is only fair that such an informal and sporty princess should not automatically fall in love with smug Prince Swashbuckle who drives a posh sportscar, wears a multi-medalled uniform and flaunts a Clark Gable-type moustache. The end reaffirms the princess's independence and rejects the picture of the narcissistic macho man as the patronizing hero of the piece.

If we agree with the assumption that gender has a cultural character, we should not underestimate the impact of fairy-tale characters or circumstances in the formation of psycho-sexual concepts of the female or male self. The device of the change of sex in *Prince Cinders* is in itself a statement about the nature of male personality when this is culturally determined as a combination of physical strength, lack of sensitive feelings, and contempt for more vulnerable males. Prince Cinders' three hairy brothers, who belong to the same category as Prince Swashbuckle, spend their time at the palace disco with their princess girlfriends while Prince Cinders is left behind to clean up their mess: Cole's highly communicative pictures show the princes' rooms scattered with empty beer cans, football and body building magazines, and cigarette ends. Cinders' wish to be "big and hairy" like his brothers exposes the dominant cultural paradigm of masculinity (based on aggressive and insensitive behaviour) as ridiculous and old-fashioned: when the inexperienced fairy godmother, a teenage school-girl in her grey uniform and tie, performs the necessary magic, he will be turned into a big hairy monkey. After the customary happy ending with the marriage to Princess Prettypenny (who believes Cinders to have scared off the big hairy monster at midnight) the hairy brothers are suitably punished by being turned into house fairies, "and they flitted around the palace doing the housework for ever and ever."

By ridiculing stereotypical and outmoded notions of masculinity and having the fairy fulfil his desires to the letter (for in fairy tales one must really be careful what to wish for), Babette Cole's retelling ironically deconstructs a traditional paradigm of male identity, in order to stress the value of individuality and self-esteem. Even though some ambiguity as to gender roles remains, as Prince Cinders is cast in the conventional role of rescuer, this is one of the few adaptations which addresses the issue of male acculturation into traditional social roles. In retellings which challenge stereotypical sexual and social roles, fairy-tale discourse becomes emancipatory and innovative, rather than a reinforcement of patriarchal culture.

Fairy stories are "elastic": they evolve revealing a process of organic reshaping around a set of core elements in response to historical and cultural influences (see Hearne 1988). Fairy-tale hypotextual classes have survived many adaptations and will outlast many more. The central issue is that, by revitalizing canonical fairy-tale values and conventions, to which they add layers of non-conventional meanings, creative retellings liberate the imaginative and subversive potential of fairy tales in contemporary child culture.

References

Ahlberg, J. and A. (1986) *The Jolly Postman or Other People's Letters*. Harmondsworth: Penguin.
Atwood, M. (1994) *Bones and Murder*. London: Virago.
Bacchilega, C. (1997) *Postmodernist Fairy Tales. Gender and Narrative Strategies*. Philadelphia: University of Pennsylvania Press.
Bernardelli, A. (2000) *Intertestualità*. Bari: La Nuova Italia.
Bettelheim, B. (1977) *The Uses of Enchantment: The Meaning and Importance of Fairy Tales*. New York: Random House.
Bremond, C. (1977) "The Morphology of the French Fairy Tale: The Ethical Model." In Janson, H. and Segal, D. (eds.) *Patterns in Oral Literature*. Paris, The Hague: Mouton, 50-76.
Clayton, J. and Rothstein, E. (eds.) (1991) *Influence and Intertextuality in Literary History*. Madison: The University of Wisconsin Press.
Cole, B. (1986/1996) *Princess Smartypants*. Harmondsworth: Penguin.
Cole, B. (1993) *Prince Cinders*. Hayes, Middlesex: Magi Publications.
Coover, R. (1973) "The Dead Queen." *Quarterly Review of Literature* XVIII, 3-4: 304-13.
Dahl, R. (1982/1984) *Revolting Rhymes*. Harmondsworth: Penguin.

Desy, J. (1982) "The Princess Who Stood On Her Own Two Feet." in Zipes, J. (ed.) (1986) *Don't Bet on the Prince: Contemporary Feminist Fairy Tales in North America and England*. New York: Routledge, 39-47.

Genette, G. (1982) *Palimpsestes. La littérature au second degré*. Paris: Éditions du Seuil.

Gilbert. S.A. and Gubar, S. (1979) *The Madwoman in the Attic: The Woman Writer and the Nineteenth-Century Imagination*. New Haven: Yale University Press.

Granowsky, A. (1996) *Giants Have Feelings, Too*. Austin: Steck-Vaughn.

Hearne, B. (1988) "Beauty and the Beast: Visions and Revisions of an Old Tale: 1950-1985." *The Lion and the Unicorn* 12.2: 74-109.

Herman, H. (1974) *The Forest Princess*. Berkeley: Rainbow Press.

Kamenetsky, C. (1992) *The Brothers Grimm and Their Critics: Folktales and the Quest for Meaning*. Athens: Ohio University Press.

Kolbenschlag, M. (1979) *Kiss Sleeping Beauty Good-bye: Breaking the Spell of Feminine Myths and Models*. San Francisco: Harper and Row.

Kristeva, J. (1970) *Le texte du roman: Approche sémiologique d'une structure discoursive transformationelle*. The Hague, Paris: Mouton.

Lieberman, M.K. (1972) "'Some Day My Prince Will Come': Female Acculturation through the Fairy Tale." In Zipes, J. (ed.) (1986) *Don't Bet on the Prince: Contemporary Feminist Fairy Tales in North America and England*. New York: Routledge, 185-200.

Lotman, J. (1980) *Testo e Contesto. Semiotica dell'arte e della cultura*. Roma-Bari: Laterza.

Napoli, D.J. (1993) *The Magic Circle*. Harmondsworth: Penguin.

Nesbit, E. (1925/1975) *The Last of the Dragons and Some Others*. Harmondsworth: Penguin.

Paterson, K. (2000) *The Wide-Awake Princess*. New York: Clarion Press.

Polacco, M. (1998) *Intertestualità*. Bari: Laterza.

Propp, V. (1928/1968) *Morphology of the Folktale*. Austin: Texas University Press.

Rodari, G. (1973/1997) *Grammatica della fantasia: Introduzione all'arte di inventare storie*. Torino: Einaudi.

Scieszka, J. (1989) *The True Story of the Three Little Pigs*. Harmondsworth: Penguin.

Scieszka, J. (1992) *The Stinky Cheese Man and Other Fairly Stupid Tales*. New York: Viking.

Segre, C. (1984) "Intertestualità e interdiscorsività nel romanzo e nella poesia." In *Teatro e romanzo*. Torino: Einaudi, 103-108.

Stephens, J. (1992) *Language and Ideology in Children's Fiction*. London and New York: Longman.

Stephens, J. and McCallum, R. (1998) *Retelling Stories, Framing Culture: Traditional Story and Metanarratives in Children's Literature*. New York and London: Garland.

Stone, K. (1975) "Things Walt Disney Never Told Us." In Farrer, C.R. (ed.) *Women and Folklore*. Austin: University of Texas Press, 42-50.

Storr, K. (1955) "Little Polly Riding Hood." In Zipes, J. (ed.) (1993) *The Trials and Tribulations of Little Red Riding Hood*. New York and London: Routledge, 234-38.

Tatar, M. (1992) *Off With Their Heads: Fairy Tales and the Culture of Childhood*. Princeton: Princeton University Press.

Thaler, M. (1997) *Schmoe White and the Seven Dorfs*. New York: Scholastic.

Thaler, M. (1997) *Hanzel and Pretzel*. New York: Scholastic.

Warner, M. (1994) *From the Beast to the Blonde: On Fairy Tales and Their Tellers*. London: Chatto and Windus.

Williams, J. (1978) *The Practical Princess and Other Liberating Fairy Tales*. London: The Bodley Head.

Worton, M. and Still, J. (1990) *Intertextuality: Theories and Practices*. Manchester: Manchester University Press.

Yolen, J. (1981/1997) *Sleeping Ugly*. New York: Putnam and Grosset.

Zipes, (1979) "The Instrumentalization of Fantasy: Fairy Tales, the Culture Industry, and Mass Media." In *Breaking the Magic Spell: Radical Theories of Folk and Fairy Tales*. Austin: University of Texas Press, 93-128.

Zipes, J. (1983) *Fairy Tales and the Art of Subversion: The Classic Genre for Children and the Process of Civilization.* New York: Routledge.

Zipes, J. (1986) *Don't Bet on the Prince: Contemporary Feminist Fairy Tales in North America and England.* New York: Routledge.

Zipes, J. (ed.) (1987) *Victorian Fairy Tales.* New York and London: Methuen.

Zipes, J. (1999) *When Dreams Come True: Classic Fairy Tales and Their Tradition.* London: Routledge.

DISNEY REVISITED, OR, JIMINY CRICKET, IT'S MUSTY DOWN HERE![1]

Betsy Hearne

I call him to account for his debasement of the traditional literature of childhood, in films and in the books he publishes:

He shows scant respect for the integrity of the original creations of authors, manipulating and vulgarizing everything for his own ends.

His treatment of folklore is without regard for its anthropological, spiritual, or psychological truths. Every story is sacrificed to the "gimmick" ... of animation....

Not content with the films, he fixes these mutilated versions in books which are cut to a fraction of their original forms, illustrates them with garish pictures, in which every prince looks like a badly drawn portrait of Cary Grant, every princess a sex symbol.

GUESS WHO FRANCES CLARKE SAYERS was talking about in 1965? This letter she published in the Los Angeles *Times* was printed as part of a longer article in *The Horn Book* (December 1965), and Walt Disney survived her attack by only one year. He died December 15, 1966. Three decades later, the single subject that will ensure debate among glazed undergraduates and exhausted graduate students of children's literature is criticism of a Walt Disney production. I have learned to muffle my salvos lest Disney devotees drop the course completely, but even so, one fan was close to tears when she exclaimed, "Can't you leave the poor man alone? He's dead!" This particular class presented me with a parting shot of three plastic figurines from the Disney Studios' *Beauty and the Beast*—plus the paperback spin-off.

---

1 From *Horn Book Magazine*, March/April 1997.

Do Sayers's assertions of 1965 need an update? She was a sharp critic, preceding by a decade and more the landmark commentary of scholarly theorists, from Kay Stone ("Things Walt Disney Never Told Us," 1975) to Jack Zipes ("Breaking the Disney Spell," 1993). Disney is continuously under attack by critics of both academia and the popular press for messing up revered literature—witness the recently skewered *Hunchback of Notre Dame*. And Disney films are more wildly popular than ever. Is this cultural schizophrenia? The pro-Disney crowds at theaters and video stores speak in cash. The anti-Disney crowds speak in print. What's happening here? And what could anyone add, besides micro-analytic details, to Sayers's articulate assessment of the structural, tonal, stylistic, and didactic alterations with which Disney and company have "revised" traditional and/or classical stories?

Perhaps we can add just a bit of perspective. Disney's films changed within the forty-three years between his first Hollywood partnership with brother Roy in 1923, the year they released a short cartoon called *Alice's Wonderland,* and his last hands-on production, *The Jungle Book,* in 1966 (released posthumously in 1967). Disney films have changed between 1966 and 1996, too, and throughout both periods, the socio-economic and aesthetic context for Disney films has been changed by almost a century of events. To the audiences of the 1920s, Disney was entertainment. To the audiences of the 1960s, Disney was an icon. To the audiences of the 1990s, Disney is myth. In the absence of a permanent electrical blackout, the Disney Olympus is centrally mapped as a pinnacle in the kingdom of childhood. With just these few words, an image may have sprung to mind of the glowing castle with myriad spires thrusting phallically toward the heavens and triangulated banners waving over all.

Well, now that we're here, let's look over the landscape. Obviously, the concept of fairy-tale revision wasn't born with Disney in Chicago, Illinois, on December 5, 1901 (the same year *Peter Rabbit* was published, speaking of landmarks). In 1697 Charles Perrault refined some lusty old tales passed on by his children's nanny. In 1812 Wilhelm and Jacob Grimm made a real hit with the stories they collected from folk and family (more family than folk, as it turns out) and then revised, sometimes radically, over the next several editions of *Kinder- und Hausmärchen*. From 1889 to 1910 Andrew Lang stamped folk and fairy tales with his own style to the tune of ringing commercial success in a twelve-volume series starting with the *Blue Fairy Book* and proceeding through Red, Green, Yellow, Violet, and all the way to Lilac (multi-color literature was only a few letters short of multi-cultural, but the time wasn't ripe yet). Perrault, the Grimms, and Lang all addressed adults as much or more than children: Perrault and Lang with a wink-wink-nod-nod, and the Grimms with an agenda of glorifying—according to their lights—a cultural heritage. Is Disney the missing twentieth-century link in a chain of clever men who borrowed stories (often from anonymous women) and broadcast them via the latest mass medium? Whatever his critics say, Disney is even more of a cultural fact now than when he was alive. Thirty years worth of successful films produced by the studio that bears his name have extended his lifetime work beyond a mortal frame.

Now, of course, Perrault, Grimm, and Lang are, if not household words, at least uncontested cultural touchstones. And yet, in earlier chapters of high culture versus popular culture, they too had their share of detractors. It may come as no surprise that the folklore we so venerate today was once viewed as common and vulgar by the educated elite of the eighteenth and nineteenth centuries (most notably the moralistic Sarah Trimmer and Mrs. Sherwood). Will the newly created field of "Disney Studies" legitimize animated versions during the last quarter of the twentieth century in the same way that "Folklore Studies" legitimized printed versions in the last quarter of the nineteenth century? Are the changes "frozen" into film from the print tradition any more deleterious than the changes "frozen" into print from the oral tradition?

Sayers's attitude was that "folklore is a universal form, a great symbolic literature which represents the folk. It is something that came from the masses, not something that is put over on the masses.... Disney is basically interested in the market." Now, the market part is certainly still true. The Disney home videos I bought to review for this article included a snowfall of glossy pamphlets advertising The Cinderella Vacation Package, Tropicana orange juice and Pillsbury products and Cheerios (there must be a connection), and, of course, lots of Disney products in print, CD-ROM, and video format: "Play with Pocahontas, Sing-Along with Pooh, Roar with Simba, and Soar with Aladdin." Favorite films are released for only a few months on the home video market and then held off the market for several years ("Sleeping Beauty is in moratorium," announced the video salesman solemnly), just to ensure ongoing consumer appetite; it's a long-term strategy that works well to create a rush on any newly released golden oldie that won't be around long. This is not to mention the myriad toy, clothing, and other products that sell because of Disney characters' copyrighted graphic motifs. Of course, in a marketplace society any product has to make money—remember that the nineteenth-century folklorist Andrew Lang was not immune to the profits from his best-selling fairy-tale series—but the sheer sophistication and international dominance of the Disney commercial machine guarantee that a Disney version of a fairy tale or classic will be THE authorized version for millions and millions of young viewers all over the world. Do we criticize Disney simply because he is so successful in shaping so many children's imaginations into one mold? In that case, shouldn't we be criticizing the capitalist/mass media system itself (the cause) rather than its cultural freight trains (the symptom)?

Probably. But in any effort to countermand the Disneyfication of storylore, dissenting parents, teachers, and librarians are often frustrated by the film company's monolithic global influence. How many children (and adults) can we reach with alternative fairy-tale variants or with classics whose originals become sausage in Disney's grinder? As he said to one of his "story men" assigned to work on *The Jungle Book*, "The first thing I want you to do is not to read it," adding later, "You can get all bogged down with these stories."

Remarks like this confirm every dissenter's objections to Disneyvision. Does this sound as curmudgeonly as Sayers's earlier remarks? Yes, but ... let's add some perspective to the rude facts, and here's where Sayers's assertions about the folk seem more questionable than her assertions about the films: "Folklore is a universal form, a great symbolic literature which represents the folk." Okay, but the folk keep changing; and although folklore is universal, the folk are not a universal unit. Further, she says of folklore: "It is something that came from the masses, not something that is put over on the masses"—as opposed to Disneylore, obviously, but that leads us to a conundrum. Disney *does* come from the masses as well as being put over on the masses, which we'll discuss further in a minute. Disney films represent the same chicken-and-egg syndrome as do the Barbie dolls his heroines so closely resemble. Our society exalts the impossible body form that Barbie represents, witness Playboy bunnies and Hollywood stars who have come closest to resembling her. Clearly, Mattel didn't originate that exalted body. But the dolls do perpetuate the exaltation through advertisement propaganda and mass distribution. Of course, there's also the little-studied question of what children do with those dolls. My kids cut off all their Barbies' hair and contorted the plastic bodies into what might benevolently be called positions of advanced yoga, but we'll try to stick to theory for a little longer and set aside the question of whether or not pernicious corporations are influencing every little girl to grow up wanting to look just like her Barbie doll (or a bald guru).

Although there's no question that private commerce manipulates public will, public will also shape private commerce, and both are shaped by social forces that influence the creation of and response to Disney's films. Dare we look at Disneylore as a grassroots movement, as electronic myth driven by social need as well as commercial greed, as formulae of exaggerated effects à la American tall tales? As even, perhaps, a form of parody, which his wry 1922 Laugh-o-Gram films of Little Red Riding Hood, Jack and the Beanstalk, Cinderella, and others so clearly were? Indeed, Disney's Hunchback of Notre Dame—based on a book that never, of course, was intended for children—takes parody to dizzying heights. Why is Jon Scieszka and Lane Smith's *The Stinky Cheese Man and Other Fairly Stupid Tales* or *The True Story of the Three Little Pigs*—along with a recent multitude of revisionist fairy tales— considered cleverly entertaining by so many children's book literati while Disney revisions, also cleverly entertaining, are deeply suspect? Why is it okay for feminists (of which I am one) to update passive heroines into active roles, or for socially sensitive library-storytellers (ditto) to omit elements of violence, racism, and other unacceptables from their story hours, and not for Disney to make changes, too? Do we really want to go graphic with heroes who trick their adversaries into eating a boiled relative, one of Brer Rabbit's escapades that somehow got left out of Disney's *Song of the South*? Can you just see animated blood dripping from the toes and shoes of Cinderella's sisters, per the Grimms' version, or two adorable little pigeons plucking out the sisters' eyes at Cinderella's wedding, one eye from each sister going into the church, and one eye from each sister coming back out? The folks at Disney want to make zippy productions and make everybody happy and make money, not hemorrhage all over the audience.

But also, you are qualified to ask, does every single story that Disney commandeers have to get so *cute* (except for the sensationally villainous scenes), no matter the tone of its ancestors? That charming little fellow we know as Jiminy Cricket, Pinocchio's conscience and commentator in Disney's film, was just an anonymous bug that got squashed in the beginning of Collodi's book. (Let me thank University of Illinois graduate student Bill Michtom for ranting and raving about this point.) Collodi's Pinocchio does bad stuff because he doesn't have a conscience; in Disney's version, he does bad stuff because of influence from villains. In other words, it's a lot easier to blame outer forces than inner forces, to see the evil in others rather than in ourselves or those with whom we identify. Is it the dark side, our own shadows, from which Disney protects the twentieth century? Are the children of today, who have never experienced a Depression or a World War, especially susceptible to a diet unbalanced toward the sprightly side with dancing teacups, singing seafood, twittering birds, and nose-twitching bunnies? Do there have to be quite so *many* animal helpers? That crowd of small mammals in *Snow White* seems on perpetual verge of stampede.

What are the real offenses Disney commits, aesthetically (distracting story gimmicks, hyperactive graphic images) and socially (violence, gender and ethnic stereotypes)? Certainly no one, not even Sayers, has objected to Disney originals such as Mickey Mouse, Donald Duck, *Lady and the Tramp*, and Roger Rabbit, for instance, or the various realistic nature/family dramas. What draws fire are the re-visions, the abandonment of past traditions for current values, which Disney reflects with unnerving accuracy. His first full-length feature, *Snow White and the Seven Dwarfs* (1937), embroidered basic fairy-tale formula with Hollywood romance, slapstick humor, and a Utopian alternative to the harsh competition engendered by the Depression (witness the cooperative work ethic of the seven miners and of the heroine's menagerie of housecleaners, an aspect that Terri Wright has explored in "Romancing the Tale: Walt Disney's Adaptation of the Grimms' 'Snow White'").

Some fifty years later, *Beauty and the Beast* has again emphasized romance and humor, but the Depression is long gone, and Disney films have long since entered the conservative mode adopted by Disney himself after World War II. Here we see cut-throat competition for Beauty's love in context of a violent society including a brutish suitor, a bloodthirsty mob, and a demonic insane-asylum director. While the household appliances are friendly, the Beast has acquired a vile temper, and even the animals have turned nasty, with a pack of wolves attacking Beauty, her father, and the Beast himself. The wolves' villainous role is particularly ironic because one of the earlier story's basic motifs was the transformational power of animal and human nature in balance.

Structurally, we've lost Beauty as hero: she who instigated the action by asking for a rose no longer asks for a rose; she who almost killed the Beast with her lack of perception but instead saved him by developing perception becomes an observer of two guys fighting over a girl. May the best man win. He does, but the woman has lost in the process. It's not enough to pay lip service to women's intelligence by propping a book up in front of a gorgeous female or showing her disdain for a macho suitor, when she's been denuded of her real power. Doesn't all this reflect an ongoing condition in our own society? Some of us don't like what we see here because we are seeing what's happening to us. Common television shows are full of it, but to watch a world-class artist like Disney glamorizing it is harder to take. On the other hand, in criticizing Disney, do we want to echo those who blame authors for producing books that reflect social problems we've created ourselves?

Without getting bogged down in a textual analysis based on scores of quotations from books and film scripts, we see over and over that Disney and company have given society not only what it will pay for, but also what it wants. The 1950 hit *Cinderella* spends as much time on Lucifer the cat chasing Gus and the other mice as it does on the main characters. Even Cinderella's return from the ball turns into a chase scene, not just the prince following her down a flight of stairs, but a wild pursuit of the king's horsemen thundering after her carriage. This device for escalating suspense is common to most of the animated features. Disney films have turned the folklore journey into a chase. What's added? Speed and competition, both key characteristics of our society. All you have to do is look at stories mythologized on television and you'll know how much our culture reverberates to chase scenes. Journeys of westward expansion turn into cowboy and Indian chase scenes; stories of crime and punishment turn into cops-and-robbers chase scenes. *Beauty and the Beast*, a television series that started with some tonal adherence to the main characters' slow-paced journeys of development, ended as a chase between Beast and the villain who stole his son (Beauty is murdered after giving birth). Disney's *Beauty and the Beast* is full of chase scenes instead of the journeys between castle and home that characterized Beauty's earlier journey of maturation.

The truth of it is that Disney's films relate less to their folkloric or literary prede-cessors than to their contemporary audience. While not all Disney's films have been equally popular, their reception does not depend on fidelity to any original. *Pinoc-chio*, *Peter Pan*, and *The Little Mermaid*, all of which veered wildly from Collodi's and Barrie's and Andersen's stories, were blockbusters. *Alice in Wonderland*, which veered wildly from Carroll's work, was a bust. The remake of *101 Dalmatians* stirred up some negative response not because it changed Dodie Smith's book, but because it changed the "original" film version! Success seems to depend on a film's fulfilling the Disney formula of visual and musical entertainment (a formula defined, circu-larly, by public response) and on fitting into the self-referential world established by the Disney canon.

This process begins with the very selection of the story itself. *The Little Mermaid* is the kind of persecuted female that Hans Christian Andersen loved to persecute even further (see also "The Red Shoes," "The Little Match Girl," etc.) and that Disney loved to rescue, sort of. Where are the swashbuckling heroines like Mollie Whuppie? Well, she's maybe a little too active, switching necklaces in the dark of night to trick her giant host into smashing the skulls of his own three daughters in-stead of Mollie and her sisters, whom he has planned to cook the next day. Tit for tat, you may say, but it would make a tough scene for the two-year-olds who swarm with their caretakers to the theater or sit propped before their electronic babysitters. A point here: the viewing crowd has gotten younger and younger over the century we're discussing, and the venues more intimate. What stranger can you trust in your children's bedroom but a film-maker whose sales figures depend on innocence and socially acceptable villainy? Murderous stepmothers seem to be okay; murderous fathers wouldn't be. Interesting, hunh? The Grimms, by the way, modulated their version of "Hansel and Gretel" through several editions to blame the children's aban-donment first on the mother and father, then on the stepmother and father, then mostly on the stepmother.

Disney's modifications originate from accurate readings of our culture. He got the address right. This is where we live. We who criticize Disney have seen the en-emy, and he is us. We are mistaken to speak as a voice removed from the rest of the population, as eighteenth- and nineteenth-century educators did in criticizing fairy tales and fiction, or to condemn artists as gulling the rest of the population. Disney belongs to us and we belong to him. What he does to fairy tales and classics is, in a sense, our own shadow. We don't have to like it and we don't have to keep quiet about it, but we do have to understand our own society and the lore it generates. The alternative is critical mustification. Popular culture and art are a vital dynamic. The past is always renegotiating with the present to become the future, and that requires the fresh air of our awareness.

"Beauty and the Beast" is a story I have loved all my life and studied for twenty years. Do I like what the Disney film has done to it? No, with qualifications. The scenes where the film-makers risk focusing on two characters' slowly maturing transformation—on the dance floor, for instance—are moving, and the animated art is rich. However, the violation of profound elements and the frenetic pace bother me in the film just as they bother me in everyday life. Does my opinion matter? Yes, but there are better ways to express it than boycotting the film or keeping it from my kids. They live here, too. They need to know what's going on, just as I do. We've watched and discussed it together; they cheer while I rant and rave. Disney is fun, they remind me. Our society craves fun, I remind them—but isn't there something else to life? Sure, Mom.

So, can we have fun and still challenge what's fun? Can we aim our criticism not at censuring/censoring an artistic reality, but at changing the self, family, and society that inspires and supports it? Sure we can, kids.

Obviously, all parents should follow their instincts about whether or not—and at what age—to expose their children to Disneyed stories. However, we may be mistaken to overestimate the changes Disney makes and underestimate the changes we can make. In one of my favorite anecdotes, from the ChildLit Listserv, Megan L. Isaac describes a four-year-old who after months of pleading was finally given Beauty and the Beast dolls that were then being promoted as merchandising tie-ins for the film. (Previously her parents had resisted purchasing a Barbie, so they were loath to give in to this similar model of female perfection.) Anyway, as the adults chatted, she sat on the floor blissfully playing with her two new dolls and creating a dialogue between them. A rough paraphrase follows:

Beast: Come on, Beauty, you have to come live in my castle.
Beauty: No, I don't want to.
Beast: You have to. I say so.
Beauty: No I don't. You're not my boss. I'm going to put you in the zoo.

Here's to the film-makers of the future!

THE END OF FAIRY TALES? HOW SHREK AND FRIENDS HAVE CHANGED CHILDREN'S STORIES[1]

James Poniewozik

ONCE UPON A TIME, IN a land near near by, there were fairy tales. Brave princes slew dragons and saved fair damsels. Princesses and scullery maids waited for brave knights and true love. The good were pretty, the evil ugly, the morals absolute. And lo, it was good. If you liked that sort of thing.

Then a hideous green monster appeared and threw the realm into chaos. Handsome princes were mocked, damsels saved themselves, and ogres and dragons were shown to be decent folks once you got to know them.

And lo, it was even better—particularly for the movie industry. The first two *Shrek* movies, which upended every fairy-tale cliché they could get their meaty chartreuse paws on, grossed more than $700 million in the U.S. alone; there's little reason to believe that *Shrek the Third* won't fill its hungry Scottish maw with hundreds of millions more after it is released May 18 [2007].

Shrek consciously rebelled against the sentimental Disney hegemony of fairy-tale movies. But today the outlaw is king: parodying fairy tales has become the default mode of telling them. 2005's *Hoodwinked!* reimagined *Little Red Riding Hood* as a crime *Rashomon*, while this year's *Happily N'Ever After* sent up *Cinderella*. Broadway smash *Wicked* posits that the Wicked Witch of the West was misunderstood. This fall Disney (*et tu,* Mickey?) releases *Enchanted,* in which a princess (Amy Adams) is magically banished by an evil queen to modern New York City, where she must fend for herself, parodying her princess foremothers as she goes. (*Snow White's Whistle While You Work* scene is re-enacted with vermin and roaches.)

All this has been a welcome change from generations of hokey fairy tales with stultifying lessons: Be nice and wait for your prince; be obedient and don't stray off the path; bad people are just plain evil and ugly and deserve no mercy. But palace revolutions can have their own excesses. Are the rules of fairy-tale snark becoming as rigid as the ones they overthrew? Are we losing a sense of wonder along with all the illusions?

Shrek didn't remake fairy tales single-handed; it captured, and monetized, a long-simmering cultural trend. TV's *Fractured Fairy Tales* parodied Grimm classics, as have movies like *The Princess Bride* and *Ever After* and the books on which *Shrek* and *Wicked* were based. And highbrow postmodern and feminist writers, such as Donald Barthelme and Angela Carter, Robert Coover and Margaret Atwood, used the raw material of fairy stories to subvert traditions of storytelling that were as ingrained in

---

1   From *Time Magazine,* 10 May 2007.

us as breathing or to critique social messages that their readers had been fed along with their strained peas.

But those parodies had a dominant fairy-tale tradition to rebel against. The strange side effect of today's meta-stories is that kids get exposed to the parodies before, or instead of, the originals. My two sons (ages 2 and 5) love *The Three Pigs*, a storybook by David Wiesner in which the pigs escape the big bad wolf by physically fleeing their story (they fold a page into a paper airplane to fly off in). It's a gorgeous, fanciful book. It's also a kind of recursive meta-fiction that I didn't encounter before reading John Barth in college. Someday the kids will read the original tale and wonder why the stupid straw-house pig doesn't just hop onto the next bookshelf. Likewise, *Shrek* reimagines Puss in Boots as a Latin tomcat—but what kid today even reads *Puss in Boots* in the original?

This is the new world of fairy tales: parodied, ironized, meta fictionalized, politically adjusted and pop culture saturated. (Yes, the original stories are still out there, but they don't have the same marketing force behind them: the Happy Meals, action figures, books, games and other ancillary revenue projects.) All of which appeals to the grownups who chaperone the movie trips and endure the repeated DVD viewings. Old school fairy tales, after all, are boring to us, not the kids. The *Shrek* movies have a nigh scientific formula for the ratio of fart jokes to ask your mother jokes; *Shrek the Third* includes a visit to a fairy tale high school where there's a Just Say Nay rally and a stoner sounding kid stumbles out of a coach trailed by a cloud of "frankincense and myrrh" smoke. More broadly, each movie gives Shrek and Fiona an adult challenge: in the first, to find love and see beyond appearances; in *Shrek 2*, to meet the in-laws; in *Shrek the Third*, to take on adult responsibility and parenthood (Shrek has to find a new heir to the throne of Far Far Away, or he will have to succeed the king).

Then there are the messages aimed at kids. What parent today wants to raise an entitled prince or a helpless damsel? Seeing Snow White turn from cream puff into kick-ass fury in *Shrek the Third*—launching an army of bluebirds and bunnies at the bad guys to the tune of Led Zeppelin's *Immigrant Song*—is more than a brilliant sight gag. It's a relief to parents of girls, with Disney's princess legacy in their rearview mirrors and Bratz dolls and Britney up ahead. It goes hand in hand with a vast genre of empowered-princess books (*Princess Smartypants*, *The Princess Knight*) for parents who'd rather their daughters dream of soccer balls than royal balls. As for the boys? Jocks have a rough time of it (a handsome prince is the villain of *Shrek the Third* and the buffoon in *N'Ever After*), supplanted by gangly emo types—fairyland Adam Brodys. "Charming" is redefined rather than repealed—Justin Timberlake voices *Third's* cute-boy hero Arthur—but at least that's some progress.

Tweaking fairy tales also allows moviemakers to tell stories about themselves without boring us. The *Shrek* movies are full of inside jokes (the kingdom of Far Far Away is essentially Beverly Hills; the first villain was widely seen as a stand-in for then Disney chief Michael Eisner). Fairy-tale parodies are safe rebellions, spoofing formulas and feel-good endings while still providing the ride into the sunset that pays the bills. In *Happily N'Ever After*, a wizard runs a "Department of Fairy-tale-land Security," seeing to it that each story—*Rapunzel, Rumpelstiltskin*, etc.—hews to the book. His bored apprentice Mambo articulates the strategy of his movie and its peers: "I just wish we could mix it up a little. Make it a little edgier! Then let 'em have their happy ending."

Sound like a formula to you? What these stories are reacting against is not so much fairy tales in general as the specific, saccharine Disney kind, which sanitized the far-darker originals. (As did *Shrek*, by the way. In the William Steig book, the ogre is way more brutal, scary and ... ogreish.) But the puncturing of the Disney style is in danger of becoming a cliché itself. The pattern—set up, then puncture, set up, then puncture—is so relentless that it inoculates the audience against being spellbound, training them to wait for the other shoe to drop whenever they see a moment of sentiment or magic. Every detail argues against seeing fairyland as something special, like the constant disposable-culture gags in *Shrek*, in which characters shop in chain stores like Versarchery and Ye Olde Foot Locker.

I feel like a traitor to my fellow parents for even saying this. These movies are made in part for me: a socially progressive, irony-friendly Gen Xer with rug rats. I thought *Hoodwinked!* and most of the *Shrek* series were hilarious, and God knows I don't want to go back to the days of suffering with my kids through a long, slow pour of Uncle Walt's wholesome syrup. But even if you ultimately reject their messages, old-school fairy tales are part of our cultural vocabulary. There's something a little sad about kids growing up in a culture where their fairy tales come pre-satirized, the skepticism, critique and revision having been done for them by the mama birds of Hollywood. Isn't irony supposed to derive from having something to rebel against? Isn't there a value in learning, for yourself, that life doesn't play out as simply as it does in fairy tales? Is there room for an original, nonparodic fairy story that's earnest without being cloying, that's enlightened without saying wonder is for suckers?

In fact, the strongest moments in *Shrek the Third* come when it steps back from the frantic pop-culture name dropping of *Shrek 2* and you realize that its Grimm parodies have become fleshed-out characters in their own right. In August, Paramount releases *Stardust*, an adaptation of a Neil Gaiman novel about a nerdy nineteenth-century lad who ventures from England to a magical land to retrieve a fallen star. The live-action movie covers many of the same themes as the ubiquitous cartoon parodies—be yourself, don't trust appearances, women can be heroic too. But it creates its own fantastic settings (a seedy witches' bazaar, a sky pirate's dirigible ship). There's a kind of surprise and unembarrassed majesty that come from minting original characters and imagery rather than simply riffing on our cartoon patrimony. In the end, that's how you make magic.

SELECTED BIBLIOGRAPHY

Anthologies/Collections

Nineteenth Century and Earlier

Afanas'ev, Aleksandr, comp. *Russian Fairy Tales*. Trans. Norbert Guterman. New York: Pantheon, 1945.

Andersen, Hans Christian. *Hans Andersen: His Classic Fairy Tales*. Trans. Erik Haugaard. New York: Doubleday, 1974.

Asbjørnsen, Peter, and Jorgen Moe, comps. *Popular Tales from the Norse*. Trans. Sir George Webbe Dasent. New York: D. Appleton, 1859.

Auerbach, Nina, and U.C. Knoepflmacher, eds. *Forbidden Journeys: Fairy Tales and Fantasies by Victorian Women Writers*. Chicago, IL: University of Chicago Press, 1992.

Basile, Giambattista. *The Pentamerone of Giambattista Basile*. 2 vols. Trans. Benedetto Croce. Ed. N.M. Penzer. London: John Lane, the Bodley Head, 1932.

Calvino, Italo, comp. *Italian Folktales*. Trans. George Martin. New York: Pantheon, 1980.

Cott, Jonathan, comp. *Beyond the Looking Glass: Extraordinary Works of Fantasy and Fairy Tale*. New York: Stonehill, 1973.

Delarue, Paul, comp. *Borzoi Book of French Folk Tales*. Trans. Austin E. Fife. New York: Knopf, 1956.

Grimm, Jacob, and Wilhelm Grimm. *Grimms' Tales for Young and Old: The Complete Stories*. Trans. Ralph Manheim. Garden City, NY: Anchor Press, 1977.

Hearn, Michael P., comp. *The Victorian Fairy Tale Book*. New York: Pantheon, 1988.

Jacobs, Joseph, comp. *English Fairy Tales*. 1890; repr. New York: Dover, 1967.

Lang, Andrew, comp. *The Blue Fairy Book*. 1889; repr. New York: Dover, 1974.

Macmillan, Cyrus, *Canadian Wonder Tales*. London: John Lane, the Bodley Head, 1918.

Mather, Powys, trans. *The Book of the Thousand Nights and One Night*. 4 vols. 2nd ed. London: Routledge and Kegan Paul, 1964.

Minard, Rosemary, comp. *Womenfolk and Fairy Tales*. Boston, MA: Houghton Mifflin, 1975.

Opie, Iona, and Peter Opie, comps. *The Classic Fairy Tales*. London: Oxford University Press, 1974.

Perrault, Charles. *The Complete Fairy Tales of Charles Perrault*. Trans. Neil Philip and Nicoletta Simborowski. New York: Clarion Books, 1993.

Straparola, Giovanni Francesco. *The Facetious Nights of Straparola*. 4 vols. Trans. W.G. Waters. London: Society of Bibliophiles, 1901.

Tatar, Maria, ed. *The Classic Fairy Tales*. New York: W.W. Norton, 1999.

Tully, Carol, ed. *Romantic Fairy Tales*. Harmondsworth: Penguin, 2000.

Zipes, Jack D., comp. *Beauties, Beasts and Enchantment: Classic French Fairy Tales*. New York: North American Library, 1989.

——, comp. *Spells of Enchantment: The Wondrous Fairy Tales of Western Culture*. New York: Viking, 1991.

——, ed. *The Complete Fairy Tales of Oscar Wilde*. New York: Signet, 1990.

——, comp. *The Great Fairy Tale Tradition: From Straparola and Basile to the Brothers Grimm*. New York: Norton, 2000.

——, comp. *The Oxford Companion to Fairy Tales: The Western Fairy Tale Tradition from Medieval to Modern*. Oxford: Oxford University Press, 2000.

——, comp. *Victorian Fairy Tales: The Revolt of the Fairies and Elves*. New York: Methuen, 1987.

Twentieth Century and Later

Block, Francesca Lia. *The Rose and the Beast: Fairy Tales Retold*. New York: Joanna Cotler Books, 2000.

Byatt, A.S. *The Djinn in the Nightingale's Eye: Five Fairy Stories*. New York: Random House, 1997.

——. *Elementals: Stories of Fire and Ice*. New York: Vintage, 2000.

Carter, Angela. *The Bloody Chamber and Other Stories*. London: Gollancz, 1979.

——. *The Virago Book of Fairy Tales*. London: Virago Press, 1990.

——. *The Second Virago Book of Fairy Tales*. London: Virago Press, 1992.

Datlow, Ellen, and Terri Windling, eds. *Snow White, Blood Red*. New York: Morrow/Avon, 1993.

——. *Black Thorn, White Rose*. New York: Morrow/Avon, 1995.

——. *Ruby Slippers, Golden Tears*. New York: Morrow/Avon, 1996.

——. *Black Swan, White Raven*. New York: Morrow/Avon, 1998.

——. *Silver Birch, Blood Moon*. Toronto: Hearst, 1999.

——. *Black Heart, Ivory Bones*. Toronto: Hearst, 2000.

——. *A Wolf at the Door and Other Retold Fairy Tales*. New York: Aladdin, 2001.

——. *Swan Sister: Fairy Tales Retold*. New York: Aladdin, 2003.

——. *The Dark of the Woods*. New York: Backpack Books, 2006.

Donoghue, Emma. *Kissing the Witch: Old Tales in New Skins*. New York: HarperCollins, 1997.

Lee, Tanith. *Red as Blood, or Tales of the Sisters Grimmer*. New York: Daw, 1983.

Lurie, Alison, comp. *The Oxford Book of Modern Fairy Tales*. Oxford: Oxford University Press, 1993.

Maitland, Sara. *The Book of Spells*. London: Michael Joseph, 1987.

Zipes, Jack D., ed. *The Outspoken Princess and the Gentle Knight*. New York: Bantam, 1994.

Poetry

Beaumont, Jeanne Marie, and Claudia Carlson, eds. *The Poets' Grimm: 20th Century Poems from Grimm Fairy Tales*. Ashland, OR: Story Line Press, 2003.

Broumas, Olga. *Beginning with O*. New Haven, CT: Yale University Press, 1976.

Dahl, Roald. *Revolting Rhymes*. London: Jonathan Cape, 1982.

Hay, Sara Henderson. *Story Hour*. Garden City, NY: Doubleday, 1963.

Mieder, Wolfgang, ed. *Disenchantments: An Anthology of Modern Fairy Tale Poetry*. Hanover, NH: University Press of New England, for University of Vermont, 1985.

Sexton, Anne. *Transformations*. Boston, MA: Houghton Mifflin, 1971.
Strauss, Gwen. *Trail of Stones*. London: Julia McRae Books, 1990.

Critical/General

Ashliman, D.L. *Folk and Fairy Tales: A Handbook*. Westport, CT: Greenwood Press, 2004.
Bacchilega, Cristina. *Postmodern Fairy Tales: Gender and Narrative Strategies*. Philadelphia, PA: University of Pennsylvania Press, 1997.
Baker, Donald. *Functions of Folk and Fairy Tales*. Washington, DC: Association for Childhood Education International, 1981.
Beckett, Sandra. *Recycling Red Riding Hood*. New York: Routledge, 2002.
Bottigheimer, Ruth B., ed. *Fairy Tales and Society: Illusion, Allusion, and Paradigm*. Philadelphia, PA: University of Pennsylvania Press, 1986.
Canepa, Nancy, ed. *Out of the Woods: The Origins of the Literary Fairy Tale in Italy and France*. Detroit, MI: Wayne State University Press, 1997.
Davidson, Hilda E., and Anna Chaudri, eds. *A Companion to the Fairy Tale*. Cambridge: D.S. Brewer, 2003.
De Vos, Gail, and Anna E. Altmann. *New Tales for Old: Folktales as Literary Fictions for Young Adults*. Englewood, CO: Teacher Ideas Press, 1999.
Dundes, Alan, ed. *Cinderella: A Casebook*. Madison, WI: University of Wisconsin Press, 1988.
——. *Little Red Riding Hood: A Casebook*. Madison, WI: University of Wisconsin Press, 1989.
Houghton, Rosemary. *Tales from Eternity: The World of Fairy Tales and the Spiritual Search*. New York: Seabury Press, 1973.
Jones, Steven Swann. *The Fairy Tale: The Magic Mirror of Imagination*. New York: Twayne, 1995.
Knoepflmacher, U.C. *Ventures into Childland: Victorians, Fairy Tales, and Femininity*. Chicago, IL: University of Chicago Press, 1999.
Lane, Marcia. *Picturing the Rose: A Way of Looking at Fairy Tales*. New York: H.W. Wilson, 1994.
Lurie, Alison. *Boys and Girls Forever: Children's Classics from Cinderella to Harry Potter*. New York: Penguin, 2003.
——. *Don't Tell the Grown-ups: Subversive Children's Literature*. Boston, MA: Little, Brown, 1990.
Lüthi, Max. *Once Upon a Time: On the Nature of Fairy Tales*. Trans. Lee Chadeayne and Paul Gottwald. New York: Frederick Ungar, 1970.
——. *The European Folktale: Form and Nature*. Trans. John D. Niles. Bloomington, IN: Indiana University Press, 1982.
——. *The Fairy Tale as Art Form and Portrait of Man*. Trans. Jon Erickson. Bloomington, IN: Indiana University Press, 1984.
McGlathery, James M. *Fairy Tale Romance: The Grimms, Basile, and Perrault*. Urbana, IL: University of Illinois Press, 1991.
Orenstein, Catherine, *Little Red Riding Hood Uncloaked: Sex, Morality, and the Evolution of a Fairy Tale*. New York: Basic Books, 2002.
Rohrich, Lutz. *Folktales and Reality*. Trans. Peter Tokofsky. Bloomington, IN: Indiana University Press, 1991.
Sale, Roger. *Fairy Tales and After: From Snow White to E.B. White*. Cambridge, MA: Harvard University Press, 1978.
Schectman, Jacqueline M. *The Stepmother in Fairy Tales*. Boston, MA: Sigo Press, 1991.
Tatar, Maria M. *Off with Their Heads!: Fairy Tales and the Culture of Childhood*. Princeton, NJ: Princeton University Press, 1992.
Thomas, Joyce. *Inside the Wolf's Belly: Aspects of the Fairy Tale*. Sheffield, UK: Sheffield Academic Press, 1989.
Tolkien, J. R. R. *Tree and Leaf*. Boston, London: Allen and Unwin, 1964.

Travers, P.L. *About the Sleeping Beauty*. New York: McGraw-Hill, 1975.

Warner, Marina. *From the Beast to the Blonde*. London: Chatto and Windus, 1994.

Yolen, Jane, *Touch Magic: Fantasy, Faerie, and Folklore in the Literature of Childhood*. New York: Philomel, 1981.

Zipes, Jack D. *Breaking the Magic Spell: Radical Theories of Folk and Fairy Tales*. 2nd ed. Lexington, KY: University Press of Kentucky, 2002.

——. *Fairy Tale as Myth: Myth as Fairy Tale*. Lexington, KY: University Press of Kentucky, 1994.

——. *Fairy Tales and the Art of Subversion: The Classic Genre for Children and the Process of Civilization*. 2nd ed. New York: Routledge, 2006.

——. *Happily Ever After: Fairy Tales, Children, and the Culture Industry*. New York: Routledge, 1997.

——, ed. *The Trials and Tribulations of Little Red Riding Hood*. 2nd ed. New York: Routledge, 1993.

——. *When Dreams Came True: Classical Fairy Tales and Their Tradition*. 2nd ed. New York: Routledge, 2007.

Brothers Grimm

Bottigheimer, Ruth B. *Grimms' Bad Girls and Bold Boys: The Moral and Social Vision of the Tales*. New Haven, CT: Yale University Press, 1987.

Ellis, John M. *One Fairy Story Too Many: The Brothers Grimm and Their Tales*. Chicago, IL: University of Chicago Press, 1983.

Haase, Donald, ed. *The Reception of Grimms' Fairy Tales: Responses, Reactions, Revisions*. Detroit, MI: Wayne State University Press, 1993.

Kamenetsky, Christa. *The Brothers Grimm and Their Critics: Folk Tales and the Quest for Meaning*. Athens, OH: Ohio University Press, 1992.

Kudszus, Winfried, *Terrors of Childhood in Grimms' Fairy Tales*. New York: Peter Lang, 2005.

McGlathery, James M., ed. *The Brothers Grimm and Folk Tale*. Urbana, IL: University of Illinois Press, 1988.

——. *Grimms' Fairy Tales: A History of Criticism on a Popular Classic*. Columbia, SC: Camden House, 1993.

Michaelis-Jena, Ruth. *The Brothers Grimm*. New York: Praeger, 1970.

Murphy, G. Ronald. *The Owl, the Raven, and the Dove: The Religious Meaning of the Grimms' Magic Fairy Tales*. Oxford: Oxford University Press, 2000.

Peppard, Murray. *Paths Through the Forest: A Biography of the Brothers Grimm*. New York: Holt, Rinehart, and Winston, 1971.

Tatar, Maria. *The Hard Facts of the Grimms' Fairy Tales*. Rev. ed. Princeton, NJ: Princeton University Press, 2003.

Zipes, Jack D. *The Brothers Grimm: From Enchanted Forests to the Modern World*. 2nd ed. New York: Palgrave Macmillan, 2003.

Perrault and the French

Barchilon, Jacques, and Peter Flinders. *Charles Perrault*. Boston, MA: Twayne Publishers, 1981.

Darnton, Robert. *The Great Cat Massacre and Other Episodes in French Cultural History*. New York: Basic Books, 1984.

Hearne, Betsy G. *Beauty and the Beast: Visions and Revisions of an Old Tale*. Chicago, IL: University of Chicago Press, 1989.

Lewis, Philip. *Seeing Through the Mother Goose Tales: Visual Turns in the Writings of Perrault*. Stanford, CA: Stanford University Press, 1996.

Morgan, Jeanne. *Perrault's Morals for Moderns*. New York: Peter Lang, 1985.
Seifert, Lewis. *Fairy Tales, Sexuality, and Gender in France, 1690-1715: Nostalgic Utopias*. New York: Cambridge University Press, 1996.
Tatar, Maria. *Secrets beyond the Door: The Story of Bluebeard and His Wives*. Princeton, NJ: Princeton University Press, 2006.

Andersen

Bredsdorff, Elias. *Hans Christian Andersen*. New York: Charles Scribner's Sons, 1975.
Gronbech, Bo. *Hans Christian Andersen*. Boston, MA: Twayne Publishers, 1980.
Lederer, Wolfgang. *The Kiss of the Snow Queen: Hans Christian Andersen and Man's Redemption by Woman*. Berkeley, CA: University of California Press, 1986.
Spink, Reginald. *Hans Christian Andersen and His World*. New York: G.P. Putnam's Sons, 1972.
Zipes, Jack D. *Hans Christian Andersen: The Misunderstood Storyteller*. New York: Routledge, 2005.

Psychological

Bettelheim, Bruno. *The Uses of Enchantment: The Meaning and Importance of Fairy Tales*. New York: Alfred Knopf, 1976.
Bly, Robert. *Iron John: A Book About Men*. New York: Vintage, 1992.
Cashdan, Sheldon. *The Witch Must Die: How Fairy Tales Shape Our Lives*. New York: HarperCollins, 2000.
Chinen, Allan B. *In the Ever After: Fairy Tales and the Second Half of Life*. Wilmette, IL: Chiron, 1989.
——. *Once Upon a Midlife: Classical Stories and Mythic Tales to Illuminate the Middle Years*. Los Angeles, CA: Jeremy Tarcher, 1992.
Dieckmann, Hans. *Twice-Told Tales: The Psychological Use of Fairy Tales*. Wilmette, IL: Chiron, 1986.
Franz, Marie Louise von. *An Introduction to the Psychology of Fairy Tales*. 3rd ed. Zurich: Spring Publications, 1975.
——. *Individuation in Fairy Tales*. Zurich: Spring Publications, 1977.
——. *Problems of the Feminine in Fairy Tales*. Irving, TX: Spring Publications, 1979.
Fromm, Erich. *The Forgotten Language: An Introduction to the Understanding of Dreams, Fairy Tales, and Myths*. New York: Grove Press, 1951.
Heuscher, Julius. *A Psychiatric Study of Myths and Fairy Tales: Their Origin, Meaning, and Usefulness*. Springfield, IL: Thomas, 1974.
Livo, Norma. *Who's Afraid...? Facing Children's Fears with Folktales*. Englewood, CO: Teacher Ideas Press, 1994.
Mallet, Carl-Heinz. *Fairy Tales and Children: The Psychology of Children Revealed through Four of Grimms' Fairy Tales*. New York: Schocken Books, 1984.
Metzger, Michael, and Katherina Mommsen, eds. *Fairy Tales as Ways of Knowing: Essays on Märchen in Psychology, Society, and Literature*. Bern: Peter Lang, 1981.

Anthropological/Folkloric/Linguistic

Aarne, Antti, and Stith Thompson. *The Types of the Folktale: A Classification and Bibliography.* Helsinki: FF Communications #184, 1961.

Degh, Linda. *Folktales and Society: Storytelling in a Hungarian Peasant Community.* Trans. Emily M. Schossberger. Bloomington, IN: Indiana University Press, 1969.

——. *Folklore and the Mass Media.* Bloomington, IN: Indiana University Press, 1994.

Dorson, Richard. *Folklore.* Bloomington, IN: Indiana University Press, 1972.

Dundes, Allan. ed. *Analytic Essays in Folklore.* The Hague: Mouton, 1975.

——. *The Study of Folklore.* Englewood Cliffs, NJ: Prentice-Hall, 1965.

Hartland, E.S. *The Science of Fairy Tales: An Enquiry into Fairy Mythology.* Detroit, MI: Singing Tree Press, 1968.

Propp, Vladimir. *The Morphology of the Folktale.* Austin, TX: University of Texas Press, 1968.

Thompson, Stith. *The Folktale.* New York: Holt, Reinhart, and Winston, 1946.

Yearsley, Percival M. *The Folklore of Fairy Tale.* Detroit, MI: Singing Tree Press, 1968.

Feminist

Estes, Clarissa Pinkola. *Women Who Run with the Wolves: Myths and Stories of the Wild Woman Archetype.* New York: Ballantyne, 1992.

Farrer, Claire, ed. *Women and Folklore.* Austin, TX: University of Texas Press, 1975.

Gould, Joan. *Spinning Straw into Gold: What Fairy Tales Reveal about the Transformations in a Woman's Life.* New York: Random House, 2006.

Haase, Donald, ed. *Fairy Tales and Feminism: New Approaches.* Detroit, MI: Wayne State University Press, 2004.

Harries, Elizabeth Wanning. *Twice Upon a Time: Women Writers and the History of the Fairy Tale.* Princeton, NJ: Princeton University Press, 2001.

Kolbenschlag, Madonna. *Kiss Sleeping Beauty Goodbye.* Garden City, NY: Doubleday, 1979.

Rusch-Feja, Diann. *The Portrayal of the Maturation Process in Girl Figures in Selected Tales of the Brothers Grimm.* Frankfurt-am-Mein: Peter Lang, 1995.

Walker, Barbara. *Feminist Fairy Tales.* New York: HarperCollins, 1997.

Zipes, Jack D., comp. *Don't Bet on the Prince: Contemporary Feminist Fairy Tales in North America and England.* New York: Methuen, 1986.

Illustration and Film

Bell, Elizabeth, Lynda Haas, and Laura Sells, eds. *From Mouse to Mermaid: The Politics of Film, Gender, and Culture.* Bloomington, IN: Indiana University Press, 1995.

Engen, Rodney K. *Walter Crane as a Book Illustrator.* London: Academy Editions, 1975.

Holliss, Richard, and Brian Sibley. *Walt Disney's "Snow White and the Seven Dwarfs" and the Making of the Classic Film.* New York: Simon and Schuster, 1987.

Meyer, Susan E. *A Treasury of the Great Children's Book Illustrators.* New York: Harry Abrams, 1987.

Nodelman, Perry. *Words About Pictures: The Narrative Art of Children's Picture Books.* Athens, GA: University of Georgia Press, 1988.

Schickel, Richard. *The Disney Version: The Life, Times, Art, and Commerce of Walt Disney*. New York: Simon Schuster, 1985.

Journals

Below are listed the major journals in which numerous articles on folk and fairy tales may be found.

Canadian Children's Literature (CanCL)
Children's Literature (CL)
Children's Literature Association Quarterly (ChLAQ)
Children's Literature in Education (CLE)
Fairy Tale Review
Horn Book
The Lion and the Unicorn (LU)
Marvels & Tales
Signal

Websites

These three websites provide a wealth of tales and reference materials.

www.pitt.edu/~dash/folklinks.html
www.pitt.edu/~dash/folktexts.html
www.surlalunefairytales.com

SOURCES

Afanas'ev, Aleksandr
"Vasilisa the Beautiful," from *The Collections of Aleksandr Afanas'ev Russian Fairy Tales*. Translated by Norbery Guterman. 2nd edition. New York: Pantheon Books, 1945. Copyright © 1945 by Afanas'ev, Aleksandr. Reprinted by permission of Pantheon Books, a division of Random House, Inc.

Andersen, Hans Christian
"The Ugly Duckling," "The Emperor's New Clothes" and "The Tinderbox," from *Hans Christian Andersen: His Classic Fairy Tales*. Edited by Erik Hauggaard. Copyright © 1974 by Erik Christian Haugaard. Used by permission of Doubleday, a division of Random House, Inc.

Basile, Giambattista
"Sun, Moon and Talia," from *The Tale of Tales, or Entertainment for the Little Ones*. Translated by Nancy L. Canepa. Illustrated by Carmelo Lettere. Detroit, Wayne State University Press, 2007. pp. 413-417. Reprinted by permission of Wayne State University Press.

Bettelheim, Bruno
"The Struggle for Meaning" from *The Uses of Enchantment*. Copyright © 1975, 1976 by Bruno Bettelheim. Used by permission of Alfred A. Knopf, a division of Random House, Inc.

Block, Francesca Lia
"Wolf," from *The Rose and the Beast: Fairy Tales Retold*. New York: HarperCollins, 2000. Copyright © 2000 by Frencesca Lia Block. Reprinted by permission of HarperCollins Publishers.

Calvino, Italo
"The Neapolitan Soldier," from *Italian Folktales: Selected and Retold*. Orlando: Harcourt, 1980. Copyright © 1956 by Giulio Einaudi editore, s.p.a. English translation by George Martin. Copyright © 1980 by Harcourt, Inc. Reprinted by permission of Houghton Mifflin Harcourt Publishing Company.

Carter, Angela
"The Company of Wolves," from *The Bloody Chamber*. London: Penguin, 1979. Copyright © 1979 by Angela Carter. Reproduced by permission of the author c/o Rogers, Coleridge & White Ltd., 20 Powis Mews, London W11 1JN.

Chang, Isabelle C.
"The Chinese Red Riding Hoods," from *Women, Folk and Fairy Tales*, Edited by Rosemary Minard. Wilmington: Houghton Mifflin, 1975.

Croce, Benedetto
"The Young Slave," from *Giambattista Basile's Il Pentamarone*. Translated by Benedetto Croce. London, John Lane the Bodley Head, 1932.

Delarue, Paul
"The Story of Grandmother" from *Borzoi Book of French Folktales*. 1956 by Alfred A. Knopf, a division of Random House Inc. Used by permission of Alfred A. Knopf.

Donoghue, Emma
"The Tale of a Handkerchief," from *Kissing the Witch*. New York: HarperCollins, 1997. Copyright © 1997 by Emma Donoghue. Reprinted by permission of HarperCollins Publishers.

Dundes, Alan
"Fairy Tales from a Folkloristic Perspective," from *Fairy Tales and Society: Illusion, Allusion, and Paradigm*. Edited by Ruth B. Bottigheimer. Philidelphia: University of Pennsylvania Press, 1986. Copyright © 1986 by the University of Pennsylvania Press. Reprinted by permission of the University of Pennsylvania Press.

Garner, James Finn
"The Three Little Pigs" from *Politically Correct Bedtime Stories*. Basingstoke: Macmillan Publishing, 1994. Copyright © 1994 by James Finn Garner. Reprinted my permission of James Finn Garner.

SOURCES

Grimm, Jakob & Wilhelm
"Little Red Cap," "Brier Rose," "Hansel and Gretel," "Snow White," "Rapunzel," "The Brave Little Taylor," "The Frog King," "The Fisherman and his Wife," "Rumpelstilskin," "The Blue Light" and "The Goose Girl," from *Grimm's Tales for Young and Old*. Translated by Ralph Manheim. New York: Doubleday, 1977. Copyright © 1977 by Ralph Manheim. Reprinted by permission of Doubleday, a division of Random House, Inc.

Hearne, Betsy
"Disney Revisited, Or, Jiminy Cricket, It's Musty Down Here!," from *The Horn Book Magazine*. March/April, 1997. Reprinted by permission of the Horn Book, Inc., www.hbook.com.

Lee, Tanith
"When the Clock Strikes," from *Red As Blood or Tales from the Sisters Grimmer*. New York: Daw Books, 1983. Copyright © 1983 by Tanith Lee. Reprinted by permission of the McCarthy Agency LLC.

Lester, Julius
"The Death of Brer Wolf," from *The Tales of Uncle Remus: The Adventures of Brer Rabbit*. Copyright © 1987 by Julius Lester. Reprinted by permission of Dial Books for Young Readers, A Division of Penguin Young Readers Group, A Member of Penguin Group (USA) Inc., 345 Hudson Street, New York, NY 10014. All rights reserved.

Lurie, Alison
"What Faries Tales Tell Us," from *Boys and Girls Forever: Children's Classics from Cinderella to Harry Potter*. New York, Penguin, 2003. Copyright © 2003 by Alison Lurie. First appeared in *American Fairy Tales: From Rip Van Winkle to the Rootabaga Series*. New York: Hyperion Books, 1998. Edited by Neil Philip, and *The Oxford Book of Modern Fairy Tales*. New York: Oxford University Press, 1993. Edited by Alison Lurie. Reprinted by permission of Melanie Jackson Agency, LLC and of Penguin, a division of Penguin Group (USA) Inc.

Luthi, Max
"The Fairy-tale Hero: The Image of Man in the Fairy Tale" from *Once Upon a Time: On the Nature of Fairy Tales*. Translated by Lee Chadeayne and Paul Gottwald. Bloomington: Indiana University Press, 1979. Reprinted by permission of Indiana University Press.

MacMillan, Cyrus
"The Indian Cinderella," from *Canadian Wonder Tales*. London: The Bodley Head, 1918.. Reprinted by permission of The Random House Group Ltd.

Maitland, Sara
"The Wicked Stepmother's Lament," from *A Book of Spells*. London: Michael Joseph, 1987. Copyright © 1987 by Sara Maitland. Reprinted by permission of Jenny Brown Associates.

Mardrus, Dr. J.C.
"The Ninth Captain's Tale," from *The Book of the Thousand Nights and One Night: Volume IV. 2nd edition*. Translated by Powys Mathers. London: Routledge, 1964. Copyright © 1964 by Routledge & Kegan Paul Ltd. Reprinted by permission of Taylor and Francis Books UK.

Marquez, Gabriel Garcia
"Sleeping Beauty and the Airplane" from *Strange Pilgrims: Twelve Stories*. Translated by Edith Grossman. New York: Alfred A. Knopf, 1993. Copyright © 1993 by Gabriel Garcia Marquez. Reprinted by permission of Knopf, a division of Random House, Inc.

McKissack, Patricia C.
Flossie and the Fox. New York: Dial Books for Young Readers, 1986. Copyright © 1986 by Patricia McKissack. Reprinted by permission of Dial Books for Young Readers, A Division of Penguin Young Readers Group, A Member of Penguin Group (USA) Inc., 345 Hudson Street, New York, NY 10014. All rights reserved.

McPhail, David
Little Red Riding Hood. New York: Scholastic, Inc., 1995. Copyright © 1995 by David McPhail. Reprinted by permission of Scholastic Inc.

Owen, Wilfred
"The Sleeping Beauty," from *The Collected* Poems. Edited by C Day Lewis. New York: Chatto & Windus, 1963. Reprinted by permission of Random House Group Ltd.

Perrault, Charles.
"Little Red Riding Hood," "Sleeping Beauty in the Woods," "Cinderella," "Puss in Boots" and "Bluebeard," from *Sleeping Beauty and Other Favorite Tales*. Translated by Angela Carter. New York: Penguin Classics, 2008. Copyright © 1992 by Angela

Carter. Reprinted by permission of the author c/o Rogers, Coleridge & White Ltd., 20 Powis Mews, London W11 1JN.

Poniewozik, James
"Is Shrek Bad for Kids?" from *Time Magazine*. May 10, 2007. Copyright © 2007, Time Inc. All rights reserved. Reprinted by permission of Time Inc.

Rowe, Karen
"Feminism and Fairy Tales." Originally published in Women's Studies 6.3 (1979): 237-58. Revised for this book. Reprinted by permission of Karen Rowe.

San Souci, Robert D.
Little Gold Star: A Spanish American Cinderella Tale. New York: HarperCollins, 2000. Copyright © 2000 by Robert D. San Souci. Reprinted by permission of HarperCollins Publishers.

The White Cat. New York: Orchard Books, 1990. A retelling of Madame la Comtesse d'Aulnoy's *La Chatte Blanche*. Copyright © 1990 by Robert D. San Souci. Reprinted by permission of Orchard Books, an imprint of Scholastic, Inc.

Scieszka, Jon & Lane Smith
"Giant Story," from *The Stinky Cheese Man and Other Fairly Stupid Fairy Tales*. Copyright © 1992 by Jon Scieszka. Illustrations copyright © 1992 by Lane Smith. Reprinted by permission of Penguin Group (UK) and of Viking Penguin, A Division of Penguin Young Readers Group, A Memeber of Penguin Group (USA) Inc., 345 Hudson Street, New York, NY 10014. All rights reserved.

Seibles, Tim
"What Bugs Bunny Said to Red Riding Hood" from *Hammerlock*. Cleveland: Cleveland State University Poetry Center, 1999. Reprinted by permission of the author and of Cleveland State University Poetry Center.

Sexton, Anne
"Cinderella" from *Transformations*. New York: Houghton Mifflin, 1971. Copyright © 1971 by Anne Sexton. Reprinted by permission of Houghton Mifflin Company. All rights reserved.

Tosi, Laura
"Did They Live Happily Ever After? Rewriting Fairy Tales for a Contemporary

ILLUSTRATION SOURCES

Tale (New York: Breslich & Foss, 2003). Reproduced by permission of Breslich and Foss, Ltd.

Figure 15: *Puss in Boots* by Stasys Eidrigevičius, from Charles Perrault's *Puss in Boots: A Fairy Tale*. Translated by Naomi Lewis. Copyright © 1990 by NordSüd Verlag AG, Zurich/Switzerland. All rights reserved. Reproduced by permission of North-South Books, Inc., New York.

Figure 16: *Puss in Boots: the Story of a Sneaky Cat* by Tony Ross. London: Andersen Press, 1981. Copyright © 1981 by Tony Ross. Reproduced by permission of Andersen Press Ltd.

Figure 17: *Giant Story* by Lane Smith from Jon Sciezka's *The Stinky Cheese Man and Other Fairly Stupid Fairy Tales*. Illustrations copyright © 1992 by Lane Smith. Reproduced by permission of Penguin Group (UK).

Figure 18: *The Princess and the Frog* by Will Eisner, retold from the Brothers Grimm. Copyright © 1999 Will Eisner Studios, Inc. Reproduced by permission of Will Eisner Studios, Inc.

Cover Image: *Into the Forest* by Anthony Browne. Reproduced by permission of Candlewick Press, Cambridge, MA, on behalf of Walker Books Ltd., London.